ResEdit™ Complete

ResEdit™ Complete

Peter Alley

Carolyn Strange

Addison-Wesley Publishing Company
Reading, Massachusetts   Menlo Park, California   New York
Don Mills, Ontario   Wokingham, England   Amsterdam   Bonn
Sydney   Singapore   Tokyo   Madrid   San Juan   Paris
Seoul   Milan   Mexico City   Taipei

Many of the designations used by manufacturers and sellers to distinguish their products are claimed as trademarks. Where those designations appear in this book and Addison-Wesley was aware of a trademark claim, the designations have been printed in initial capital letters.

Library of Congress Cataloging-in-Publication Data

Alley, Peter, 1956-
    ResEdit complete / Peter Alley, Carolyn Strange.
      p.   cm.
    Includes index,
    ISBN 0-201-55075-X
    1. Macintosh (Computer)--Programming. 2. ResEdit. I. Strange,
Carolyn. II. Title.
QA76.8.M3A446 1991
005.265--dc20
                                           90-22135
                                             CIP

Sponsoring Editor: Carole McClendon
Technical Reviewer: Craig Carper
Cover Design: Ronn Campisi Design
Set in 10.5 point Palatino by Shepard Poorman Communication Corporation

6 7 8 9 10–MW–96959493
Sixth printing, February 1993

To our parents

Contents

▶ **PART SIX Customizing ResEdit 421**

▶ **APPENDICES**

▶ **AFTERWORD 535**

▶ **INDEX 537**

Acknowledgments

Among the people who helped us with this project, two truly stand out. Craig Carper and Alexander Falk contributed to this book in a variety of ways. Certainly, their competent technical input, and numerous good suggestions improved the manuscript. Alexander suggested several *leiwand** ResEdit tricks—truly fun and practical additions—and provided valuable comments on early drafts. Craig's thorough and thoughtful technical review helped us smooth the final manuscript, and he user-tested projects on a different Macintosh model than those we used to write the projects. He was always ready to check (or fix) something in ResEdit for us. Thanks guys. We really appreciate your enthusiasm and support.

Thanks also to the whole ResEdit team for your efforts on version 2.1: Craig Carper, Tom Chavez, Dave Curbow, Alexander Falk, Laurel Frischman, Jack Littleton, Larry Nedry, Keith Nemitz, and Jon Singer.

Many people offered encouragement and moral support, but we would especially like to thank Scott Knaster, Clayton Lewis, and Stephen Hart.

We can't let Michael Tibbott escape notice for his germinal role in this project.

---

*leiwand—(German, pronounced: LIGH-vond) expression for "neat" or "cool" used in Vienna, Austria.

To friends and family, neglected for months and months while we were chained to our Macs, we apologize. Again.

Last, but by no means least, the folks at Addison-Wesley deserve credit not just for seeing the book through, but for helping to see us through. Carole McClendon provided the impetus (and a great deal of optimism) for this project, and her enthusiasm helped keep it, and us, going. Rachel Guichard cheerfully attended to numerous loose ends. We appreciate Joanne Clapp Fullagar's patience with us, and with tight schedules and last-minute revisions due to software changes. Her encouragement and support helped us, and her thoughtful suggestions and editing improved the book. Finally, we are grateful for Mary Cavaliere's attention to so many details—expected and otherwise—as she shepherded these pages through the production process.

PART ONE

▶ **ResEdit Basics**

1 ▶ Introduction

As friendly as the Mac is, and as much as you love it, there may very well be some things about it that have always bugged you. Go on, admit it. Maybe a confusing, perhaps grammatically incorrect, screen message has always set your teeth on edge. Perhaps you've always wished you had a keyboard equivalent for a certain command, or that you could change existing Command-key assignments. Why is a certain alert's default "Yes" when it should be "No"? Then there's that stupid-looking icon, and the menu that bewilders. Wouldn't it be nice if you could see more and longer file names in standard file directory dialogs? Come to think of it, sometimes you wish your mouse responded more quickly than the Control Panel's fastest setting. And why can't you permanently add a new desktop pattern to the Control Panel?

You can.

You can change every one of these things and more. All these user interface components are stored in resources, and you can change them with ResEdit, the Resource Editor.

If you're a programmer you're probably already familiar with ResEdit. But you might be wondering whether you're getting the most out of it as you develop the user interface for your applications. From creating and editing standard resources, to designing your own templates, or even writing your own resource editor, ResEdit is a powerful ally to help you in your work.

▶ Introducing ResEdit 2.1

"What is ResEdit anyway?" some may ask. As the name implies, ResEdit is an application that allows you to create and edit resources, which are an important part of what makes the Macintosh the friendly, malleable machine it is. Just about everything you see on your screen can be (in fact *should* be) stored in resources. Figure 1-1 shows just some of the changes you can make to common graphic resources. But resources control more than just visual effects. Sounds are resources, too. By using ResEdit to change the appropriate resources, you can modify your Mac's time and date format, your keyboard's character layout, and the default paper sizes you choose from the print dialog, just to name a few possibilities. In short, ResEdit can help you create a customized Macintosh environment that's a pleasure to work in.

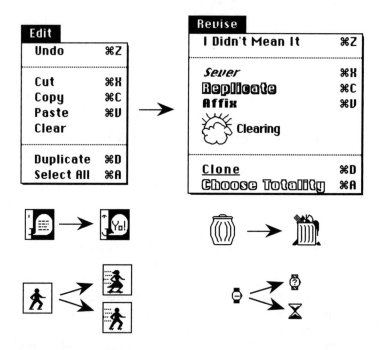

Figure 1-1. The changes you can make with ResEdit range from reasonable to radical.

ResEdit has undergone a major overhaul and version 2.1 is truly New and Improved, as Figure 1-2 points out. If you've used old versions of ResEdit, you're in for a pleasant surprise. If you've never used ResEdit, be glad you waited until now to start. Although ResEdit may once have deserved a reputation as somewhat of a doomsday program, those days are gone. Even though it has become much safer and friendlier, ResEdit remains a powerful program that you use on very valuable files—your applications. But there's no reason to fear ResEdit; like any powerful tool, it can be used safely and profitably if treated with the proper respect.

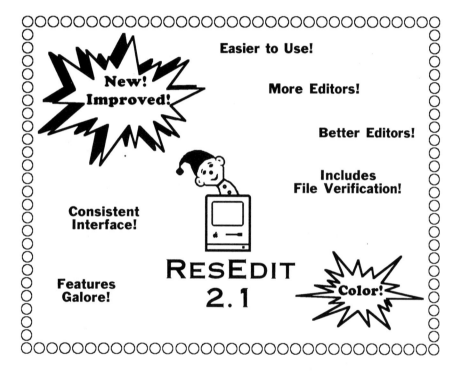

Figure 1-2. Introducing ResEdit 2.1.

▶ Is This Book for You?

We've addressed this book to two general types of readers. If you're a Macintosh user who wants to customize your work environment for greater enjoyment and productivity, this book is for you. If you're a programmer interested in learning fast, efficient ways to create and edit resources for the applications you're developing, this book is for you. Of course, these audiences overlap—programmers customize their Macs for increased enjoyment and productivity, too!

The first part of the book is aimed at both audiences and focuses on editing resources for purposes of customization. We've included enough information to keep programmers interested, but not so much that everyone else drowns in technical details. The last part of the book is aimed at programmers and focuses on creating resources, programming with ResEdit, and customizing it to create and edit unique resource types.

To sum up, if you have any interest in creating or changing aspects of the Macintosh user interface, this book is for you.

▶ How to Use This Book

This is a modular, task-oriented book and the chapters are organized functionally by grouping related resource types together. Generally, each chapter describes one or more related resource types and how they're used, explains how to edit them, and includes some projects you might want to try. We encourage you to browse and try whatever projects interest you—dip into chapters as you please—but bear in mind that the chapter topics and projects gradually increase in difficulty and complexity. If you've never used ResEdit, you should probably gain a little experience nearer the beginning of the book first rather than diving right in to later chapters.

The section about color resource types assumes you're familiar with corresponding black-and-white resource types. If you have a black-and-white Mac, you won't miss anything by skipping the color section, but if you have a color monitor, you'll have to read about black-and-white resource types in order to understand the color ones.

First we need to get you oriented and set some ground rules. Following our advice will not only help you get more out of this book, more out of ResEdit, and ultimately more out of your Macintosh, but will also help prevent unfortunate mistakes with important files.

▶ What You Need to Know

This book contains six parts. Readers interested in customizing their Macintoshes will find Parts 2 through 4 most useful. Readers interested in programming with ResEdit will find Parts 3, 5, and 6 most useful. *No matter who you are, you should read all of Part 1, ResEdit Basics.* All of the subsequent chapters assume you've read Part 1, which covers the basic information you need to understand how to use ResEdit effectively and safely. Besides, if you skip it you'll miss out on several helpful hints for working with ResEdit. (Appendix A lists a collection of ResEdit shortcuts and hints, but it's not a substitute for reading the chapters.)

Every book is built upon at least a few assumptions, and this one is no different. To help you use this book more effectively, we've summarized several of our most important assumptions.

- You didn't get your Macintosh yesterday. You're experienced and comfortable using it. You've probably used a paint or draw program, and navigating in the Mac user interface is second nature, or very nearly so. Therefore, we won't waste your time rehashing basics described in your user manuals.

- The sections directed at programmers, especially Parts 5 and 6, assume you're already familiar with programming the Macintosh. Part 6 also assumes familiarity with Apple's Macintosh Programmer's Workshop (MPW).

- Our discussions and examples assume you're using at least System 6.0 or later, which seems like a safe bet. We've tested all the projects and examples with either 6.0.4 or 6.0.5. Most projects probably work just fine with Systems earlier than 6.0, but weren't tested that way so we can't vouch for them.

- We address pertinent changes the System 7 revolution brought about, but we don't dwell on the new System. Unless we specifically mention System 7, you can assume we're talking about System 6.

▶ Warnings

Even though we've tested the projects and examples we present, we couldn't possibly test all of them on every possible hardware configuration with every possible assortment of software. Your system may very well be unique—in fact, that's one of the joys of the Macintosh and part of the purpose of this book. It's your Macintosh, and you can make it work the way you want it to. You spend a lot of time setting up your machine just the way you like it, so you should protect that investment by maintaining backups of all your important files. If you have a hard disk, you should have copies of all your files backed up on floppy disks, a separate hard disk, or tape. If you work from floppy disks, you should have copies of all your files backed up on a second set of floppy disks. It's up to you whether you use a backup program or your own scheme.

We also recommend that you always have a "rescue disk" to restart your machine if disaster strikes. In Chapter 4 we give more specific directions for creating a rescue disk.

We assume you already follow this sage advice, but we generally suggest that before you work on a file with ResEdit you make another copy anyway—especially in the beginning. Because the book is modular, we can't assume readers will try things in any particular order, so we've sprinkled reminders and warnings throughout the book. Our intent with warnings is not to frighten, but to remind you that you're using a powerful tool on valuable files. In any undertaking, mistakes are notoriously easy to make, especially for beginners, and accidents can always strike anyone, anytime. Be sure you read and understand the following warning because it's the only full-length version; the rest of them are abbreviated reminders.

Warning ▶	**Changing resources can cause unpredictable and disastrous results. Never change resources in your only copy of a file. Always work on an expendable copy.** ResEdit is a programmer's utility; it actually changes application programs. Altering most resources shouldn't affect how your program works. However, some applications may rely on complex relationships and interactions between various software components, so the final results of your changes may not always be entirely predictable. Although side effects are rare, they can be serious. That's why you should work only on an extra copy of any application.

Making a copy is analogous to using a seat belt when riding in an automobile. It doesn't take much time or effort, and it just might save your file. Make a copy first.

Hint ▶	Before you use ResEdit to open a file, use the Finder's Duplicate command to make a copy. Keep a spare copy until you're sure your changes are working correctly and you want to keep them.

Here's another good rule to follow: Avoid changing things you don't understand. If you feel you must change things "just to see what happens," make sure you're prepared to deal with the consequences. (OK, we admit that changing things just to see what happens can be educational and fun, but since we have no idea what you're going to change, we have to be clear that if you do this you're on your own.) To follow-up with the automobile analogy, don't go joy-riding with ResEdit. Try to be clear about where you're going and have a plan for getting there. You want to be wide-awake and sober when you take ResEdit out for a spin.

Approaches to Working on Files

There are three possible approaches to editing files with ResEdit; we recommend only the first two.

1. Safest: You have a backup of the file, but you make another copy before you work on it with ResEdit.

    The advantage of this approach is that if you don't like your changes, restoring the original is a snap. Even if some accident befalls you, you won't have to start over from the backup. This is definitely the best approach for inexperienced ResEdit users.

2. Safe: You have a backup, so you go ahead and work on the file with ResEdit.

    If you're absolutely positive you have a recent backup, then technically, the copy you work with is an expendable copy. But if you have an accident or need to switch back to the original, you'll have to start all over from the backup, which may be a nuisance. Once you become familiar with ResEdit and understand more about what you're doing, you'll be better able to gauge the seriousness of the tasks you undertake. For someone experienced with ResEdit who's performing only simple changes, this approach is usually adequate.

3. Dangerous: You don't have a backup, but you go ahead and work on your only copy of the file anyway.

    If you know people who do this, don't let them near your Mac.

| Hint ▶ | Why not consider keeping a log of all the changes you make using ResEdit? If your Mac or applications begin to behave strangely weeks or months later, such a log could prove valuable in helping you track down and eliminate problems. |

Debunking a Myth

Before we conclude the warnings, we have to debunk a myth you may have run across. You may have read that you should only use ResEdit on files stored on floppy disks, suggesting that you can somehow "break" your hard disk.

Even if you suffer a tragic mental lapse and somehow manage to destroy data on your disk, all you lose is time as long as you have a rescue disk and backups. In any case, these gloomy scenarios just don't reflect reality. We routinely use ResEdit on files or copies of files right on our hard disks, and we've never had to resort to our backups or rescue disks.

▶ The Disk with This Book

ResEdit 2.1 occupies most of the disk with this book, but a few other files of interest to programmers are also included. ResEdit comes with a set of code examples that can help you write your own pickers and editors. Usually you can just make a few changes and you'll have your own picker or editor up and running in almost no time. Chapter 26 provides an introduction to what's in the Examples folder.

This book went into production a few months before the final version of ResEdit was completed. Because of the continued work on the program during this time lag, you may notice slight differences between the ResEdit we describe and the ResEdit on the disk with this book.

▶ Summary

This chapter introduces ResEdit and briefly describes in general terms some of the things you can do with it. This modular, task-oriented book is aimed at two general audiences: all users interested in customizing their Macintoshes for enjoyment and productivity, and programmers interested in using ResEdit to create resources for applications they're developing. Topics are organized functionally by grouping related resource types together in chapters that generally increase in difficulty or complexity as you progress through the book. Because ResEdit is a powerful program, this chapter also warns you to make copies of files before editing them. Finally, we describe what's on the disk with this book.

2 ▶ What Are Resources?

So far we've talked about resources in rather general terms. Now it's time to get a little more specific. To understand how your Macintosh applications work and, more importantly, how ResEdit works on those applications, you need to know something about resources.

Resources are one of the most powerful and innovative ideas in the Macintosh programming world. They're an essential key to the design of Macintosh software and form the foundation of every application. Properly written applications store as much as possible in resources, including all the familiar user interface components. The apt term *resource* can apply to anything of use to an application—including the program code itself. In fact, you could say that a Macintosh application is a collection of resources. Before the Macintosh, everything an application needed, including user interface components such as menus, was buried in bulky chunks of program code, or "hard-coded." Macintosh applications, on the other hand, are split into numerous building blocks, such as dialog and alert boxes and their messages, fonts, menus, icons, and patterns, as well as the program code. In other words, Macintosh applications are modular. Each of these resource modules is created, stored, and modified separately.

▶ Advantages of Using Resources

Dealing with resources separately gives software much greater flexibility. This modular, resource-based approach to software design offers several advantages.

- Foreign language translation—Using resources for the user interface makes translation into foreign languages easier. All screen messages and menu items are separate from the program code, so non-programmers can translate the pertinent text. With the "hard-coded" approach used in the non-Macintosh community you have to change the program itself, then recompile it after each translation—a time-consuming, laborious process.

- Shared resources—Standard data, such as mouse pointer shapes, fonts, or Open and Save dialogs can be made available to every application. Sharing resources promotes consistency between applications and saves disk space because standard building blocks are stored only once, usually in the System file. You may think of the System file as a hog because it takes up so much space, but actually it saves space by functioning as a library, therefore allowing applications to be smaller.

- Responsive memory management—The Mac can manage memory more efficiently because it doesn't have to store whole applications; it can store just the bits and pieces required at a given time. Application developers can designate resources that aren't being used at the moment as purgeable, and if the Mac needs more memory for a specific task, it can clear those resources from memory.

- Customization—As a spin-off benefit, using resources enables Mac owners to personalize applications. "So much for shared resources promoting consistency between applications," you may be muttering to yourself. But wait a minute. Consistency and customization don't really conflict; they're just useful at different times. Consistency between applications is one of the reasons novices can sit down with a new Macintosh application and become productive in almost no time. But most people eventually settle into their own preferred ways of doing things. As you become more adept at using your computer and applications, you can harness more of your Macintosh's power by creating the individualized working environment that best suits you. You don't have to take things as they come—after all, it's *your* Macintosh.

▶ Resource Basics

Chaos would inevitably result if you tossed the bazillion or so possible resources together in a big box labeled simply, "Resources," as Figure 2-1 illustrates. Rummaging through such a multitude of building blocks becomes easier for both you and your Mac when there's some basis for categorizing them. Macintosh resources are identified by their type and their ID number. Resources can also have names, but they're optional.

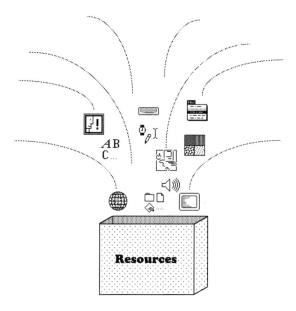

Figure 2-1. Simply throwing unidentified resources together would lead to chaos.

▶ Resource Types

Resources are grouped logically into resource types. Each type performs a particular function and holds a particular kind of data. You're probably already familiar with some of the resource types shown in Figure 2-2. All that the various resource types have in common is that they are chunks of specially formatted data and are identified by four-character names. Some common resource types may appear to have only three characters in their names, but the fourth may be a non-printing character, such as the space in the 'PAT ' (pattern) and 'snd ' (sound) resources. Non-printing characters, which can occur in any of the positions in the resource type, are just as important as printing characters. Case (upper or lower) also matters. For example, the Mac won't recognize 'font' or 'Font' as the 'FONT' resource type. Appendix B lists the standard resource types, but you may encounter others because software developers are free to define new ones as necessary. By convention, resource types are written enclosed in single quotation marks; the marks are not part of the type.

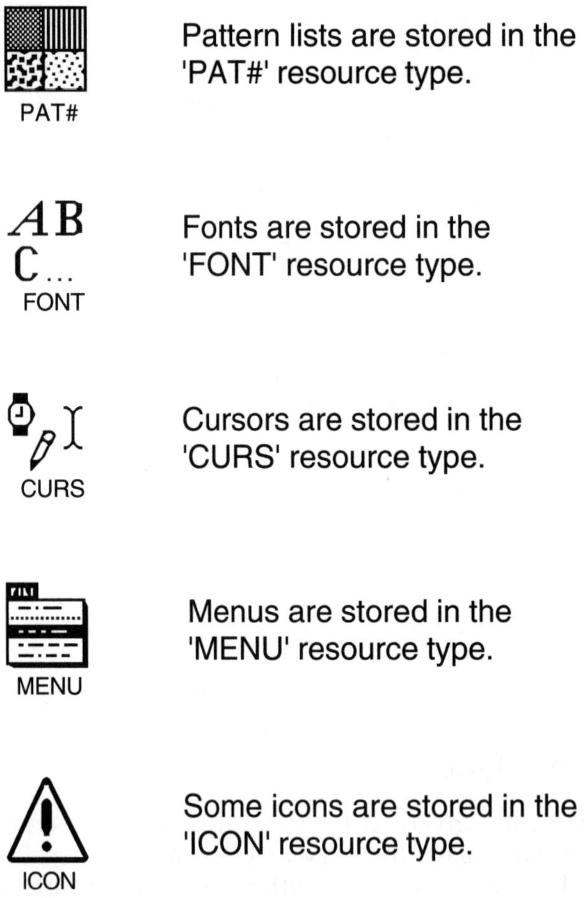

PAT#

Pattern lists are stored in the 'PAT#' resource type.

FONT

Fonts are stored in the 'FONT' resource type.

CURS

Cursors are stored in the 'CURS' resource type.

MENU

Menus are stored in the 'MENU' resource type.

ICON

Some icons are stored in the 'ICON' resource type.

Figure 2-2. Resources are grouped logically by their function and identified by their type.

In the early days of the Macintosh, the resource types Apple created had all uppercase letters, such as 'MENU' and 'FONT'. Later, when the Mac II came out, Apple switched to using lowercase letters, such as 'cicn' (color icon) and 'ppat' (pixel pattern). Currently, Apple reserves for its use all resource types having only lowercase letters.

Sooner or later (and probably sooner) you will come across a resource type containing a pound sign (#). By frequently ignored convention, this symbol means that resources of that type contain a collection or *list* of similar elements. For instance, the 'PAT#' resource type stores pattern lists, and the 'STR#' resource type stores lists of strings. These lists can contain any number of elements.

Although 'ICN#' was initially defined as a law-abiding icon list, this resource type doesn't follow the rules anymore. The 'ICN#' type is now defined for Finder icons and always contains exactly two elements, the icon and its mask.

For nearly every list resource type, there's a corresponding resource type that contains only one such element per resource. For instance, a 'PAT ' resource contains only one pattern, an 'STR ' contains only one string and an 'ICON' contains only one icon. Now you're probably scratching your head wondering why you need two types of resources to handle one kind of data. From a programmer's point of view, each approach has pluses and minuses. In a nutshell, list resource types come in handy because they allow you to group a large number of related elements together and to save space both in memory and on disk. For example, 20 patterns stored in separate 'PAT ' resources occupy more space than those same 20 patterns stored in a single 'PAT#'. On the other hand, a 20-pattern list resource takes up a good chunk of space if you only need one pattern at a time.

▶ Resource IDs

Within each resource type, individual resources are identified by a resource ID number. The ID should be unique within each resource type, but resources of different types can have the same ID. With just these two pieces of information, an application can find any resource it needs. 'MENU' ID 2 refers to a unique menu resource within an application, just as 'DLOG' ID 2 refers to a unique dialog. An application doesn't say "OK, the user wants to see the Set Margins dialog," it says, "OK, the user wants to see 'DLOG' ID 32." The usual way the application knows which particular resource to display or use in any situation is by type and ID. (It's also possible to look for a resource by type and name instead of ID, but not many applications do that.) That's why you have to keep track of ID numbers carefully as you substitute resources to personalize your applications. We'll show you how to substitute your custom resources and change their resource IDs in later chapters.

We mentioned that one of the advantages of using resources is that applications can share the resources stored in the System file. But they don't have to. Just because there's a certain resource in the System file doesn't mean an application has to use it. Because of the way it searches for resources, the Macintosh gives you a way to override the System resource with a custom resource specific to your application. As illustrated in Figure 2-3, when an application needs a resource, the Mac normally begins its search with the file opened most recently, and works backward to the System file, which opens at startup. (We said "normally" because an application can change where the search starts.) Therefore, if an application resource has the same type and ID number as a System file resource, the application resource is used, otherwise the System resource is used. Keep this search order in mind as you modify resources. If the change you made in the System file doesn't show up in your application, maybe you need to modify the corresponding resource in the application.

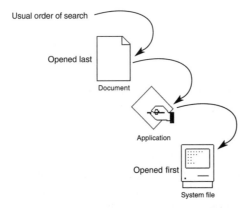

Figure 2-3. The Mac usually searches for resources starting with the file opened most recently.

Numbering Conventions

Although resource IDs can fall between -32,768 and 32,767, resources don't acquire their ID numbers willy-nilly. Resource IDs follow certain rules, which are summarized in Table 2-1. Other restrictions may also apply; for instance, if you want to put an icon in a menu, the icon's ID has to be greater than 256, but less than 512.

Table 2-1. Guidelines for Allocating Resource IDs

Resource ID Range	Use
-32,768 to -16,385	Reserved by Apple
-16,384 to 127	Used for System resources
128 to 32,767	Available for applications

As you become familiar with ResEdit you'll notice that whenever you ask it to create or duplicate a resource, it seems to always hand out the same number for the new resource's ID. Well, it doesn't just seem to, it usually does. When it has to assign a new resource ID, ResEdit starts with 128, the lowest number available for use, and increases by one until it finds a number that isn't already taken by a resource of that type in that file.

▶ Forked File Structure

Now you know a bit about how resources are identified, but you may be wondering where and how they're stored. Macintosh files are unique in that every one can have two parts, or *forks:* the *data fork* and the *resource fork.*

Either fork of a file can be empty. The resource fork of an application file, for instance, normally contains all the resources the application uses, including the program code. The data fork can contain anything the application puts there, but often it's empty. (For example, ResEdit has no data fork.) Many of the documents that applications create have no resource fork. For instance, the text you type into a word processing document is stored in the data fork. Some applications may use their documents' resource forks to store customized settings that pertain only to that document.

By the Way ▶ The System file's resource fork contains the standard resources shared by all applications and by the Macintosh Toolbox, which is the built-in software that makes the Macintosh user interface available to programmers and their applications. Some resources that are too big to fit in ROM (Read-Only Memory) have to be stored in the System file instead. Other resources may also exist in the various ROMs but are duplicated in System software releases for the sake of compatibility with machines that don't have the newer ROMs. If you want to be sure you only copy resources you need when updating to a new System, use Apple's Installer.

A file's two forks handle their assigned data differently. The data fork contains one big chunk of unstructured data. The resource fork, on the other hand, is divided into two parts, as illustrated in Figure 2-4. The *resource map* is the table of contents or index your Mac uses to find the individual resources that are stored in the *resource data* part of the resource fork.

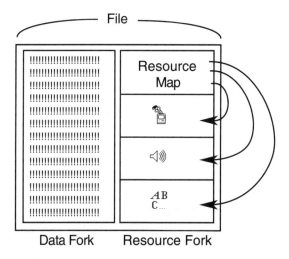

Figure 2-4. The resource map tells the Mac where to find individual resources.

By the Way ▶ The resource map is part of the reason that list resources take up less memory. Each entry in the map requires a 12-byte parcel of memory. So 20 'PAT ' resources take up 240 bytes in the resource map, plus the space needed for the pattern resources themselves. Those same 20 patterns stored in a 'PAT#' resource require the same amount of space for the patterns, but only take up one 12-byte parcel in the resource map.

This forked file structure may sound a little schizophrenic. To confuse matters, people sometimes refer to the forks as files (the "data file" or the "resource file"). You can relax, though, because you never have to worry about keeping tabs on the two parts of your files. Your Mac takes care of that for you.

▶ What ResEdit Does

ResEdit is a general-purpose resource editor that provides understandable representations of resources so you can edit them and, in the case of graphic resources, immediately see how they'll look. ResEdit lets you browse through a file's resource fork, open any resource present, and change it. Because changing a file's resources can have unpredictable and disastrous results, you should always edit an expendable copy. Like any powerful tool, ResEdit can be dangerous if used carelessly.

By the Way ▶ Although ResEdit only opens a file's resource fork, for convenience we generally say that it opens the file.

The resources in a file are specially formatted chunks of data that your Mac can understand, but they're incomprehensible to most people, and at best unwieldy to the rest. ResEdit makes those chunks of data understandable by presenting usable representations of them. For instance, the data that describes an icon can be displayed several ways, two of which are shown in Figure 2-5. It can be displayed literally (as a series of hexadecimal characters), or graphically. Most people would choose to work with the more understandable graphic representation.

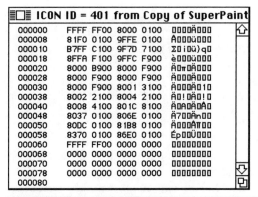

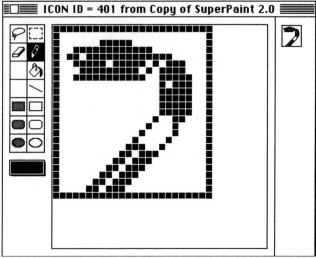

Figure 2-5. ResEdit's hexadecimal editor (top) and 'ICON' editor (bottom) display two very different representations of the same icon. Which one would you rather edit?

ResEdit has three general ways it can show you a resource. First, it has numerous resource-specific special editors, and it automatically opens a resource in the corresponding special editor if one exists. For example, a 'MENU' resource opens in the 'MENU' editor, which provides all the tools you need for editing menus, but no others. While you're editing a menu, you won't trip over the tools required for editing icons, dialogs, patterns or other resources. ResEdit also presents resources in templates—windows that resemble big dialog boxes. A template is like a blueprint; it's a list of parameters used to build a particular resource, but it's not the resource itself. You can create or edit more than 60 resource types using specific templates. Each resource type has its own kind of template, and each individual resource is characterized by its unique values within the template. Finally, if ResEdit doesn't have a special editor or a template for a resource (meaning it doesn't know about the resource's structure), it will present the resource to you as a sequence of characters in its hexadecimal editor. This book covers all the special editors and includes several chapters on templates. Appendix C covers the basics of working with hexadecimal numbers in the hexadecimal editor.

▶ What You Can't Do with ResEdit

You can do a wide variety of things with ResEdit—that's what this whole book is about. But there are still a few things you can't do. You're bound to be happier as you customize your Mac if you keep in mind what ResEdit can't do and why.

You can change a resource's content, ID, name, and certain other attributes, but generally you can't change its type. That would be tantamount to software alchemy. You can't turn lead into gold, nor can you turn menus, pointers, icons, or dialog boxes into each other. Fortunately, the usual Macintosh magic still works where it makes sense, however. You can copy certain components of some resources to resources of other types. For instance, you can copy the bits that make up the image in one graphic editor and paste them into another graphic editor.

ResEdit only works on resources, so if an application doesn't use resources for the user interface components you want to change, ResEdit can't help you. The fewer resources an application uses, the more that has been "hard-coded," the less flexible and customizable an application is. (Register your complaints with the developer of the offending software.)

Although program code is stored in resources, ResEdit isn't useful for editing code. Besides needing to understand how to program a Macintosh, you need some sort of a software development environment (such as Apple's MPW or Lightspeed C, from Symantec) before you tackle changing program code.

ResEdit allows you to edit existing resources as well as create new ones. But you usually can't just create a new resource and expect an application to use it. For example, an application that doesn't have an animated cursor will just ignore the clever 'acur' resource you add. Likewise, devising a new menu won't change the functions an application can perform. The application doesn't know what to do with the new resource. In fact, it doesn't even know to *look* for the resource. Remember, applications look for resources by resource type and ID, so generally you can only substitute customized versions of existing resource types. You can either change the existing resource or substitute a new version. We'll tell you how to do that in the next chapter.

▶ Summary

This chapter presents an overview of Macintosh resources: what they are, the advantages of using them, and how they're identified—by type and ID. We touch on the forked structure of Macintosh files, and how resources are stored in the resource fork. Finally we describe in general terms how ResEdit works on the resource fork of a file and summarize the few things that ResEdit can't do.

Now that you're familiar with resources, you're ready to find out how to use ResEdit.

3 ▶ How to Use ResEdit

In most respects, ResEdit works just like any other Macintosh application, so you can forget whatever frightening or mystical references you may have read on various electronic bulletin boards or in trade magazines. It's actually fairly simple: With word processing applications you create and edit text, with paint and draw programs you create and edit pictures, and with ResEdit you create and edit the resources found in most files. The important difference to remember is that rather than working on documents, you generally use ResEdit on valuable application files, so you have to be careful. Manipulating resources can be as simple as adding a keyboard shortcut for a common operation in your favorite application, or as complicated as editing a custom resource for an application you're writing. Although ResEdit behaves like a typical Mac application in most respects, it has some special characteristics because it does a unique job. This chapter describes ResEdit's features, and tells you how to use it so you'll feel comfortable taking it out for a spin.

One of the ways ResEdit differs from most Macintosh applications is that it can open any file. Text processing applications show you only text files in the standard file directory dialog, and graphics applications show you only graphics files. ResEdit isn't so picky. It shows you every file because every file can have a resource fork, and it can open any of them. This ability gives ResEdit great power and utility, but it's also one of the reasons why careless joy-riding with ResEdit can be dangerous. We recommend that you only open *copies* of files so that you don't accidentally damage important files and applications. Later, when you become a ResEdit pro, you'll know when you have to make a copy and when you don't. (Any time you wonder whether you should make a copy, you should.) We'll give more specific instructions for working on important files such as your System file in the next chapter.

| By the Way ▶ |

Although ResEdit can open any file (or, more precisely, any file's resource fork), it can do so only if the file isn't already open. If you think about it, this is just as well. You wouldn't *want* to tweak an application's resources while it's running (unless you like living dangerously). However, there are two important files that ResEdit can open even though they're already running. ResEdit can open the System file's resource fork and it can open its own resource fork. (Of course, the System file is always open whenever your Mac is running.) Still, we recommend that you always work on copies of these files.

▶ Starting ResEdit

When you open ResEdit you see a splash-screen which includes, in addition to the animated ResEdit Jack-in-the-Mac, the version number and other information. Virtually anything you do, such as pressing a key or clicking the mouse, causes the splash screen to disappear so you can select a file to edit. While the splash-screen is displayed, ResEdit can also act on any Command keys that make sense, such as shortcuts that open files you work on frequently. Once you find the file (or preferably a copy of the file) you want to examine or edit, you can double-click and ResEdit will open it. But before you can find your way around in ResEdit comfortably, you need to understand how it presents information, so you should become familiar with its windows.

▶ ResEdit's Windows

ResEdit has three general kinds of windows: pickers, editors and info windows. Each kind of window has two or more subkinds. If you understand how ResEdit displays information, and know what you can and can't do from certain windows, you'll be able to accomplish more work with less wheel spinning. Figure 3-1 gives you a preview of how

ResEdit's pickers and editors work together. The rest of this section introduces pickers, editors, and info windows in more detail.

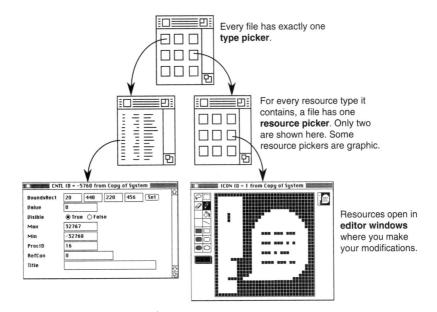

Figure 3-1.   ResEdit's pickers and editors open in a predictable, hierarchical order.

▶ Pickers

Pickers are windows that list text or icons, and they behave much like windows in the Finder. They have zoom boxes and size boxes so you can adjust their size and shape, and you can change how the window contents are displayed by choosing options from the View menu. You can also change size characteristics of pickers with the Preferences command on the File menu. Some commands apply only in pickers, such as the Edit menu's Select Changed item. There are two kinds of pickers: the type picker (one per file) and resource pickers (one for each resource type in a file). You pick the type of resource you want to edit from the type picker. You pick the individual resource you want to edit from the resource picker. Although there are many kinds of resource pickers, they all work similarly.

The Type Picker

The *type picker* is the first window you see any time ResEdit opens a file. The type picker lists the types of all the resources the file contains. You can view this list either by icon, as shown in Figure 3-2, or by resource type, as shown in Figure 3-3. As you can see in Figure 3-2, ResEdit has two generic icons it uses for resource types for which it doesn't have editors. You can edit such resources only using the hexadecimal editor (see Appendix C). Any other icon represents a resource type for which ResEdit has a special editor, or a template you can fill in using the template editor.

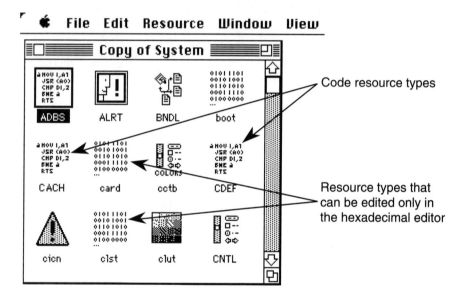

Figure 3-2. The type picker, view by icon. Some icons represent more than one resource type.

In the By Type view you can see more information about the contents of a file. You see not only the four-character names of the resource types, but also how many resources of that type exist in the file. You can also tell ResEdit to show you the total size (in bytes) of the resources, as shown in Figure 3-4. This can be useful for analyzing the contents of a file, but sometimes displaying resource sizes can be slow. For example on a Mac Plus, opening a file that contains a large number of resources can take several seconds or longer. Furthermore, any time ResEdit redraws part of a window (for instance, if you change the size of a window or scroll) it has to recalculate these sizes. If delays associated with displaying resource sizes become too annoying, simply turn off the Show Size With Type option on the View menu.

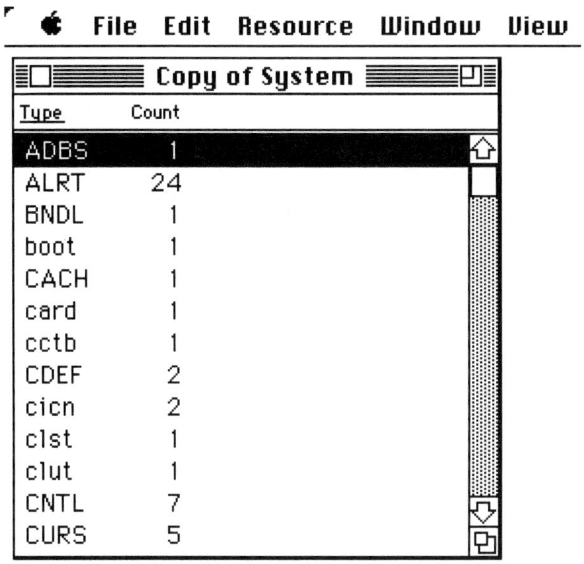

Figure 3-3. Type picker, view by resource type.

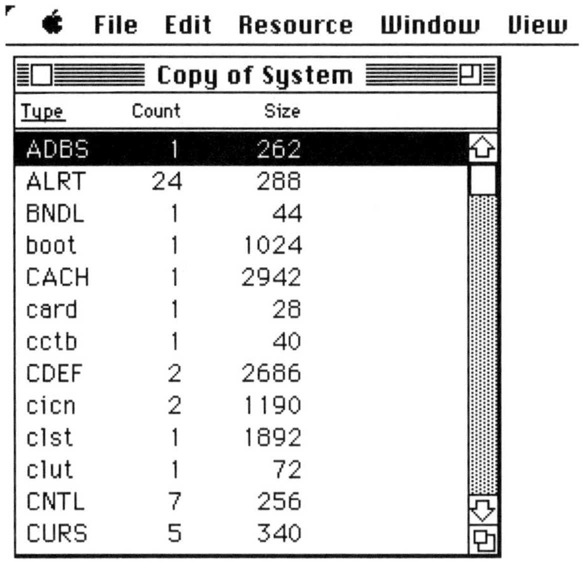

Figure 3-4. The type picker, showing size (in bytes) with type.

When you've found the resource type you want to open, double-click it or choose Open Pickers from the Resource menu. (The command's text varies slightly, depending on what's selected. Don't choose Open from the File menu or use Command-O—that opens files, not the resources within them.) The window that opens next is the other kind of picker—a resource picker.

Resource Pickers

Resource pickers show you all the resources in a file that are of the type chosen from the type picker. The list displays the ID, size, and name for each resource, as shown in Figure 3-5. In many cases resources don't have names, so the right side of the window is blank. The View menu for resource pickers gives you more options than the one available for type pickers. You can sort resources by ID, Name, Size, or Order in File. Viewing by Order in File gives you a chronological list of resources, with the resource added to the file most recently listed first. You can also view some resource types in special pickers that give you more information. Pickers for graphical resources for instance, default to a graphical view (sorted by ID) that shows you what each resource looks like. For example, the 'ICON' picker is shown in Figure 3-6. On some systems (notably the Mac Plus) the By Name and By Size views may be a bit slow.

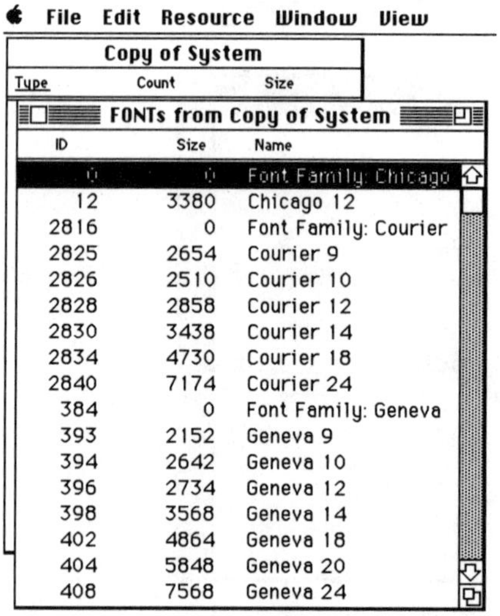

File Edit Resource Window View
Copy of System
Type Count Size
FONTs from Copy of System
ID Size Name
0 0 Font Family: Chicago
12 3380 Chicago 12
2816 0 Font Family: Courier
2825 2654 Courier 9
2826 2510 Courier 10
2828 2858 Courier 12
2830 3438 Courier 14
2834 4730 Courier 18
2840 7174 Courier 24
384 0 Font Family: Geneva
393 2152 Geneva 9
394 2642 Geneva 10
396 2734 Geneva 12
398 3568 Geneva 14
402 4864 Geneva 18
404 5848 Geneva 20
408 7568 Geneva 24

Figure 3-5. The 'FONT' picker, a resource picker for 'FONT' resources.

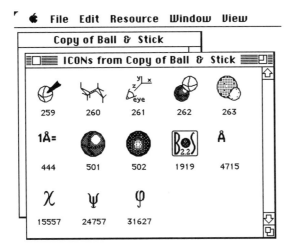

Figure 3-6. A resource picker, view by 'ICON'.

The last item on the View menu is the Show Attributes command, which is available for any non-special view. Choosing this item tells ResEdit to display more detailed resource information, shown in Figure 3-7, that's generally useful only for programmers. You can't change this information here, but you can choose Get Resource Info from the Resource menu to change the attributes for any resource. (For more on resource attributes, see Chapter 23.)

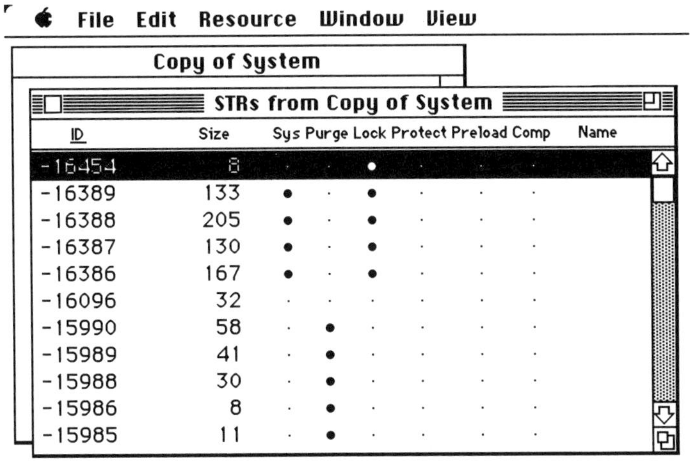

```
   ▶  🍎  File  Edit  Resource  Window  View

            ┌───────────────────────────────────────┐
            │          Copy of System               │
        ┌───┴──────────────────────────────────────┐│
        │▤ □    STRs from Copy of System         ▣▤ │
        ├──────────────────────────────────────────┤
        │  ID      Size   Sys Purge Lock Protect Preload Comp   Name │
        ├──────────────────────────────────────────┤
        │ -16454     8     .    .    ●    .    .    .        ⇧│
        │ -16389   133     ●    .    ●    .    .    .         │
        │ -16388   205     ●    .    ●    .    .    .         │
        │ -16387   130     ●    .    ●    .    .    .         │
        │ -16386   167     ●    .    ●    .    .    .         │
        │ -16096    32     .    .    .    .    .    .         │
        │ -15990    58     .    ●    .    .    .    .         │
        │ -15989    41     .    ●    .    .    .    .         │
        │ -15988    30     .    ●    .    .    .    .         │
        │ -15986     8     .    ●    .    .    .    .        ⇩│
        │ -15985    11     .    ●    .    .    .    .        ▱│
        └──────────────────────────────────────────┘
```

Figure 3-7. Resource pickers can show the attributes of resources.

Hints on Making Selections in Pickers

You won't have any trouble making selections in pickers, but a few tricks and shortcuts could make your life easier. Just as in the standard file directory dialogs found throughout the Macintosh environment, if you know the name of what you want to find, you can just type it instead of fiddling with the scroll bar. The same trick works with ID numbers or names in resource pickers; just type them.

Knowing how to select more than one item can also come in handy. You can open multiple resource types from type pickers, and you can open multiple resources from resource pickers, too. The techniques generally work any time you see a list in ResEdit, which will mostly be in pickers. As usual in the Macintosh world, Shift-click extends a selection. To select items that aren't next to each other, use Command-click. If an item is already selected, Command-click deselects it without deselecting other items.

▶   Editor Windows

After you select one or more resources from the resource picker, you can double-click or choose Open Resource Editor from the Resource menu to edit the resource(s). Each resource editor provides different features depending on the kind of information it handles. In many cases the editors look and behave similarly. For example, the 'ICON' and 'ICN#' editors are quite similar, and you can use the same editing techniques in both. You can think of each editor as a mini-application. It may have its own additional menus, and may appear different from most other editors. Of course, many things are the same for all editors. We'll discuss editors in general terms here, and cover individual editors in more detail in chapters devoted to them.

| By the Way ▶ | As you browse files with ResEdit, you should be aware that color resource editors, such as 'cicn' and 'ppt#', open only on machines that have Color QuickDraw (for instance, SE/30s and Mac IIs). Also, for those of you lucky enough to have two monitors, you can choose (in the Preferences dialog) which screen ResEdit's color pickers and editors use. If you decide to have them automatically open on the screen able to display the most colors or grays, that's where they open—even if that monitor isn't turned on. This can be confusing, but unfortunately the Mac doesn't have a mechanism for letting an application know whether a monitor is on. |

ResEdit has many *graphical editors*, which let you manipulate visual representations of resources. Some examples are the editors that you use to work on menus, windows, alert and dialog boxes and their contents, and keyboard character maps. The graphical editors used for patterns, icons, fonts, and pointers (or cursors) are fatbits editors. These editors always give you at least two views of the resource you're editing—an enlarged fatbits editing area and at least one actual-size view. In addition, editors that work on list resources (such as the patterns in a 'PAT#' resource or the small icons in an 'SICN' resource) supply a method for selecting the item you want to work on from the list.

A handful of non-graphical editors allow you to edit all the remaining resources. The editors for date, time, and number formats ('itl0' and 'itl1' resources) resemble elaborate dialog boxes. The two most general editors, the hexadecimal editor and the template editor, can edit a wide variety of resources. In fact, if you know what you're doing, you can edit *any* resource using the hexadecimal editor. Most users won't find the hexadecimal editor very helpful, however, because it represents resources as a series of numbers. (For more on the hexadecimal editor, see Appendix C.)

The template editor is another story. This one editor comes with more than 60 templates, each one representing a different type of resource (and you can add more). Although templates aren't graphical and may not be intuitively obvious, they're quite easy to edit. We've included an entire chapter (Chapter 15) on one particularly handy example, the 'LAYO' resource, which controls the Finder's layout of files and folders. Another example is the template used for animated cursors ('acur' resources). See Chapter 14 for more information on templates and the template editor.

▶ Info Windows

The three kinds of info windows, which behave like dialogs, allow you to find and set a variety of characteristics for resources, files, and folders. For information about a file or a folder, you would choose the Get File/Folder Info item on the File menu. However, unless you're a programmer, you probably won't use these windows very often. For more information, see Chapter 23.

To access the Resource Info window, choose Get Resource Info from the Resource menu. This command only becomes available after you've opened a resource picker (and selected a resource), or an editor. Like the other info windows, this window, which is shown in Figure 3-8, is most useful for programmers. But anyone serious about customization will find two fields in this window particularly useful. In experimenting with various resources you may have to change their ID numbers; this is where you do it. We guide you through the steps later in this chapter. You may also want to name some of the nameless resources you encounter as you browse through your files.

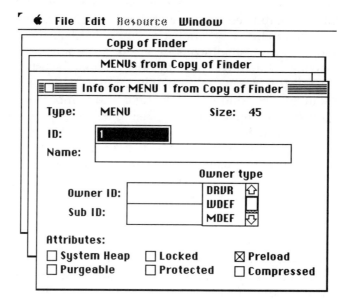

Figure 3-8. The Resource Info window.

Hint ▶

Naming unnamed resources can be a big help as you peruse your files because the names appear in any non-graphic resource picker view. You won't have to waste time repeatedly opening resources just to find out which ones they are. Simply choose Get Resource Info from ResEdit's Resource menu and type a name in the Name field of the Resource Info dialog. You can do this either from resource pickers or from editors. But never change an existing name! Remember that sometimes applications look for resources by type and name rather than type and ID, so play it safe and leave existing names alone. For this same reason, don't use a name already taken by another resource of the same type.

▶ Using ResEdit's Windows

Working with ResEdit's windows will become second nature in no time. Just remember there's a hierarchy, as you saw in Figure 3-1. When you open a file with ResEdit, the first window you always see is the type picker for that file. From there (and only from there) you open the resource picker(s). Only after you've selected a resource in the resource picker can ResEdit open the appropriate editor. You can open as many windows as memory accommodates. Except for info windows, which you can open from more than one place, there's a predictable sequence to how the windows open. Finally, in your adventures with ResEdit, don't forget about the View menu and the Window menu. (There's more information about them later in this chapter, in the "Menus" section.) These menus exist to help you manipulate windows, so take advantage of them.

| Hint ▶ | Closing a window also closes all the windows that were opened from it. |

▶ **Clipboard Operations**

At the beginning of this chapter we mentioned that ResEdit differs from most Macintosh applications in a few important ways. One difference is that it can open any file. Another is the way it handles the clipboard. In fact, in order to carry out its unique mission, ResEdit has to maintain its own clipboard to get around limitations of the Macintosh's main Clipboard. Fortunately, you don't have to worry about keeping track of clipboards—all that's taken care of for you. But you should understand a few important points about how clipboard operations work.

The Macintosh's main Clipboard can only contain one resource of each type because it doesn't keep track of ID numbers. To enable you to cut and paste multiple resources, ResEdit operates its own clipboard that can handle ID numbers. As long as you do your cutting, copying, and pasting within ResEdit, you shouldn't face any surprises because you're dealing only with ResEdit's clipboard. (See the Paste command in the "Menus" section, later in this chapter, for more details.)

You have to pay a little more attention, however, when you set out to move things to or from applications other than ResEdit because then you're using the main Clipboard. As you've probably surmised, you can't, for example, copy more than one 'PICT' resource at a time into your paint program, because the main Clipboard can only handle one resource of any type at a time.

The reverse situation, pasting a selection from an application into an open file in ResEdit, carries its own unique problem because many applications send more than one representation of a selection to the main Clipboard when you cut or copy. For example, MacDraw sends an 'MDPL' resource to the clipboard in addition to a 'PICT' resource. This approach works most of the time because when you paste from the Clipboard these applications look for their preferred representations. MacDraw looks for an 'MDPL' on the clipboard when you paste, but it will settle for a 'PICT'. ResEdit has no preferred representation, so if you're pasting into a type picker, it takes everything on the clipboard. Thus, you may get more than one resource when you paste to a type picker, and any extras will clutter up your file and take up space. If you know to look for them, you can purge any duplicate resources masquerading under assumed names—or more precisely, assumed *types*.

| By the Way ▶ | If you copy just one resource, ResEdit puts it on the Mac's main Clipboard. If you copy more than one, however, ResEdit *clears* the main Clipboard. |

| Hint ▶ | How can you find all the aliases a paste operation from another application gives you? One way is to first try pasting into a new, empty file temporarily created with ResEdit just for that purpose. Another approach is to choose Select Changed from the Edit menu, which shows you the resources that have changed since you last saved the file. |

Of course, the best way around the problem is to avoid it altogether, if you can. If you know what resource type you're interested in, and you also know that the application you're copying from can give you that resource type, just paste it into the resource picker for that type ('PICT' in the MacDraw example). When pasting to resource pickers, ResEdit pastes only resources of the corresponding type. For more information, see the section on the Paste command in the Edit menu later in this chapter.

▶ Resource Checking

When ResEdit opens a file, it automatically verifies the integrity of the resource fork. This preliminary checking is somewhat analogous to having a food taster check your food: If ResEdit tries to open a "poisoned" file, it may choke or die. Unlike the food taster, however, ResEdit's verification feature includes the ability to repair some damage—which not only prevents ResEdit from crashing, but recovers resources from corrupted files!

The resource verification feature includes two levels of checking. You can determine whether ResEdit performs the brief or full check by choosing the appropriate option in the Preferences dialog. Also, the Verify command on the File menu lets you carry out a full check without opening a file.

| **By the Way ▶** | The brief check verifies the basic structure of the resource fork. It checks the location of the resource map and checks to see that all the data fit within appropriate bounds. If any of the basic checks fail, the full test is automatically performed.

The full resource check does a more thorough walk through the resource map and verifies that the type list, the reference lists, and the name list are consistent, and that all resource data areas can be located and don't exceed the available space. It also checks for duplicate types and duplicate IDs within a type.

If you're familiar with Apple's MPW development environment, you may notice that the verification is similar to that performed by MPW's RezDet tool. ResEdit's resource verification feature can sometimes recover resources when RezDet can't even find a resource in the file. It can do this because it uses several techniques to locate the resource map, whose existence and location is critical to the resource recovery process.

▶ Resource Fork Repair

ResEdit alerts you if it finds any damage in a file and gives you the opportunity to repair it, as the alert shown in Figure 3-9 illustrates. You would see a similar alert, but without the Continue button, if you had checked the file using the Verify menu item. Most users should avoid the Continue button.

Warning ▶

Neither test can verify the contents of individual resources, because only the structure of the resource fork is tested. When repairing damage, the integrity of individual resources can never be guaranteed, so you should always restore a backup of the file if you see a "damaged file" alert. The repair facility is intended as a last resort if you don't have any backups but still need to recover some resources.

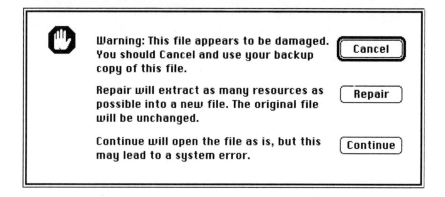

Figure 3-9. This alert warns you of possible damage encountered when opening a file and gives you the option of attempting to repair it. Most users should avoid the Continue button.

When repairing a file, ResEdit doesn't do anything to the damaged file itself, but instead copies all the resources it can to a new file. It renames the damaged file with an extension of "(damaged)." ResEdit apprises you of its progress with a variety of alerts. If it can't extract all the resources in a damaged file, it tells you so. If only one resource can't be copied, ResEdit tells you its type and ID. Another possibility is that the file may be damaged beyond repair.

ResEdit does work directly on a damaged file in one situation: when a resource fork wasn't closed properly (perhaps the application bombed). Such damage is so minimal that ResEdit performs the repair without even asking your permission, but it informs you that it has done so.

Now you're familiar with how ResEdit presents information in its windows, how it deals with clipboard operations, and how it checks your files. Even though you're probably eager to take it out for a spin, you should first spend a few moments to become familiar with the controls on ResEdit's instrument panel—the menus.

▶ The Menus: Once Over Quickly

ResEdit opens showing the four standard menus it always shows: File, Edit, Resource, and Window. But the menus and menu items available to you in ResEdit vary depending on the situation because ResEdit encompasses many applications in one. The changes aren't capricious, but depend on where you are within ResEdit and what you're doing. For instance, why should you work around menus and commands having to do with color icons when you're modifying a dialog? We'll go over the basic menus here, and cover specific, resource-related menus in chapters devoted to those resources.

▶ The File Menu

As you can see in Figure 3-10, most of the File menu's commands let you manipulate files or folders, and they're probably familiar to you from other Macintosh applications. However, a few of the commands are unique to ResEdit or behave a little differently than you might expect.

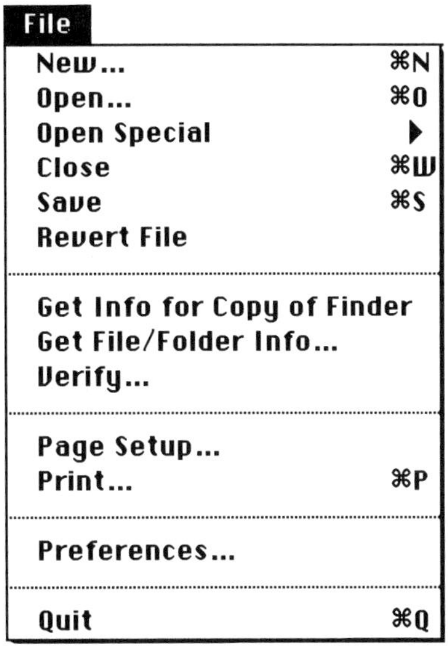

```
┌──────────────────────────────┐
│ File                         │
├──────────────────────────────┤
│ New...                   ⌘N  │
│ Open...                  ⌘O  │
│ Open Special              ▶  │
│ Close                    ⌘W  │
│ Save                     ⌘S  │
│ Revert File                  │
├──────────────────────────────┤
│ Get Info for Copy of Finder  │
│ Get File/Folder Info...      │
│ Verify...                    │
├──────────────────────────────┤
│ Page Setup...                │
│ Print...                 ⌘P  │
├──────────────────────────────┤
│ Preferences...               │
├──────────────────────────────┤
│ Quit                     ⌘Q  │
└──────────────────────────────┘
```

Figure 3-10. ResEdit's File menu.

New

The New command displays the standard file directory dialog, which allows a new file to be created. This behaves a bit differently from most applications because ResEdit asks you to name the new file before opening it.

Open

The Open command works the same in ResEdit as in most other applications. The only difference is that every file is visible in the standard file directory dialog. Remember, ResEdit can open *any* file, not just ones of a specific type.

Open Special

If you get tired of sifting through the standard file directory dialog every time you want ResEdit to open a certain file you work on frequently, you'll like this item. The Open Special menu item displays a hierarchical menu that you can customize by filling in the names of files you work on frequently, as in the example shown in Figure 3-11. To get going even more quickly, you can assign Command-key shortcuts that you can type as soon as ResEdit's splash-screen appears.

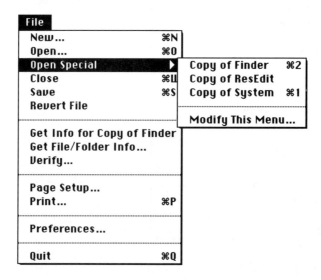

Figure 3-11. The Open Special menu item lets you create custom shortcuts to files you work on frequently.

When you first select the Open Special item, all you see on the hierarchical menu is the Modify This Menu command. As you add files, that command gets pushed further down. There's no limit—within reason— to the number of files you can add. When you select Modify This Menu, ResEdit displays the dialog shown in Figure 3-12. This dialog contains everything you need to add and remove files and Command-key shortcuts on the Open Special menu.

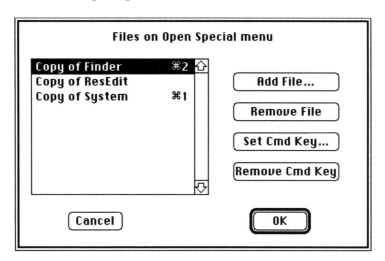

Figure 3-12. The Modify This Menu command displays this dialog, which you use to change the files and Command-key shortcuts on your Open Special menu.

When you click the Add File button, ResEdit displays a standard file directory dialog so you can locate the file you're after. Once you find it and double-click, ResEdit adds the file to the menu and remembers where to find it. ResEdit even lets you have two files with the same name on the menu. It keeps track of them by showing you the path it follows to get to each file. If you move a file or change its name, ResEdit will not be able to find it. (When this happens, ResEdit displays a fairly standard "File not found" alert.) The file remains on the Open Special menu, however, so before you can reteach ResEdit where the file is, you should remove the file name from the menu. To remove a file from the menu, simply select it and click the Remove File button.

Convenience is the whole point of the Open Special menu, so ResEdit also lets you assign Command-key shortcuts so you can quickly open the files you work on frequently. If you want to add a Command-key shortcut, first select the file, then click the Set Cmd Key button. ResEdit displays a dialog like the one shown in Figure 3-13. The dialog vanishes when you press a key, and you see your shortcut beside the file name in the Open Special dialog. If you press a key that's already in use, ResEdit warns you. (Even though the warning gives you the option of using the key anyway, we advise you not to.) To remove a Command-key shortcut from a file, simply select the file and click the Remove Cmd Key button.

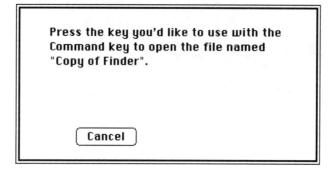

Press the key you'd like to use with the Command key to open the file named "Copy of Finder".

[Cancel]

Figure 3-13. Clicking the Set Cmd Key button causes this dialog to be displayed.

By the Way ▶

You'll probably want to avoid using the Option Key when you assign shortcuts. If you've checked Verify files when they are opened in the Preferences dialog, pressing the Option key when you open a file causes the file verification hidden diagnostic window to appear. (For more information, see Chapter 13.) There's nothing dangerous about this, it just slows you down a bit.

Close

Selecting this command is the same as clicking the active window's close box. If the active window is a type picker, ResEdit closes the file. If you haven't saved, ResEdit gives you the opportunity before closing the file.

Hint ▶

Pressing the Option key when you close a window closes all windows for the file except the type picker. Also remember that closing a window closes all the windows you've opened from it.

Save

The Save command saves the file associated with the active window. If you have several files open, ResEdit saves only the file associated with the active window. You can't save individual resources within a file; you save the whole file.

Revert File

Use this command if you have inadvertently deleted a resource or made some other change you're not happy with and want to get back to a known good file. This command reverts the active file to its last saved state. All open windows for that file will close except the type picker. If you only want to restore certain resources, but you don't want to revert the entire file, use the Revert Resource command on the Resource menu.

Get Info for <filename>

ResEdit provides a shortcut with this command. It works just like Get File/Folder Info (see next command), except that it automatically applies to the active file.

Get File/Folder Info

Unless you're a programmer, you probably won't use this command much. It displays a standard file directory dialog that allows you to choose the file or folder you'd like to get information about. If you select a folder (you must use the dialog's Get Info button because double-clicking opens the folder), you get the Folder Info window. If you select a file (double-clicking works here), you get the File Info window. These windows allow you to set various attributes of files and folders. For more information, see Chapter 23.

Verify

This command displays a standard file directory dialog to let you select a file to verify. The selected file will be scanned to make sure that its resource fork is valid. For more information, see "Resource Checking" earlier in this chapter. If you're having trouble opening a file with ResEdit, try using this command to make sure the file hasn't been corrupted. To have ResEdit automatically verify files as they're opened, see the Preferences command later on this same menu.

Page Setup

The Page Setup command allows you to set the standard page setup information. This is where you tell your printer what size paper you're using, among other things. As usual, the dialog you get depends on the printer you're using.

Print

This command displays a standard print dialog that varies with the printer you're using. Here's where you tell your printer how many copies you want, and so on.

Printing in ResEdit is not intended to give you a beautifully arranged picture of your resource suitable for framing. Instead, you simply get a convenient record of the information you can refer to later. At least that's the intent. In many cases ResEdit just prints a copy of what you see in the active window and adds a title that's the same as the title of the window being printed, along with a page number if you print multiple pages. In a few cases ResEdit takes a slightly more sophisticated approach. For instance, printing from the hexadecimal editor gives you a copy of the whole resource. Similarly, printing from pickers gives you a listing of all the resources or types displayed by the picker. Try printing from the pickers or editors you're interested in and see what you get.

ResEdit accomplishes most printing by creating a bitmap that represents the window—taking a snapshot—and sending it to the printer, so if you're using a high resolution printer you may occasionally have some problems associated with printing bitmaps. The problem stems from discrepancies between screen resolution (usually about 72 dots per inch) and the resolution at which most laser printers print (300 dots per inch). If you have unusual results, try selecting Precision Bitmap Alignment in the Page Setup dialog. If this doesn't help, just remember that even though you may have a few stray bits on your picture, at least you have a record of the information you need.

For a fancy output with headers, footers, and variable margins, you can copy the information from ResEdit and paste it into your favorite word processing application. The easiest way to do this is to take a screen snapshot using Command-Shift-3. This produces a file called Screen0 (up to Screen9 if you take several snapshots) that you can open in your paint program. Then you can touch up the screen shot, select what you want of it, and paste it into your document.

Hint ▶

Remember, Command-Shift-3 only works in black and white. If you have a color or gray-scale monitor, set it to black-and-white before using Command-Shift-3. Or use a third-party screen capture utility, such as Flash-It.

Preferences

The Preferences command displays a dialog, shown in Figure 3-14, that lets you customize several ResEdit characteristics.

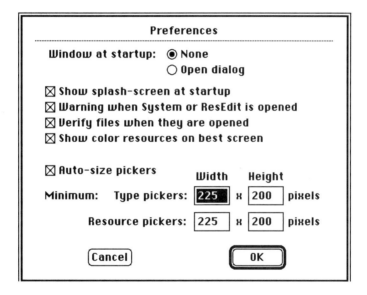

Figure 3-14. The Preferences dialog lets you adjust several ResEdit characteristics.

The Window at startup item lets you decide whether you want ResEdit to display the standard file directory dialog when it starts up. If you would rather have it start up with no dialog, click the None radio button. The next item lets you turn off ResEdit's splash-screen.

Because modifying the active System file or the version of ResEdit you're currently running can be disastrous if you make a mistake, ResEdit displays a warning when you open either of these files. If you open these files frequently, and know for certain you won't mess them up, you can turn off the warning. Simply click the check box in front of Warning when System or ResEdit is opened.

As you may remember from the "Resource Checking" section, ResEdit always performs a quick resource check when you open a file. If you want it to routinely carry out the more thorough check, simply click the check box in front of Verify files when they are opened. Selecting this option increases the length of time necessary to open files, but only slightly if you have a hard disk. Opening files from floppy disks can take much longer, however, so if you don't have a hard disk, you may not want to take advantage of this option.

The next item, Show color resources on best screen, is useful only for those Mac II owners with two monitors. If it's checked, color pickers and editors automatically open on the screen capable of displaying the most colors or grays. If it's not checked, color pickers and editors always open on the same monitor as their parent window. This command applies only to those pickers and editors displaying resources that *require* color. Color-optional resources, such as 'MENU's, always open on the same monitor as their parent window.

When you check Auto-size pickers, ResEdit optimizes the size of picker windows, making them just large enough to show every item, or to show as much as possible, depending on the file and your screen size. For pickers containing only a few items, ResEdit uses the minimum sizes set in the Width and Height fields at the bottom of the dialog. If you turn off the Auto-size feature, these minimum sizes become the default sizes for all pickers.

Quit

The Quit command behaves like a typical Macintosh Quit command. It asks you if you want to save any files you have modified, and then exits ResEdit.

▶ The Edit Menu

The Edit menu, shown in Figure 3-15, behaves as you would expect it to behave in most Macintosh applications. An important point to keep in mind, however, is that the commands work differently depending on what kind of window is active. For example, if a type picker is active and a resource type is selected, Cut will cut all resources of that type. But if an editor is active, Cut applies only to selected resource components within the editor. Fortunately, because Cut, Copy, Paste, Clear, and Duplicate always work on a selection, it's always easy to tell what will be affected.

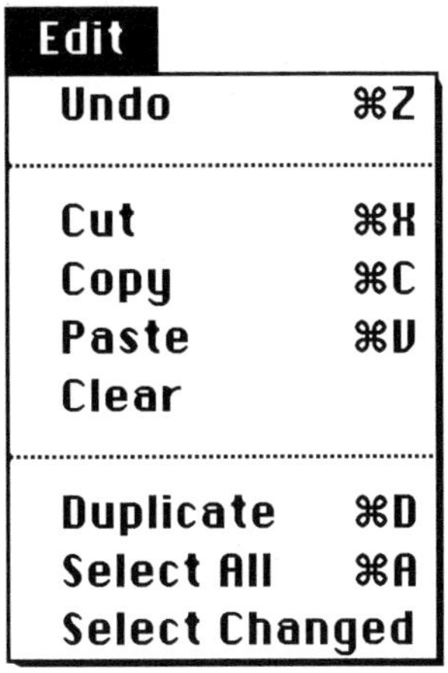

```
┌─────────────────────────┐
│ Edit                    │
├─────────────────────────┤
│  Undo          ⌘Z       │
│·························  │
│  Cut           ⌘H       │
│  Copy          ⌘C       │
│  Paste         ⌘U       │
│  Clear                  │
│·························  │
│  Duplicate     ⌘D       │
│  Select All    ⌘A       │
│  Select Changed         │
└─────────────────────────┘
```

Figure 3-15. The Edit menu.

Undo

With few exceptions, the Undo command will undo the last editing command. There are a few cases in which Undo is not available and is dimmed in the menu. For example, you can't undo cutting and clearing in pickers. You can achieve the same result, however, with the Revert command on the Resource menu. Most of the special editors fully support Undo.

Cut and Copy

These commands put the current selection or a copy of it onto ResEdit's clipboard. If you cut or copy from a type picker, you'll get *all* the resources of the selected type(s). From a resource picker, you get only the resource(s) selected. If you don't want to replace the clipboard contents with a new selection, Option-Command-X and Option-Command-C append the selection to what's already on the clipboard. (Appending works with the menu commands, too; just be sure to press the Option key before you pull down the Edit menu.)

Paste

What happens with this command depends on what you're pasting and where. That sounds more iffy than it really is because, fortunately, what the Paste command does makes sense when you think about it. If you paste to a type picker, you'll get all the resources of any type from the clipboard. If you paste to a resource picker, you only get resources of the corresponding type. You can also paste certain resource components into editors. For instance, you can paste bits (which become 'PICT' resources when cut or copied) into any of the fatbits editors.

Clear

As in most of the Macintosh world, choosing Clear is the same as pressing the Delete key. Nothing goes to the clipboard and in many cases you can't undo it.

Duplicate

Duplicate is available from resource pickers and some editors. In resource pickers, this command makes a copy of each selected resource, but instead of sending them to the clipboard as Copy does, it gives the duplicates new ID numbers and puts them in the same window. In editors, the command makes a copy of the selected resource component and keeps it within the resource. For instance, you can duplicate a menu item in a 'MENU', or duplicate a pattern in a 'PAT#' pattern list.

Select All

When you know you want to select everything in a picker window, this is the command to choose. (It also works in a few editors.) If you want all but a few, choose Select All then deselect the ones you don't want by using Command-click.

Select Changed

The first time you close a file and ResEdit asks if you want to save, causing you to mistakenly exclaim, "But I didn't change anything!" you'll be glad you have this memory-jogging command. Available from picker windows, this command selects resources (in resource pickers) or types (in the type picker) you've altered since you last saved the file.

▶ The Resource Menu

The Resource menu, shown in Figure 3-16, is ResEdit's most dynamic menu, but then resources are what ResEdit is all about. Although variable menu items may seem unsettling at first, they're intended to prevent confusion. ResEdit can perform such a variety of functions that generic commands would be almost meaningless. So, when necessary, menu items become more specific to let you know how they work in the current active window.

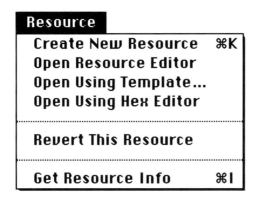

Figure 3-16. The Resource menu (as seen from a resource picker).

Create New Resource

What this command does when you're in a resource picker is probably obvious—it creates a new resource of that type, gives it a unique ID, and opens it in the appropriate editor. When you're at the editor level, the command will either be dimmed, or it will allow you to create a new component to add to the resource you're editing. For example, in a small icon list ('SICN') this command changes to Insert New Icon. In templates it changes to Insert New Field.

From the type picker, this command displays the dialog shown in Figure 3-17, which lets you create any new resource type, whether or not that resource type already exists in the file. (Remember, this may not do you any good unless you can write some program code that uses the resource.) You can scroll through the list or you can enter the resource type in the editable field. ResEdit creates the new resource for you, gives it a unique ID, and opens it in the appropriate editor. ResEdit picks the first available number greater than or equal to 128 for the new resource ID. You can even create a completely new resource type by entering a unique four-character name. When ResEdit doesn't have a special editor for a resource type, it opens in the hexadecimal editor.

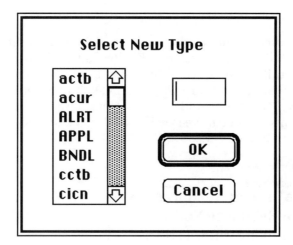

Figure 3-17. From the type picker, the Create New Resource command displays this dialog.

Open Resource Editor

When no resource type is selected in the type picker, this command is dimmed. As soon as you select a resource type, the item becomes available and the text changes to reflect your selection (Open 'MENU' Picker, Open 'ICON' Picker, and so on). If more than one type is selected, it becomes Open Pickers. The result of choosing this command remains the same—ResEdit opens the selected resource picker(s). Once you're in the resource picker, the command changes to Open Resource Editor. This item is also available from certain editors, where it will open an associated resource or a more detailed part of the same resource. For example, from the dialog ('DLOG') editor you can open the dialog item list ('DITL') editor, and from there you can open a dialog item. In short, this command (which is usually equivalent to double-clicking) gets you to the next deeper level, if there is one.

Open Using Template

This command, which is available from resource pickers and some editors, displays a dialog that allows you to choose a template from Res-Edit's template list, which is shown in Figure 3-18. This dialog is similar to the one in Figure 3-17 for the Create New Resource command, except that the types list includes only template resources. Occasionally, you may want to open a resource as a template even if a special editor exists, because sometimes you can edit infrequently changed parts in the template that you can't edit in the special editor. Option-Command-double-clicking a selection has the same result as choosing this command.

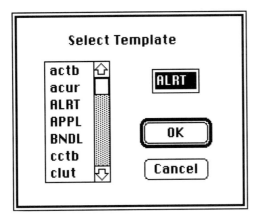

Figure 3-18. The Open Using Template command displays this dialog.

Open Using Hex Editor

The hexadecimal editor displays resources as a series of hexadecimal numbers. Programmers can open and edit any resource using the hexadecimal editor, but most users won't find it very helpful. This command is available from resource pickers and some editors. Option-double-clicking a selection has the same result as choosing this command.

Revert This Resource

If you've made a mistake and want to start over from the last saved version, choose this command. What this command affects depends on where you are when you invoke it, however. When you're in resource pickers and editors, this item says Revert This Resource, or Revert These Resources, depending on how many resources you've selected. In the type picker this item changes to Revert <type> Resources, or Revert Resource Types if you've selected more than one type. Every change to all resources of the selected type(s) will be discarded. To revert more specifically, go to the resource picker, where you can revert individual resources.

Get Resource Info

Use this command, which is available from resource pickers and editors, to see or set a variety of resource characteristics. It displays the Resource Info window, shown in Figure 3-19, in which you can change ID numbers and names of resources. Generally, the rest of the fields, which are discussed in Chapter 23, are useful only to programmers.

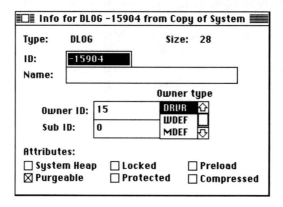

Figure 3-19. Unless you're a programmer, the Resource Info window is useful only for changing the names and IDs of resources.

▶ The Window Menu

The Window menu can help you find your way around a screen plastered with lots of windows. It lists, in an organized way, all the windows you've got open, as in the example shown in Figure 3-20. Windows in the list are indented according to the order in which you opened them, with each subsequent window name appearing below and to the right of the name of the window from which you opened it. The most recently opened window in each category appears at the top. File and folder info windows are in a class by themselves and appear grouped at the top of the menu. A check mark designates the active window. Selecting a window name brings that window to the front, making it the active window. When you close a window, all the windows indented under it in the window menu (all the windows opened from it) also close.

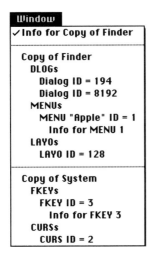

Figure 3-20. If you've got a lot of windows open, the Window menu can help you find the one you want.

▶ The View Menu

The View menu, shown in Figure 3-21, lets you tell ResEdit how to display the contents of pickers. (The section on pickers earlier in this chapter describes much of this in more detail.) The View menu lets you display the contents of a type picker either by icon or by type. If you want to see resource sizes (in bytes), you can choose Show Size With Type.

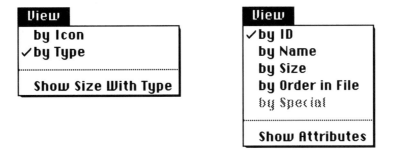

Figure 3-21. The View menu changes depending on whether the active window is a type picker (left) or a resource picker (right).

In resource pickers, the View menu lets you sort a list of resources by ID, Name, Size, or Order in File. You can also view some resource types in special pickers that give you more information. For instance, graphical pickers, such as those for icons or pointers, default to a graphical view (sorted by ID) that shows you what each of the resources looks like. The dimmed "by Special" item changes to the appropriate resource type, for instance, "by ICON." The last item on the resource pickers' View menu, the Show Attributes command, is available for any non-special view. Choosing this option tells ResEdit to display more detailed resource information that's generally useful only for programmers. (For more on resource attributes, see Chapter 23.)

▶ Substituting Resource IDs

Now that you're familiar with ResEdit's windows and menus, you're ready to learn a simple procedure you'll use frequently. Often you'll want to substitute a custom resource for the original one. You can customize the original, of course, and doing that is often just fine. But the advantages of keeping the original are twofold: You have it for reference, and you can switch back to it if you need or want to. The more complicated the resource, the more important preserving the original becomes.

As you recall from the previous chapter, applications generally look for resources by type and ID. So if you want an application to use your custom resource, it has to have the right ID. Let's say you want to customize the Tweak menu in some application, and you want to keep the original version, too. Here's the easiest way to do it:

1. Open a copy of your file with ResEdit, find the 'MENU' type in the type picker, and double-click it to open the 'MENU' resource picker.

2. In the 'MENU' picker, find the Tweak menu, let's say it's ID 17, and duplicate it. (First select it, then choose Duplicate from the Edit menu.)

3. ResEdit makes a copy of the resource and, starting with 128, gives it the first available (unused) ID. Keep this one as your spare, and make your changes to ID 17.

4. To help you keep track of what you've done, and so you can find it later, why not label the spare? Simply click it, then choose Get Resource Info from the Resource menu. You'll see a dialog like the one you saw in Figure 3-19. Click in the name field and type

"Original Tweak" or "Spare Tweak," or whatever makes sense to you. Similarly, you can label your custom Tweak menu. If the original resource had a name, you should preserve that name in your custom resource and rename the spare—just in case the application looks for resources by name instead of ID.

5. When you're through, close the file (saving your changes) and quit ResEdit. You can now try out your new menu in the application you changed.

If you want to switch back to the original Tweak menu and save your custom version, you'll have to shuffle both resource IDs around.

1. Open a copy of your file with ResEdit, find the 'MENU' type in the type picker, and double-click it to open the 'MENU' resource picker.

2. In the 'MENU' picker, find your custom Tweak resource, ID 17, and select it.

3. Choose Get Resource Info from the Resource menu. Click the ID field and type in a number that hasn't been used, let's say 129. (ResEdit warns you if you pick a number that's taken.) Close the window.

4. Now select the original Tweak resource, ID 128, and once again choose Get Resource Info from the Resource menu. Click the ID Field and type 17. Remember, if the resource originally had a name, you should change it back too.

5. Close the file (saving your changes) and quit ResEdit. Next time you use the application, you'll see the original Tweak menu.

The same steps apply no matter what resource type you're working with. Just be sure to remember what the original ID should be!

▶ Summary

This chapter describes ResEdit's features and style of presenting information. ResEdit has three kinds of windows: pickers, editors, and info windows. You pick what you want to work on from pickers. There's one type picker per file, and one resource picker for every resource type in a file. You make your changes in the various editor windows. Info windows are specific dialogs that allow you to see or set a variety of file, folder, and resource characteristics. This chapter also provides a guide to ResEdit's menus. The menus are dynamic; ResEdit adds, changes, and removes options depending on what kind of window you're working in, so you'll understand how the commands apply in the given situation, and so you don't trip over menus or commands you don't need.

Now that you're familiar with ResEdit's features and instrument panel, you're ready for a test drive. In the next chapter we'll give you a few more rules of the road and describe how to safely cruise through changing familiar and vital files you'll probably return to frequently—the System and Finder.

4 ▶ Editing the System, Finder, and Other Files

Some of the most useful customization projects you can tackle involve resources found in important files, such as the System and Finder, located in your System Folder. In fact, the System Folder and the Desktop file contain all the resources needed to initialize your Macintosh when you turn it on. Although the same rules apply to any application file, you must take special care when editing system files because a mistake can easily cripple your computer. With proper precautions, however, you can browse and modify to your heart's content. Table 4-1 lists selected customization projects, the system file in which you find those resources, and the chapter that discusses the project. In this chapter we describe a few more basics for editing any kind of file, then we explain how the Macintosh uses the System, Finder, and Desktop files, and how you can change them.

Table 4-1. Where to Start for Selected Customization Projects

Chapter	File	Project
5	System	Changing your scroll bar pattern and permanently adding a desktop pattern to the Control Panel
6	Finder	Changing the animated watch pointer
7	System	Customizing icons in alert boxes
7	Finder	Replacing the Trash icon
9	System	Moving keyboard characters
10	System	Customizing the size of standard file directory dialogs
15	Finder	Personalizing the Finder's layout
16	System	Speeding up your mouse response
18	System	Colorizing icons in alerts
19	System/ Finder	Adding color to the user interface

▶ Creating a Rescue Disk

All Macintosh owners should take the precautions of maintaining backups and having a rescue disk. You should always have a floppy disk that you can use to start your Mac just in case disaster strikes. This rescue disk should have a System Folder containing at least a System file and a Finder file. You can just use the System Tools disk that came with your Macintosh or the latest System software update. (You could easily generate a rescue disk using the Installer.) An even better approach is to create your own special rescue disk with a copy of your personalized System file and Finder so you don't have to reinstall all your fonts and desk accessories. In fact, as you set about customizing your System and Finder, you should update your rescue disk to preserve your custom resources. Follow these steps to create a rescue disk.

1. Initialize a floppy disk and name it "Rescue Disk."
2. Create a folder on this floppy and name it "System Folder."
3. Copy your customized System and Finder files (from the System Folder on your hard disk or your favorite start-up disk) into the System Folder on the rescue disk.

Now you've got a basic rescue disk. Depending on how big your System file is, you'll have room for more files on the floppy. You might want to include your hard disk initialization software, Apple's Disk First Aid, a disk recovery program, or other files from your System Folder. (Of course, you need to be sure all the other files in your System Folder are backed up, too.) Slide the tab on the floppy disk to the locked position so you don't accidentally erase it, then put the disk somewhere safe.

Hint ▶

As you customize resources in the System and Finder, why not save copies of your masterpieces in a special backup so you can easily replace them when you update to a new System software release? Simply create a file with ResEdit, calling it something like "Custom System (or Finder) Resources." Then, whenever you customize a resource, paste a copy of it into your special file. After you update to new System software, you can copy your own resources into the new files.

▶ Always Work on a Copy

When you first start to use ResEdit, and any time you're planning to make complicated changes, always make a copy of the file you're going to edit. ResEdit is a powerful program that has no limitations on the kinds of modifications you can make to resources. This power gives you the flexibility to change anything you want, but it also means you can destroy valuable data with the slip of a finger. Even though ResEdit can revert your file to the saved version, this only works if you catch your error soon enough. Mistakes using ResEdit can cause problems in a variety of ways. The most obvious mistake is to delete an important resource that the System or your application needs. Many more subtle problems stem from unforeseeable side effects of changes, due to complex interactions between resources and applications.

Hint ▶

Before you use ResEdit to open a file, use the Finder's Duplicate command to make another copy. Keep a spare copy until you're sure your changes are working correctly and you want to keep them. If you're working from a floppy disk, be sure to keep a copy of the file you're going to modify on a different disk.

As you become more familiar with using ResEdit, you'll learn when you don't absolutely have to make a copy before editing. For example, if you're just going to change the location of a dialog box, you might decide not to work on a copy since you wouldn't be making any irreparable changes. Remember, you should always have a backup copy so you can restore the original contents of the resource if you should decide you want to change back. Once you've tested your changes for a while and you're positive you like them and will never need the original resources, you should back up your customized file.

Until you have some experience using ResEdit, play it safe and work only on a copy.

▶ The System File

The System file is the brain, heart, and soul of your Macintosh. Without this file, the Mac won't even start. It contains part of the operating system (the rest is in ROM), fonts, desk accessories, keyboard layouts, pointers, icons, patterns, and many other resources you normally think of as integral parts of your Macintosh's personality. Many resources found here, such as the wristwatch pointer and the scroll bar definition, are provided for applications to use. Others, such as fonts and desk accessories, you add as you customize your environment. Because the System file contains so many important resources, you'll find many of the most interesting resources to customize here. As Table 4-1 shows, you'll find resources that control a variety of aspects of your Macintosh's appearance and behavior.

Your Mac needs this vital file to function, so you should be especially careful when making changes. You may remember that the System file is one of the files that ResEdit can open even though it's already open. (Of course, the System file is open any time your Mac is on.) Although it's possible to edit the active System file, we don't recommend it. Treat the System file just like any other file you've spent time modifying—keep a backup copy in case something should happen to the one you're using. But don't be afraid to play with it just because it's an important file or you'll miss out on some of the most useful ways you can customize your Mac.

▶ Editing the System File

Since the System file is indispensable, you should make a copy before making changes. You can use the following steps to modify your System file.

1. Use the Finder's Duplicate command to make a copy of the System file, and leave it in your System Folder.
2. Use ResEdit to modify the copy of the System file.
3. When you're done making your changes, save the file and quit from ResEdit.
4. Drag your original System file out of the System Folder and onto the desktop (or into any folder you want). You can't throw the System file into the Trash yet because it's still the currently active System file. Besides, you don't know if your changes will work properly, so keeping the original version is a good idea.
5. Rename your Copy of System file to "System."
6. Restart your Mac to activate your new System file.
7. If everything works as you planned, you can throw your original System file into the Trash or, better yet, hold onto it for a backup just in case your changes misbehave in the future.

By the Way ▶

You *can* edit the active System file directly, and occasions may arise when you'll want to do just that. You should still make a copy first, but you can keep it as a handy backup and work on the original. The advantage is that you can try out your changes immediately without having to drag files around and restart, because as soon as you save the System file in ResEdit, your changes take effect. The disadvantage is that it's much riskier because your changes may inadvertently make conflicting demands on your Mac, causing it to freeze up in confusion. If you're confident of your ability to recover in the event of a mishap, and you have good reasons for working on the original, you can take this approach for making simple changes.

▶ The Finder

When you're not using any other application, you'll always find yourself using the Finder, the application that manages your desktop. It helps you use your Mac by providing such things as folders and desktop icons, and housekeeping services such as emptying the Trash, copying or renaming files, and restarting your computer. You can customize many aspects of the Finder and, in fact, Chapter 15 is devoted entirely to customizing the Finder's layout. Although many substitute applications have been developed to replace the Finder, in this book we assume you're using the standard Finder provided by Apple.

▶ MultiFinder

If you have enough memory, MultiFinder can be a big help because it allows you to have more than one application open at a time. For example, you can have applications and printing (with a LaserWriter) continue in the background while you work on something else.

But MultiFinder creates a couple of situations you should be aware of when you're modifying resources in system files. You should be especially careful about editing the System file while using MultiFinder. If another application is open while you're editing the System file, you may inadvertently change a resource that the other application is using. The resulting confusion is usually not a pretty sight. Also, while Multi-Finder is running, you can't edit the Finder or the Desktop file. Remember that, with the exceptions of itself and the System file, ResEdit can't open files that are already open. Under MultiFinder the Finder is always open. (Of course you can, and in most cases should, always edit a copy.) Nor can you edit MultiFinder itself, but that's not a problem since there's nothing to change anyway.

| By the Way ▶ | Under System 7, MultiFinder is always running—you don't have the option of using the original Finder. |

▶ Editing the Finder

Since the Finder is an indispensable system application, you should make a copy before making your changes. You can use the following steps to modify your Finder.

1. Use the Finder's Duplicate command to make a copy of the Finder itself, and leave it in your System Folder.

2. Use ResEdit to modify the copy of the Finder.

3. When you're done making your changes, save the file and quit from ResEdit.

4. Drag your original Finder out of the System Folder and onto the desktop (or into any folder you want). You can't throw the Finder into the Trash yet because it's still the currently active Finder. Besides, you don't know yet if your changes will work properly.

5. Rename your Copy of Finder file to "Finder."

6. Restart your Mac to activate your new Finder.

7. If everything works as you planned, you can throw your original Finder into the Trash or, better yet, keep it for a backup just in case your changes misbehave in the future.

By the Way ▶

You *can* edit the Finder directly if you're not running MultiFinder, and occasions may arise when you'll want to do just that. You should still make a copy first, but you can keep it as a handy backup and work on the original. The advantage is that you can try out your changes immediately without having to drag files around and restart, because as soon as you quit ResEdit your new Finder will start up. The disadvantage is that it's riskier. If you're confident of your ability to recover in the event of a mishap, and you have good reasons for working on the original, you can take this approach. Chapter 15 gives more details.

▶ The Desktop File

The Finder uses the Desktop file to store information about which kinds of documents belong to which applications. When you double-click a document, the Finder looks in the Desktop file to determine which application to launch. Each mountable volume (such as a floppy disk, a hard disk or a server volume, if you're connected to a network) has its own Desktop file that stores information about applications and files it has encountered. You haven't seen this file lying about anywhere because the Finder makes it invisible. It's also the one system file not stored in the System Folder. Instead, it's located at the "root," or top level (not in any folder) on each volume. You can see and modify it from within ResEdit, of course, but you usually won't have much reason to edit it. The Desktop file contains the desktop icons for any application that has ever been on the volume, as well as the icons for each application's documents.

▶ Browsing and Updating the Desktop File

Browsing the Desktop file can be interesting just to see all the icons your applications might use. Remember that ResEdit can't open the Desktop file if MultiFinder is running, so you must restart your Macintosh without MultiFinder. Because the Desktop file is invisible, you can't use the Finder to make a copy first, so remember to be very careful.

| Hint ▶ | You can turn off MultiFinder two ways. One way is to choose the Set Startup command on the Finder's Special menu, click the Finder radio button, then restart. Or you could just hold down the Command key while restarting. (Hold it down until the Finder appears.) |

Generally you won't have any reason to use ResEdit's editors on the Desktop file. If you want to edit an application's icons, you should do that in the application file itself and then update the Desktop file. If you hold down the Command and Option keys when you restart your Macintosh (or when you insert a floppy disk) the Finder automatically rebuilds the disk's Desktop file However, when you update your Desktop file this way, you lose any information you've entered into the Finder's Get Info boxes. Chapter 7, which discusses icon customization, describes a manual way of updating the Desktop file that preserves comments in the Get Info boxes.

| By the Way ▶ | System 7 did away with the Desktop file, replacing it with a desktop database that's considerably faster, especially on large volumes storing lots of applications (and therefore lots of icons). The best way to update the Desktop database is to have the Finder rebuild it for you, the same way versions of the Finder prior to System 7 rebuild the Desktop file. To do this, hold down the Command and Option keys when you restart. |

▶ Summary

This chapter describes a few precautions to take before editing files, and discusses some of the most important files stored in your Macintosh—the System, Finder, and Desktop files. Some of the most fun and productive customization projects you can undertake involve resources in the System and Finder. We explain how to make a rescue disk, and remind you to always work on copies of files you edit. The System file is the brain, heart, and soul of your Mac, so you should be especially careful when editing System resources. Editing the Finder, another vital file, can get tricky, but the chapter explains how to go about it. The Desktop file is an important file to the Finder, and we describe one way to update it.

PART TWO

▶ Customizing Your Macintosh

5 ▶ Playing with Patterns

Without patterns, the Macintosh wouldn't be the Macintosh. They're everywhere. The desktop and scroll bars are filled with patterns. The Control Panel and About the Finder box use them. Tones—such as the white, black, dark gray, gray and light gray that are always available to any application on the Mac—are also generated using patterns. Then, of course, there are all the designs and pattern possibilities available in paint and draw programs.

Patterns, along with other graphical resources such as icons, fonts, and mouse pointers, are some of the most fun and rewarding resources to customize. You edit these graphical resources in fatbits, and ResEdit provides more than 10 fatbits editors. These editors have so much in common that once you know how to use one fatbits editor, you'll have a good grasp of all of them. (We'll cover specific features unique to the color fatbits editors in the color section.) This chapter introduces the fatbits editors in general, then tells you about pattern resources and what you can do with them.

▶ Using the Fatbits Editors

Figure 5-1 shows two representative editors, the 'ICON' editor and the 'PAT ' editor. Fatbits editors always give you at least two views of the resource you're editing—an enlarged fatbits editing view, and one or more actual-size views. A tool palette runs along the left side of the window. In addition, editors that work on list resources (such as the patterns in a 'PAT#' resource or the small icons in an 'SICN' resource) supply a scrolling selection panel so you can select the item you want to work on from the list. A dark outline around the list tells you when the list is active so you know when the Edit menu commands apply to the list instead of to the fatbits editing area. Fatbits editors also add the Transform menu to the menu bar. We discuss these features in more detail in the following sections, but first let's clarify a few details about how copying, cutting, and pasting work in fatbits editors.

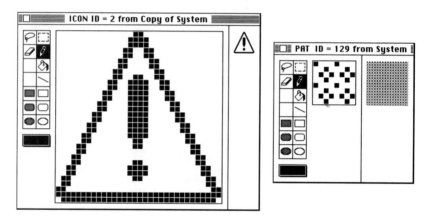

Figure 5-1. These representative examples illustrate some common features of the fatbits editors: an enlarged fatbits editing view, at least one actual-size view, and a tool palette.

Copying, cutting, and pasting fatbits resources will work without a hitch if you're clear about the difference between copying resources and copying selections of bits from resources. When you choose Copy from an editor or picker, the selected resource is copied to the clipboard *as a resource* of a certain type. You can paste that resource into a type picker, or a matching resource picker, but you can't paste it into another resource. On the other hand, if you have fatbits selected in an editor when you choose Copy, your selection goes to the clipboard *as bits*. Res-Edit handles a selection of bits as a 'PICT' resource, just as paint programs do. You can paste those bits into any fatbits editor or into a paint program document. So, although you can't paste an 'ICON' into an 'ICN#', for example, you can paste the bits from an 'ICON' into an 'ICN#'. You can find the tools you need in the tool palette.

▶ The Tool Palette

Most of the standard tools in the palette probably look familiar to you. The top two, the lasso and selection rectangle, are for selecting irregularly shaped and rectangular sections of bits, respectively. The eraser comes in handy for getting rid of lots of black bits, while the pencil lets you click black bits white or white bits black in a more precise fashion. The paint bucket pours black or white bits, or a selected pattern, into an enclosed area. The gray-filled shapes tools work the same as the empty shapes tools, except that the rectangles or ovals you draw will be filled with the selected pattern.

Hint ▶

The tool palette has some built-in shortcuts that may already be familiar to you from paint and draw programs.

- Double-clicking the rectangle selection tool gives the same result as Select All on the Edit menu—the entire image becomes selected.
- Double-clicking the eraser clears the entire view.
- Pressing the Shift key constrains several of the tools. For example, the rectangle tools draw only squares when you press the Shift key. Similarly, you can constrain ovals to circles, and lines to 45- or 90-degree angles. The eraser's action is constrained to a straight line. (*Wanting* to constrain the paint bucket or lasso makes no sense.)

▶ The Pattern Palette

The swatch under the tool palette tells you what color (black or white, except for color editors) or pattern the filled shapes and paint bucket tools will use. To change the pattern setting, click the swatch and the pattern palette pops up, as shown in Figure 5-2. Simply drag the mouse pointer to the pattern you want to use, and then release the mouse button. The swatch under the tool palette reflects your choice. You can also "tear off" the pattern palette, and move it to any convenient spot on the screen. Just click the palette's close box when you're through.

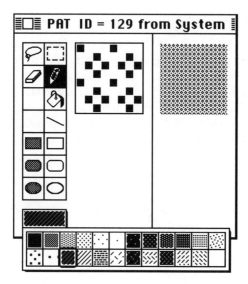

Figure 5-2. Pull down the swatch under the tool palette to select a pattern from the tear-off pattern palette.

By The Way ▶

ResEdit lets you add or change patterns in the pattern palette. Simply open a copy of ResEdit and open its 'PAT#' type, where you see all the patterns in the palette. By the end of this chapter you'll know how to edit this resource type. If you significantly customize the patterns, you might want to consider copying the 'PAT#' resource to the ResEdit Preferences file in your System folder. That way you won't lose all your work when you update to a new version of ResEdit.

▶ The Transform Menu

To give you more ways to manipulate the bits and images you're working with, the fatbits editors add the Transform menu, shown in Figure 5-3, to the menu bar.

The Flip, Rotate, and Nudge commands all work on selections, so they're dimmed until you've selected something for them to work on. Flip Horizontal flips the selection so that what was on the right appears on the left and vice versa. (The flip axis is vertical, but the fatbits move horizontally.) Flip Vertical flips bits from top to bottom and vice versa.

Rotate moves the selection counterclockwise. You can always move a selection by dragging it with the hand pointer, but the Nudge commands offer finer shifts. They move the selection by one bit in the chosen direction. The arrow keys do the same thing.

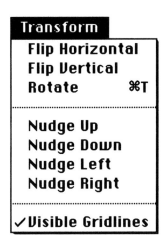

Figure 5-3.   The commands on the Transform menu help you manipulate selections in a fatbits editor's window.

When you have the Visible Gridlines option turned on (indicated by the presence of a check mark), each bit is outlined by a tiny strip of white space. This white grid lets you see exactly where the bits are, so you can position the editing tools more easily.

That's all you need to know about the fatbits editors. Now you're ready to edit patterns.

▶ Pattern Resources

A *pattern* is an 8-by-8-bit image used to define a repeating design (such as stripes or plaid) or tone (such as gray). They can draw lines or fill areas. When the Mac draws patterns, it aligns them so that adjacent areas of the same pattern blend into a single continuous pattern with no seams. (If only wallpaper worked as well!)

There are two kinds of black-and-white pattern resources. In the 'PAT ' type each resource is a pattern, whereas in the 'PAT#' type each resource is a list or collection of patterns. (Remember that resource names are always four characters long. 'PAT ' has a space at the end of its name.) 'PAT#' resources come in handy for offering pattern options and flexibility to users. Applications generally use 'PAT ' resources to store only a few consistently used patterns when flexibility is not a concern. We discuss the color versions of these resources, 'ppat' and 'ppt#', in Chapter 19.

How do applications keep all the patterns in a 'PAT#' resource straight? Remember, applications don't keep track of individual patterns—that would defeat the purpose of using a resource—instead, they keep track of position in the list. For instance, the Finder uses the second and twenty-second patterns from the System's 'PAT#' resource to fill in the memory graph bars in the About the Finder box. If you rearrange patterns or add new ones, you alter the order of the patterns. Figure 5-4 shows an example of one possible unexpected change. That's why it's a good idea to add new patterns to the end of a 'PAT#' list.

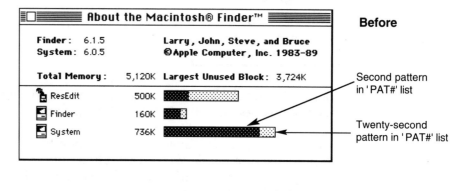

Before

Second pattern in ' PAT#' list

Twenty-second pattern in 'PAT#' list

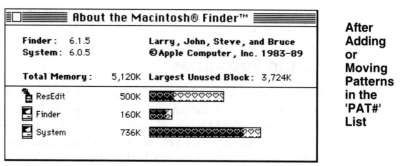

After Adding or Moving Patterns in the 'PAT#' List

Figure 5-4. If you rearrange patterns in lists, you might change things you didn't mean to change.

▶ 'PAT ' Resources

As you would expect, opening the 'PAT ' type from the type picker opens the 'PAT ' resource picker, shown in Figure 5-5. Simply double-clicking the pattern you want to alter opens the 'PAT ' editor, which you've already seen in Figures 5-1 and 5-2. The 8-by-8-bit editing field sits beside a sample field that shows you the results of your changes.

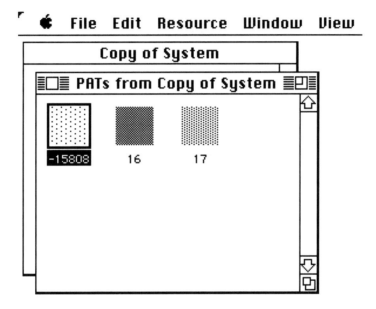

Figure 5-5. The 'PAT ' resource picker.

If you browse through your applications using ResEdit, you may not find many 'PAT ' resources. Most programs that use patterns use 'PAT#' resources so they can offer users flexibility. The System uses its 'PAT ' resources to keep track of the current desktop pattern and to fill things that stay the same, as shown in Figure 5-6, such as scroll bars and the background in the Control Panel. With ResEdit, however, you can change them. We'll show you how later in the chapter.

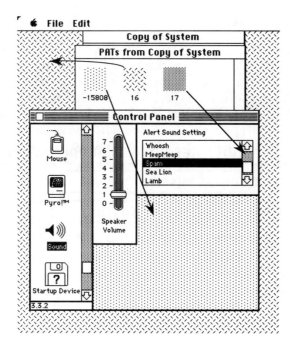

Figure 5-6. Uses of the System file's 'PAT ' patterns.

▶ 'PAT#' Resources

If you open a copy of your System file with ResEdit and open the 'PAT#' resource, you'll see a window that looks something like Figure 5-7. This is the 'PAT#' picker, but in this case there's only one 'PAT#' resource, one pattern list, to pick. Some paint programs may have more than one, so the window would look somewhat different, as shown in Figure 5-8.

You can enlarge the window or click the zoom box to show more of the patterns, but 'PAT#' resources can be so long that you may not be able to see the whole list unless you have a large screen. That's OK, because you can browse through all the patterns in the 'PAT#' Editor.

Hint ▶	As you work on patterns in the 'PAT#' Editor, remember that Revert applies to the whole resource—the whole list of patterns—not just the pattern you're currently working on. If you're planning a multi-pattern editing session, saving after changing each pattern would be a good idea.

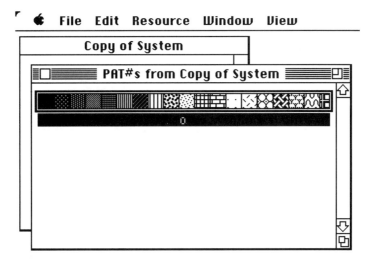

Figure 5-7. The System file has only one 'PAT#' resource, but it contains nearly 40 patterns.

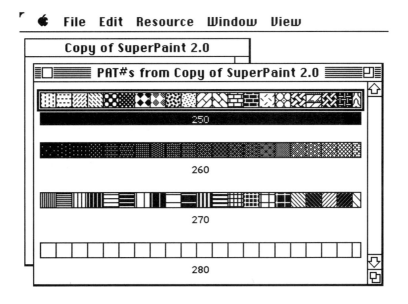

Figure 5-8. Some paint programs have more than one 'PAT#' resource.

To open the 'PAT#' editor, double-click the patterns list, or select Open Resource Editor from the Resource menu. The editor always opens on the first, or leftmost pattern, so it doesn't matter where on the list you double-click. This editor, shown in Figure 5-9, is similar to the 'PAT' editor, except that it also has a scrollable panel on the right to help you find your way through the list of patterns. The pattern that's first, or leftmost, in the resource picker becomes the topmost pattern in the scrollable list. The selected pattern has an outline around it. If you want to select another pattern, simply scroll to it, click it, and it will fill the editing field.

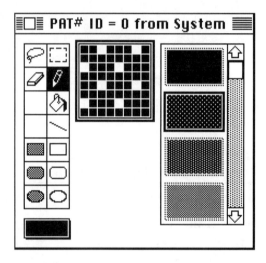

Figure 5-9. The 'PAT#' editor.

Hint ▶ You can select more than one pattern in the list for copying, cutting, or deleting (but not for editing, obviously). Also, you can move a pattern in the list simply by dragging it around in the scrollable selection panel. Don't do this in your System file, though, because you'll rearrange the order of the list.

In addition to editing existing patterns, you can create entirely new ones. Simply scroll to the bottom of the pattern list and select Insert New Pattern from the Resource menu. Of course, you can insert a new pattern anywhere you want to, but you might change something like the About the Finder box (and who knows what else) if you add to the first part of the list. If you want to keep both the original and modified versions of a pattern, copy the original pattern, paste it at the end of the list, then modify. The next section gives more details about working with patterns.

▶ Copying and Pasting Patterns

Maybe you found a nifty pattern in HyperCard or somewhere else that you'd like to add to your paint program or spread across your desktop. Or perhaps you stumbled across an interesting visual effect in your paint program by airbrushing a pattern or overlapping two patterns—in effect creating a new pattern without going to a pattern editor. Although paint programs may offer you the option of creating or editing patterns, in some cases the custom pattern stays with the document. Even if you can create new default patterns, copying a pattern from another application may not work. With ResEdit you can copy patterns within and between applications, and preserve swatches of new patterns as resources.

ResEdit allows a great deal of flexibility for moving patterns around in files. Normally, if you want to copy one fatbits resource image into another fatbits resource type, you have to select and copy the bits. With pattern resources, ResEdit makes an exception. You can copy a pattern from a 'PAT ' picker into the scrollable selection panel in the 'PAT#' editor. Picking up a swatch of a pattern from a paint program is easy, too. Just use a selection tool to grab a chunk of the desired pattern and copy it. Keep in mind that you're pasting it into an area only 8-by-8-bits square. If you paste a selection larger than 8-by-8, you can slide it around in the editor to position it. Once you deselect it, it's trimmed to 8 by 8.

Pasting and positioning patterns can be slightly trickier, but fortunately these operations work basically the same in both of ResEdit's pattern editors.

1. Once you've copied the pattern you're interested in, use ResEdit to open the appropriate pattern resource in the application to which you want to add it.

2. If you're pasting bits, you have to create a new, blank pattern in which to paste them. To do this, choose from the Resource menu either Create New Resource (from the 'PAT ' picker) or Insert New Pattern (from the 'PAT#' editor). If you fail to first insert a new pattern, the bits will end up pasted into the currently selected pattern.

3. Choose Paste from the Edit menu. If you copied bits, the pattern you copied will appear in the editing field surrounded by a selection marquee. (The marquee may be hidden if the pasted selection is larger than 8-by-8 bits, but the mouse pointer will be the grabber hand.) As long as the marquee or hand pointer is present, you can slide the pattern about in the editing field using the mouse, the Nudge commands, or the arrow keys.

Hint ▶	You can create brand new patterns just by repositioning patterns and selections in the editors. Because patterns repeat, almost any change can make a pattern look different.

As you're playing with patterns, remember that any time you'd like to see your new creation spread over your desktop (temporarily) all you have to do is choose Try Pattern from the 'PAT ' or 'PAT#' menus. When you choose the command again (or close the editor) your desktop returns to its original pattern.

▶ Changing Your Scroll Bar Pattern

Follow these steps to change the pattern in your scroll bar to something like that shown in Figure 5-10, or any other pattern you like.

Hint ▶	If you make your scroll bar black or mostly black, you won't be able to see the scroll box outline moving along with your pointer during repositioning. If you don't miss that feedback and really want a dark scroll bar, go ahead.

1. Open a copy of your System file with ResEdit and open the 'PAT ' resource type. If you think you might want to return to the original scroll bar pattern, duplicate resource ID 17 first. (Choose Duplicate from the Edit menu.)
2. Double-click pattern ID 17 to open the 'PAT ' editor.
3. Arrange and rearrange the bits to your heart's content.
4. When you're satisfied with your results, save your changes and quit ResEdit.

5. Now, simply reinstall the copy of your System file. (If you need a refresher, see Chapter 4.)

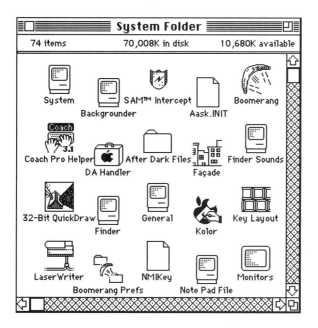

Figure 5-10. Your scroll bar can have any pattern you like.

After you restart, you should see your new scroll bars. Try moving the scroll box and clicking the up and down arrows. Remember that scroll bars also work horizontally. If your eyes cross or your stomach turns when the scroll box moves over your new pattern, you can just repeat these steps to edit and test the pattern until you're pleased with your results.

By the Way ▶

Changing your scroll bar pattern would obviously be easier if you worked on the active System file instead of a copy because you wouldn't have to reinstall your System file and restart to see your changes. If you're having trouble visualizing how your new pattern will look in a scroll bar, this is a case in which experienced users (or brave novices) might want to go ahead and *carefully* edit the active System file. Since patterns generally aren't vital resources, you ought to be OK. Just make sure you have a backup and don't change anything else!

▶ Adding a Desktop Pattern to the Control Panel

Not everybody uses the variety of desktop patterns available from the Control Panel. If you always keep the same desktop pattern, you might want to skip this part. This task is for those people who not only like to switch among the desktop patterns provided, but who also long to permanently add custom patterns. Have you ever created a desktop pattern that you wanted to keep but didn't necessarily want to look at all the time? As soon as you switch from your custom pattern, it's lost. For example, maybe you don't want to have to recreate festive seasonal desktop patterns like those shown in Figure 5-11 every year before the holidays. Here's how to add patterns to the 'PAT#' resource your Mac uses for drawing the desktop.

1. Open a copy of your System file with ResEdit and open the 'PAT#' resource.
2. Double-click anywhere on the patterns list (the bar of patterns) in the 'PAT#' picker to open the 'PAT#' editor.
3. Scroll to the end of the patterns list, and choose Insert New Pattern from the Resource menu.
4. Now you're ready to create a new pattern by clicking fatbits or to paste in a pattern copied from somewhere else. Remember that dragging a selection can create new patterns and visual effects.
5. Once you're satisfied with your results, just reinstall the copy of your System file.

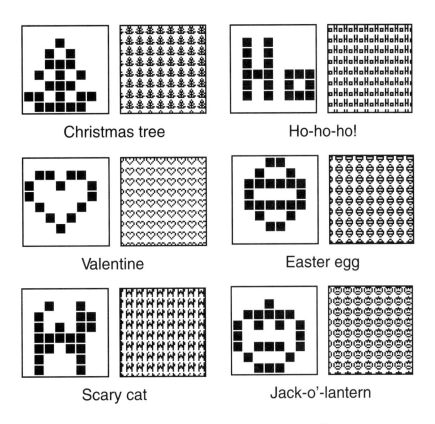

Christmas tree   Ho-ho-ho!

Valentine   Easter egg

Scary cat   Jack-o'-lantern

Figure 5-11. You don't have to recreate your festive seasonal desktop patterns every year.

▶ Summary

This chapter introduces ResEdit's fatbits editors and describes their common features. They always give you at least two views of the resource: an enlarged, fatbits editing view and at least one actual-size view. They have a tool palette and a tear-off pattern palette. The commands on the Transform menu, which these editors add to the menu bar, are also explained. Then we discuss the two types of pattern resources, 'PAT ' and 'PAT#', and their editors. We describe how to change your scroll bar pattern and how to permanently add desktop patterns to your Control Panel.

6 ▶ Personalized Pointers

The mouse is so integral to the Macintosh user interface that you probably don't think that much about it anymore. Just point and click, or click and drag. No big deal, right? Right! But as with so much about the Mac, you can customize aspects of the mouse user interface.

The small icon that indicates the mouse position is called the *pointer*. People often call it a cursor and, in fact, pointers are stored in 'CURS' resources. Pointers come in many different shapes but only one size, 16 by 16 bits. You can find them in applications, the System File, and the ROM. You can't modify the most common pointer, the arrow, because it's in the ROM. But you can modify three other common pointers—the wristwatch, I-beam, and crosshairs—because they're in the System file. You've no doubt encountered a variety of pointers in various Macintosh applications, so the examples in Table 6-1 probably look familiar.

As with many other types of resources, you have to keep a few things in mind when you set out to change a pointer. Not all applications use standard resources. Some (such as MacPaint) have their own copies of the pointers stored in the application. Others (such as Microsoft Word) don't use resources for their pointers. Still, you can modify most pointers you encounter.

Table 6-1. Some Macintosh Pointers

Pointer	Use
▶	The arrow is the standard pointer.
Ⅰ	The I-beam is used with text.
+	The crosshairs is used by graphics applications.
⌚	The wristwatch indicates that an application is busy.
✖	The beachball also indicates that an application is busy.
◁	The paint bucket is used by paint programs.
✋	The hand is used to move objects.
?	The question mark indicates that a help mode is active.
☺ 🄿 ⚔	Other pointers can be substituted just for fun.

By the Way ▶

If you look in HyperCard, you'll notice that there's a 'CURS' resource for the hand pointer. However, HyperCard doesn't use this for its hand pointer. The hand is actually stored in a 'FONT' resource (an 'NFNT' in HyperCard 2.0). So, to modify HyperCard's hand pointer, you actually need to modify ASCII character number 152 (ò) in HyperCard's font resource. For more details, see Chapter 13.

▶ The 'CURS' Editor

The 'CURS' editor is one of ResEdit's fatbits editors. (Even if you don't want to play with patterns, flip to the first part of Chapter 5—if you haven't already done so—for an introduction to the fatbits editors.) When you open a 'CURS' resource you see a window like the one shown in Figure 6-1.

This editor is a little more complex than the pattern editors, because a 'CURS' resource includes three parts—the pointer, the mask, and the hot spot. Each of these is a separate, editable entity. The fatbits view can display either the pointer itself or the shadow-like *mask* that determines how the pointer looks on various backgrounds. Immediately to the right of the editing area you see actual-size views of the pointer and the mask. Just click the one you want to edit. The dark outline and inverted name indicate which one is displayed in the fatbits view. To create a mask, simply drag the pointer view down onto the mask view. ResEdit makes a copy of the pointer and fills in all the enclosed areas. In most cases, this default mask will meet your needs. In any case, it's a good mask to start from.

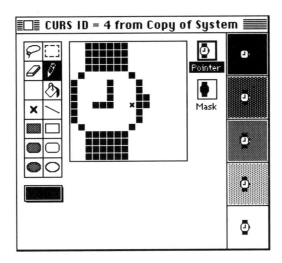

Figure 6-1. The 'CURS' editor.

The fatbit marked with an X shows the hot spot. The *hot spot* is the whole purpose of a pointer—it's the bit that positions the results of the pointer's actions. It's where the pointer truly points. You position the hot spot by using the hot spot tool (the X-shaped tool on the tool palette) to click the bit you want to set as the hot spot. Along the right side of the window the pointer appears on different backgrounds to give you an idea of how it will look in various situations.

The 'CURS' menu, which appears when the 'CURS' editor opens, has only one command on it. Try Pointer lets you test drive the pointer you're working on. ResEdit substitutes your pointer for the arrow it normally uses so you get to see how it feels and looks moving over various backgrounds. You can even edit your pointer during your test drive. When it's over the fatbits view, the pointer turns into the selected tool, as you would expect. But when you move the pointer outside the editing area, you can see the results of your changes. You can switch back to the normal arrow pointer by choosing Try Pointer again or by closing the editor window.

▶ Mask Hints

The mask determines how the pointer looks as it passes over non-white backgrounds on the screen. The only parts of the background affected are those where either the pointer or the mask contains black bits. That's why a pointer without a mask can look transparent; the background hasn't been masked, so it shows through. You can obtain interesting effects by altering the mask, but usually you'll want the mask to be the filled-in copy of the pointer that ResEdit automatically makes for you when you drag the pointer down onto the mask.

If you're careful, you can creatively modify the mask to improve a pointer's usefulness and visibility on various backgrounds. For example, if you make the mask one bit bigger than the pointer in all dimensions, the pointer will always have one bit of white around it. This white halo makes the pointer stand out much better against most backgrounds, as shown in Figure 6-2.

Putting a hole in the mask allows one bit of underlying data to show through. If the hole corresponds to the location of the hot spot, as is the case in Figure 6-2, you'll be able to position the pointer more precisely. This trick is particularly useful in graphics applications where you want to know exactly which bit you'll select when you press the mouse button.

You can also eliminate the mask entirely. The crosshairs and I-beam pointers stored in the System file don't have masks. A pointer is normally drawn by erasing the bits covered by the mask and then inverting all the background bits that correspond to black bits in the pointer. If there's no mask, the black bits in the pointer will be white on a black background, as Figure 6-3 shows, or black on a white background. Such a pointer can be confusing on varied backgrounds, such as text and some patterns.

Some pointers can give unexpected results when you drag the pointer onto the mask view to create an automatic mask. ResEdit makes a copy of the pointer and fills in all enclosed areas. But with a pointer like the hand (🖐), ResEdit simply produces a copy of the pointer that's not filled in. How can it fill the hand with bits if they all leak out the wrist? To avoid this, simply draw a line across the bottom of the hand, create the mask (which will now be filled in), then remove the extra line in the pointer. For any type of pointer, just make sure the picture forms an enclosed area before creating the mask. If the enclosed area in the pointer is filled in, however, or if the pointer is identical to the mask, it can disappear on black backgrounds. You can solve this problem by turning some enclosed bits white in either the pointer or the mask, or by making the mask larger.

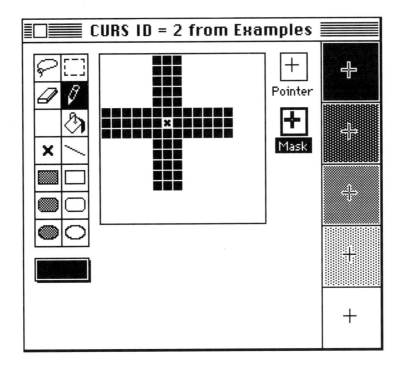

Figure 6-2. By altering the mask, you can make a pointer and its hot spot more visible.

| Mask | Pointer | Pointer and Mask |
| Alone | Alone | Combined |

Figure 6-3. The mask erases background bits, and the pointer inverts background bits. When they're combined, the mask makes a hole in the background first, then the pointer is drawn.

▶ Hot Spot Hints

The fatbit marked with an X in the 'CURS' editor shows the location of the business part of the pointer—the hot spot. It's the bit that indicates the exact spot pointed to when you click the mouse. For example, the hot spot on the arrow pointer is at its tip. Interestingly, every pointer has a hot spot, even if you can't use it for positioning the mouse's actions. The familiar watch and other special pointers that some applications display while they carry out lengthy operations illustrate this point. Essentially, these pointers say "please wait." Because the application is busy, you can't *do* anything with such pointers, but they still have hot spots.

By the Way ▶	You can locate the hot spot anywhere in the 16-by-16-bit field. It doesn't have to correspond to a black bit in either the pointer or its mask.

Moving a pointer's hot spot can make your interactions with an application less frustrating. Sometimes the pointer just doesn't position your mouse click's action exactly where you think it should. For instance, do you ever run into situations where the insertion point ends up in the wrong place after you click the mouse? The I-beam pointer that text processing applications use illustrates this problem. If the hot spot is too high in the I-beam, sometimes you end up putting the insertion point on the line above the one you were aiming for. You can fix this easily enough by simply editing the pointer and moving the hot spot toward the center of the I-beam. (Unfortunately, if you use Microsoft Word, you're stuck with the I-beam Microsoft thinks you should have. Remember, Word doesn't often use resources, so you can't customize it with ResEdit.)

▶ **Personalizing the Watch Pointer**

You're probably familiar with the watch that many applications display to indicate that they're busy. That watch is set at 9:00—what if that's not your favorite time of day? Here's how you can reset the hands, put stripes on the watchband, or even change the pointer to an hourglass, shown in Figure 6-4.

1. Use ResEdit to open a copy of the System file, and then open the 'CURS' type.

2. From the 'CURS' resource picker, select the watch pointer (it should be ID 4) and duplicate it (from the Edit menu). Having a duplicate means you can easily restore it later if you don't like your new creation.

3. Double-click the original watch cursor (ID 4), which opens in the 'CURS' editor and should look something like Figure 6-1.

4. Edit the pointer to suit yourself.

5. You can edit the mask, too, but ResEdit creates a mask automatically if you drag the actual-size view of the pointer straight down onto the actual-size view of the mask. If you're only resetting the watch's hands, the original mask will still work.

6. You can move the hot spot by setting the bit of your choice, but there's not much point since you can't use this pointer for selecting things anyway.

7. If you choose Try Pointer from the 'CURS' menu, you can test-drive your new pointer. Return to the normal arrow pointer by choosing Try Pointer again, or by closing the editor window.

8. When you're happy with your pointer, save your work, quit ResEdit, and reinstall your System file. Your new pointer should appear in place of the watch pointer in any application that uses the System file's 'CURS' resource.

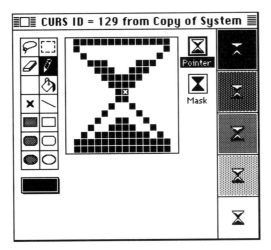

Figure 6-4. You can create an hourglass—or anything else you like—and substitute it for the watch pointer.

Hint ▶	Have you ever wished you could flip certain pointers (the pencil, for instance, or other tool palette pointers) to make them left-handed? You can! Just use the Flip Horizontal command on the Transform menu. Don't forget to move the hot spot, too.

▶ Animated Pointers

Some applications take the watch pointer one step further—they display an animated pointer when performing a lengthy task. For example, the Finder displays a watch with a rotating hand, and some other applications display a rotating beach ball. In most applications, you can easily modify these animated pointers to display any animation you can fit into a series of 16-by-16-bit pointers. If you get annoyed with an application's performance, why not change its pointer to a rotating pig face, such as the example in Figure 6-5?

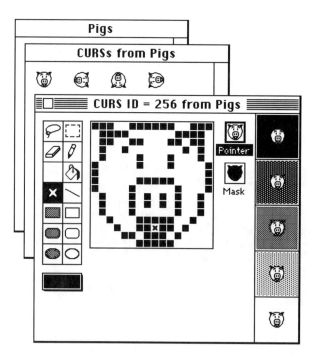

Figure 6-5. You can change an animated pointer to a rotating pig face, or any other animation sequence you design.

An 'acur' (Animated CURsor) resource controls pointer animation. (Remember, you can only modify existing 'acur' resources; you can't add an animated cursor to an application that doesn't already have one.) This resource determines how many pointers the animation sequence uses and lists their ID numbers in the order they should be displayed.

▶ The Finder's Animated Watch

Let's look at the Finder's animated watch to illustrate how this works. Like any 'acur' resource, the one that controls the Finder's animated watch uses several ordinary 'CURS' resources to make up the animation sequence. Figure 6-6 shows the Finder's 'CURS' resources.

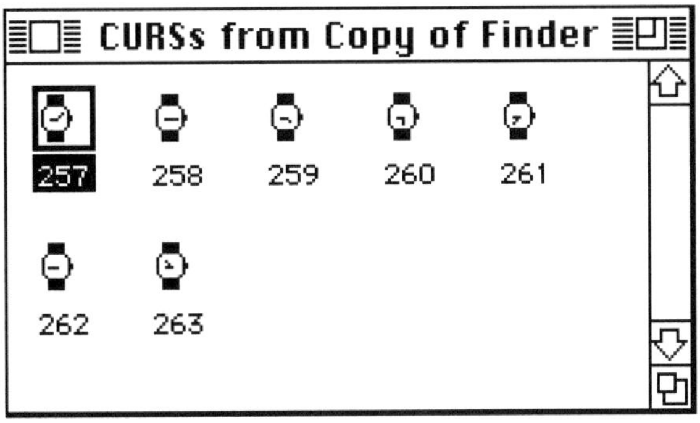

Figure 6-6. The Finder uses these watches for its animated pointer.

The Finder's 'acur' resource, which is shown in Figure 6-7, organizes these pointers into the sequence we recognize as animation. The 'acur' resource is an example of a template resource. You can learn more about using templates in Chapter 14. The first field contains the number of individual pictures or *frames* used in the animation sequence, in this case, eight. The second field controls the speed of animation; smaller numbers produce faster animation. Next, the IDs of the frames are listed in order. The first frame follows the last frame, and the sequence plays over and over until the application returns to the usual pointer.

By now the wheels are probably starting to turn in your head. Yes, all you have to do to make the hand rotate backwards is reverse the order of the pointers' IDs in the 'acur'. (This will not make time go backwards, of course, but you already knew that.) You can also substitute a completely different animation sequence. Perhaps you liked a series of pointers or other 16-by-16-bit images you saw in one of the miscellaneous resource collections you downloaded from a bulletin board. Or maybe you'd like to develop your own animated cursor.

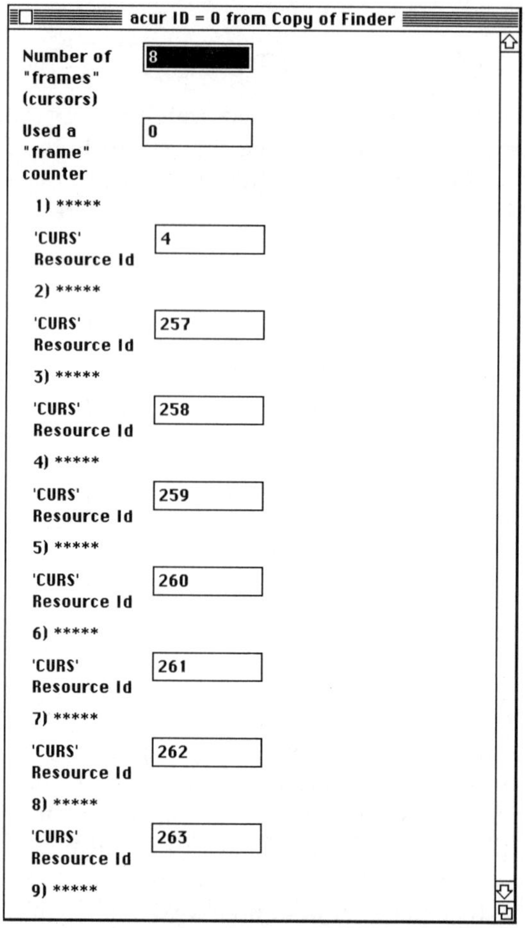

Figure 6-7. An 'acur' resource organizes the series of pointers used in an animated pointer sequence.

One way to devise your own animated sequence is to go to the 'CURS' editor and create a series of pointers that advance some action a little bit with each successive image. (The Rotate command on the

Transform menu comes in handy for pointers that rotate.) Perhaps you'd like to follow up on the hourglass pointer. The first frame would have all the sand at the top, and successive frames would show more and more sand flowing to the bottom. Finally, in the last frame, the sand fills the bottom and the top is empty. If you really want a fancy hourglass animation sequence, rotate the hourglass at the end so the part full of sand is on top again. You can create and store this set of frames in the (copy of) Finder's 'CURS' resource type, or you can create an "Experimental Resources" ResEdit file and work on the project in there.

| By the Way ▶ | You've probably noticed that although the 'acur' resource uses eight pointers, only seven watches appear in the Finder's 'CURS' picker. The first pointer in the 'acur', ID 4, is the old familiar 9:00 watch. "But I just changed that to an hourglass (or something)!" you cry. Relax. You don't have to worry about ruining the Finder's animation sequence. You may remember from Chapter 2 that System resources usually override ROM resources. However, in this instance the Finder reprioritizes to make sure that it gets the watch from the ROM. |

▶ Customizing the Finder's Animated Watch

Follow these steps to substitute the animation sequence you've designed for the Finder's rotating watch hands. (See Chapter 4 if you need to refresh your memory before modifying the Finder.)

1. Use the Finder's Duplicate command to make a copy of the Finder itself, and leave it in your System Folder.

2. Use ResEdit to open your copy of the Finder and open the 'CURS' resource type. You should see the seven watches shown in Figure 6-6. If you created your new pointers in this file, you'll also see them, and you can skip the next step.

3. If you created your animation sequence in another file, paste the new pointers you want the Finder to use into the 'CURS' picker. You may want to switch back to using the watches later, so be sure you don't overwrite any of them. (ResEdit will warn you if any of your new pointers happen to have the same ID as the watch pointers. Just be sure to click the Unique ID button in the dialog.)

4. Select all the pointers you just added to the Finder and choose Get Resource Info from the Resource menu. Make sure that the Locked and Preload check boxes are checked in the Resource Info window

for each pointer as shown in Figure 6-8. This guarantees that the Finder can always find the pointers when it needs them.

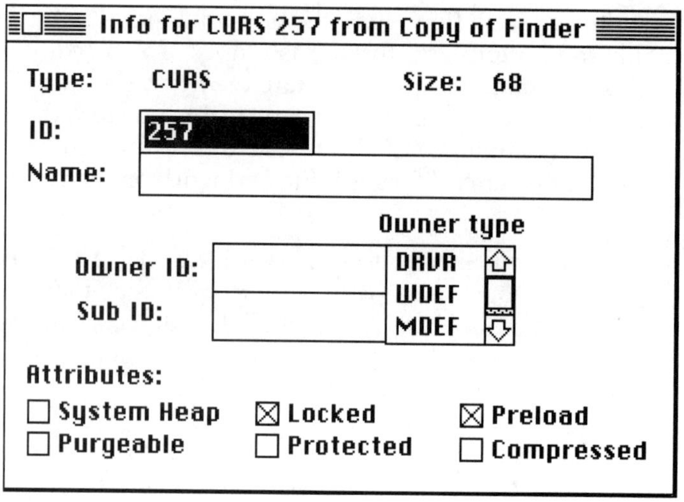

Figure 6-8. Make sure the Locked and Preload check boxes are checked for each 'CURS' resource you use in your animation sequence.

5. Make a note of the resource ID for each of your pointers and also the order in which they should appear.

6. Open the Copy of Finder's 'acur' picker and duplicate the 'acur' with ID 0. You should now have two 'acur's—one with an ID of 0, and one with an ID of 128. The one with an ID of 128 will be your spare if you want to return to using the watches. (You can label it as such by giving it a name with Get Resource Info on the Resource menu.)

7. Open the 'acur' resource with an ID of 0 and change it so it contains the appropriate number of frames and the IDs of your new pointer resources. List your pointers' IDs in the order you want them to appear. If you need to remove items, select the row of five asterisks (*****) above the item to be removed and press the Delete key. If

you need to add items, select the last ***** and choose Insert New Field(s) from the Resource menu. (For more information about using templates, see Chapter 14.)

8. Close the copy of the Finder, save your changes, and quit ResEdit. Drag your current Finder to the desktop, and rename your copy (it should still be in the System Folder) "Finder."

9. Restart, and you should be able to see your new animated pointer whenever the Finder performs a lengthy operation.

10. Once you have restarted, you can throw the old Finder (the one on the desktop) into the Trash.

▶ Restoring the Watch Pointer

If you decide you're tired of your new pointer, you can easily restore the Finder's original rotating watch.

1. Make a copy of the Finder.

2. Open the copy with ResEdit, and open the 'acur' resource type.

3. Select the 'acur' resource with ID of 0 and choose Get Resource Info from the Resource menu.

4. Change the ID to 129 (or the next available number).

5. In the same way, change the ID of the 'acur' with ID of 128 (you did save it, didn't you?) to 0. If you left all the watch pointers in the file, you shouldn't have to worry about them.

6. Reinstall your new Finder and restart.

By the Way ▶

A delightful shareware desk accessory called Cursor Animator lets you have animated cursors in every application. The program includes a large collection of clever animated cursors to suit every taste, and it even lets you add your own. With ResEdit and Cursor Animator you'd never be at a loss for animated cursors. Cursor Animator is available on most electronic bulletin boards, from many Macintosh user groups, or from Wilhelm Plotz, Siedlungstrasse 21, 4222 St. Georgen a.d. Gusen, Austria.

▶ Summary

This chapter introduces *pointers*, the small icons that indicate mouse position. They're often called cursors, and are stored in 'CURS' resources. A 'CURS' resource has three editable parts: the pointer, the shadow-like mask that determines how the pointer looks on various backgrounds, and the hot spot—the bit that positions the pointer's actions. To handle this added complexity, the 'CURS' editor has a few more parts than the pattern editors, but it's still an easy-to-use fatbits editor. We show how to change the watch pointer that many applications use to indicate they're busy. Some applications use animated pointers, which are stored in 'acur' resources. The Finder's watch with its rotating hand is one example. We describe how to substitute your own animation sequence for the Finder's animated watch.

7 ▶ Ideal Icons

As you customize your favorite applications, why not customize their icons, too? Modifying icons is one of the most popular and rewarding things you can do to personalize your Mac, and you've probably been itching to dig in. Changing icons can not only satisfy your urge to personalize, but it can add information. An application's Finder icon can include a version number, your initials, or any other identifying information you're clever enough to fit into the space you've got. Icons play an important role throughout the Macintosh environment. You're familiar with their use in the Finder to represent files and devices such as disk drives. These icons can show up on the desktop or within folders. But icons also appear in dialog and alert boxes, and occasionally in menus.

The Mac uses many different kinds of icon resources. Ultimately, they all describe a set of bits that are copied to the screen, but each resource type contains slightly different information. Icons come in two basic sizes, large (32-by-32-bit) and small (16-by-16-bit), except for one type of color icon ('cicn'), which can vary in size. Table 7-1 briefly lists all the icon resource types.

Table 7-1. Types of Icon Resources

Type	Description
ICON	32-by-32-bit icon used in dialogs, alerts, and menus.
SICN	16-by-16-bit small icon lists used in menus and some applications.
ICN#	32-by-32-bit icon the Finder uses on the desktop. Includes a shadow-like mask.
cicn	Color icon. Size can vary (from 8-by-8- to 64-by-64-bit). Can include a black-and-white version used when color isn't available. Usable only on machines with Color QuickDraw (Mac II, Mac IIcx, Mac SE/30, etc.). Used in dialogs, alerts, and menus.

These came into existence along with Finder 7.0:

icl4	32-by-32-bit icon, 16 colors.
icl8	32-by-32-bit icon, 256 colors.
ics#	16-by-16-bit icon. Black-and-white, includes a mask.
ics4	16-by-16-bit icon, 16 colors.
ics8	16-by-16-bit icon, 256 colors.

To handle all these icon types, ResEdit has five editors. Each of the first four icon types listed in Table 7-1 has its own editor. The last five icon types are related, so you can edit them all in one editor, the icon family editor. We'll talk about the color icon editors ('cicn' and icon family) in Chapter 18. Similar editing methods work in all the icon editors, so we'll review a few techniques first, then progress through the icon types, and give you some ideas for what you can do with them.

▶ Creating and Editing Icons

Almost any time you want to create a totally new icon, you can head for the first item on the Resource menu, Create New Resource. The command isn't available from editors, so you may have to go back to the icon picker. (Creating new icons within 'SICN's is a little different, but we'll explain that in the section on 'SICN's.) If you're working in a file that doesn't have the icon type you're interested in, you'll have to go back to the type picker and create the icon type there. But first, decide whether this makes sense. Remember, with rare exceptions, you can't just create a new resource type and expect an application to use it. Whether you do it from the type picker or the resource picker, ResEdit creates a new resource, gives it a unique ID, and opens it in the editor. Now you can happily click away using normal fatbits techniques. (For a refresher on how to use ResEdit's fatbits editors, see the first section of Chapter 5.)

You might also want to create an icon in a paint program. Maybe you find drawing easier in paint and draw applications (just remember the icon size you're limited to). Or perhaps you've come across part of a picture you'd like to turn into an icon. Once you've got the desired art, use a selection tool to grab the picture and copy it. You don't have to worry about trying to select an area exactly the size of the icon because you'll have a chance to position things later. Next, use ResEdit to create a new icon resource in your target file and paste your selection into the blank editor. If the selection was too large, or if you only want an edge of it, use the Nudge commands on the Transform menu (or the arrow keys) or the mouse to slide the selection to where you want it. When you deselect it (for instance by selecting another tool), any bits not visible in the editor are discarded.

Why not try out these basic editing techniques on one of the simplest types of icons, the 'ICON' resource.

▶ 'ICON' Resources

With a few clicks in the 'ICON' editor, you can give the Find File person a skateboard and speedy streaks or make the talking head in dialogs friendlier, as shown in Figure 7-1. You can find these two icons, along with several others you may want to change, in the System file.

Figure 7-1. In the 'ICON' editor you can change the icons you see in dialogs, alert boxes, and some menus.

Figure 7-2, which shows the System file's 'ICON' picker, gives you an idea of the 'ICON's the System file contains. When you double-click an 'ICON' resource, ResEdit opens it in the 'ICON' editor, shown in Figure 7-3. The editing field is just the right size to hold a 32-by-32-bit image, and the editor works just as you would expect.

The next section describes how to use this editor to change icons in alert boxes.

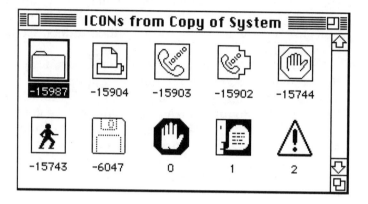

Figure 7-2. The System file has many 'ICON's you might want to change.

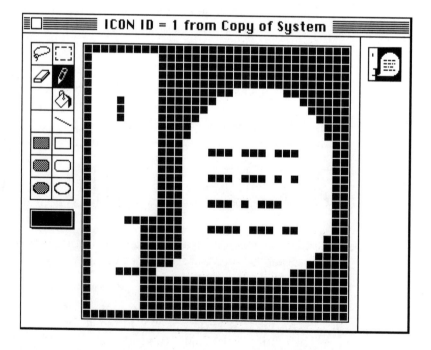

Figure 7-3. The 'ICON' editor is a prototypical fatbits editor.

▶ Changing Icons in Alert Boxes

You can easily modify any of the alert icons shown in Figure 7-4. (In Chapter 18 we'll show you how you can make them appear in color!)

Figure 7-4. Alert boxes can employ one of these three icons from the System file.

By the Way ▶ Macintosh applications generally use four kinds of alert boxes. One kind contains no icon. For the other three, the icon in the upper left corner of the alert indicates the type of alert, as shown in Figure 7-4.

If you're not experienced with modifying System files, now would be a good time to flip to Chapter 4, Editing the System, Finder, and Other Files, to review procedures and precautions.

1. Use ResEdit to open a copy of your System file.
2. Open the 'ICON' picker. You should see something similar to the icons you saw in Figure 7.2.
3. Select the icon you want to alter and duplicate it. That way you'll always have a copy of the original in case you need to start over or want to switch back.
4. Double-click the icon you just duplicated to open the 'ICON' editor. (If you work on the original instead of the duplicate, you won't have to change IDs.)
5. Edit the icon until you have exactly what you want.

6. Close the file, save your changes and quit ResEdit.

7. Install your modified System file and restart to see your changes.

▶ Small Icon Lists ('SICN' Resources)

Applications can use 'SICN' (Small ICoN) resources in a variety of places, but you're most likely to see them in menus or palettes. Each 'SICN' can contain any number of small (16-by-16-bit) icons. (This is an example of a list resource that doesn't have a pound sign (#) in the resource type.) Although many applications don't use any 'SICN's at all, others have quite a few. FullWrite Professional has eight 'SICN' resources, one of which includes well over 30 icons. MORE II contains 20 'SICN's, many with ten or more icons. So, if the icon you want to modify is small and doesn't seem to have a big counterpart, checking the file's type picker for the 'SICN' resource type could prove worthwhile.

| By the Way ▶ | Until the 'cicn' and Finder 7.0 small icons came along, the only way applications could have a small icon was to use an 'SICN' resource. The icons the Finder uses for its small icon view aren't 'SICN's; they're reduced 'ICN#' icons—which is why they sometimes look clumpy. System 7 got around this problem by defining a whole new set of icons, which includes both small black-and-white and small color icons. For more information on this icon family, see Chapter 18. |

Like a typical picker for a list resource, the 'SICN' picker displays the first several icons for each 'SICN' in the file, as shown in Figure 7-5. The Finder's 'SICN' lists are short enough to fit, but others may be much longer, as mentioned previously. You can enlarge the picker window or click the zoom box to show more of the icons if you need to, but 'SICN' resources can be so long you may not be able to see the whole list even if you have a large screen. That's OK, because you can browse through all the icons in the 'SICN' Editor.

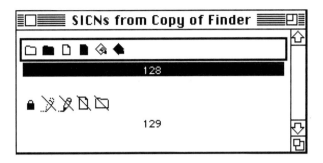

Figure 7-5. The Finder has only two 'SICN' resources, but each one contains many icons.

When you open an 'SICN' resource, you see the first icon in the list in the fatbits editor window, and a list of actual-size icons displayed along the right side in a scrollable panel, as shown in Figure 7-6. Where you double-click an 'SICN' resource doesn't matter, the editor always opens on the first (leftmost, or topmost) icon in the list. Use the scrollable list along the right to select the icon you want to modify. The selected icon has a dark box around it. To edit a different icon, simply click it. An outline around the scrollable list tells you when it's active, meaning the Edit menu's commands apply to it instead of to the fatbits editing area.

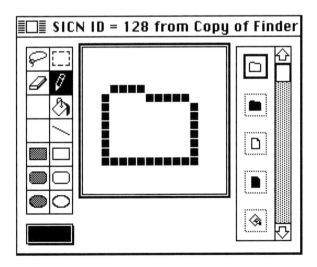

Figure 7-6. The 'SICN' editor displays a fatbits view of the selected icon and a scrollable list.

You may remember from the introduction to list resources in Chapter 2 how an application decides which icon to use in an 'SICN' resource. Applications don't keep track of specific icons—that would defeat the purpose of using a list resource—instead, they keep track of position in the list. Therefore, be careful not to rearrange icons or otherwise alter their order because that can lead to chaos. When an application fetches and displays the wrong icons, you quickly realize how much you depend on these little pictures. Any substitutions or rearrangements should be the result of a conscious effort, not an accident.

By the Way ▶

If you're familiar with the pattern list resource ('PAT#'), some of this may sound familiar. However, there's an important difference in the way applications employ these two list resource types. Generally, applications make patterns available for users to use, but they use 'SICN's themselves. So, patterns might exist in 'PAT#' resource lists without ever being used, but any icon that exists in an 'SICN' resource has a purpose, presumably, or it wouldn't be there. That's why you don't want to take a cavalier attitude toward rearranging icons in 'SICN' resources.

Choosing Insert New Icon from the Resource menu adds a new small icon just after the currently selected one. Of course, that rearranges the order of icons in the resource, but if you're a programmer, we're assuming you'll figure out how to make your application do the right thing. Even if you're not a programmer, you can still add new icons if you keep the list in order by adding them at the very end.

A question probably just sprang to your mind: "What good does it do me to add icons to the end of the list if the application won't use them anyway, because it won't know they're there?" Icons at the end of the list can serve as "extras." For example, you can keep the original icon handy while you put your modified version into service. Even though you've got a backup copy of the file (you do, don't you?), storing the spare icon in the same resource is awfully convenient if you want to switch back. The end of the list is also a great place to store or create experimental icons.

OK, so maybe it makes sense, but how do you go about it? You can scroll to the very last icon and choose Duplicate (from the Edit menu), or choose Insert New Icon (from the Resource menu). Either way you end up with a spare spot to play around with, and more options.

Keeping track of where the list of "real" or in-service icons ends might be a good idea. You can do that any number of ways, but just leaving a blank icon as a spacer easily does the trick, as shown in Figure 7-7.

Hint ▶	As you work on icons in the 'SICN' editor, keep in mind that, as with all list resources, Revert This Resource applies to the whole resource—the whole list of icons—not just the icon you're currently working on.

Hint ▶	Remember to pay attention to the location of the dark outline in the editor (either around the fatbits editing area or the scrollable list) so you'll know whether you're copying a whole icon or a selection of bits from an icon. When you paste an *icon* (that is, when you've copied it from the scrollable list), ResEdit pastes it just after whatever icon is currently selected. When you paste a selection of *bits* (that is, when you've copied bits from any of the fatbits editors or from a paint program), ResEdit pastes the selection into the currently selected icon, thus overwriting it. If you're pasting bits, create a new empty icon to paste into. Menu item text also gives you clues as to what will happen. For example, the Edit menu says "Paste PICT" for bits and "Paste Icon" for an icon.

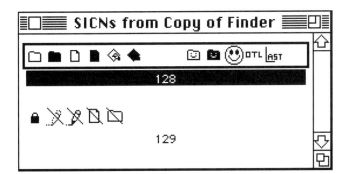

Figure 7-7. If you store experimental small icons at the end of an 'SICN' list, you might leave a blank icon spacer to mark the end of the in-service icons.

▶ Changing the Icons the Finder Uses in Its Text Views

The Finder uses icons even in its text views. You may have recognized the folder, file, and application icons in Figures 7-5, 7-6, and 7-7. But maybe you feel that those blank little document icons don't really represent the amount of work you put into your documents. You can change that. You can add pictures or lines of text. While you're at it, you can touch up the other icons, too, perhaps making your folders look happier, as Figure 7-8 illustrates.

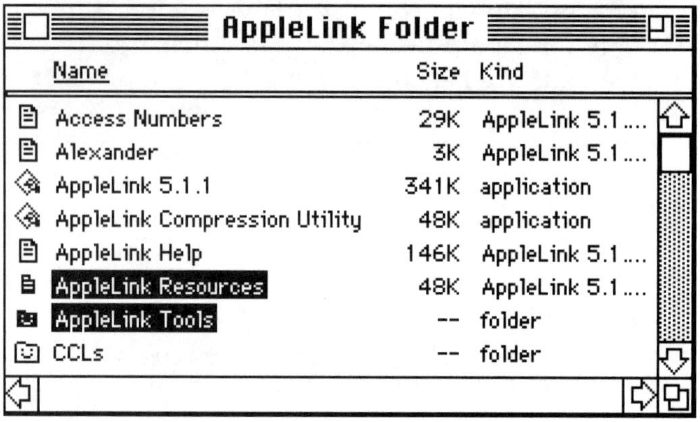

Name	Size	Kind
🗎 Access Numbers	29K	AppleLink 5.1....
🗎 Alexander	3K	AppleLink 5.1....
AppleLink 5.1.1	341K	application
AppleLink Compression Utility	48K	application
🗎 AppleLink Help	146K	AppleLink 5.1....
AppleLink Resources	48K	AppleLink 5.1....
AppleLink Tools	--	folder
CCLs	--	folder

Figure 7-8. You can touch up the icons the Finder uses in its text views.

When you set out to beautify your Finder, remember to make sure the icon pairs match. The all-black icon in the pair should be a perfect silhouette, the same size, shape, and orientation as the other icon. This is important, unless you like your Finder looking screwy. The shadow-like black icon acts as a *mask* so that the icon looks right when the file it represents is selected. You don't have to worry about what a mask is just yet. You can learn all about masks in the next section about 'ICN#' resources—the big Finder icons. For now, just remember to keep the icon pairs in the Finder's 'SICN' resource matched.

One more thing to keep in mind before you dive in is that, for cosmetic reasons, your new icons shouldn't use the whole 16-by-16-bit space. The default spacing in the Finder doesn't accommodate full-sized small icons without overlapping. You can change this spacing, however. See Chapter 15 for more details.

By the Way ▶	Perhaps you're wondering why Finder 'SICN' icons need mask-like partners but System ones don't. Part of the Finder's job is to let you know which files are selected, not selected, or selected and open, and so on. To convey these different states, the Finder draws the icon several ways, using the mask where necessary. The 'SICN' icons that other applications use generally don't have to go through this complicated change of appearances.

If you're not experienced with modifying your Finder, now would be a good time to flip to Chapter 4 to review the section about working on the Finder.

1. Make a copy of your Finder, as explained in Chapter 4.
2. Use ResEdit to open the copy of your Finder, then open the 'SICN' resource type. You should see two resources that look something like the ones you saw in Figure 7-5.
3. Double-click the resource with ID 128. ResEdit opens the 'SICN' editor. You should see something like Figure 7-6.
4. Edit the icon pair(s) you're interested in.

Warning ▶	Be sure to preserve the order of the icons in the resource as you edit and substitute your new icons. The only way the Finder knows which icon to use where is by its position in the list.

5. When you're satisfied with your new icons, save your changes and quit ResEdit.
6. Install your modified Finder and restart.

You should see your snazzy new icons any time the Finder displays one of its text views.

▶ Finder Icons ('ICN#' Resources)

Some of the most prominent icons you work with are those displayed on your desktop, including the Trash, file and folder icons, and the specific icons associated with applications. These icons are stored in 'ICN#' resources, and, because the Finder is responsible for drawing them, people sometimes call them Finder icons. Most applications have their own special icons, but you can personalize them to make them uniquely yours.

ResEdit can edit 'ICN#' resources in two different editors, but which one you see depends on your Macintosh. On any of the "classic" Macs and up through the SE, 'ICN#' resources open in the 'ICN#' editor, a strictly black-and-white editor. But if your Mac's ROM has Color Quick-Draw (which SE/30s and all MacIIs do), 'ICN#' resources open in the icon family editor, discussed in more detail in Chapter 18.

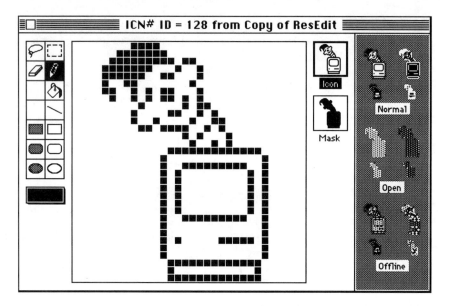

Figure 7-9. The 'ICN#' editor can show the icon or its mask in fatbits, and combines them in actual size to show how the Finder would draw them in various situations.

When you open an 'ICN#' resource you see a window containing a magnified view of the icon, and several actual-size views along the right side of the window, as shown in Figure 7-9 for the 'ICN#' editor and Figure 7-10 for the icon family editor. The fatbits view can display either the icon itself or the shadow-like *mask* that determines how the icon looks on various backgrounds. Immediately to the right of the editing area you see actual-size views of the icon and the mask. To select the one you want to edit, simply click it. A dark outline and a highlighted label indicate which one is displayed in the fatbits view. The mask determines how the icon looks when drawn on various backgrounds and in various states. (More on this in a minute.) You can edit the icon and mask using normal fatbits techniques.

Along the right side of the window you see the selected icon as it would appear in several different states. As the labels indicate, the top views show the icon in its normal state (closed), the middle views show it open, and the bottom views show it offline (ejected but still mounted).

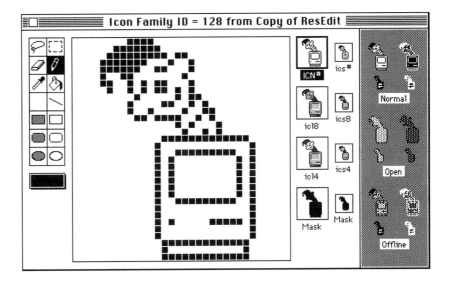

Figure 7-10. On Macs with Color QuickDraw, you edit 'ICN#' resources in the icon family editor.

In each case, the left side shows the icon unselected and the right side shows it selected. Underneath you see the shrunken version of the icon. You can change the background on which the samples are drawn to white, gray, black, or your current desktop pattern with the aid of the 'ICN#' (or Icons) menu.

| By the Way ▶ | When the Finder needs a small icon for its small icon view, it simply shrinks the large icon (and its mask) by half. |

▶ Creating the Mask

You may be wondering how the mask works. In a nutshell, when the Finder draws an icon, it uses the shape of the mask to erase a hole in the background, then draws the icon in the resulting hole. An icon without a mask may become transparent—or even disappear altogether—depending on the background and the state of the icon (for instance, selected or not). So when you change an icon, remember to change its mask, too. The only mask guaranteed to work properly under every circumstance is a filled in version of the icon itself. You can easily create such a mask by dragging the boxed icon (just to the right of the editing panel) straight down onto the box labeled "Mask." Of course, you can also experiment with trying to get interesting effects by altering the mask. Browsing through your applications' icons may give you more ideas for techniques to try.

Hint ▶	If the icon you design contains open shapes, you may be puzzled over the results you get when you drag the icon down onto the mask box. To create a mask, ResEdit makes a copy of the icon, then fills it in, which works fine with a closed shape. But if the shape of the icon is open, ResEdit can't fill it in—all the bits leak out! This doesn't have to cramp your creative style, however. Simply close up the icon before you make the mask, then open it again afterward. (You can also enclose areas of the mask using the pencil tool, then fill them using the paint bucket.)

▶ Changing an Application's Icons

Changing the icons of your applications or data files can be fun as well as informative. For example, you could add the version number of an application to its icon. If you want to add a document icon to an application, or if you're creating your own application, refer to Chapter 22.

Hint ▶	An easy way to find all the 'ICN#' resources an application uses is to open the 'BNDL' editor. See Chapter 22 for more information.

1. Use ResEdit to open a copy of the application whose icon you want to change.

2. Open the 'ICN#' type and select the icon you want to change. Duplicating the original icon before you make changes is a good idea just in case you want to switch back later.

3. Make your changes (to the original, not the duplicate, so you won't have to change IDs).

4. Close the file and save it.

As you can see, changing an icon is relatively easy. Getting the Finder to use your new icon can be somewhat trickier. Before you can convince the Finder to use your new icons, you need to know a little about how it interacts with icons.

▶ Understanding Finder Icons

Clearly, the Finder can't magically know the icons for every application possible, so a mechanism exists for acquiring and keeping track of these icons. Applications generally supply icons for themselves and for the documents they create. The Finder uses these icons to represent the application and its documents, and it stores them in its invisible Desktop file.

▶ How the Finder Finds Icons

To link icons with their appropriate files, the Finder makes use of two identifiers. These identifiers, which every file has, are four-letter codes called the Type and Creator. Applications always have the Type APPL, but their Creators give each application a unique signature. For example, ResEdit's Creator is RSED and MacPaint's is MPNT. A document has the same Creator as the application that created it, so the Finder knows where to look for its icon. The Finder uses the Creator to associate a document with the appropriate application.

An application's documents may have various Types, and these tell the Finder which icon of the application's set of icons to use for which type of document. For example, in FullWrite Professional, the FW Dictionary file's Type is FWDI, whereas a stationery file has a Type of FWST. The Finder uses file types to display different icons for each kind of file. Table 7-2 lists a few examples to illustrate these relationships. For more information about associating icons with file types, see Chapter 22.

Table 7-2. Types and Creators Used to Match Icons and Files

Icon	Type	Creator	Kind of File
	APPL	FWRT	FullWrite application
	FWST	FWRT	FullWrite stationery
	FWDI	FWRT	FullWrite dictionary
	APPL	MWII	MacWrite II application
	MW2D	MWII	MacWrite II document

Although the Finder gets icons and information from applications, it doesn't repeat the fetching process every time it encounters a file. Instead, it maintains a list of every application it has ever encountered. This list includes every application's icon for itself and the icons for all its documents. The Finder stores this roster in an invisible file known as the Desktop file. Thus, the Desktop file contains a history of every file Type and Creator that has ever resided on the disk.

By the Way ▶ Much of this story changed with System 7. To find out what's different, see Chapter 18.

When the Finder encounters a file, for example when you copy a file to a disk, it checks the file's Creator and Type. Then it scans the Desktop file to see if the copied file is related to anything it has ever encountered before. If the file is a document, the Finder determines whether it has ever encountered the creator application, and if it has, it uses the icon previously stored in the Desktop file. The process is similar for a previously encountered application—the Finder uses the icon from the Desktop file. When the Finder encounters a new application, it adds the new icons, Type(s), and Creator to the Desktop file's roster. When it can't find specific icons, the Finder uses the generic icons shown in Figure 7-11 to represent files. It uses the generic document icon when it encounters a document whose creator application has never been on your disk, or whose creator application doesn't specify a special document icon. The Finder uses the generic application icon when an application doesn't contain an icon for itself.

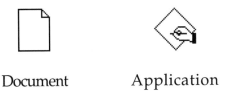

Document   Application

Figure 7-11. The Finder contains two generic icons that it uses when it can't find specific "brand-name" icons.

You may be wondering why the Desktop file is invisible. The intent is to prevent tampering. Most of the time nobody needs to see this important file or do anything to it. But the Finder won't use your custom icons until you make it update the Desktop file.

▶ Updating the Desktop File

Now you know why the Finder seems to ignore your new icon masterpieces. Actually it doesn't ignore them, because it doesn't even look for them. It continues to use old stored versions until you make it update its Desktop file. There are two ways to make the Finder update the Desktop file: an easy way and a hard way. As you might have guessed, the easy way has a potential drawback. (The hard way constitutes its own drawback.)

Updating the Desktop File the Easy Way

If you hold down the Command and Option keys when you restart your Macintosh (or when you insert a floppy disk), the Finder automatically rebuilds the disk's Desktop file and includes any new icons you've added. (To be sure the Finder uses your new icon, don't leave the original copy of the file on the same volume. Move the original to a different disk.) Unfortunately, the Finder also throws away any comments you've added to the Get Info windows. If you can live without those comments, or if you've never added any, go ahead and let the Finder do the dirty work for you.

Hint ▶	If you only store short comments (one or two lines), try putting them in 'vers' resources instead of the Finder's Get Info windows. These resources survive when you let the Finder rebuild your Desktop file. For more information, see "Adding Version Information to Documents" in Chapter 13.

Updating the Desktop File the Hard Way

Updating the Desktop file the hard way is more tedious. Plus, you have to repeat Steps 2 through 10 for each icon you've changed. To manually update the Desktop file, follow these steps.

1. Make sure you're not using MultiFinder. Restart while pressing the Command key if you normally use MultiFinder. (Hold it down until your desktop appears.)
2. Use ResEdit to open the (copy of the) application file you modified, and then open the 'ICN#' type.
3. In the 'ICN#' picker, select the icon you modified and copy it.
4. Close the application file.
5. Use ResEdit to open the Desktop file, which is located at the top level (not within any folders) of your disk. Every disk has its own Desktop file, so make sure you open the correct one. This will be the Desktop file of the disk from which you launch the application.
6. Open the 'ICN#' type, find the old icon you want to replace, and write down the ID number you see beneath the icon.
7. Now select the old icon (a black box will appear around it), and use the Clear command or the Delete key to remove it.
8. Paste in the icon you copied from the application file.
9. Select the new icon (it should be selected).
10. Choose Get Resource Info from the Resource menu, and change the ID of the icon to the number you wrote down.
11. Close the file, saving your changes, and you're done.

When you quit from ResEdit, the Finder should display your new icon.

▶ Personalizing Other Desktop Icons

In addition to application icons, the Finder draws several other icons commonly found on the desktop, as shown in Figure 7-12, and these are obvious targets for customization. Many people play with the Trash can, making it overflow, turning it into a toilet, or turning it into an IBM PC. Figure 7-13 shows fatbits versions of some possible Trash can substitutes. Before you edit the Finder's icons, review the procedures described in Chapter 4, Editing the System, Finder, and Other Files.

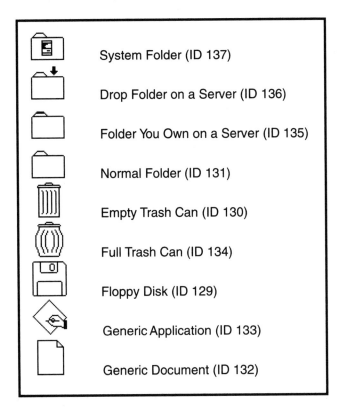

System Folder (ID 137)

Drop Folder on a Server (ID 136)

Folder You Own on a Server (ID 135)

Normal Folder (ID 131)

Empty Trash Can (ID 130)

Full Trash Can (ID 134)

Floppy Disk (ID 129)

Generic Application (ID 133)

Generic Document (ID 132)

Figure 7-12. You can find these familiar desktop icons in the Finder's 'ICN#' resource type.

Remember to create a mask before saving the icon. (Drag the icon straight down onto the box labeled "Mask.")

By the Way ▶

Whatever substitute you choose for the Trash can, you may be able to carry the metaphor further. Let's say you substituted a toilet icon. You can modify the Finder's Special menu so that it says Flush instead of Empty Trash. You can also change all the Finder's messages that refer to the Trash by searching in the 'STR ' and 'STR#' resources. For information about modifying menus, see Chapter 8. For information about changing string resources ('STR ' and 'STR#'), see Chapter 16.

Figure 7-13. Here are some potential substitutes for the Finder's Trash can. You can copy these or create your own.

▶ Summary

This chapter discusses three types of icon resources and how they're used and edited: 'ICON', 'SICN' and 'ICN#'. 'ICON' resources often appear in dialogs, alerts, and menus, and we show you how to customize the ones that appear in alerts. Applications use 'SICN' resources in menus, palettes, and other parts of the user interface. We describe how to change the 'SICN's the Finder uses for its text views. The Finder keeps track of desktop icons—'ICN#' resources—in its Desktop file. How to change an application's desktop icons, and how to update the Desktop file so the Finder will use the new icons, are also described.

8 ▶ Modifying Menus

One of the features of the Macintosh is that the user interface remains the same from one application to another. Mostly. But let's face it—not all software developers follow the same user interface guidelines. One result is that menus tend to vary and keyboard shortcuts are inconsistent—even within an application type, such as text processing. As you become more familiar with the programs you use frequently, keyboard shortcuts can speed up your work. But some of your most-used menu commands might not come equipped with Command-key equivalents. Plus, you can run into problems if Command-P means "Plain Text" in WizzyWrite, "Print" in FingerPaint, and "Propagate" in ZowieCalc. If you absent-mindedly type Command-P without remembering where you are, you could end up with unsettling results—and increased appreciation for Command-Z (which is always Undo).

In many cases, you don't have to put up with annoying menus or keyboard shortcuts. With ResEdit you can add menu icons and Command-key shortcuts, and modify the names, text style, and colors for menu items to increase consistency between applications, to streamline your work, or just to suit your style, as Figure 8-1 shows.

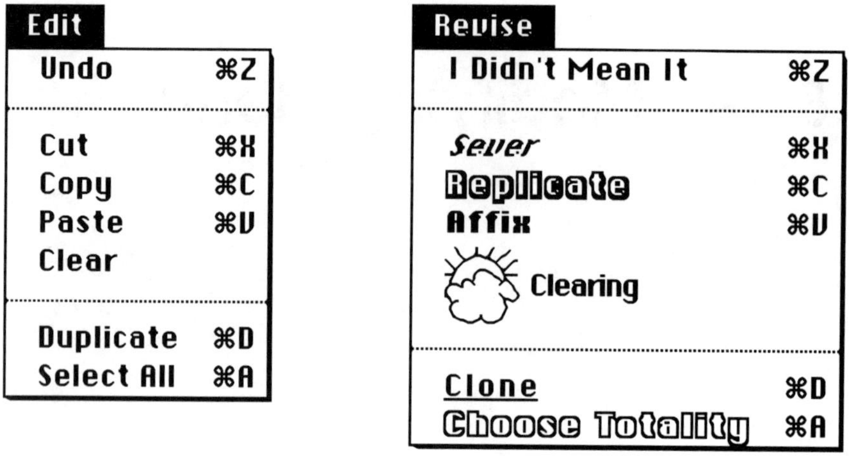

Edit	
Undo	⌘Z
Cut	⌘X
Copy	⌘C
Paste	⌘U
Clear	
Duplicate	⌘D
Select All	⌘A

Revise	
I Didn't Mean It	⌘Z
Sever	⌘X
Replicate	⌘C
Affix	⌘U
☁ Clearing	
Clone	⌘D
Choose Totality	⌘A

Figure 8-1. With ResEdit you can customize menus to suit yourself.

▶ Macintosh Menus

Much of your communication with Macintosh applications is through menus, which tell applications what operation to perform next. Whether or not they use resources for their menus (most do), applications work with the Macintosh's Menu Manager, the user interface middleman that sets up and manages menus. When you select a menu item, either by pulling down on a menu or by typing a keyboard equivalent, the application calls the Menu Manager, which highlights that menu's title (by inverting it), and does all the other things that make menus behave like menus. The application doesn't know which menu item you chose until the Menu Manager tells it. The split-second interchange goes something like this:

Application: Yo, Menu Manager? The user just typed "Command-X." What is this?

Menu Manger: OK, I'll check into it so I can do some user interface stuff and get back to you. Let's see . . . that's menu 3, item 2.

Application: Item 2 on menu 3? Gotcha. The user wants to cut.

In other words, applications can't read menus, and the Menu Manager doesn't understand application commands. The bottom line is that you can't add new commands to menus just by typing them into

'MENU' resources. You can't rearrange the order of menu commands either. Moving the *text name* of a menu command doesn't change the instructions the application associates with that *location* in the menu. For example, if you swap the names of Cut and Copy in the Edit menu, the application will still cut when you select the second menu item, even though you made it read "Copy."

| By the Way ▶ | Applications written with newer versions of MacApp will have 'CMNU' (Command MeNU) resources instead of 'MENU' resources. With 'CMNU's, each menu item has a unique command number associated with it, and that number is what counts. 'CMNU's allow you to rearrange items in menus, and even move items to different menus, because all that counts is the command number. When you find 'CMNU's in your applications, you can edit them with ResEdit just as you would edit 'MENU' resources. The 'CMNU' editor looks almost the same as the 'MENU' editor, except for the addition of a field that allows you to specify a command number. |

ResEdit won't let you get at every menu, and there are some you can't or shouldn't try to modify. For example, you can't do much that's useful to the Apple menu, or to various Font and Size menus, because they're designed to contain information that varies. In these cases the application has to get that changeable information from somewhere else, usually your System file. (For a tip on rearranging Font menus—by changing font names—see Chapter 13.) Finally, some applications (such as Microsoft Word) don't use any menu resources, but employ special code for their menus instead. You won't be able to change such menus with ResEdit.

▶ Command-key Shortcut Considerations

Perhaps one of the most popular uses for ResEdit is assigning keyboard equivalents for menu commands. Some people like to create Command-key shortcuts for the Finder's Special menu, such as, Command-R for Restart and Command-S for Shutdown. Of course, if you're running MultiFinder and get distracted, you could wind up turning off your machine instead of saving the file you *thought* you were in. Fortunately, as usual, the Macintosh protects you from such blunders by asking if you want to save before quitting, so you won't lose anything. You'll probably realize your mistake, click Cancel in the Save dialog, and continue working. Then, some time later, when you quit from the application, your Mac will shut down. Surprise!

Which brings up an important point. To try to avoid surprises, consider Command-key shortcuts carefully before implementing them. Generally, it's a good idea to try to avoid confusing yourself or your Mac. As you contemplate your modifications, keep several things in mind.

First, get an overview of your existing keyboard commands so you don't inadvertently duplicate key combinations you already have. Clearly, you need to check the application you want to tweak, but also remember that desk accessories may have hot keys assigned, and you may have created global shortcuts in MacroMaker or other macro utilities. When faced with conflicts, what does your Mac do? Let's say you add Command-E to the Finder's Special menu so you can quickly Empty Trash. But Command-E is already taken by Eject on the File menu. How does the Mac decide whether to empty the Trash or stick its floppy out at you? The Menu Manager looks at Command-key shortcuts from right to left across the menu bar, so Command-E would work for the Special menu, not the File menu.

Once you figure out which Command-key shortcuts are already taken, you can get down to the business of assigning some new ones. Ideally, the keyboard shortcuts you choose should make sense to you so they'll be easy to remember and use. You can use almost all the letters and numbers on the keyboard for Command-key shortcuts. However, the Menu Manager ignores the Shift key, so Command-+ is the same as Command-=. Consequently, you can *not* use most punctuation characters for keyboard equivalents because they're Command-Shift-number combinations. Recall, for example, that Command-Shift-1 and -2 eject disks, and Command-Shift-3 takes a screen snapshot no matter what application you're running. These key combinations are not handled by the Menu Manager, so it can't return any information to the application. (If you really want to use punctuation, Chapter 9 contains a solution to this problem.)

Even though you can't use the Shift key, you still have the Option key. Check the Chicago font in the Key Caps desk accessory if you want to get an idea of the possibilities. (Menus use the System font, which is Chicago unless you change it. To find out about changing the System font see Chapters 12 and 13.) Let's say you use Save As frequently in an application, and want a keyboard shortcut. Command-S is taken for Save, but you can add Command-Option-S to that application's File menu. Option-S gives you a "ß" character, so you'll see "⌘ß" after Save As on your customized menu. Bear in mind that some keys just give you an empty box character when pressed with the Option key. Seeing "⌘□" on the menu won't help much if you forget the key you assigned.

Having an extended keyboard doesn't extend your range of options. All the FKeys put the same character—an apple—in your menus, which doesn't help much.

Before you set to work, with a gleam in your eyes, to assign and change Command-key shortcuts, remember that sometimes you may wish you had left well enough alone. While it's true that you'll probably be able to change things back, (assuming you have the suggested copies and backups), that's sort of like saying you can heal after you shoot yourself in the foot. Consider, too, that most Macintosh users are familiar with certain standard Command-key shortcuts. If you aren't careful, the more you customize your Macintosh or your applications with nonstandard "improvements," the more likely you are to flummox yourself up with inconsistencies and bewilder other people who may someday use your software and equipment. It's your system, and customization is one of the major benefits of the Mac and ResEdit—just try to think through your modifications.

Finally, for cosmetic reasons, always type in capital letters when assigning keyboard shortcuts. Even though the Menu Manager doesn't distinguish between capitals and lowercase (because it ignores the Shift key), lowercase letters will look out of place in the menus.

▶ 'MENU' Resources

Besides Command-key shortcuts, you can modify menu items in a variety of other ways. You can change a menu item's name or text style so that it stands out or makes more sense to you. Maybe an icon to the left of a menu item would provide a helpful visual reminder of that item's function. Exploring the menu editor will give you an idea of the possibilities, but first you need to know a bit more about 'MENU' resources. Then, after some examples, you can branch out on your own.

To find the menu resources you want to edit, you first have to start up ResEdit and use it to open up (a copy of) the application you're interested in. Find the 'MENU' resource type and open it. ResEdit opens the 'MENU' picker, shown in Figure 8-2, which displays the top of every menu in the file. Searching through the 'MENU' picker for the particular menu you want to modify takes almost no time, but you need to remember a few things. You may find that some applications contain more than one 'MENU' resource for the same menu. The Finder, for instance, has two 'MENU' resources for the Special menu. (It uses a different Special menu on the portable Mac.) Also, an application might have more menus to sift through than just what's along the menu bar because some dialog boxes use 'MENU' resources for pop-up menus. So, sometimes you may have to open a 'MENU' resource to make sure you've found the right one. If you've got the right one, you're ready to work. (If it's not the right one, just click the close box and choose the next likely candidate from the 'MENU' picker.)

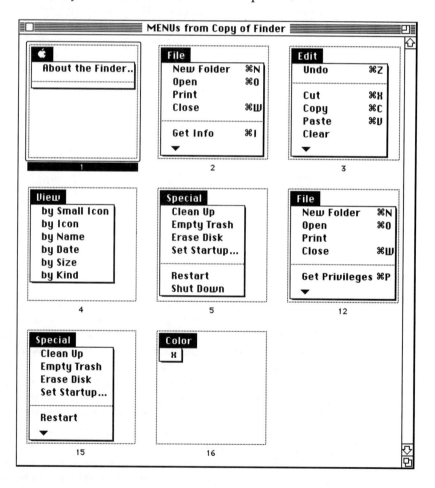

Figure 8-2. The 'MENU' picker, view by 'MENU'.

▶ The 'MENU' Editor

The 'MENU' editor, shown in Figure 8-3, opens showing a likeness of the selected menu with the menu's title already highlighted. If you wanted to change the menu's title, you could do that now by typing the new name into the Title field. Programmers use the radio button with the apple icon when they're creating the Apple menu for an application, but most users won't have much reason to click it. For information about the Enabled box, see Chapter 21. If you want to add color to your menus, see Chapter 19. Off to the right on the menu bar ResEdit displays a test version of the menu you're modifying. You can pull it down as you edit to see the effect of your changes.

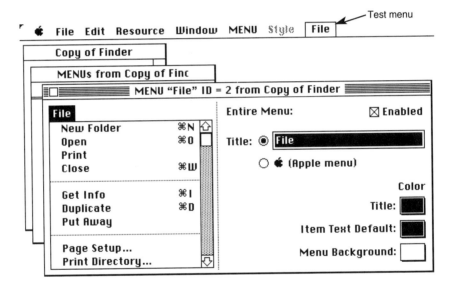

Figure 8-3. The 'MENU' editor with a menu title selected.

To edit a menu item, simply click it. But be careful not to drag menu items around within the editor! Remember, moving the *text name* of a menu command doesn't change the instructions the application associates with that *location* in the menu. As Figure 8-4 shows, the 'MENU' editor offers more options for modifying menu items than it does for menu titles. The Style menu becomes available, allowing you to change menu item text to any combination of seven text styles. The Choose Icon item in the 'MENU' menu (see next section) also becomes available. Unless you are a software developer, however, you won't use the other available options. You'll want to confine your modifications to four areas: setting Command-key shortcuts with the Cmd-Key field, changing the text name and style of menu items, adding icons, and changing the colors used to draw the menu.

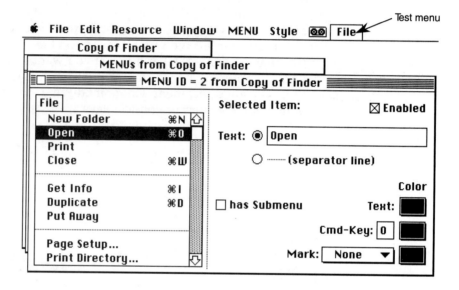

Figure 8-4. The 'MENU' editor, menu item selected. Menu items have more options for customization than menu titles do.

In other words, stay away from the Enabled, has Submenu, and Mark boxes. For more information on these, see Chapter 21 in the Programming section. Also, be careful not to click the radio button that could obliterate a menu command with a separator line. (You can, however, change an existing separator line into a "command" that does nothing. We're not sure why you'd want to do this, but it seems relatively harmless, so here's how: Simply click on the separator line to be replaced, click the radio button by the Text field and type in "Bogus" or whatever name you choose.)

The menus in some applications have submenus, and you can modify those, too. Figure 8-5 shows a menu that makes extensive use of submenus. To edit a submenu, double-click the menu item that the submenu is attached to. Another MENU editor window opens containing the submenu, which you can edit just as you would any other menu.

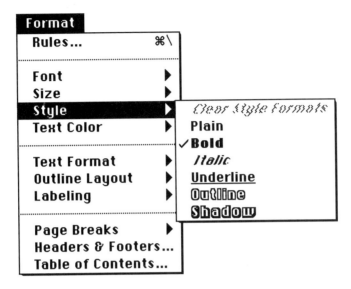

Figure 8-5. This menu from MORE II has several submenus.

▶ The 'MENU' Menu

When the 'MENU' editor opens, it adds a new menu, shown in Figure 8-6, to ResEdit's menu bar. Programmers use the first item, Edit Menu & MDEF ID, when they are developing the menus for an application. (For more information, see Chapter 21.) This item has no customization potential, and, in fact, unless you're developing software, you should leave it alone. You can use the next two items, Choose Icon and Remove Icon, to add and remove icons in your menus. We'll talk more about menu icons a bit later in this chapter. The last item, Use Default Colors, is useful when you're working with color in your menus, which is described in Chapter 19.

▶ Changing Menu Item Text

To modify the text of a menu item, click in the Text field. You don't have to select the text to apply styles. If the blinking insertion point is in the text field, ResEdit applies whatever text style(s) you choose from the Style menu to the text of the entire menu item. You can't apply styles to individual words within a menu item. The change will show up to the left within the editor window and in the test menu to the right on the menu bar, but not in the text field. If you don't like what a menu item says, select the existing text and type in something you like better. The 'MENU' editor's Text field allows you to type in more characters than you'll ever need or want. Once you get beyond 15 to 20 characters, or overflow the Text field, further text won't show up within the 'MENU' editor. The Menu Manager can make menus as big as necessary, however, so you can check the test menu to see how your lengthy menu item looks.

```
┌─────────────────────────────┐
│ MENU                        │
├─────────────────────────────┤
│ Edit Menu & MDEF ID...      │
│ Choose Icon...              │
│ Remove Icon                 │
│ Use Default Colors          │
└─────────────────────────────┘
```

Figure 8-6. The 'MENU' editor adds its own menu to ResEdit's menu bar to help you modify 'MENU' resources.

▶ Assigning Command-key Shortcuts

Adding or changing Command-key shortcuts is a snap. Simply click the menu item you want to change, click the Cmd-Key box, and type in the character you desire. Remember: Use capital letters, for cosmetic reasons. Also, you can't use Command-Shift-number combinations because they're already taken for built-in FKeys like Command-Shift-3, which takes a screen shot no matter what application you're using. (If you must use punctuation characters, see Chapter 9.)

▶ Adding Menu Icons

Icons, which appear to the left of menu item text or alone if there is no text, can give valuable visual clues about the function a menu command performs. Figure 8-7 illustrates how icons can help. Few applications use them, perhaps because they can take up so much space, but any menu item can have an icon. You can add three types of icons to menus. Normal icons are 'ICON' resources, which are 32-by-32-bit pictures. Reduced icons are normal icons reduced to 16-by-16-bit pictures. Small icons are 'SICN' resources, which are also 16-by-16-bit pictures. For more information, see Chapter 7. Normal icons may look too big and give the menu an off-balance appearance, so reduced or small icons tend to look better. But if you also want a keyboard equivalent for your illustrated menu item, you have no choice: You have to use a normal icon. You can't have a Command-key shortcut with reduced or small icons.

By the Way ▶

Menus on the original Macintosh didn't include provisions for small or reduced icons. To add this capability, another part of the 'MENU' resource had to be reassigned. You guessed it; the Command-key shortcut lost its place. Reduced and small icons can only be used in Systems 5.0 or later. Reduced icons are the ones MultiFinder uses in the Apple menu.

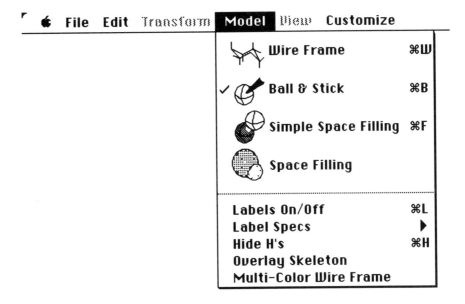

Figure 8-7. This menu from Ball & Stick, a chemistry molecular modeling program, shows a good use of menu icons.

| By the Way ▶ | Actually, you can add four types of icons to menus. If you're interested in color icons, you can substitute a 'cicn' for an 'ICON'. See Chapter 18. |

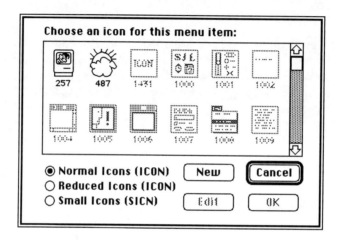

Figure 8-8. You select icons to add to menus from the Choose Icon dialog.

Menu icons can come from a number of places. You can use an existing icon, create an icon from scratch in ResEdit, or copy a picture from a paint or draw program. Whichever way you choose, you'll need to become familiar with the Choose Icon dialog and the icon editors.

When you select Choose Icon from the 'MENU' menu, ResEdit displays the dialog shown in Figure 8-8, which asks you to do just that. What you see next depends on the application. ResEdit shows you all the 'ICON' (but not 'ICN#') resources in that application or the first icon in each 'SICN' list it finds. The dialog defaults to show Normal Icons, but you only have to click the radio buttons to move between the three types of icons. Most icons you see will probably be dimmed, indicating you can't use them because they don't have suitable ID numbers. In menus, you can only use icons with IDs from 257 to 511. Then again, you may not see any icons. MacPaint, for example, doesn't have any icons of the types used in menus. The Finder only has two small icons, and they're dimmed. (Of course, if there aren't any Normal Icons, there won't be any Reduced Icons either, since both come from the same 'ICON' resources.)

Using Existing Icons

If you happen to come across an icon you like and it's not dimmed, simply double-click it, and ResEdit will add the icon to the currently selected menu item—you're all set. If you want to use an icon that's dimmed, you can copy it and give it a suitable ID. Here's how.

1. Go back to the type picker.
2. Look for the 'ICON' or 'SICN' type, whichever type matches the icon you're after, and open it.
3. Find your icon in the icon picker and select it (click once). Duplicate the icon (from the Edit menu), and give the duplicate an ID between 257 and 511 (using Get Resource Info from the Resource menu). If you need to brush up on how to use the Resource Info window to change IDs, see Chapter 3.

When you go back to the 'MENU' editor and select Choose Icon, your icon won't be dimmed, so you'll only have to double-click it.

You can also use an icon from a different application. Just use ResEdit to copy it from the icon picker of the original application into the icon picker of the application you're modifying, giving it an appropriate ID if necessary. (Be careful not to cut or delete icons!) When you go back to the 'MENU' editor, you'll be able to edit the icon or add it to your menu as is. Icons don't appear in the 'MENU' editor window, so you'll have to check the test menu to see how it looks.

Creating and Editing Icons

When you click the New button in the Choose Icon dialog, or select an icon and then click the Edit button, ResEdit opens either the 'ICON' or 'SICN' editor, depending on the radio button selected. These two editors behave like ResEdit's other fatbits editors and are covered extensively in Chapter 7. The 'SICN' editor is shown in Figure 8-9, and the 'ICON' editor is shown in Figure 8-10.

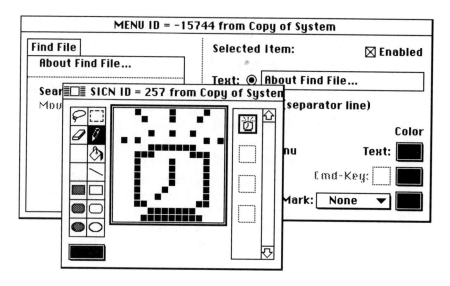

Figure 8-9. When you edit a Small Icon for a menu item, the 'MENU' editor uses the 'SICN' editor.

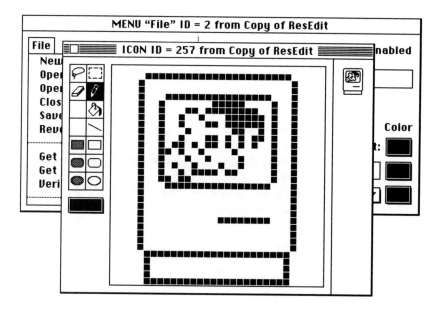

Figure 8-10. When you edit a Normal Icon for a menu item, the 'MENU' editor uses the 'ICON' editor.

Actually, ResEdit does more than just open an icon editor when you click the New button; it creates an icon and assigns it an ID number in the appropriate range. In other words, from within a 'MENU' resource you create an icon resource. If you never click one fatbit, you'll still have a new, all-white icon, which will precede the menu item text. If you fiddle with the fatbits a while, and then decide you don't want the icon after all, you can't just throw it away from here. Remove Icon on the 'MENU' menu only takes the icon off the menu item you're editing, but there will still be an icon resource cluttering up your file. Revert This Resource on the Resource menu applies only to the 'MENU' resource open, not the icon ('ICON' or 'SICN') resource. You can select Revert File from the File menu, but of course that throws away all the changes you've made to any resources in that file.

So it's a little easier to make messes than it is to clean them up. Fortunately, throwing out an icon isn't very hard. Simply go back to the type picker and double-click the appropriate icon type ('ICON' or 'SICN') to open that icon picker. You can toss unwanted icons from there, or Revert this Resource to get rid of your changes. If you're planning a major icon-editing session, you might consider going directly to the icon editor via the icon picker, instead of the 'MENU' editor.

▶ Adding a Command-key Shortcut to ResEdit

Why not modify one of ResEdit's menus by adding a keyboard shortcut to the Revert This Resource item on ResEdit's Resource menu? Such a shortcut will probably come in handy as you play around with ResEdit. This is one of the rare occasions when you don't have to make a copy first—*if* you follow the steps exactly and don't make any other changes, and if you have a backup in case of disaster.

"Use ResEdit on itself?!" you exclaim. Sure, it's a little like doing brain surgery on yourself, but hey—ResEdit's a powerful program.

1. Start up ResEdit and use it to open ResEdit. You'll see a warning dialog that reminds you to be careful. Click OK and remember to be careful.

2. Find the 'MENU' resource type and open it.

3. From the 'MENU' picker, open the 'MENU' resource for the Resource menu (ID 128, Named "Resource"), and ResEdit will open the 'MENU' editor. You might notice that the Enabled box is not checked. That's OK; leave it alone. (The Resource menu

remains disabled—dimmed—until a resource is selected/opened. At that point, ResEdit enables the menu.)

4. Click the Revert This Resource item in the 'MENU' editor's window (not the one on the menu bar). Next, click the Cmd-Key box and type a capital R.

Warning ▶	Be careful not to click and drag items around within menus! Remember, moving the text name of a menu command doesn't change the instructions the application associates with that location in the menu.

5. Close all ResEdit's windows or just quit, making sure to save. Next time you start ResEdit, you can try out your new shortcut as you poke around an application's resources.

Now you're armed with a quick way to revert resources as you embark on customizing menus—or any other resources you tackle.

▶ Summary

This chapter describes 'MENU' resources, and briefly explains how the Macintosh works with them. With ResEdit's 'MENU' editor you can add or change Command-key shortcuts, edit the names of menu titles and commands, alter the text style of menu items, and add icons to menu items. (Changing the colors used to draw menus is discussed in Chapter 19.) We conclude the chapter by showing you how to add a Command-key shortcut to one of ResEdit's menus.

9 ▶ Modifying Your Keyboard Layout

There has never been and never will be a keyboard layout that can please everyone. Most people probably wish they could move at least one character. The good news is that ResEdit allows you to move characters around to your heart's content. The bad news is that moving the physical key caps is not nearly as easy. In fact, it's almost impossible to move most key caps because they're difficult to remove without breaking and because they're sculpted to fit their location, so they wouldn't feel right even if you were able to move them.

Even without moving the key caps, you can make some useful changes to the keyboard layout. Wouldn't it be nice if you could type "P.O. Box" without having to release the Shift key for each period? Or how about making the curly (printer's) quotes more accessible? You can make small changes such as these without worrying about moving key caps. If you're interested in more radical changes, such as converting your keyboard to a Dvorak layout (a layout that minimizes the distance your fingers need to travel for common characters, thus allowing you to type five to ten times faster), you should look for a new keyboard instead of trying to remap the keys. (If you just want to try out a Dvorak keyboard layout, a customized keyboard layout is available from many user groups and bulletin boards.)

First, a bit of definition is in order. As we're using it here, a "key" is a physical key on the keyboard labeled with a symbol, such as "A." A "character" is what your application receives when a key is pressed. A key in a given keyboard location can be labeled differently and can produce different characters, depending on what country's System software you're using and what changes you've made to the resources we'll describe shortly. For example, on the U.S. keyboard, the first key in the second row of keys produces a *q* character, whereas in France it produces an *a* character.

To allow for many different keyboards and languages, the translation of a key pressed on your keyboard into a character that can be displayed by your application involves a couple of steps, each controlled by a different resource. Figure 9-1 shows the path a character takes from the keyboard to the application. The 'KMAP' resource maps the key pressed on the keyboard to a "virtual" keycode that's independent of the type of keyboard being used. The 'KCHR' resource is next in line. It translates the virtual keycode into a character that can be used by an application. Because of this, you can take advantage of the 'KCHR' resource to change the layout of your keyboard. In fact, the 'KCHR' resource is used to customize the Macintosh for different countries. No matter what country you live in, you can probably modify your 'KCHR' resource to make your life a bit easier. We'll mention a couple of modifications for U.S. keyboards here.

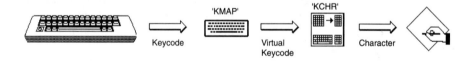

Figure 9-1. A character's trip from the keyboard to your application.

The 'KCHR' resource determines keyboard and character assignments—which key on your keyboard produces which character. This is a complex resource, but ResEdit's editor allows you to avoid most of the complexity if you only want to make simple changes. Because it was designed to allow Apple to change the keyboard layout for different languages and countries, the 'KCHR' editor can handle complex situations you'll never encounter while customizing. This chapter first explains the 'KCHR' resource and how the editor works and then shows you some examples of how you can remap your own keyboard. We've included more detailed information at the end of the chapter for those who want to make more significant changes.

By the Way ▶	Each country has its own 'KCHR' resource provided by Apple. The name of the resource is usually the same as the name of the country or region that uses the resource. The resource ID is the same as the country's Country Code (a unique number assigned to each country by Apple). For example, the 'KCHR' for the United States has an ID of 0 and is named "US," whereas Switzerland has two 'KCHR's, either ID 18 ("Suisse Romand") or 19 ("Deutsche Schweiz"). If you have more than one 'KCHR' resource, you can use the Keyboard Control Panel device to choose which 'KCHR' your Mac uses.

▶ The Main Window

The main 'KCHR' window is divided into five parts, as shown in Figure 9-2. You'll mainly be concerned with the Character Table and the Keyboard, so we'll only briefly mention the other parts of the window. You can find more information about the modifier key tables later in this chapter.

▶ Character Table

The character table contains a spot for each of the 256 characters that a font can contain. Most fonts don't define every possible character, and you'd probably have trouble remembering all the key combinations even if they did. The font shown in the character table doesn't matter—you're mapping your keyboard, not your font. But if you're looking for a certain special character, you can switch to the appropriate font. The character table is initially filled in with the characters from the application font (usually Geneva), but you can use the Font menu to switch to any available font. It's from the character table that you get the characters to assign to keys on the keyboard.

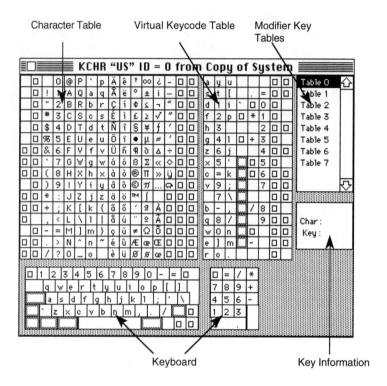

Figure 9-2. The 'KCHR' window has five parts.

Hint ▶

The 'KCHR' window is normally displayed using the application font (usually Geneva). You'll notice, however, that many of the characters in the character table aren't defined (they just contain a box character). If you use the Font menu to change the font to Helvetica, all the empty spots in the table will be filled in with the special accented characters supported by the Apple extended character set.

▶ Keyboard

The keyboard area of the window shows a picture of a keyboard. You can change to a different keyboard picture by selecting the View As command from the 'KCHR' menu. The View As dialog is shown in Figure 9-3. The keyboards listed in the dialog correspond to the 'KCAP' resources found in the Key Layout file in your System folder. (The 'KCAP' resources contain the physical layouts of the keyboards displayed by the Key Caps desk accessory.) In versions of the Key Layout file that came with Systems earlier than version 6.0.4, the resources weren't named, so you'll see only the IDs of the resources in the dialog. If you don't see keyboard names in the dialog, you can use Figure 9-3 to help you decide which keyboard to pick. Remember, no matter what keyboard you display, you're still editing the same 'KCHR' resource, so you can't set it up differently for each keyboard.

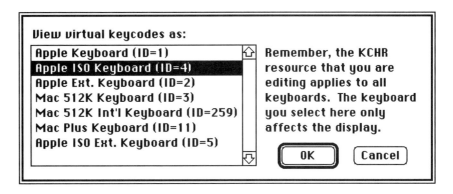

Figure 9-3. The View As dialog lets you pick a keyboard layout.

▶ Modifier Key Tables

Each 'KCHR' resource contains several modifier key tables that are used to translate virtual keycodes to characters. Every keyboard has several modifier keys such as the Shift, Command, Caps Lock, Option, and Control keys. Each modifier key combination is associated with one of the tables. For example, there is one table for the Shift key and one for the Shift-Option key combination. Several modifier key combinations (such as Control, Control-Shift, and so on) can share the same table.

Warning ▶ | Don't click on the table numbers! Clicking on a table number in this list changes the table used for the current modifier key combination. There's more information about how to use these tables later in this chapter.

▶ Virtual Keycode Table

The virtual keycode table shows the translation from virtual keycode to character for the current modifier key table (the one that's highlighted in the list). (Remember, virtual keycodes are just numbers that represent the keys on the keyboard. They're "virtual" because they're independent of the keyboard used.) Each spot in the table corresponds to a different virtual keycode and can contain any character from the character table. For example, the first position in the table corresponds to the virtual keycode for the key labeled *A* on the U.S. keyboard. In Figure 9-2, this entry in the table contains the character *a*.

▶ Key Information

The Key Information field shows the ASCII code and the virtual keycode of any key you press.

▶ Making a New 'KCHR' Resource

If you have more than one 'KCHR' resource in your System file, you can use the Keyboard Control Panel to switch to the one you want to use. This is convenient if you work with different countries or if you want to make your own customized keyboard layout. If you're going to modify your 'KCHR' resource, it's convenient to make a copy of the original resource so you can switch back to it if you have any problems with your modified version. Because you're going to work only on a duplicate resource, it's probably OK to edit the System file directly in this case. As always, you should be very careful not to change any other resources and to keep a backup of your System file. If you edit the System file directly, you'll be able to make changes and try them out quickly without reinstalling your System file and restarting. Here's how you can make your own 'KCHR' resource.

1. Use ResEdit to open your System file. (You can make all these changes in a copy of your System file, but you'll have to reinstall your new System file and restart to see the results of your changes.)
2. Select the 'KCHR' resource. (Its name should be the same as the name of your country or region.)
3. Duplicate the resource using the Duplicate command on the Edit menu.

4. Select the new resource and choose Get Resource Info from the Resource menu.

5. Change the name to something new, like "My KCHR."

6. Close and save the System file.

7. Open the Keyboard Control Panel. You should see your new resource listed under the "Keyboard Layout" label. Selecting it activates it immediately—you don't have to restart to see your changes.

Hint ▶

If you've made a new 'KCHR' resource and selected it in the Keyboard Control Panel's Keyboard Layout list, further changes you make might not take effect immediately. That's because you need to tell the Mac that it needs to get a new copy of the resource. You can do this in the Keyboard Control Panel by selecting the original 'KCHR' resource and then reselecting your new one.

▶ Changing Shift-Period to a Period and Shift-Comma to a Comma

Shift-period is usually a > character, and Shift-comma is usually a < character. If you're like most people, you don't use these characters very often, and you might like not having to release the Shift key to type periods within abbreviations like U.S.A., P.O., or D.C. Here's a simple way to make better use of these keys.

1. Use ResEdit to open your System file (or a copy).

2. Open the 'KCHR' resource you created in the previous task, "Making a New 'KCHR' Resource." You should see a window similar to the one shown in Figure 9-4. (Table 1 won't be selected until you press the Shift key.)

3. If the picture of the keyboard doesn't look like your keyboard, select the View As command from the 'KCHR' menu. If you have a version of the System software later than 6.0.4, you'll see the names of the keyboards, and you can pick the one you're using. If you're using an earlier version of the System, use Figure 9-3 to help you find the right keyboard.

4. Press the period key and notice where the period character is in the character table (it's in the lower-left part of the character table).

5. Now press and hold the Shift key. While you hold the Shift key down, drag the period from the character table and drop it on the key on the keyboard displaying the right angle bracket character, as shown in Figure 9-4.

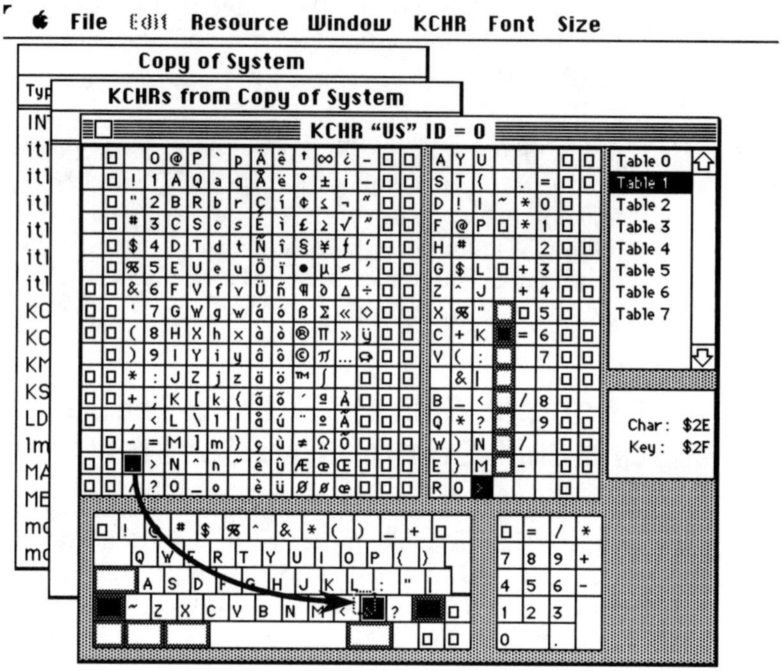

Figure 9-4. Changing the > character to a period.

You've now replaced the > character (Shift-Period) with a period, and you can follow the same procedure to replace the < with a comma. Of course, now you have no way to type the < and > characters. If you think you might occasionally need these characters, you should map them to some other key combination. A good place might be Option-Shift-Period and Option-Shift-Comma since most fonts don't use these key combinations.

Now all you have to do is select your new 'KCHR' in the Keyboard Control Panel to make your changes take effect. (If your new 'KCHR' was already selected, don't forget to select the original 'KCHR' and then reselect your new 'KCHR'.) If you worked on a copy of the System file, you'll need to reinstall it as your current System file and restart.

▶ Making Curly Quotes Easy to Type

A document looks more professional if you use "real" curly quotes instead of the normal "straight" quotes. These characters are always available on the keyboard but aren't very convenient. Normally, you can use the curly quotes by typing these key combinations:

- Option-[for open double quote (")
- Option-Shift-[for close double quote (")
- Option-] for open single quote (')
- Option-Shift-] for close single quote or apostrophe (')

If you're like most people, you probably don't use the square ([and]) and curly ({ and }) bracket characters very often, so why not put the curly quote characters there, where you can easily get to them? Even if your word processing program has an automatic curly quote feature, you might wish you could type them more easily in all your applications. Since the quotes already use the Option-] and Option-[keys, you can just switch the quotes and the brackets, as shown in Table 9-1, and you'll still have access to all the characters.

Table 9-1. Suggested Character to Key Assignments

Key	Character
{	"
}	"
[	'
]	'
Option-[	[
Option-Shift-[	{
Option-]	]
Option-Shift-]	}

You can accomplish this switch in the same way outlined earlier for Shift-period—just hold down the modifier keys you want to use while you drag a character from the character table to the key on the keyboard.

▶ Using the Modifier Key Tables

So far we've talked about some simple changes you can make to your keyboard. But what if you want to make more complex changes? Since the 'KCHR' resource was designed to support the myriad differences between languages and keyboards in different countries, chances are it will support any change you want to make. For example, you might want to make the punctuation characters (like ! and *) available for use as Command-key equivalents. Or you might want to change the special accent characters (generated by the so-called "dead keys" described shortly) to get to extra characters in a font.

When you press the *A* key or the Option-*A* key, your Mac has to have some way of deciding what character it should send to the application. Since a keyboard has many modifier keys (Command, Option, Control, Caps Lock, Shift, and so on), the translation from virtual keycode to character is a complex process. (Remember, the keycode from the keyboard is translated into a virtual keycode using the 'KMAP' resource.) The Macintosh performs the translation using the Modifier Key Table that applies to the modifier keys held down when the key is pressed. For example, when you press the Option-*A* key, your Mac finds the Modifier Key Table for the Option key and looks up the *A* virtual keycode. The character it finds in the table is the one it sends to your application. Every key on the keyboard has a spot in the table that contains the character to be generated when that key is pressed. (To find the spot in the table, just press the key.) The tables are kept in the 'KCHR' resource and are displayed in the Modifier Key Tables section of the 'KCHR' editor window, shown in Figure 9-2.

The same table is often used for several key combinations, as you can see in Table 9-2.

| By the Way ▶ | There's no way to find out which modifier key combinations have been assigned to a particular table, other than pressing all combinations in turn and seeing which tables are selected. |

Table 9-2. Modifier Key Tables and Their Use in the U.S. 'KCHR'

Table Number	Modifier Key Combinations
Table 0	Command, Command-Shift, Command-Shift-Caps Lock, or none
Table 1	Shift, or Shift-Caps Lock
Table 2	Caps Lock, or Command-Caps Lock
Table 3	Option
Table 4	Option-Shift, Command-Option-Shift, Option-Shift-Caps Lock, or Command-Option-Shift-Caps Lock
Table 5	Option-Caps Lock, or Command-Option-Caps Lock
Table 6	Command-Option
Table 7	Control plus any other modifier key(s)

These tables can be confusing to use, but they're worth the small extra effort it takes to understand them. Remember, the selected table is the active table for the modifier keys you've pressed. You can't select a table to see what it contains; if you click a table, you'll reassign it. For example, in the U.S. 'KCHR' resource, if you press the Option key, Table 3 is selected. If you click Table 4 while still pressing the Option key, you'll reassign the Option key to use Table 4 instead of Table 3. The virtual keycode table area of the window shows the contents of the current modifier key table, as shown in Figure 9-2. (In the figure, no modifier keys are pressed.)

Now that you understand something about how the modifier key tables work, you can safely change them a bit.

▶ Making the Punctuation Characters Available for Menu Commands

Adding extra Command-key equivalents to your menus is often convenient (see Chapter 8 for details about how to do this), but you may quickly run out of meaningful characters. When this happens, you can start using Command-Option characters like Σ or ƒ, but will you really remember how to type these characters? The problem with such characters is that pulling down the menu doesn't help remind you of the shortcut because it doesn't indicate which keys to type, anyway! To solve this problem, you can use the number keys, but sometimes the punctuation characters (such as ! and *) might be easier to remember. You can't use Command-Shift numbers because they're already defined to be FKeys (such as print screen) by the System, but you can make these characters available from Command-Option number. Here's an example of how it would work. To type the @ you would still press Shift-2, but to use @ as a keyboard shortcut you would press Command-Option-2. Option-2 would still produce the ™ character; you would have changed only what Command-Option-2 produces.

1. Use ResEdit to open your System file (or a copy).

2. Open the 'KCHR' resource you created earlier. (Use the Duplicate command to make a copy of the 'KCHR' resource, if you haven't already.) You should see a window similar to the one shown in Figure 9-4, except that Table 0 will be selected.

3. If the picture of the keyboard doesn't look like the keyboard you're using, set the correct keyboard from the View As item on the 'KCHR' menu.

4. Press the Command and Option keys and choose Duplicate Table from the 'KCHR' menu. This makes a duplicate of Table 6 (since it was selected) and names it Table 8. If you want to duplicate a different table, hold down the set of modifier keys that selects that table before choosing Duplicate Table from the 'KCHR' menu.

5. Now hold down the Command and Option keys (which cause Table 6 to be selected) and click the new table in the table list. An alert appears asking if you're sure you want to switch tables. Click the OK button.

6. You now have a new table, but the behavior is exactly the same as the old one since it's a duplicate table. Hold down the Command and Option keys and drag the punctuation characters from the character table to the corresponding number keys on the picture of the keyboard. The standard characters are: !, @, #, $, %, ^, &, *, (, and).

Hint ▶

You can locate the characters in the Character Table by holding down the Shift key and pressing the appropriate key on the keyboard. For example, hold down Shift-1 and you see that the ! character is in the upper left part of the Character Table.

7. Close and save the System file.

8. Activate your new 'KCHR' by selecting it in the Keyboard Control Panel. (If you worked on a copy of the System file, install the copy in your System folder and restart your Mac.)

▶ Changing Dead Keys

Even on a U.S. Macintosh you can use many accented characters, such as é or â. You enter these characters by pressing two keys in succession: The first key tells your Mac what accent you want and the second key tells it what character to accent. So, for example, to type the é character you type Option-e followed by e. The first key (Option-e in this example) is called a *dead key* because it doesn't produce any character by itself, but instead modifies the character generated by the next key typed. In general, there's one dead key for each accent mark. Dead keys are indicated by a dark outline in both the virtual keycode table and the keyboard picture (the gray outlines indicate the modifier keys). The U.S. 'KCHR' resource uses the Option key for all the dead keys, as shown in Figure 9-5. 'KCHR' resources for other countries may use other modifier key combinations to access the dead keys.

Your Mac needs some way of knowing what the final, accented character should be. It finds out by looking in a dead key table. Each dead key has its own table that indicates which characters can have the indicated accent. To see a dead key's table, just press the dead key or click it in the picture of the keyboard. A window similar to the one shown in Figure 9-6 appears to let you edit the dead key. You can also select the dead key you're interested in from a list if you choose the Edit Dead Key command from the 'KCHR' menu.

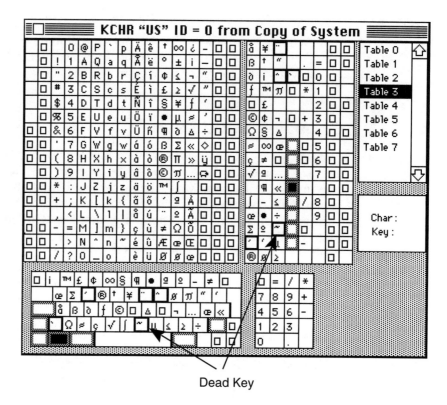

Figure 9-5. Dead keys in the U.S. 'KCHR' resource.

The substitution character table contains the pairs of characters that determine what character is produced by the dead key. For example, if Option-~, the dead key shown in Figure 9-6, is followed by a character from the first column of the substitution character table, the result will be the character shown in the second column. To change either part of a substitution pair, just drag a character from the character table to the appropriate spot in the substitution character table. If you want to create a new pair, just drag a character into one of the empty gray squares. If you want to delete a pair, drag either character into the Trash.

If a dead key is followed by a character that's not found in the substitution character table, the No Match character is used instead. This character is shown in the upper-right part of the dead key window and can be changed by dragging a new character over the existing one.

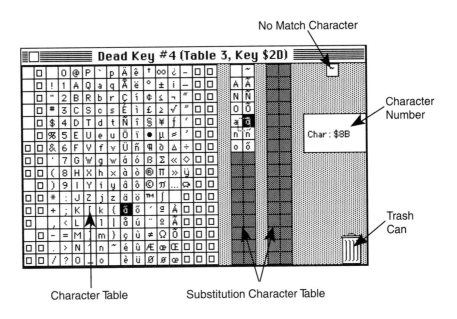

Figure 9-6. The dead key editor window for Option-~.

▶ Summary

This chapter explains how the 'KCHR' resource is used to translate a key typed on your keyboard into a character that appears in your application. We explain the parts of the 'KCHR' editor window and show you how to make some commonly used characters easier to type by modifying the 'KCHR' resource in your System file. Next, we explain the modifier key tables and show you how to make a new table so you can use punctuation characters for menu shortcuts. Finally, we discuss dead keys—the keys that modify other keys so you can type accented characters.

10 ▶ Customizing Windows, Dialogs, and Alerts

The ways that you can customize windows, dialogs, and alerts may not rate as the flashiest, but they definitely rank among the most practical. If you continually find yourself moving a certain window that always opens in the same awkward place on your screen, change its default location and save yourself some time and annoyance. If you wish you could see more file names in the standard file directory dialogs, you can enlarge the dialog's list box so you'll spend less time scrolling. If you're always using the mouse to click the Yes button in a certain alert, change the default to Yes so you can simply press Return. This chapter tells you how you can do all these things.

The editors for windows, dialogs, and alerts are closely related, and we suggest you read about them in order because the discussion for each successive editor builds upon the last. In other words, understanding how to edit windows, or 'WIND' resources, helps you learn the basics for editing dialogs ('DLOG'), which in turn helps you understand how to work with alerts ('ALRT'). Dialogs and alerts get their contents from a fourth resource type, called a dialog item list ('DITL'), and this chapter covers that editor, too. Some of these are no doubt more familiar to you than others, so we'll start with some brief definitions.

- A *window* defines a rectangle's size and location on the screen, and can include a bit of other associated information, such as a title.

- *Dialogs* appear when an application needs more information from you in order to carry out a command. Dialogs may or may not be *modal*. A modal dialog is one you must respond to before you can do anything else. Modeless dialogs behave pretty much like document windows. A dialog consists of a rectangle that defines the dialog's size and location, an optional title, and the ID of a 'DITL' (Dialog ITem List) resource.

- Applications use *alerts*, a special subset of dialogs, to report errors or give warnings. They're always modal. Alerts contain only buttons, some text, perhaps an icon, and sometimes a sound signal. There are no fancy controls and no boxes or fields to fill in.

- A *dialog item list* is a collection of the various items a dialog or alert contains, such as text, pictures, icons, buttons, check boxes, and other controls. The 'DITL' specifies a size and window-relative location for each item.

With these definitions to build upon, you're ready to dive in.

▶ Windows

Windows are relatively simple resources, so there are only a few ways you can customize them. Changing a window's default size and location are the two most useful changes you can make. (You can also change a window's colors. See Chapter 19 if you're interested.) If you have a large screen, you can change the window size in your favorite application so you can use all that space. If a certain window always appears in the same awkward place, you can change where it appears.

As with many resources, you need to remember a few caveats. Because the Macintosh provides applications with other, more convenient ways of drawing windows, many applications avail themselves of those instead, and you can't customize those windows. Applications that do use 'WIND' resources may already enlarge some windows automatically to take advantage of bigger screens. They may also keep track of where you last left certain windows, in effect automatically resetting the default. You can still make useful changes in many applications, however, once you know how.

▶ The 'WIND' Editor

The 'WIND' editor, shown in Figure 10-1, is pretty easy to understand. Across the top of the editor window, under the title bar, you see a row of small pictures of windows. These window pictures are actually buttons that allow you to choose from a variety of window types. Simply click a different picture to choose that window type. In most cases, however, you'll want to leave the window-type buttons alone, unless you're a programmer. Choosing a new window type with a size box or a close box won't do you any good, anyway. You'll see the boxes, but they won't work unless the application has been designed to support them.

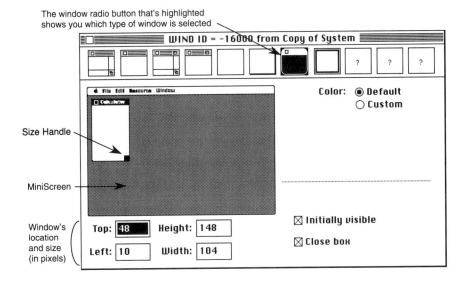

Figure 10-1. The 'WIND' editor showing the 'WIND' resource for the Calculator DA, scaled for an SE screen.

By the Way ▶ The Calculator DA is an example of an application that keeps track of where you left the window (by updating the 'WIND' resource). Also, it's one that you should not change the size of, because the contents (the calculator) won't fit right if you do. The only thing you can customize is the window title.

Beneath the window-type buttons on the right are the radio buttons that allow you to control window colors. You can learn about them in Chapter 19. Unless you're a programmer, you'll want to stay away from the two check boxes in the bottom right. (For more information, see Chapter 20.) Four fields in the bottom left corner of the editor window allow you to set the size and location of the *content area* of the window. (In other words, the space a title bar takes up is "extra.") Above these four fields is the MiniScreen, a miniature likeness of a Macintosh screen, complete with menu bar. You can change the size and position of the window on the MiniScreen in two ways. You can simply drag it to its new location and resize it by pulling on its size handle. As you do so, the values in the size and location fields are updated. Alternatively, you can type in new size and location values, and the window changes size and jumps to the new spot.

Hint ▶	If you want to use the size and location fields, it helps to understand that the top left corner of the screen is defined as the origin (0,0), and everything is measured from there in pixels. The menu bar covers the first 20 pixels down from the top (in most Western languages), so remember to position tops of windows at 21 or more pixels. Also keep in mind that the values in these fields indicate the size and location of the *content area* of a window, so a title bar or other window frame needs extra space. (Title bars vary, but generally take up about as much space as the menu bar.) Keep in mind that if you change the position of the top of the rectangle without also changing the position of the bottom, you can inadvertently squash the window. If that particular window has contents, they probably won't fit properly anymore. You can avoid squashing the window if you choose Show Height & Width (instead of Show Bottom & Right) from the 'WIND' menu. Or you can just drag it to its new position.

This editor adds two menus to ResEdit's menu bar. You can set characteristics of the MiniScreen using the MiniScreen menu. The 'WIND' menu lets you control a variety of characteristics of the 'WIND' editor and the resource you're editing.

▶ The MiniScreen Menu

ResEdit uses the same MiniScreen menu, shown in Figure 10-2, for the 'WIND', 'ALRT', and 'DLOG' editors. The MiniScreen defaults to an SE screen, but you can change it to any of the standard Apple monitor sizes listed. Their dimensions are shown in pixels. If you have a monitor that's not listed (or if you want to create a screen so you can see magnified details), choose Other from the MiniScreen menu. You see the dialog shown in Figure 10-3, which allows you to set another screen size (in pixels), and even add it to the menu if you wish. The editor appropriately scales the MiniScreen and the window it contains to whatever screen size you select, as shown in Figure 10-4. When you set the MiniScreen size for any one of the 'WIND', 'ALRT', or 'DLOG' editors, you set it for all of them, because ResEdit saves your choice in its Preferences file.

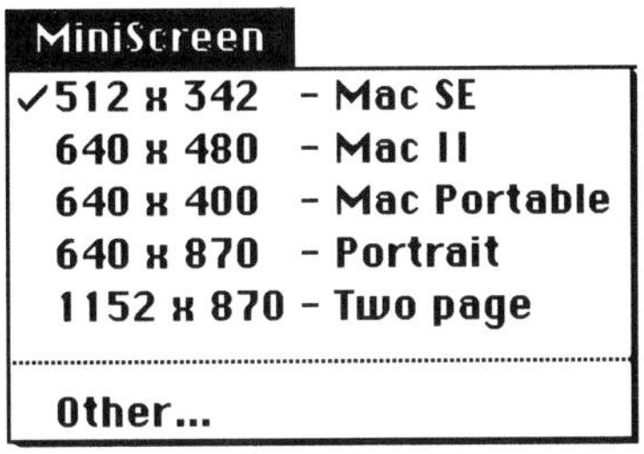

MiniScreen
✓512 x 342 - Mac SE
640 x 480 - Mac II
640 x 400 - Mac Portable
640 x 870 - Portrait
1152 x 870 - Two page
Other...

Figure 10-2. The MiniScreen menu lets you set the scaled screen size displayed in the 'WIND', 'ALRT', and 'DLOG' editors.

MiniScreen Size
Height: 240
Width: 240
Add to menu
Cancel
OK

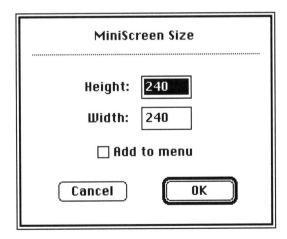

Figure 10-3. This dialog, which is displayed when you choose Other from the MiniScreen menu, allows you to set a custom screen size.

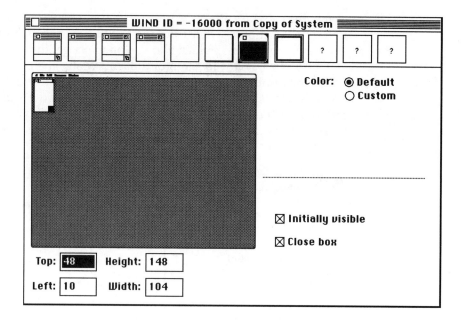

Figure 10-4. The 'WIND' editor showing the 'WIND' resource for the Calculator DA, scaled for a two-page screen. (Compare with Figure 10-1.)

▶ The 'WIND' Menu

The 'WIND' menu, shown in Figure 10-5, allows you to control certain characteristics of 'WIND' resources and the 'WIND' editor. The first item, Set 'WIND' Characteristics, causes the dialog shown in Figure 10-6 to be displayed. If you want to change the title of a window, perhaps changing the "Calculator" DA to the "Abacus" DA, here's where you make the change. Unless you're a programmer, you should leave the other two editable fields alone.

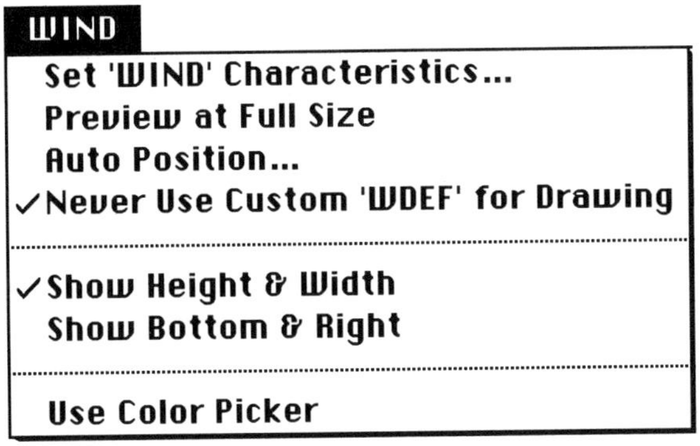

Figure 10-5. The 'WIND' menu helps you manipulate resources in the 'WIND' editor.

The Preview at Full Size command temporarily displays the 'WIND' you're editing at full size and in the location specified. Clicking the mouse or typing a key makes the preview disappear.

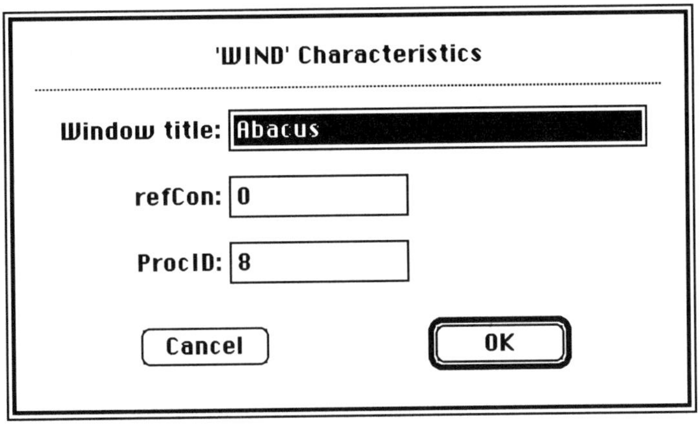

Figure 10-6. This dialog, which is displayed when you choose Set 'WIND' Characteristics, allows you to edit the title of a window.

The Auto Position command displays the dialog shown in Figure 10-7, and as indicated, this feature only works with System 7.0 or later. The pop-up menu on the left in the dialog determines the positioning, and the three choices in the pop-up menu on the right determine whether the selected position is relative to the Main Screen, the Parent

Window, or the Parent Window's Screen. If you choose Center, the 'WIND' is centered both vertically and horizontally, relative to the selected window or screen. Alert position is also centered left-to-right, but higher. Stagger moves the 'WIND' down and to the right. Auto position overrides the default position set in the bottom left corner of the editor, so if you're using System 7, experiment with this command to reposition 'WIND's (also 'DLOG's and 'ALRT's) that annoy you.

The next command in the menu, Never Use Custom 'WDEF' for Drawing is a Programmers Only item. For more information, see Chapter 20. One of the next two items on the 'WIND' menu is always checked—checking one unchecks the other. They let you choose how to display the size of the 'WIND', either in terms of the location of its bottom and right sides, or in terms of its height and width. We discuss the last command, Use Color Picker, in Part 4.

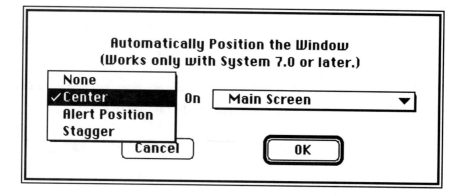

Figure 10-7. The two pop-up menus in the Auto Position dialog let you tell System 7.0 (or later) how to automatically position a 'WIND'.

▶ Changing Where a Window Appears

The document window in MacWrite 5.0 automatically takes advantage of a larger screen, but its Clipboard, Header, and Footer windows don't. And they always appear in the same place, which might not be exactly where you'd like them. You might prefer to have the Footer and Clipboard windows open at the bottom of your screen—or somewhere else. Here's how to make that happen.

1. Use ResEdit to open a copy of MacWrite 5.0, then open the 'WIND' resource type.
2. You see four 'WIND' resources listed in the resource picker. The resource with ID 303 is the Footer window, and ID 304 is the Clipboard window. If you want to change the Header window, it's ID 302. (There's not much you can do to the Untitled document window, ID 301, because it already takes advantage of a larger screen.) Open the 'WIND' you want to alter.
3. The 'WIND' editor opens, displaying the resource you selected. Make sure the editor's MiniScreen matches your screen. Pull down the MiniScreen menu and choose your screen size, if it isn't already checked.
4. Now you can drag the image of the window to where you'd like it to appear. If you want to change the size, drag the size handle in the lower right corner to reshape the window until it suits you. You can also make adjustments by typing directly into the size and location fields below the MiniScreen.
5. Quit ResEdit, saving your changes.
6. Launch your copy of MacWrite and test the new window size and location. If it's not quite right, or if you'd like to customize another window, simply repeat these steps. (You don't have to repeat Step 3. ResEdit remembers your MiniScreen selection.)

▶ Dialogs

When you see the 'DLOG' editor, you'll probably have a vague feeling that you've seen it before, and actually you have. As you can see in Figure 10-8, this editor looks almost exactly like the 'WIND' editor. Add a field in which to specify the ID of an associated 'DITL' resource, and essentially you've got yourself a 'DLOG' editor, which makes sense, because a 'DLOG' is basically a 'WIND' plus a 'DITL'.

Virtually everything you just learned for 'WIND' resources applies to 'DLOG' resources, too. Changing the window type for a dialog (using the window-type buttons across the top of the editor) usually doesn't do you any good. You can change the colors. (See Chapter 19 if you're interested.) You shouldn't change the check boxes in the lower right-corner of this editor, either. The MiniScreen menu is the same, and the 'DLOG' menu is completely analogous to the 'WIND' menu.

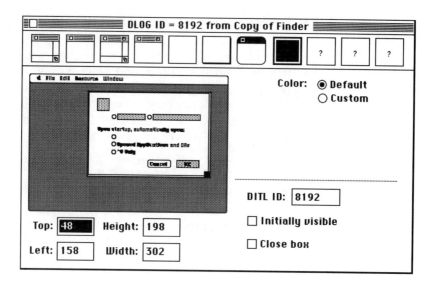

Figure 10-8. The 'DLOG' editor closely resembles the 'WIND' editor. (Compare with Figure 10-1.)

| Hint ▶ | If you change a dialog's location, but the new position doesn't seem to "stick," it might be because the application employs special procedures for moving or centering its dialogs. In fact ResEdit does this, so don't bother trying to reposition its dialogs. Any time you open a 'WIND', 'DLOG', or 'ALRT' and find it jammed up in the top left corner of the MiniScreen, you can bet that the application has its own procedures for positioning the window. You can go ahead and customize its contents, if any, but don't bother trying to tweak its position. |

One important way the 'DLOG' editor differs in appearance from the 'WIND' editor is that the rectangle appearing on the MiniScreen usually shows some items inside. Everything in a 'DLOG' is stored in an intimately associated resource called a dialog item list, or 'DITL'. In other words, the 'DITL' is the business part of the dialog, and the 'DLOG' is the box in which the 'DITL' is packaged. The main inference you can draw from this apt analogy is that, unless you significantly change the size of the product (the 'DITL'), you don't have to worry about changing the package (the 'DLOG').

Translating software for foreign markets gives an example of this relationship. When you want to change the text of a dialog, you do that in the associated 'DITL'. Often text translated from English occupies more space, however, so the text item has to become larger. To make room for the translated text, you have to enlarge the text item in the 'DITL'. Then, to make room for the bigger text item in the 'DITL', you have to enlarge the dialog's rectangle which you can do either in the 'DLOG' editor or in the 'DITL' editor. (For more information about translating software, see Appendix E.) To understand how all this works, you have to understand how to edit the meat of a dialog, its 'DITL'. We cover that in the next section.

▶ Dialog Item Lists

Manipulating dialog items in a 'DITL' is almost as easy as manipulating files in the Finder or objects in a program like MacDraw. Before you can do anything to an item, you have to click it to select it. Once an item is selected, you can drag it to reposition it. You can also select groups of items by dragging out a rectangle that encloses the items you want to select. (Any item even partly inside the selection rectangle becomes selected.) Most kinds of items have size handles in their bottom right corners that you can drag to resize the item. You see the size handle only when a single item is selected because you can resize only one item at a time.

| Hint ▶ | When an item, or group of items, is selected, each touch of one of the arrow keys moves the selection by one pixel in the chosen direction. |

Dialog item lists are made up of collections of nine different kinds of items (ten items in System 7) that can be arranged any number of ways within the 'DLOG' or 'ALRT' window they're associated with. Table 10-1 summarizes what you can and can't do when customizing dialog item lists (without changing the application's code). The next section describes the 'DITL' editor and gives more details.

Table 10-1. What You Can and Can't Do When Customizing 'DITL's

Safe
- You can reposition items in a 'DITL'.
- You can change the size of items in a 'DITL'.
- You can add or change static items (static text, icons, pictures).
- You can make some items invisible (by dragging them out of the window).
- You can change the text in any item: buttons, radio buttons, static text, and so on.

Dangerous
- Do not change item numbers in a 'DITL'.
- Do not remove items from a 'DITL'.
- Do not change item types; for instance, don't change a button to a check box.
- Do not change pairs of characters such as ^0 or ^1 (You may see numerals 0 through 3). These markers tell the application where to insert text, such as file names, error numbers, or text from string resources ('STR ' or 'STR#').

▶ The 'DITL' Editor

You can open the 'DITL' editor in a few different ways. You can open it from the 'DITL' picker if you know the ID of the 'DITL' you want to edit. By convention, a 'DITL' resource should have the same ID number as the 'DLOG' or 'ALRT' it's associated with. You can also open the 'DITL' editor three ways from the 'DLOG' editor. You can choose Open 'DITL' Editor from the Resource menu, you can double-click the picture of the dialog on the MiniScreen, or you can press the Return or Enter key.

What you see when the DITL editor opens depends on the 'DITL' you're editing. The size of the 'DLOG' or 'ALRT' rectangle determines the window size of the associated 'DITL'. Figure 10-9 shows the 'DITL' associated with the 'DLOG' you saw in Figure 10-8. Other 'DITL's contain different items. No matter what 'DITL' you edit, you should understand the additional menus, item palette, and item editor.

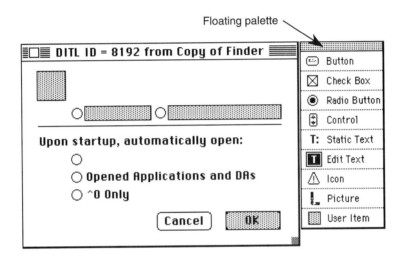

Figure 10-9. The 'DITL' editor shows all the items in a dialog.

The 'DITL' Menu

The 'DITL' menu, shown in Figure 10-10, offers extensive options for manipulating dialog items. Many of the commands are useful only to programmers, however, so they're not described here. (For more details, see Chapter 20.) For instance, the first group of commands, (down to the first separator line) are all concerned with item numbers. Since you should never change item numbers when customizing a 'DITL', you have no use for any of these commands.

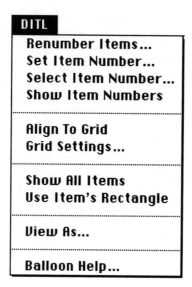

Figure 10-10. The 'DITL' menu helps you manipulate dialog items.

The next two commands can help tidy up the appearance of a dialog you're customizing by letting you align items to an invisible grid. Align to Grid causes the upper left corners of items to snap to the grid corners when you move the items. Grid Settings displays a simple dialog that allows you to set the size (in pixels) of the grid. (Remember, screens vary, but there are roughly 72 pixels per inch.)

The Show All Items command temporarily expands the 'DITL' window so you can see items that may be hidden outside the dialog's or alert's rectangle. The next item, Use Item's Rectangle, applies only to dialog items that are resources: icons, controls, and pictures ('ICON's, 'CNTL's, and 'PICT's). This command causes the 'DITL' to use the resource's rectangle instead of the rectangle set in the 'DITL'. This command comes in handy if you change pictures, streamlining the rectangle for an automatic fit.

The View As command lets you see how the 'DITL' would look in a different font or font size. Control Panel dialogs, for instance, use 9-point Geneva, so you might want to use that font when you edit the 'DITL' for a Control Panel dialog. (This command could also come in handy if you change your System font, as described in Chapter 16.)

The Balloon Help command is useful only to programmers developing applications to run under System 7.

The Alignment Menu

Making dialogs look nice is the whole point of the Alignment menu, shown in Figure 10-11. All but the last two commands on this menu apply to selections of two or more items, and the menu icons give you good visual clues about what the commands do.

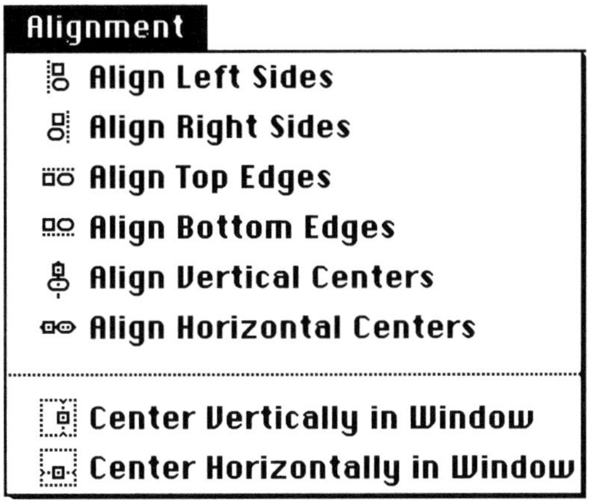

```
┌─────────────────────────────────────────┐
│ Alignment                                │
├─────────────────────────────────────────┤
│  ⌷  Align Left Sides                     │
│  ⌷  Align Right Sides                    │
│ ⌷⌷  Align Top Edges                      │
│ ⌷⌷  Align Bottom Edges                   │
│  ⌷  Align Vertical Centers               │
│ ⊙⊙  Align Horizontal Centers             │
│ ⋯⋯⋯⋯⋯⋯⋯⋯⋯⋯⋯⋯⋯⋯⋯⋯⋯⋯⋯⋯⋯⋯⋯⋯⋯⋯⋯ │
│  ⌷  Center Vertically in Window          │
│  ⌷  Center Horizontally in Window        │
└─────────────────────────────────────────┘
```

Figure 10-11. The Alignment menu helps line up dialog items.

The first four commands align items relative to each other. Choosing Align Left Sides lines up the left sides of all selected items to the position of the leftmost item. Similarly, Align Top Edges aligns the tops of all selected items so that they line up with the highest of the selected items. The other commands work analogously.

The next command, Align Vertical Centers, shifts the selected items horizontally so that their centers line up. ResEdit lines them up halfway between the center of the leftmost item and the center of the rightmost item. Align Horizontal Centers works analogously.

The last two commands work on single or multiple-item selections, aligning the items relative to the window rather than to each other.

The Item Palette

The item palette, shown in Figure 10-12, is a floating window that you can drag anywhere on your screen. To add a new item to a dialog, click the appropriate item in the palette and drag it into position in the 'DITL'. When you're customizing an existing 'DITL', however, you can only add three kinds of items: icons, pictures, and static text. For information about the other items, see Chapter 20.

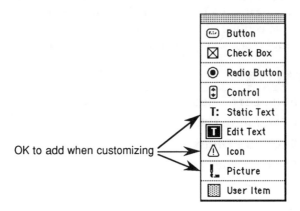

Figure 10-12. You can drag items into a 'DITL' from the floating item palette.

The Mac uses lots of kinds of icons, but if you're thinking about adding one to a 'DITL', you have to find (or create) an 'ICON' resource in the same file. Adding pictures is similar, but the resource type is 'PICT' and it's not limited to a certain size, as icons are. Static text items, as the name suggests, are the text items that you see but can't change when the dialog is in use. (The name distinguishes them from edit text items, which are fields that you can type into when the dialog is in use.)

Hint ▶

If you're copying a picture from a paint or draw program, paste it into the file's 'PICT' picker. Remember that when you send a selection of bits to the clipboard, it's handled as a 'PICT'. If the file doesn't have any 'PICT's (and therefore doesn't have a 'PICT' picker), paste into the type picker.

Dragging an item into the 'DITL' from the item palette reserves a spot for it, but you still need to set its individual characteristics. To set an item's characteristics, double-click it to open the item editor. (You can also select an item, then choose Open as Dialog Item from the Resource menu.) The item editor is where you fill in the unique text of a static text item, or the ID of the particular 'ICON' or 'PICT' you want to use.

▶ The Item Editor

The item editor, shown in Figure 10-13, is a pretty simple editor. The current selection on the pop-up menu indicates the type of item you're editing. The four fields in the lower right probably look familiar to you because they're similar to the ones in the 'WIND', 'DLOG', and 'ALRT' editors. These fields allow you to set the size and location of the dialog item, but note that the origin for these measurements is the upper left corner of the dialog (or alert) window, not the screen. You can choose between showing the height and width or bottom and right of the item, just as you've seen for other editors, using the two commands on the Item menu. The Enabled check box is a Programmers Only item.

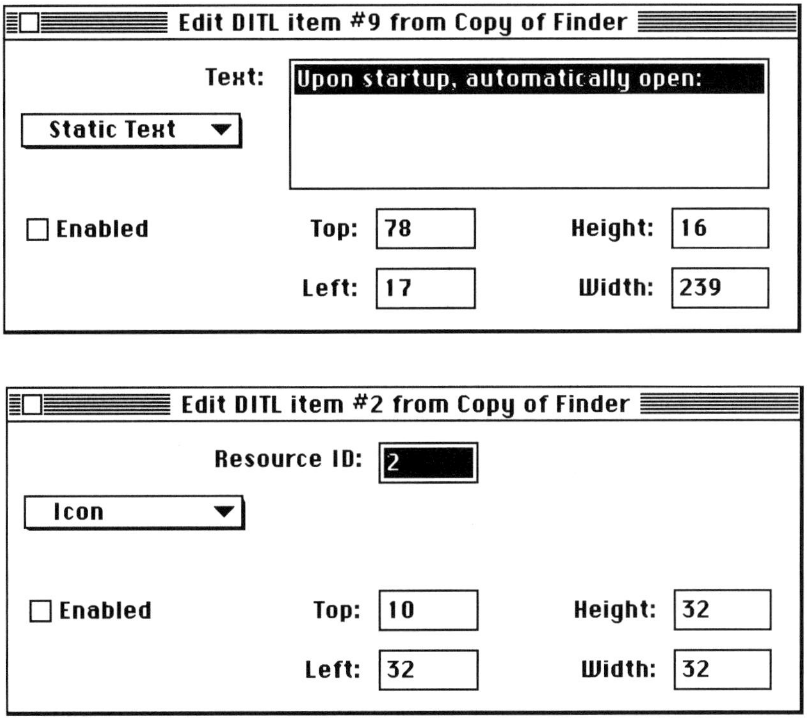

Figure 10-13. Two views of the item editor showing different kinds of items.

You edit or type the text you want to see in the Text field. If you run across things like "^0," remember not to change them. These are the place holders applications use to figure out where to insert text that varies. The Text field scrolls to accommodate more lines of text (In fact, it can hold 255 characters), but generally, if you have to scroll you're probably entering too much text. Remember, if your text item grows, you can always enlarge and reposition the static text item in the 'DITL'. If necessary, you can also enlarge the 'DLOG' or 'ALRT', too. Finally, the Resource ID field is where you enter the ID of the 'ICON' or 'PICT' you want to see in the dialog.

▶ Enlarging the List Box in a Standard File Directory Dialog

Do some standard file directory dialogs seem cramped to you? If you would like to be able to see more and longer file names, you can enlarge the list boxes in these dialogs. This section describes how to modify one of these resources in the System file. Some applications have their own standard file list boxes that override those in the System file, so you may want to change those, too.

If you need to revert at some point, remember that you're changing *two* resources—a 'DLOG' and a 'DITL'.

1. Use ResEdit to open a copy of your System file, then double-click the 'DLOG' resource type.
2. Find ID -4000 in the 'DLOG' picker and double-click it. You see the Open dialog, which should look something like the window shown in Figure 10-14.
3. Make sure the editor's MiniScreen matches your screen. Pull down the MiniScreen menu and choose your screen size, if it isn't already checked.
4. Double-click the dialog on the MiniScreen to open the 'DITL' editor.
5. Drag the size handle (the black square) on the 'DITL' window down and to the right, as shown in Figure 10-15. (You'll have to move the item palette first.) That makes the associated 'DLOG' rectangle bigger so it can accommodate a longer and wider list box.

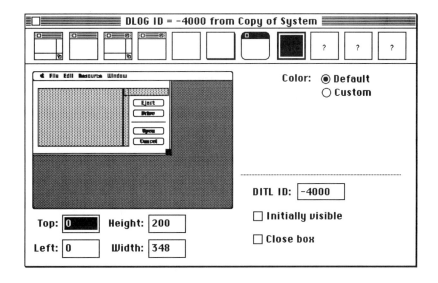

Figure 10-14. Many applications use this Open dialog from the System file.

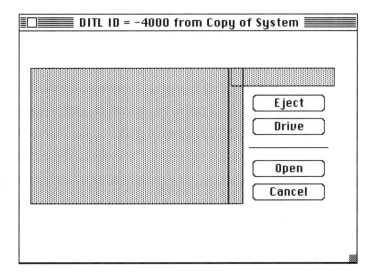

Figure 10-15. Dragging the 'DITL' editor's size handle down and to the right makes the associated 'DLOG' rectangle bigger.

6. Now you can move and enlarge dialog items to take advantage of the extra space you added on the bottom and right. Click the smallest gray rectangle (this horizontal user item is where the disk name goes) and drag it to the right (or use the right-arrow key). Select the four buttons and the separator line and drag them to the right under the item you just moved, and down a bit. (The easiest way to select these items is to drag the mouse pointer in a rectangle that encloses all of them.) In a similar fashion, select the tall, skinny gray rectangle (this is where the scroll bar goes) and drag it to the right. Exact placement doesn't matter just yet. Your 'DITL' should now look something like Figure 10-16.

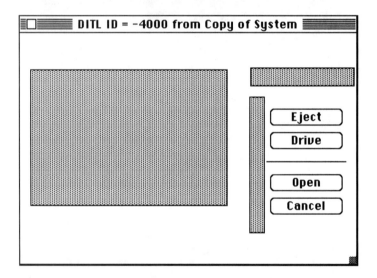

Figure 10-16. Drag peripheral dialog items into the space you added.

7. You're ready to enlarge the list box. Click the large gray rectangle. When it's selected, you'll notice a darker spot in the lower right corner. Drag this size handle down and to the right, but don't crowd the other items. Even though it looks like there's room, don't reposition the list box upward. Your Mac needs the space above for telling you which folder you're in.

8. Once you've got the list box sized and positioned, you can drag the scroll bar user item back over. You need to make the scroll bar's rectangle the same height as the list box, but don't change its

width. You can change its size the same way you did for the list box. Position it right next to the list box.

9. For cosmetic reasons, you might want to consider spreading out the buttons a little. Simply click each one and drag it into position, or use the arrow keys. Remember, the Alignment menu and the Align To Grid command on the 'DITL' menu can help you tidy up the items. Figure 10-17 shows one possible new look.

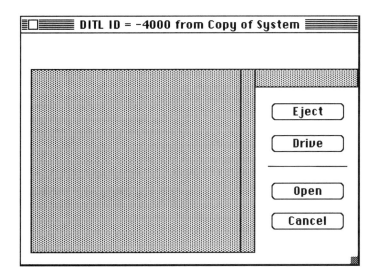

Figure 10-17. An enlarged list box surrounded by appropriately rearranged companion dialog items.

10. Close all the windows, save your work, and quit ResEdit. When you reinstall your System file, you'll see your new enlarged list box in any application that uses the System resource for its open dialog. If you want to reposition something in the dialog, just repeat the appropriate steps.

▶ Alerts

Alerts are a special subset of dialogs, so if you've read the preceding sections you know a lot about them already. The same guidelines apply for moving or changing the size of an alert's window and for editing the 'DITL's in which alerts store their contents. As you search through your files for the alerts you want to customize, you should be aware that alerts aren't always stored in 'ALRT' resources. Dialogs can easily masquerade as alerts, and often do. Just because 'ALRT's offer a convenient way of showing a modal dialog window doesn't mean applications have to use them. Something else to be aware of is that many applications make their 'ALRT's do extra duty by substituting different text strings, depending on the situation. For instance, Figure 10-18 shows a 'DITL' from an alert that the Finder can use as it pleases, and there's not much you can do to change it.

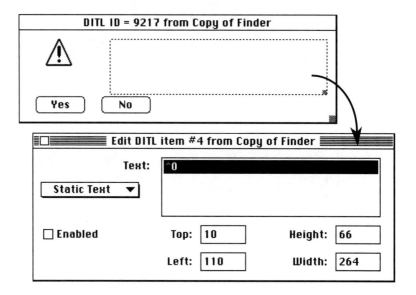

Figure 10-18. This 'DITL' from an 'ALRT' gives the Finder great flexibility but offers users little possibility for customization.

Numerous alerts offer greater customization potential than this, however, and you can make several useful changes to them.

▶ The 'ALRT' Editor

The 'ALRT' editor, shown in Figure 10-19, resembles a streamlined 'DLOG' editor. The most conspicuous difference is the absence of the window-type buttons across the top of the editor window because alerts automatically and unchangeably have modal windows. The MiniScreen menu works just as in the 'WIND' and 'DLOG' editors. You can edit associated 'DITL' resources just as you would for any dialog. To make changes unique to alerts, you have to go to the 'ALRT' menu.

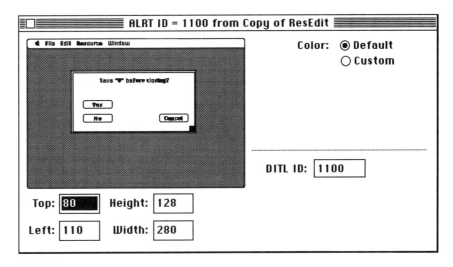

Figure 10-19. The 'ALRT' editor resembles the 'DLOG' editor.

▶ 'ALRT' Menu

The 'ALRT' menu, shown in Figure 10-20, is almost completely analogous to the 'WIND' and 'DLOG' menus. Choosing the first menu item, Set 'ALRT' Stage Info, causes the dialog shown in Figure 10-21 to be displayed.

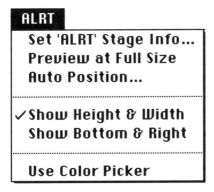

Figure 10-20. The 'ALRT' menu.

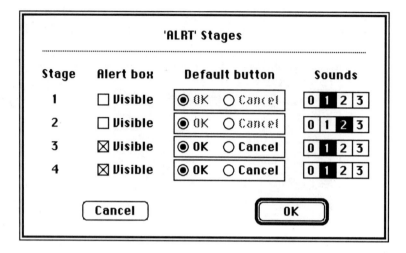

Figure 10-21. The 'ALRT' Stage Info dialog contains several useful settings.

A glance at the 'ALRT' Stage Info dialog may give you ideas for a variety of changes you can make to alerts. As you can see, an alert can beep from zero to three times, and the alert box doesn't have to be visible. This dialog is also where you set an alert's default button, the dark-bordered button you can activate by pressing Return or Enter.

You may be wondering what an alert stage is. Actually, you probably already know, because anyone who has used a Macintosh for a while knows on some level what alert stages are. Let's say you type a letter in a field that can only accept numeric characters. The application assumes you've simply made a mistake, so it beeps. Stage 1 settings are used for the first occurrence of a problem. If you do it again, the application still gives you the benefit of the doubt, and beeps again, using Stage 2 settings. If you try this three times, the Stage 3 settings assume you probably really don't understand the situation, so it's time to make an alert visible that explains the problem. The Stage column in the dialog lists the four possible Macintosh alert stages. An alert can do something different at each stage, but it doesn't have to.

To make an alert invisible, simply click the Visible check box to uncheck it. However, if an alert contains any buttons besides an OK button, do not make it invisible! The only kind of alert that should be invisible is one that contains only an OK button. You can't get into too much trouble changing sounds. Simply click the number that represents the number of beeps you want to hear.

If the beeping of a certain alert annoys you, you can decrease the number of beeps, or even turn the beep off. Open the offending 'ALRT' resource and choose Set 'ALRT' Stage Info from the 'ALRT' menu. In the Sounds part of the dialog, click the number of beeps you want to hear.

An alert has to have a default button, but you can change which button it is. The radio buttons in the Default button section of the dialog are labeled OK and Cancel, which follows Apple's suggested human interface guidelines for buttons in an alert. However, you might find it easier to think about OK as Button 1 and Cancel as Button 2, since obviously the text in alert buttons can say anything. To find out which alert button is Button 1, open the associated 'DITL' and press the Option key to see the item numbers, as shown in Figure 10-22.

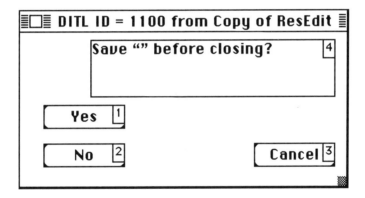

Figure 10-22. Press the Option key to see the item numbers in the 'DITL'.

You may have noticed that all buttons in a 'DITL' look the same, causing you to wonder at what point the default button in an alert acquires its dark outline. The Dialog Manager, one of the Macintosh's user interface middlemen, takes care of it using the information set in the 'ALRT' Stage Info dialog. Because no such setting exists for regular dialogs, applications have to resort to other means for marking the default button.

▶ Changing the Default Button in an Alert

Do you frequently face an alert that seems like it has the wrong button set as the default? For instance, some people get annoyed by the alert shown in Figure 10-23, which you see if you use an existing name in a Save As dialog. As the figure illustrates, you can change the default button, making it easier to overwrite existing files.

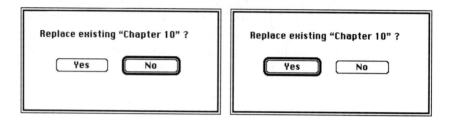

Figure 10-23. If you are annoyed by having to use the mouse to click Yes in this alert, you can change the default button, which allows you to quickly press Return.

Follow these steps to make the change shown in the figure.

1. Use ResEdit to open a copy of your System file, then double-click the 'ALRT' resource type.
2. Find ID -3996 in the 'ALRT' picker and double-click it. You see the Replace existing "^0"? alert in the 'ALRT' editor.
3. Choose Set 'ALRT' Stage Info from the 'ALRT' menu. You see a dialog similar to the one you saw in Figure 10-21.
4. Click all four radio buttons labeled Cancel, because the Yes button is item number 2.
5. Close all the windows, save your work, and quit ResEdit. After you reinstall your System file, you'll see your new alert in any application that uses the System resource.

If you decide you want to change things back, just repeat these steps, except click the radio buttons labeled OK.

▶ Summary

This chapter covers four types of interrelated resources and how to edit them: 'WIND's, 'DLOG's, 'ALRT's, and 'DITL's. Windows ('WIND') define a rectangle having a specified size and location on the screen. Their window frames can vary, and they can have an optional title. Dialogs ('DLOG') and alerts ('ALRT'), which are a special subset of dialogs, store their contents in dialog item lists ('DITL). Generally the bulk of dialog customization takes place in the 'DITL' editor, where you can add or change icons, pictures, and certain text items. You can also reposition and resize dialog items. This chapter shows how to change the size and location of a 'WIND' and how to enlarge the list box in standard file directory dialogs by changing the appropriate 'DLOG' and 'DITL'. The chapter concludes with alerts and shows you how to change a default button in a System file 'ALRT' resource.

11 ▶ Changing Time, Date, and Number Formats

Your Macintosh comes with resources that set the standard date, time, and number formats for your country. Every application that displays a date, time, or number should use these resources. If they don't, getting the application to work in different countries becomes much more difficult. The Finder's text views, Microsoft Word's Glossary command, FullWrite Professional's Variables command, Full Impact's date and time functions, and the SuperClock shareware program all use the 'itl0' and 'itl1' resources. In general, you can expect most major applications and many smaller ones to follow the rules and use these resources. The only way to find out for sure whether an application uses them is to change the resources and see if the application changes. Each country has its own 'itl0' and 'itl1' resource, but the standard formats for your country may not be exactly what you want. For example,

- In the U.S., the default date format includes the day of the week (Saturday, June 29, 1991), which is often not desirable.

- The U.S. default time format is 12-hour, with AM and PM, but in many cases (especially for the military or when communicating with other countries) a 24-hour format is desirable.

- If you do business with people in other countries, you may want to use their currency symbol rather than yours in your communications.

179

- In the U.S., negative numbers are placed within parentheses, but you might want them preceded by a minus sign.

You can change any of these formats by modifying the 'itl0' and 'itl1' resources in your System file.

The 'itl0' resource contains the defaults for the format of numbers, short dates (1/16/91), and time. Figure 11-1 shows the U.S. 'itl0' resource. The numbers and times shown in a different font on the left side of the window are examples of the current settings. As you make changes, the examples change to show you what the new settings will look like. You should not change the Country Code field unless you are actually creating a resource for a new country. You can type any character you want into the editable fields (for example, you could make your decimal point be shown as "x" instead of ".").

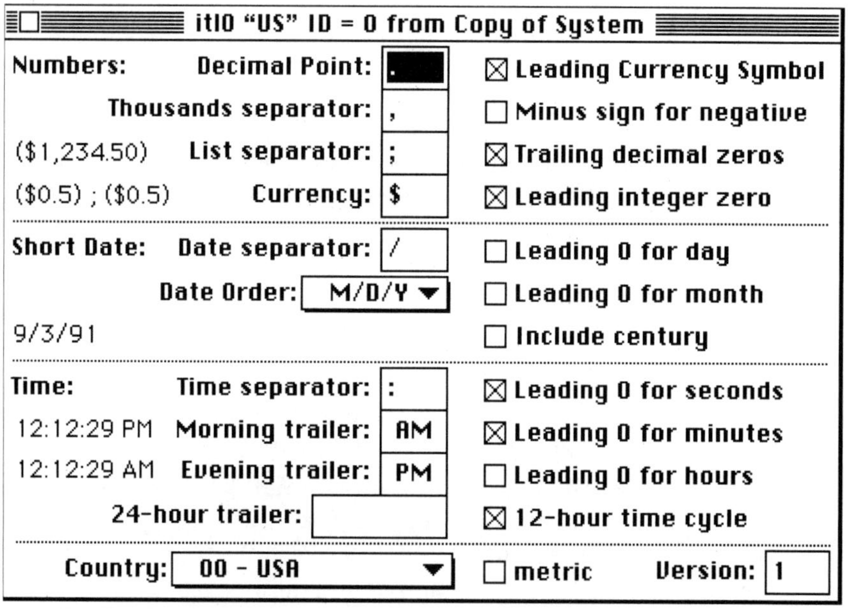

```
┌─────────────────── itl0 "US" ID = 0 from Copy of System ───────────────────┐
│ Numbers:        Decimal Point: [.  ]      ⊠ Leading Currency Symbol        │
│            Thousands separator: [,  ]      ☐ Minus sign for negative        │
│ ($1,234.50)    List separator: [;  ]      ⊠ Trailing decimal zeros         │
│ ($0.5) ; ($0.5)    Currency: [$  ]         ⊠ Leading integer zero           │
│ ................................................................ │
│ Short Date:    Date separator: [/  ]       ☐ Leading 0 for day             │
│                 Date Order: [ M/D/Y ▼ ]    ☐ Leading 0 for month           │
│ 9/3/91                                      ☐ Include century               │
│ ................................................................ │
│ Time:          Time separator: [:  ]       ⊠ Leading 0 for seconds         │
│ 12:12:29 PM   Morning trailer: [ AM ]      ⊠ Leading 0 for minutes         │
│ 12:12:29 AM   Evening trailer: [ PM ]      ☐ Leading 0 for hours           │
│            24-hour trailer: [     ]         ⊠ 12-hour time cycle            │
│ ................................................................ │
│ Country: [  00 - USA          ▼ ]   ☐ metric      Version: [1 ]            │
└─────────────────────────────────────────────────────────────────────────┘
```

Figure 11-1. The U.S. 'itl0' resource.

Manipulating this resource is as easy as filling in a dialog box. For example, changing to 24-hour time is a simple matter of clicking the 12-hour time cycle check box to turn it off. You may wonder what the side effects of your changes might be. For example, will the AM and PM indicators go away when you switch to 24-hour time? The examples on the left side of the window show exactly what your new format will look like.

The 'itl1' resource shown in Figure 11-2 contains the defaults for the long date format, including the names of the months and days and the order of the month, day, and year. The date in the lower left corner in a different font shows an example of the abbreviated and long date formats. These examples change as you enter new values. As with 'itl0', you should not change the Country Code field unless you're making a resource for a new country. The fields lined up across the middle of the window represent the order of the parts of the date, and the separators that should be used. The date has four parts (day, month, date, and year), and they can appear in any order. Simply reset them using the pop-up menus. You can also have any separator you want (up to three or four characters, depending on the field), including spaces. For example, the separator between Day and Month in Figure 11-2 is a comma and a space character.

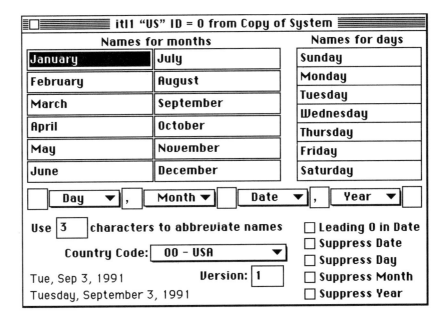

Figure 11-2. The U.S. 'itl1' resource.

Again, as with the 'itl0' resource, making changes is simply a matter of filling in a dialog box. For example, to show only the month, day, and year and not the day of the week, simply click the Suppress Day check box in the lower right corner of the window. You can substitute anything you want in the Names for Months and Names for Days fields. For example, if you type "banana" in place of Wednesday, every time you would normally see the word Wednesday, you'll see the word "banana" instead. Substituting for foreign languages is just as easy. Figure 11-3 shows the French 'itl1' resource.

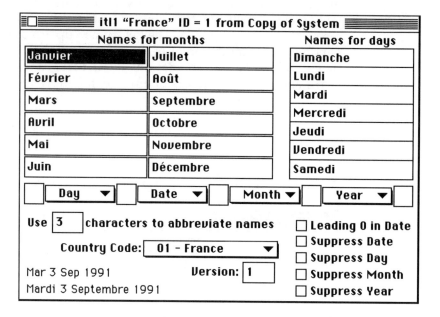

Figure 11-3. The French 'itl1' resource.

▶ Reordering Your Date

Here's an example of how you could change your date format from Sunday, February 10, 1991 to 10 February 1991 (with no day name).

1. Use ResEdit to open a copy of your System file.
2. Open the 'itl1' resource with ID 0.
3. Across the middle of the window is a row of four pop-up menus and five editable fields that define the date format (as shown in Figure 11-2 and Figure 11-3). Change the second pop-up menu from the left to Date instead of Month.

4. Change the third pop-up menu to Month instead of Date. You have now switched the date and month parts of the date format.

5. Click the Suppress Day check box to remove the day of the week from your date.

6. Remove the comma between the month and year. You don't need to worry about the comma between the day of the week and date— since you're not using a day of the week, the System knows not to use the comma.

7. That's it! Close and save the file, reinstall it in your System Folder, restart your Mac, and you should see your new date format.

▶ Saving a Couple of Different Formats

If you only occasionally need to change the format of the date or time, you can create alternate versions of the 'itl0' and 'itl1' resources that you keep in your System file. When you want to switch, simply install your alternate resource.

1. Use ResEdit to open the System file. (It's OK to edit the System file directly this time since you won't be changing any resources it's currently using.)

2. Open the 'itl0' or 'itl1' picker.

3. Use the Duplicate command on the Edit menu to get a spare version of the resource.

4. Open your new spare resource and make whatever changes you will occasionally want to use.

5. Close and save the System file.

You can use the 'itlb' resource to tell the System to use your new 'itl0' or 'itl1' resource. Just follow these steps.

1. Open the System file with ResEdit.

2. Open the 'itlb' picker.

3. Open the 'itlb' resource with ID of 0. (If you're using a System software version before 7.0, you may see an alert warning you that the template needs more data. Just click OK.) You should see a window similar to the one shown in Figure 11-4.

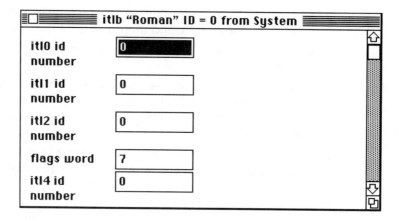

Figure 11-4. Change the 'itl0' and 'itl1' numbers for your new resources.

4. The first two fields (itl0 id number and itl1 id number) contain the resource IDs of the 'itl0' and 'itl1' resources used by the System. Change one or both fields to contain the resource IDs of your new resources.

5. Close and save the System file and restart your Mac.

When you want to change back, just restore the original resource ID numbers in your 'itlb' resource.

Hint ▶

You can use a different approach if you want to use your special format only in certain applications. Make a copy of the application and use ResEdit to install your custom 'itl0' and 'itl1' resources with ID 0 right into the copy. In most applications (including HyperCard, Microsoft Excel, and MacProject II), the new formatting will be used the next time you use the copy of the application. This allows you, for example, to keep your Macintosh in French but use a U.S. copy of Microsoft Excel.

▶ Using the International Control Panel

If you have the International Control Panel that Apple includes with all systems shipped outside the United States, you can switch between resources much more easily. The International Control Panel shown in Figure 11-5 displays a list of the names of all 'itl0' resources found in the System file. If you create a custom 'itl0' or 'itl1', just give it a unique name (with the Get Resource Info command), and you can use the Control Panel to activate your special formatting. Keep in mind, though, that the International Control Panel only lists 'itl0' resources, even though it switches both 'itl0' and 'itl1' resources. If you only want to change your 'itl1' resource, you'll need to duplicate your original 'itl0' resource and give it a unique name and ID that's the same as your new 'itl1' resource. (The International Control Panel's Sorting Order list lets you pick the way your Mac sorts text strings. It lists the 'itl2' resources in your System file. These are code resources that you can't edit.)

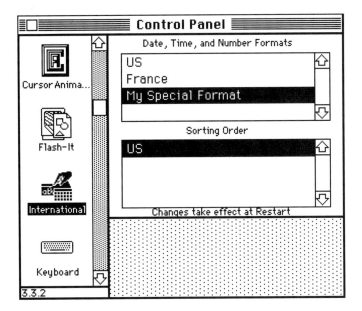

Figure 11-5. The International Control Panel

▶ Summary

In this chapter we show you ways you can customize your time, date, and number formats. The 'itl0' resource lets you change your number, short date, and time format. The 'itl1' resource lets you change your long date format. These resources are intended to allow your Macintosh to be localized for other countries, but you can use them to make sure your times, dates, and numbers are formatted just the way you want them.

12 ▶ Fiddling with Fonts

The variety of fonts and text styles available on the Macintosh has certainly contributed to its popularity. Despite this embarrassment of riches, at times you may have wished you could change some letters in your favorite fonts, or add a few special characters or symbols. Maybe you'd like to add a fraction or a mini-icon, or put a slash through the zero in a certain font so you can distinguish it from an uppercase *O*.

Whole books have been written about fonts and typography, so obviously a thorough treatment of the topic goes beyond the scope of this chapter. That's why we skip the terminology distinctions between typefaces and fonts, and don't mention kerning, proportional fonts, or fractional character widths. (Well, OK, we just mentioned them, but that was *it*.) ResEdit's 'FONT' editor is a good tool, but if you're interested in heavy-duty font projects, you should look into the various font editing software packages available. ResEdit can help you adjust many fonts, but not all of them. There are two general kinds of Mac fonts, and you need to understand the difference before you can figure out which fonts you can attempt to restyle with ResEdit. Knowing a few basics about fonts will not only help you figure out which fonts you can modify, it will help you understand ResEdit's 'FONT' editor. Our goal here is simply to give you a basic understanding you can apply when tinkering with your fonts.

▶ Two Ways to Draw Text

It may sound strange, but the Mac can do so much with text partly because it doesn't have what's called a text mode on more primitive computers. The Mac treats everything, including text, as graphics. QuickDraw, the graphics wizard residing in ROM, controls what your Mac draws on the screen, as well as what some printers, such as the ImageWriter, print. When QuickDraw sends a character to a screen or a printer, it sends a bitmap of the character. Such fonts are often called *bitmap fonts* or *screen fonts*.

There's another way to draw fonts. Some fonts are made up of mathematical descriptions of characters rather than bitmaps. Such fonts are often called *outline fonts* or *laser fonts*. (The misleading term *laser font* probably arose partly because PostScript, a standard page description language for drawing outline fonts, is included in the ROM in some laser printers.) For our purposes in this chapter, all you need to know about outline fonts is that you can *not* edit them with ResEdit. You may be able to edit their corresponding screen fonts, however, which are bitmap fonts. Just remember that such changes won't affect the printer's output.

In fact, if you have Adobe Type Manager or Apple's TrueType you can probably skip this chapter. Both of these products solve the schizophrenia of screen *versus* printer fonts because they use outline fonts to create both. As a result, you can't do any useful editing with ResEdit.

By the Way ▶	If you need to edit outline fonts, look for applications specifically developed to do just that. Fontographer (Altsys Corporation) is one such program.

▶ Bitmap Fonts

Having dispensed with outline fonts, let's focus on bitmap fonts. There are two types of bitmap font resources: 'FONT' and 'NFNT' (New FoNT), which came along with the 128K ROM. This resource type has the same format as the 'FONT' type but can accommodate many more fonts. (You can find out about 'NFNT' resources in the "Font Manager" chapters of *Inside Macintosh*, Volume IV, Chapter 5, and Volume V, Chapter 9.) Although you can open 'NFNT' resources in ResEdit's 'FONT' editor and browse through them, you can't seriously edit them. (You can alter the characters somewhat, but you can't change their sizes at all.) Commercial 'NFNT' editors are available if you really need to edit 'NFNT' fonts.

Lest you should feel you're left with typographical dregs, rest assured that many of the most familiar Mac fonts—including all the "city name" fonts such as New York, Athens, San Francisco and Cairo—are stored in 'FONT' resources. After a few more font basics, the rest of this chapter is devoted to these and other 'FONT' resources and what you can do with them.

▶ Font Basics

When you're deciding how to display text, you choose the font by its name, such as New York or Chicago, and you choose a size. The *font size*, as shown in Figure 12-1, is the distance between the *ascent line* (the height of the tallest characters) and the *descent line* (the lowest point that the "tails" of letters like *g* and *y* touch). Depending on the font, individual characters may vary in width.

By the Way ▶ Font size is measured in *points*, a typographer's term that roughly equals 1/72 of an inch. But two fonts with the same font size may not actually be the same size on the screen or when printed. Font sizes tend to be most useful for distinguishing between sizes within the same font.

Figure 12-1. The size of a font is the distance between the tops of the tallest characters (the ascent line) and the bottoms of the lowest characters (the descent line).

Although you keep track of fonts by their names, your Mac keeps track of font numbers. All the different sizes of a font belong to the same *font family*, which has a unique font number. The resource ID for a font family is calculated from its font number. Each size of a font is stored as a separate resource, as you can see in Figure 12-2, which shows a 'FONT' picker. Because every size of a font is a separate resource, you have to remember to modify each size you use. The figure also shows that the ID of a 'FONT' resource is always equal to the font family's resource ID plus the point size. We'll explain more about font numbering later.

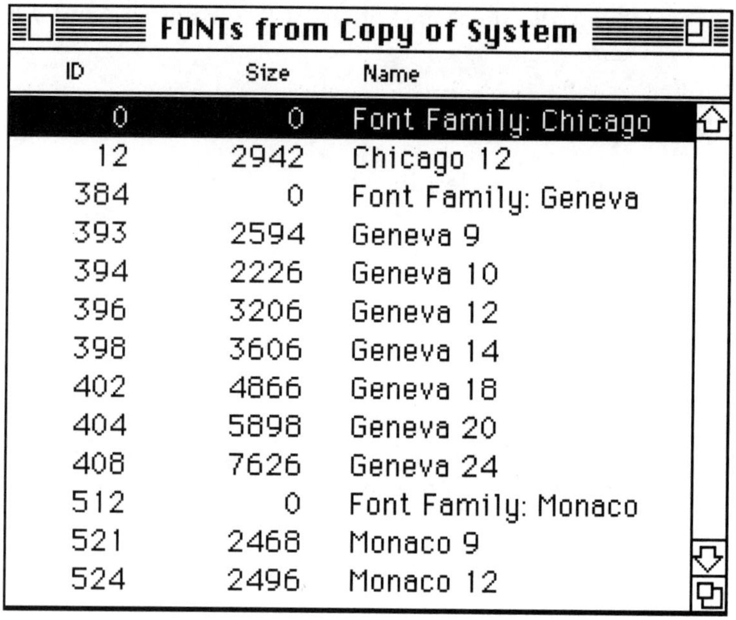

ID	Size	Name
0	0	Font Family: Chicago
12	2942	Chicago 12
384	0	Font Family: Geneva
393	2594	Geneva 9
394	2226	Geneva 10
396	3206	Geneva 12
398	3606	Geneva 14
402	4866	Geneva 18
404	5898	Geneva 20
408	7626	Geneva 24
512	0	Font Family: Monaco
521	2468	Monaco 9
524	2496	Monaco 12

FONTs from Copy of System

Figure 12-2. The 'FONT' picker shows that each size of a font is a separate resource.

You may also choose a style, such as italic or bold, when you're deciding how to display text. You can get styled text two ways. Font families may include styled fonts as separate resources, such as an italic Athens. If styled fonts aren't available, your Mac can apply the style, achieving italics, for instance, by slanting the characters. The important thing to remember is that you can't edit styled text unless it's a separate font resource.

Hint ▶

Remember that to get the best results with your ImageWriter you need an installed font twice as large as the size you want. This is because the ImageWriter prints 144 dots per inch, which is twice the typical screen resolution of 72 pixels per inch. (The ImageWriter LQ needs a font three times as large, and other printers may have other requirements.) For example, if you want 9-point text to look as good as possible in Best mode, you should have an 18-point font installed. So if you edit the 9-point resource, you should also edit the 18-point resource if you want to see your results on the printer and the screen.

A font can contain 255 unique characters, but every character need not be defined. (All the font sizes in a font family don't have to contain exactly the same set of characters, either.) The standard Macintosh characters and their ASCII (American Standard Code for Information Interchange) numbers are shown in Figure 12-3. As you might expect, certain fonts made up of symbols or pictures correspond only minimally with the ASCII chart. Every font contains a missing symbol (an empty rectangle character) in addition to the maximum 255 distinct characters. The Mac draws the missing symbol if you type a character that's missing from the font.

	0	16	32	48	64	80	96	112	128	144	160	176	192	208	224	240
0			space	0	@	P		p	Ä	ê	†	∞	¿	–	‡	
1		⌘	!	1	A	Q	a	q	Å	ë	°	±	¡	—	·	Ò
2		✓	"	2	B	R	b	r	Ç	í	¢	≤	¬	"	‚	Ú
3		◆	#	3	C	S	c	s	É	ì	£	≥	√	"	„	Û
4		(Apple)	$	4	D	T	d	t	Ñ	î	§	¥	ƒ	'	‰	Ù
5			%	5	E	U	e	u	Ö	ï	•	µ	≈	'	Â	ı
6			&	6	F	V	f	v	Ü	ñ	¶	∂	Δ	÷	Ê	ˆ
7			'	7	G	W	g	w	á	ó	ß	Σ	«	◊	Á	˜
8			(	8	H	X	h	x	à	ò	®	Π	»	ÿ	Ë	¯
9			)	9	I	Y	i	y	â	ô	©	π	…	Ÿ	È	˘
10			*	:	J	Z	j	z	ä	ö	™	∫		⁄	Í	˙
11			+	;	K	[	k	{	ã	õ	´	ª	À	¤	Î	˚
12			,	<	L	\	l	|	å	ú	¨	º	Ã	‹	Ï	¸
13			-	=	M	]	m	}	ç	ù	≠	Ω	Õ	›	Ì	˝
14			.	>	N	^	n	~	é	û	Æ	æ	Œ	fi	Ó	˛
15			/	?	O	_	o		è	ü	Ø	ø	œ	fl	Ô	ˇ

Figure 12-3. To find the ASCII number of a character in the standard Macintosh character set, add the character's column number to its row number. (For example: R = 80 + 2 = 82.)

Another thing to remember is that, depending on which Mac you have, some fonts may reside in ROM. (Appendix D lists the resources stored in ROM.) Although some fonts and some sizes may be duplicated in the System file (for the sake of older, smaller ROMs), editing these System file font resources would usually be pointless because ROM fonts override them. However, even though you can't edit resources in ROM, you can make your Mac ignore them. A section later in this chapter shows you how to override ROM 'FONT' resources and suggests a couple of fun changes you can make in the System font—the font used for window titles, the menu bar, and most dialog and alert boxes. If you want to use an entirely different 'FONT' resource for the System font, you can find instructions in Chapter 13.

▶ The 'FONT' Editor

As you can see in Figure 12-4, the 'FONT' editor has three panels and a fairly standard tool palette. The sample text panel displays text in the font and size you're editing. If the character you're working on isn't represented in the sample, simply click the panel and type some new text. The text sample gets updated as you edit, so you can always see your changes in the context of surrounding characters.

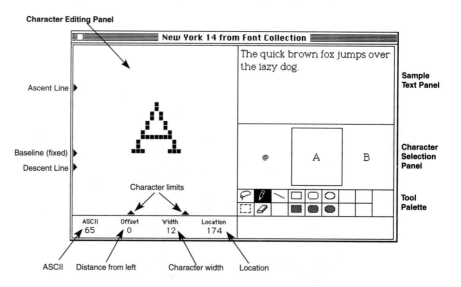

Figure 12-4. The 'FONT' editor has three panels and a standard tool palette.

The character selection panel shows a three-character section of the list of characters in a font. (They're listed in ASCII order.) The selected character occupies the middle position and has a box around it. The box is drawn with solid lines to indicate when this panel is active, otherwise the box is dotted. When this is the active panel, you can select a character simply by typing it, using whatever key combination is necessary. You can also scroll through the character list by clicking the end characters. To scroll quickly, click one of the end characters and drag the pointer outside the selection panel.

The character editing panel shows a fatbits enlargement of the selected character. The three black triangles along the left edge of the window mark the ascent line, the baseline, and the descent line, as described in Figure 12-1. You can move the ascent or descent lines by dragging them, but doing so alters the font size for the entire font, not just the character you're editing. Any bits you click outside these limits are ignored, which can be a little confusing since the bits do appear. The two black triangles along the bottom mark the left and right limits of the character, and the distance between them is the character width. We recommend that you avoid changing character widths, because doing so affects how the characters look when flanked by other characters. If you want to see how a character is spaced relative to one of these five limit lines, click and hold the appropriate triangle marker to make a dotted limit line appear across the editing panel.

| Hint ▶ |

This editor doesn't have all the features of the other fatbits editors, and some things work a bit differently. The differences are minor, so you might not notice at all, but then again you might have an unsettling, slightly confused feeling. Since knowledge is the best weapon to fight confusion, here's a list of a few of the differences.

- In the other fatbits editors, the eraser can knock out up to four bits at a time. The 'FONT' editor's eraser can only erase one bit at a time. (You'll quickly figure out which corner is the important one.) When in use it looks different, too, so you have a visual reminder.

- There's no hand pointer. When you want to move a selection, you get the arrow pointer.

- The 'FONT' editor doesn't have the tool palette mouse shortcuts described for the other editors in Chapter 5 (such as double-clicking the eraser to clear the editing panel).

- You can't use the arrow keys to nudge a selection.

Information about the current character is listed across the bottom of the panel. Its ASCII number is on the left, followed by the offset, which is the distance (in pixels) from the left limit to the first pixel of the character. The character width and its location in the font data are also listed. As you edit, your changes are reflected in the sample text and the character selection panel—as long as your monitor is set to show just black and white. ResEdit alerts you if your monitor is set to display more than two colors, explaining that you won't get to see the results of your changes.

Now you're ready to start improving your fonts.

Hint ▶   If you don't see your changes reflected in the sample text, it's probably because the System is using a ROM version of the same font. You can find out how to override ROM fonts later in this chapter.

▶ Editing a Character

In many fonts (Chicago and Monaco, for example) you can't tell the difference between a zero and an uppercase *O*. Sometimes there's a similar problem with lowercase *l* and uppercase *I*. Context doesn't always help you out, and even if it does, the momentary confusion slows you down. Besides, why should you have to resort to context? Why not put a slash through the zero so you'll always know which character you're looking at? You probably have Chicago 12 in your ROM, so you can't change its zero unless you override the ROM font with the System file font, as described later in this chapter. The same holds true for Monaco 9, so for now, let's fix Monaco 12. Of course you can fix other fonts, too, and the steps are the same.

As always, the safest course is to work on a copy of the resource. If you have your fonts installed with a program like Suitcase II, you can just copy the file that has Monaco in it. If you've installed your fonts with Font/DA Mover, you can work on a copy of your System file. Once you become familiar with ResEdit and the 'FONT' editor, you probably don't have to work on a copy, if you're making a simple change like this, and if you're very careful.

1. Use ResEdit to open the font file you copied. Open the 'FONT' type to get to the 'FONT' picker.

2. Open the 'FONT' resource that's named "Monaco 12." (More than likely, it will have ID 524.)

3. The font resource opens in the 'FONT' editor, with the letter A selected. To move to zero, type a zero.

4. Click the pencil tool if it's not already selected and add the diagonal slash to the zero, as shown in Figure 12-5. If you want to try out your new zero, click the sample text panel and type in something appropriate.

5. Save your changes and quit ResEdit.

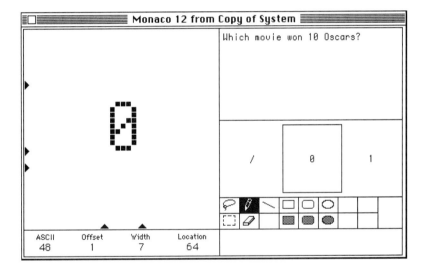

Figure 12-5. Adding a slash to a zero helps you distinguish it from an uppercase O.

After you reinstall your altered font file, you'll be able to distinguish zeros from uppercase Os in Monaco 12. If you work on a font having multiple sizes, remember you have to individually edit each size.

▶ Adding a Character to a Font

Adding a special character to a font can be almost as easy as editing an existing one. You can create the character right in the font, or you can copy the bits from another font or even from a paint or draw program. You just have to do a little preparation first to figure out where in the font to add it. In this example, we'll add the Command key symbol (⌘), to New York 12. Make a copy of the appropriate font file(s) before you start.

1. Open the Key Caps desk accessory and look at the font you want to change. You're looking for easy-to-remember key combinations that aren't already taken. Control or Option-Shift often have lots of openings. Make a mental or written note of the available spot(s) you want to use. You may also want to verify that you know the location of the character you want to copy. You can find the Command-key symbol at Control-q in Chicago. As it turns out, Control-q is available in New York too, which is easy to remember. (The Control key is usually available because it's reserved for terminal emulation and other software. If you use the Control key for terminal emulation or any other purposes, maybe you should stick with Option-Shift. Also, if you have a Mac Plus, your keyboard doesn't have a Control key, so you should definitely stick with Option-Shift.)

| By the Way ▶ | You can also look for likely key combinations using the 'KCHR' editor, if you're familiar with it. Just be sure to switch to the particular font you're interested in. For more information, see Chapter 9. |

2. Use ResEdit to open (a copy of) the file containing Chicago. Open the 'FONT' resource type, and then open Chicago 12. (Most likely, it will have ID 12.)

3. When Chicago opens in the 'FONT' editor, scroll to the Command key symbol by dragging the box in the character selection panel, or simply type Control-q, to select it. (If you have a Mac Plus, you can't type Control-q, so you have to scroll. The ASCII number you're heading for is 17.)

4. Click the selection tool, drag the marquee around the character, and copy it. Close the Chicago 'FONT' resource.

5. Now open a copy of the font you want to add to, New York 12. Type the key combination you're adding the character to, in this case Control-q.

6. Paste the copied character and, if necessary, position it by dragging.

7. The new character has a character width of 0, which means it will appear right on top of the surrounding characters. (You can test this by typing in some sample text.) The left and right character limits (indicated by the black triangles) are stacked on top of each other in the bottom center of the editing panel. To give the character width, just drag one triangle to the left and the other to the right. Leaving an extra one-bit space on each side is nice, but it's up to you.

8. If you want to do any final positioning, simply drag the selection marquee around the character, then drag the selection where you want it, keeping an eye on the sample text.

9. When you're satisfied with your work, save the file and quit ResEdit.

You can add the symbol to all the other sizes of New York following this same procedure. For larger sizes, you'll need to redraw the symbol to enlarge it so it won't look dwarfed by surrounding characters. (You could scale the character by pasting it into a larger or smaller selection rectangle, but you'll probably have to touch it up anyway.) You can also try adding fractions, scientific or mathematical symbols, mini-icons, or your monogram. You're limited only by your imagination and the space within the font.

Hint ▶

Many fonts have unusual characters that you can type by pressing Option-Shift-tilde (~). Robots, hearts, flowers, Macs, apples, borders, and various animals are just some of what you'll find. Different sizes of the font may contain different characters, but Key Caps only shows you one font size. You can find all these "hidden" characters, and copy them if you wish, using the 'FONT' editor.

▶ Overriding Your ROM Font

The System font, usually Chicago 12, is the font used for window titles, the menu bar, and most dialog and alert boxes. Because it's stored in ROM, you can't change it. But several of its characters can be fun or useful to modify, as you have seen. Fortunately, you can tell your Mac to ignore the 'FONT' resource in ROM and use the one stored in the System file instead. Here's how to override your ROM font.

1. Use ResEdit to open a copy of your System file.

2. Open the 'ROv#' picker (double-click the 'ROv#' resource type).

3. You should see a list of several 'ROv#' resources. Each resource specifies the ROM overrides for a different version of the ROM. Since you probably don't know what version of the ROM you have, you should make your changes in *every* 'ROv#' resource. Open the first resource. You should see a window similar to the one shown in Figure 12-6.

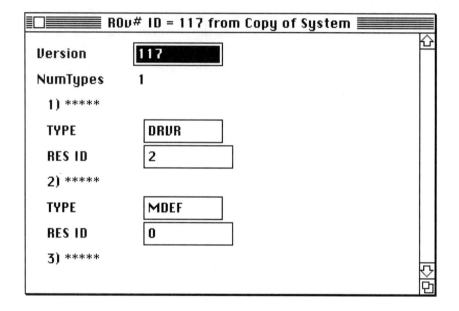

Figure 12-6. A ROM override resource from the System file.

4. Click the last row of asterisks (*****) in the window and select Insert New Fields from the Resource menu. (This is a template resource. For information about working with templates, see Chapter 14.)

5. Fill in the two new fields with the 'FONT' resource type and the resource ID of the System font (12 for 12-point Chicago). Your window should now look like the one shown in Figure 12-7.

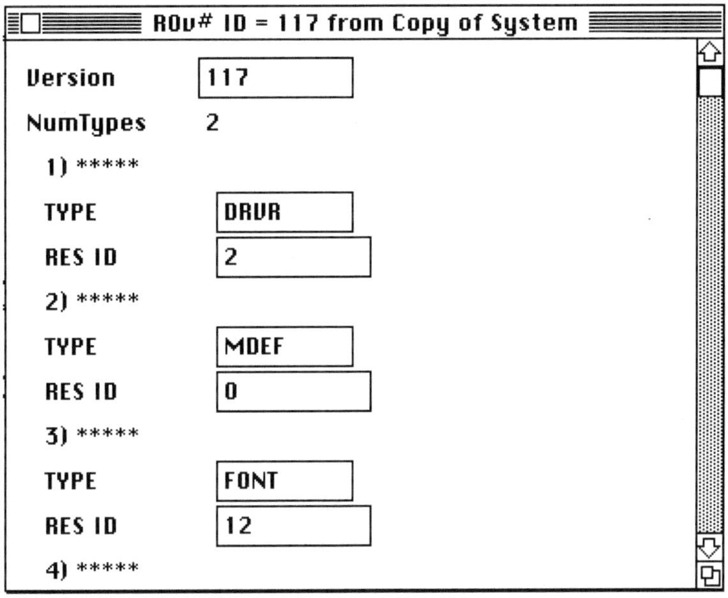

Figure 12-7. Add an override for the 'FONT' resource with ID 12.

6. Repeat steps 4 and 5 for every 'ROv#' resource in your System file.
7. Close and save the file, and quit ResEdit.
8. Install your modified System file, and restart your Macintosh. You won't see any difference after you restart, but you will be using the System 'FONT' from the System file rather than the ROM. You can now edit the Chicago 12 'FONT' in your System file and see your changes in the menu bar, in window title bars, and in most dialog boxes.

Now that you're not using the ROM font anymore, what changes can you make? As with every other font, you can change any of the characters to look any way you like. For instance, we already showed you how to make the zero and the uppercase *O* look different. Maybe you'd also like to fix the uppercase *I* and lowercase *l* that look exactly alike. Even better, why not substitute your initials for the apple character that's used for the title of the Apple menu? You can also change the ⌘ character that menus use to show Command-key equivalents to a character since both symbols are on the key cap anyway. These last two changes are illustrated in Figure 12-8.

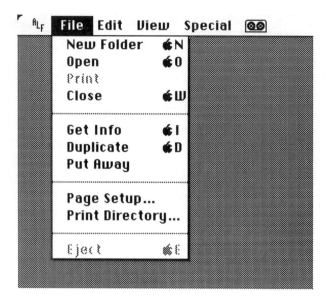

Figure 12-8. Why not use your initials instead of the apple in the Apple menu title, and apples instead of the ⌘?

If you open Chicago 12 in the 'FONT' editor, you can find the character by typing Control-t and the ⌘ character by typing Control-q. Simply copy the character to Control-q, then go back and substitute (or create) your monogram in place of the apple at Control-t. Remember, you'll lose the ⌘ character forever unless you first copy it to an empty spot in the font, or keep a copy of the Chicago 'FONT' resource.

| Warning ▶ | Remember, when you change Chicago for your menus, you change it for everything else, too—you're changing the font itself. So that means if you ever use Chicago in documents, and if you use these characters, you'll have to type Control-q instead of Control-t to get the apple. If you type Control-t, you get your monogram. But if you then take your documents to another Mac, you won't get the apple, you'll get the ⌘ character instead. You can still get all the characters you need, but they're in different places. Obviously, keeping track of what's where can make your head spin, so you should consider the ramifications before you make your changes. |

▶ The 'FOND' Resource

For most of what you'll do with the 'FONT' editor the only resource type you need to know about is the 'FONT'. Some projects, however, may involve another resource, too. If you add a new font resource to a font family or create a new font (both potentially major undertakings!), you need to update or create an associated 'FOND', which is sort of a font bookkeeping resource.

One 'FOND' resource is associated with each font family, and it can store a great deal of information about the 'FONT' (or 'NFNT') resources it "owns." You can edit this information in a 'FOND' template. (For more information about using templates, see Chapter 14.) Each 'FOND' has a unique ID, which is the same as the font number your Mac uses to keep track of fonts. Table 12-1 shows the standard font numbers for some common fonts. The resource IDs of 'FONT' and 'FOND' resources in a family are related. The ID of the parent 'FOND' multiplied by 128 gives you the Font Family resource ID; add the point size of a 'FONT' to determine that 'FONT' resource's ID. (Font number x 128 + point size = 'FONT' resource ID. For Geneva 10: 3 x 128 + 10 = 394)

Because of the way 'FONT' resource IDs are calculated, 'FOND' resources can have IDs only from 0 (Chicago, the default System font) through 255. Only half those numbers are available for third-party font families, however, because Apple reserves IDs 0 through 127. Because the number of existing bitmap fonts exceeds the number of IDs available, conflicts are unavoidable. When you move fonts around with the Font/DA Mover, it changes font numbers to make sure no two fonts have the same number. ('NFNT' resources avoid this problem. The IDs of 'NFNT's are not calculated from the resource IDs of their parent 'FOND's, so more IDs are available for both 'NFNT's and 'FOND's.)

We'll touch on only a few of the fields in the 'FOND' template. Many of the fields are optional. For more information, see the "Font Manager" chapters of *Inside Macintosh*, Volumes IV and V.

▶ Creating or Updating a 'FOND'

We don't encourage you to try to create a whole new font using ResEdit. At best it's a long, tedious process, and as we mentioned early in this chapter, other software packages are better suited to the task. Still, you may want to keep a small collection of characters or symbols handy all in one place. If you gather them together into a 'FONT' resource, you'll be able to use the Key Caps desk accessory to jog your memory about which characters are available and where.

Table 12-1. Standard font numbers for some common fonts.

Font number	Font Name
0	System font (Chicago)
1	Default application font (usually Geneva)
2	New York
3	Geneva
4	Monaco
5	Venice
6	London
7	Athens
8	San Francisco
9	Toronto
11	Cairo
12	Los Angeles
13	Zapf Dingbats
14	Bookman
15	N Helvetica Narrow
16	Palatino
18	Zapf Chancery
20	Times
21	Helvetica
22	Courier
23	Symbol
33	Avant Garde
34	New Century Schlbk

Hint ▶

Remember, the font you create will eventually be listed in your Font menu, so the name matters a little. Normally the menu font is Chicago, but with some utilities, such as Suitcase II, you can make the fonts write their own names. For cosmetic reasons, you might make a point of creating the characters that allow the font to spell its own name. That way you won't see the missing symbol rectangles on your font menu!

1. As always, the safest first step is to make a copy of the file to which you'll add your new 'FONT'.
2. Use ResEdit to open the file, and create a new 'FONT' resource.

(Choose Create New Resource from the Resource menu.) Remember, you can do this from the type picker or from the 'FONT' picker. You see the alert shown in Figure 12-9. Click OK.

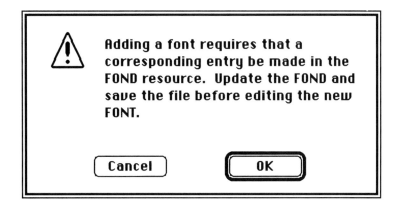

Figure 12-9. If you create a 'FONT', you have to update (or create) the associated 'FOND' resource, as this alert box reminds you.

3. Next you see the dialog shown in Figure 12-10. Fill in the new name and point size, then click OK. ResEdit then opens the 'FONT' editor.

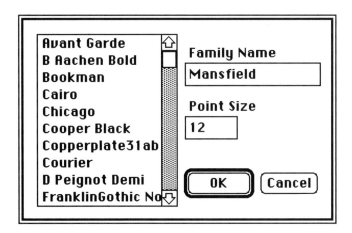

Figure 12-10. You name your new font family in this dialog.

4. You can create and edit your new characters now or later, or you can divide the work into several sessions. Before you can experiment with your new font outside the editor, you've got to create a new 'FOND' resource. Close the 'FONT' editor and go back to the 'FONT' picker.

5. In the 'FONT' picker you can see that, in addition to your new 'FONT' resource, ResEdit automatically created the Font Family resource (which has a size of 0) and is required for a font to be recognized. Make a note of both ID numbers. You have to enter the 'FONT' resource ID into the 'FOND' you're about to create, and you need the Font Family resource ID to calculate what the ID of the 'FOND' should be.

6. Go back to the type picker, open the 'FOND' picker, and create a new 'FOND' resource. (Choose Create New Resource from the Resource menu.)

7. Choose Get Resource Info from the Resource menu. Type the name of your new font in the Name field. (If you need a refresher, see the end of Chapter 3.) Divide the Font Family resource ID (you made a note of it in Step 5) by 128 and enter the result in the ID field. Close the Resource Info window.

8. Now you're ready to fill in a few fields in the 'FOND' template. Figure 12-11 shows the first part of a fairly typical 'FOND' template. In the Family ID field, enter the resource ID of the 'FOND'. You can enter $4000 (for a monospaced font) or $6000 (for a proportional font) in the Flag word field, or you can just leave these and the other fields blank.

9. Scroll to the bottom of the template and click the row of five asterisks you see just above the field called "The Tables." Choose Insert New Field(s) from the Resource menu, and the three fields shown in Figure 12-12 are inserted. Fill in the appropriate values for Font Size, Font Style (generally 0 for plain, unstyled characters), and Resource ID (you made a note of it in Step 5).

10. Save your changes, quit ResEdit, and install the font file you've altered. When you restart, you should see your new font on the font menu!

If you add a new 'FONT' resource to an existing font family, you have to update the associated 'FOND' to make sure your Mac can find your new 'FONT'. Just open the existing 'FOND' and follow Steps 9 and 10.

```
┌──────────────────────────────────────────────┐
│ ▤□▤▤ FOND "Monaco" ID = 4 from Copy of System ▤▤│⇧│
│                                                    │▓│
│  Flag word      │$6000              │             │▓│
│                                                    │▓│
│  Family ID      │4                  │             │▓│
│                                                    │▓│
│  First Char     │$0000              │             │▓│
│                                                    │▓│
│  Last Char      │$0000              │             │▓│
│                                                    │▓│
│  Ascent         │0                  │             │▓│
│                                                    │▓│
│  Descent        │0                  │             │▓│
│                                                    │▓│
│  Leading        │0                  │             │▓│
│                                                    │▓│
│  WidMax         │0                  │             │⇩│
│  Offset to      │$00000000              │         │▫│
│  width tables                                      │ │
└──────────────────────────────────────────────┘
```

Figure 12-11. The first few fields of a typical 'FOND' resource.

```
┌──────────────────────────────────────────────┐
│ □▤▤ FOND "Mansfield" ID = 26 from Copy of System ▤▤│⇧│
│                                                    │▓│
│  # of Font         0                              │▓│
│  entries                                           │▓│
│                                                    │▓│
│    1) *****                                        │▓│
│                                                    │▓│
│    Font Size      │12               │             │▓│
│                                                    │▓│
│    Font Style     │0                │             │▓│
│                                                    │▓│
│    Res ID         │3340             │             │▓│
│                                                    │▓│
│    2) *****                                        │ │
│                                                    │ │
│  The Tables    $│                        │        │⇩│
│                                                    │▫│
└──────────────────────────────────────────────┘
```

Figure 12-12. You have to add this set of three fields (Font Size, Font Style, and Resource ID) to the corresponding 'FOND' any time you create a new 'FONT'.

▶ Summary

This chapter describes some basic information about fonts to give you enough background to successfully tinker with your fonts in the 'FONT' editor. You can edit only bitmap fonts with ResEdit, and because each size of a font is stored in a separate resource, you have to edit each size individually.We describe how to edit an existing character, how to add a character or symbol to a font, and how you can override fonts in ROM. We also explain how to create a new font. Creating new 'FONT' resources requires that you create or update the corresponding 'FOND', so we explain how to do that, too. Now you're ready to have fun fixing fonts.

13 ▶ Tips and Tricks

This chapter contains a collection of unrelated projects to help you get the most from your Macintosh. Most other chapters also contain projects related to their topics, so be sure to scan the Table of Contents for the tips that interest you.

▶ Using Other Paint Programs With MacPaint Files

The MacPaint file format has become a standard on the Macintosh. Most clip art comes as MacPaint files, and taking a picture of the screen with Command-Shift-3 creates a MacPaint file. If you own MacPaint and like to use it as your main painting program, this isn't a problem (and you can skip this tip). If you use one of the other popular paint programs, however, this gets annoying pretty quickly. Instead of simply double-clicking a file to open it, you have to find your paint program, open it, and then open the file. Here's a way around the problem. (The next tip shows you how to make Command-Shift-3 create a file in other formats.)

1. Make a copy of your paint application.
2. Start ResEdit and choose Get File/Folder Info from the File menu.
3. Select the copy of your paint program and click the Get Info button. You'll see a window similar to the one in Figure 13-1.

4. Write down the four-character Creator type you see on the right side of the window (you'll need this if you want to restore your application later). For example, Figure 13-1 shows that SuperPaint's Creator type is 'SPNT'.

5. Change the creator to 'MPNT' for MacPaint (be sure to type it in capital letters).

6. Save and quit ResEdit.

7. From the Finder, open the folder that contains the copy of your application. If the folder is already open, close and reopen it. This forces the Finder to notice your change.

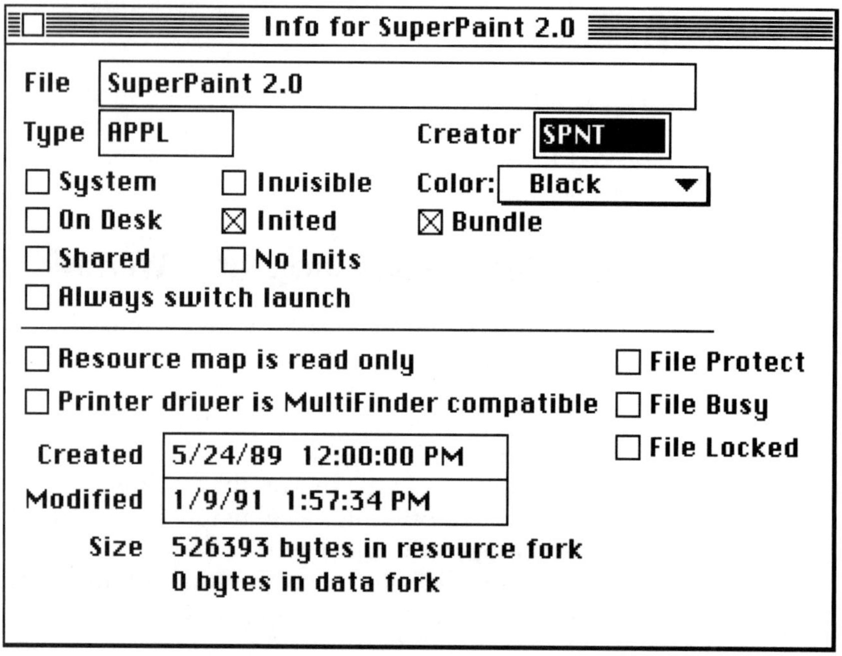

Figure 13-1. Change the Creator field to 'MPNT'.

Now when you double-click a screen shot created with Command-Shift-3 or any other MacPaint file, your paint program starts instead of MacPaint. The only problem with this approach is that if you want to open a file created with your paint program, it'll no longer work because the Finder now thinks your program is MacPaint. One way to get around this problem if you have a hard disk with enough spare room is to keep both the old and new versions of your application. When you edit a MacPaint document your Mac uses your new, modified copy, and when you edit a normal document your Mac uses your original application. Be sure to give your modified copy a name (like SuperPaint-MPNT) that lets you distinguish between your original application and your modified copy.

This approach won't work if you have a copy of MacPaint on your disk, but then, if you did, you wouldn't have to worry about any of this.

▶ Reading Screen Shots into Your Paint Program

If you ever make screen shots to include in your documents and you don't use MacPaint, you've probably been frustrated by the fact that you can't double-click the screen shot file to start your paint program. A way to solve this problem for any MacPaint file is detailed above. This approach has the problem that you need to keep two copies of your paint program. If you're only worried about screen shots, here's a better approach.

1. Start ResEdit and choose Get File/Folder Info from the File menu.
2. In the standard file directory dialog that appears, select your paint program (the one you want to open when you double-click a screen shot).
3. Write down the four characters shown in the Creator field on the right side of the window. (For example, as shown in Figure 13-1, SuperPaint's creator is 'SPNT'.)
4. Use ResEdit to open a copy of your System file.
5. Open the 'FKEY' resource with ID 3 (this is the Command-Shift-3 screen shot 'FKEY'). The 'FKEY' resource opens in the hexadecimal editor. Appendix C explains how to use the hex editor, but we'll give you the basics here.
6. Choose Find ASCII from the Find menu.
7. Enter 'MPNT' (be sure to type it in capital letters) and click the Find Next button.
8. Click the window that's showing your 'FKEY'. You'll see 'MPNT' highlighted in the lower right part of the window, as shown in Figure 13-2.
9. Change 'MPNT' to the four characters you found in the Creator field of your paint program ('SPNT' for SuperPaint). You can do this by

typing your new characters over the selected characters in the right part of the window. Copy the characters (uppercase or lowercase) exactly. Be sure not to make any other changes in this window. (If you accidentally change something else, choose Revert This Resource from the Resource menu and try again.)

10. Close and save the file.

11. Install your modified System file and restart.

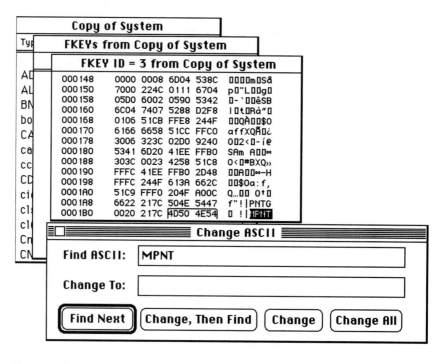

Figure 13-2. Use the Find dialog to find 'MPNT'.

Now when you use Command-Shift-3 to take a screen shot, you can double-click the resulting file and your paint application will be launched. If you use a desk accessory such as Camera or a different 'FKEY', you should still be able to use this trick. If you use a desk accessory, you can use the following steps to find the characters you need to change.

1. Find the Creator of your paint application, as described previously.

2. Use ResEdit to open the suitcase file containing the DA you want to modify.

3. Open the 'DRVR' type picker.

4. Choose the Open Using Hex Editor command on the Resource menu to open the 'DRVR' resource you want to change. The resource's name should be the same as the name of the desk accessory.

5. Find and change 'MPNT' to your paint application's Creator type, as previously described.

▶ Changing Graphical Elements in HyperCard

HyperCard contains many special icons and pointers you might want to fiddle with, but they aren't stored where you would expect. If you want to change, say, the hand pointer, in most applications you would look for a 'CURS' resource, but in HyperCard you must look in a 'FONT' resource. HyperCard keeps all its graphical elements in a 'FONT' resource. Like Cairo and Zapf Dingbats, the characters in the HyperCard font display pictures instead of the usual alphabetic characters. For example, typing an *A* displays a picture of a padlock. The contents of the 'FONT' for HyperCard version 1.2 are shown in Figure 13-3.

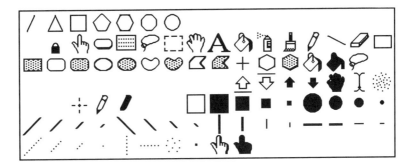

Figure 13-3. Graphics in the HyperCard font.

By the Way ▶ HyperCard 2.0 uses an 'NFNT' resource instead of a 'FONT' resource. As you may remember from Chapter 12, you can use the 'FONT' editor to change the characters in an 'NFNT' resource, as long as you don't change their sizes.

Before we tell you how to find and change the item you're looking for, you need a bit more information about editing this particular font. From ResEdit's point of view, this is a very strange font. Not only is it not part of a normal font family, but it doesn't even have a font family record—the resource with a length of zero that contains the name of the font family. Because of this, when you open this font the 'FONT' editor won't show you any of the special characters on the right side of the window in the list or example text as illustrated in Figure 13-4. Don't worry about this—the changes you make will still show up in the font. Instructions at the end of this section describe how to make a few changes so ResEdit can correctly display the examples.

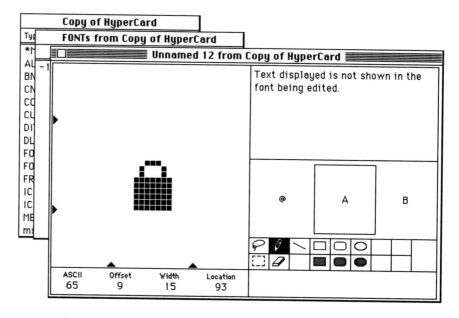

Figure 13-4. HyperCard's font contains graphics instead of characters.

Note that this section shows you only how to change HyperCard. If you want more details about how to modify fonts, please refer to Chapter 12.

Also note that by following these instructions you'll be changing the pictures HyperCard uses. Except for the brush shapes, however, you can't change the actions HyperCard performs when it uses the pictures. Changing this font is really only useful if you want to change one or more of the available brush shapes, if one of the pointers doesn't suit you, or if you just like to fiddle with your applications.

First, let's open up a copy of HyperCard and look at what's in the font.

1. Use ResEdit to open a copy of HyperCard.
2. Open the 'FONT' picker.
3. You should see one 'FONT' resource with resource ID -16500. Open this font.

You can browse through the font to see which pictures it contains. Remember, to get a different character to appear in the fatbits area of the window, you can either click a different character in the list in the middle of the right part of the window or press the key whose corresponding symbol you want shown. If you press the Z key, for example, the picture that's in the spot normally occupied by Z appears. If you want to move quickly through the list, just click the right or left character in the list and, while still holding down the mouse button, drag the pointer out of the list rectangle.

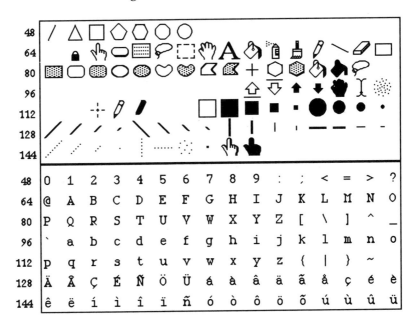

Figure 13-5. Graphics and their corresponding normal characters in the HyperCard font.

The top of Figure 13-5 shows the pictures in the font, and the bottom part shows their corresponding normal characters. For example, to move to the spray can, find the spray can in the top part of Figure 13-5; notice that it's in the row labeled 64. Now look down the page to the row labeled 64 in the table of normal characters at the bottom of the figure, and you'll see that you should type a J. The numbers on the left side of Figure 13-5 are the ASCII numbers of the first picture in each row. The selected character's ASCII number appears in the lower left corner of the 'FONT' editor window.

Now you know how to get to all these pictures—but where are they used?

The pictures in Figure 13-6 are used in the small dialog that appears when you choose the Polygon Sides command from the Options menu.

Figure 13-6. HyperCard polygon sides.

Figure 13-7 shows the picture that's displayed on the menu bar when the current stack is locked.

Figure 13-7. HyperCard's locked stack symbol.

Figure 13-8 shows the pictures used in the Tools menu. The gray filled shapes are used when you choose Draw Filled from the Options menu.

Figure 13-8. The HyperCard Tools menu.

Figure 13-9 shows the graphics used in the Brush Shape dialog. By changing these items, you can actually change the shapes HyperCard uses. For example, if you change one of the circles to an X shape, you'll be able to draw with an X-shaped pen.

Figure 13-9. HyperCard brush shapes.

Figure 13-10 shows the pointers HyperCard uses. The all-black shapes are the pointers' masks (see Chapter 6 for an explanation of masks and pointers). Changing these pictures in the font changes them in all your stacks, whereas changing them in a HyperCard script with Set Cursor only changes them temporarily. When you change these pointers, remember that since HyperCard doesn't use a 'CURS' resource, you can't change the hot spot. (The hot spot is the place on the pointer, such as the tip of the finger or the point of the pencil, that actually determines what's selected.) No matter what you do to the pointer, the hot spot won't move. Keep this in mind when you design your new pointers so the hot spot remains in a logical place relative to the new pointer symbol.

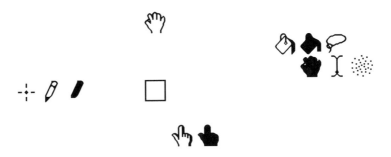

Figure 13-10. HyperCard's pointers.

▶ Changing the Font

Now let's look at an example of how to change one of the pictures in the font. If you want to change a different one, just follow these steps, substituting the picture you want to change. We'll look at how to change the pointing hand pointer.

  1. Use ResEdit to open a copy of HyperCard.

2. Open the 'FONT' resource, as described previously.

3. Type *ò* to move to the pointing hand. (Press Option ` — Option-back quote—followed by *o*.)

4. Modify the cursor any way you like.

5. Click the next character in the list, the *ô*.

6. Change this mask to be a filled-in copy of your new pointer. You can do this by copying your new pointer, pasting it into the mask, and filling it in. (Selecting the entire editing area before you copy assures that the selection is aligned properly when you paste.)

7. Close and save the file.

From now on, when you use your new copy of HyperCard, you'll see your new pointer instead of the normal hand.

▶ Making the HyperCard Font into a Normal Font

It's much easier to understand the contents of the HyperCard font if you can see what you're editing. All you need to do is temporarily change the resource ID of the font to some reasonable positive value so ResEdit can treat it like a normal font. Let's go through what you need to do step by step.

1. Use ResEdit to open a copy of HyperCard. Working on a copy is very important, because you may need to go back to your original to recover the font.

2. Open the 'FONT' picker.

3. Write down the resource ID of the font.

4. Select the 'FONT' resource and choose Get Resource Info from the Resource menu.

5. Change the resource ID to 3212.

6. Close the Resource Info window.

7. Open the 'FONT' resource—you should now see the graphical characters in both the selection list and the example text as shown in Figure 13-11.

8. Make your changes to the font.

9. Close the 'FONT' editor.

10. Once again, select the 'FONT' resource and choose Get Resource Info from the Resource menu.

11. Change the resource ID back to its original value so that HyperCard can find it.

12. Close and save the file.

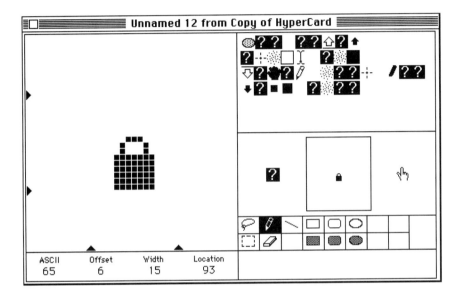

Figure 13-11. The HyperCard 'FONT' resource as it should look in the 'FONT' editor after assigning it a valid resource ID.

Any time you want to make changes to the font you'll need to follow these steps to be able to see the results of your changes. Before you use this version of HyperCard, be sure to change the ID of the font back to what it was originally. If you don't, you'll get some interesting results—instead of familiar pictures on the Tool menu, you'll see letters. The letters will work the same as tools, but you won't know which "tool" does what!

▶ Displaying a Color Picture at Startup

If you have a Mac II, you can display just about any picture you want while your Mac is starting up—including one in full color. All you have to do is create a file in your System Folder that contains a 'PICT' resource with ID 0. This is a neat idea but has a couple of drawbacks. The biggest problem is that many inits (startup documents that the System loads) clear the screen when they're loaded. If you have any inits that do this, enjoyment of your startup picture might be limited to a couple of seconds. Even if an init doesn't clear your picture, your normal desktop replaces it anyway as soon as startup is completed. A better approach is to use an init such as ColorDesk that displays a picture for your desktop instead of the normal pattern. But, if you don't have ColorDesk and you'd like to see your company logo or your spouse's face when you start your Mac, you can follow these instructions.

1. Start your favorite paint program and copy the picture (or part of a picture) that you want to use for your startup screen.
2. Start ResEdit, and create a file in your System Folder called "StartupScreen."
3. Paste in the 'PICT' resource that you copied in your paint program.
4. Double-click the 'PICT' resource type to open the 'PICT' picker and select the resource you just pasted.
5. Select Get Resource Info from the Resource menu.
6. Change the resource's ID to 0.
7. Close and save the file.

Next time you restart your Mac you'll see your picture during the startup process.

By the Way ▶ Even if you don't have a Mac II, you can still have a startup screen displayed when you start your Mac. Unfortunately, you can't use ResEdit to create the startup screen because the picture isn't stored in a resource. (It's stored in the data fork.) All is not lost, however, because many paint programs (including MacPaint and SuperPaint) let you save a picture as a startup screen. Just make sure you save the picture in a file called StartupScreen in your System Folder.

▶ Changing Your Printer's Default Number of Copies

When you ask an application to print, you always see the same print dialog, with the number of copies set to 1. But if you routinely print duplicates, or some other number of copies, you may want to change this default. If you have a LaserWriter or ImageWriter, here's how you can change your printer's default number of copies.

1. Use ResEdit to open a copy of the LaserWriter or ImageWriter file

in your System Folder. Open the 'DITL' resource type, and then open resource ID -8191. You'll see a window that looks almost exactly like your print dialog.

2. Double-click the field to the right of the word "copies." Another window opens in which the default copy number is already selected. Simply type the number you want to change it to.

3. Close all ResEdit's windows, save your changes, and quit ResEdit.

You can throw away the original printer file, but you might want to leave both versions in your System Folder. They'll both show up in the Chooser, so if you know you'll be doing a lot of printing requiring one of these preset numbers of copies, you can just choose the appropriate printer file. If you keep more than one version, rename alternates appropriately. Put the distinguishing feature early in the name, because the Chooser doesn't have room to show you more characters at the end.

▶ Reordering Your Apple Menu

Have you ever wished you could move your favorite desk accessories to the top of the Apple menu? How about putting the ones you hardly ever use near the bottom? Or how about grouping your desk accessories by function so you can find the one you want out of that long list? Maybe you'd just like to make some of the names more meaningful for you. Any of these changes are possible (and even easy), but you can't use the 'MENU' editor to change the Apple menu. The Apple menu is a special menu the System constructs when you start your Macintosh. It's built from the names of all the desk accessories you've installed in your System file (or opened with Suitcase II or a similar program).

The Apple menu lists the names of desk accessories in alphabetical order, so you can put the desk accessories in any order you want by changing their names. Adding a punctuation character or a space to the front of the name moves it to the top of the list. Adding a z or a • (Option-8) in front of the name moves it to the end of the list. With this technique, you can set up your Apple menu in any order you want.

If you use the Font/DA Mover to install desk accessories in your System file, it's safest to use the Font/DA Mover to copy the desk accessory into a separate suitcase file before you make any changes. When you're done changing the name, you can use the Font/DA Mover to reinstall your edited desk accessory. If you use a program like Suitcase II or Font/DA Juggler Plus, you can change the name in the suitcase file and then reopen it with Suitcase II or Font/DA Juggler Plus.

You can follow these steps to change the name of a desk accessory.

1. Using ResEdit, open the file containing the desk accessory whose name you want to change. Be sure to keep a backup copy of the file before you modify it. If your desk accessories are installed in your System file, open the System file. If you use Suitcase II or a similar program, open the suitcase file containing the desk accessory.
2. Open the 'DRVR' picker (double-click the 'DRVR' resource type).
3. Select the 'DRVR' resource with the name that's the same as the name of the desk accessory you're looking for.
4. Select the Get Resource Info command from the Resource menu. You should see a window similar to the one shown in Figure 13-12.

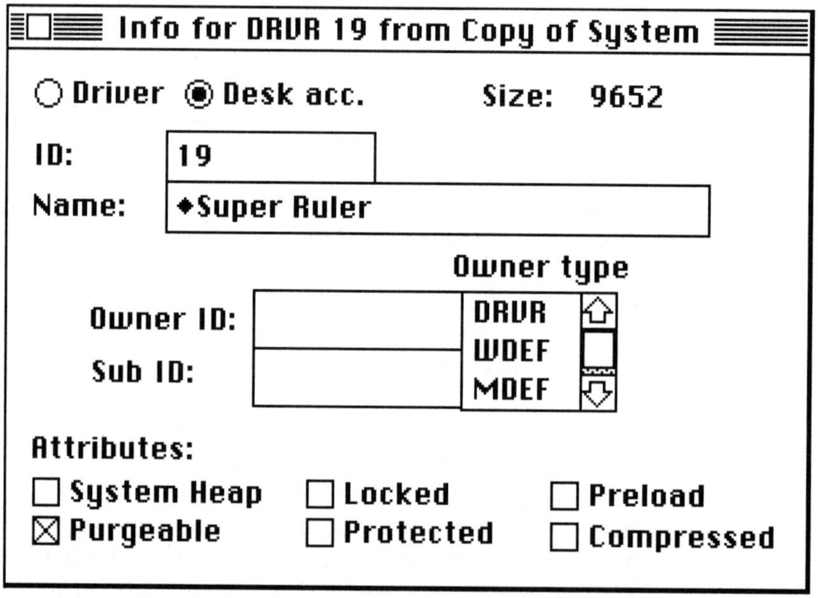

Figure 13-12. Change the names of desk accessories to move them to the top of the Apple menu.

5. Change the name to anything you like. Try a space or ◆ (Control-s) to move the desk accessory to the top of the menu. Try • (Option-8), ◊ (Option-Shift-v) or   (Option-Shift-k) to move it to the end of the list. Be sure to leave the other fields in the Resource Info window alone.

6. Close and save the file. If you modified the System file, you'll need to restart your computer to see the effect of your changes. (If you're using the Finder, instead of MultiFinder, simply exiting ResEdit is enough to update the Apple menu.) If you use a program like Suitcase II, just use that program to close and reopen the suitcase.

▶ Adding Version Information to Documents

Many times, it's useful to keep some information about a document in the comment area of the Finder's Get Info window. The problem with this comment is that it's easily lost. For example, when you rebuild your Desktop file you lose all your Get Info comments. Don't worry, there's a better way! Every application has a 'vers' resource that contains, among other things, a string that the Finder displays in the Get Info window. You can use ResEdit to add 'vers' resources to your documents to keep track of a version number or just to record some information about the file. (For more information about 'vers' resources, see Chapter 22.) Here's how to add a 'vers' resource to your document.

1. Use ResEdit to open your document.

Hint ▶

Many document files don't have a resource fork, so you'll need to add one to store a 'vers' resource. When you open a file that doesn't have a resource fork, ResEdit displays a dialog asking you if you want to create one. All you have to do is click the OK button and then proceed with the steps outlined.

2. Choose Create New Resource from the Resource menu.
3. A dialog appears to let you select the resource type for the resource you're creating. Enter 'vers' and press the OK button.
4. You should see a window like the one shown in Figure 13-13. The last field labeled Long version string is the one you're interested in. You can leave the rest of the fields blank. Enter any string you want for the Long version string. There's room for at most two lines of text. You can separate the lines by pressing the Return key if you like.

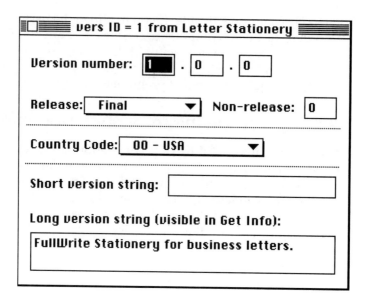

Figure 13-13. The editor window for a 'vers' resource.

5. After you've entered your string, close the editor window. In the resource picker, select the resource you just created, and choose Get Resource Info from the Resource menu. In the Resource Info window, change the resource ID to 1. While you're there, check the Purgeable check box so the resource will be removed from memory when the Finder's done with it.

6. Close and save the file. From the Finder, select the file and select Get Info from the File menu. You should see a window like the one shown in Figure 13-14.

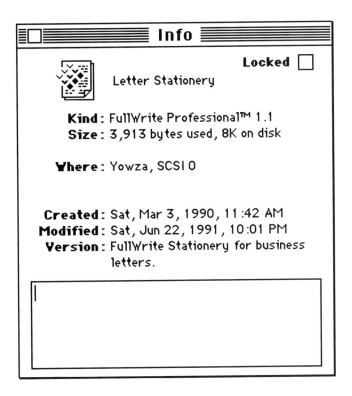

Figure 13-14. The Finder's Get Info window with a custom version string.

▶ Creating a Debugger 'FKEY'

If you're a programmer or just like poking around inside your Macintosh, you've probably spent some of your time using MacsBug, Apple's low-level debugger. In this tip, we show you how to add an 'FKEY' to your System file that causes you to enter MacsBug. An 'FKEY' is more convenient than trying to find the programmer's switch on your Mac (especially if you accidentally press the wrong button as often as most people do).

As you probably know, the Macintosh treats Command-Shift-0 through Command-Shift-9 in a special way. When you press one of these key combinations, the Mac looks for an 'FKEY' resource in the System file with the same ID as the number you pressed. Your Mac comes with a couple of 'FKEY' resources built in that you're probably familiar with. For example, Command-Shift-3 takes a snapshot of your screen and saves it to a file, and Command-Shift-4 prints a snapshot of your screen on a printer (as long as the printer is an ImageWriter). If you look in your System file, you see two 'FKEY' resources, one with ID 3 and one with ID 4, that correspond to the Save Screen and Print Screen commands. (Command-Shift-1 and Command-Shift-2 eject disks from floppy disk drive one or two, but these don't use 'FKEY' resources.) You can follow these steps to make Command-Shift-6 break into MacsBug.

1. Use ResEdit to open your System file (or a copy).
2. Open the 'FKEY' picker (double-click the 'FKEY' type).
3. Select Create New Resource from the Resource menu.
4. You should see a window similar to the one shown in Figure 13-15. Type "A9FF4E75". Don't press Return or put in any spaces. (This is just a Debugger trap followed by an RTS instruction.)

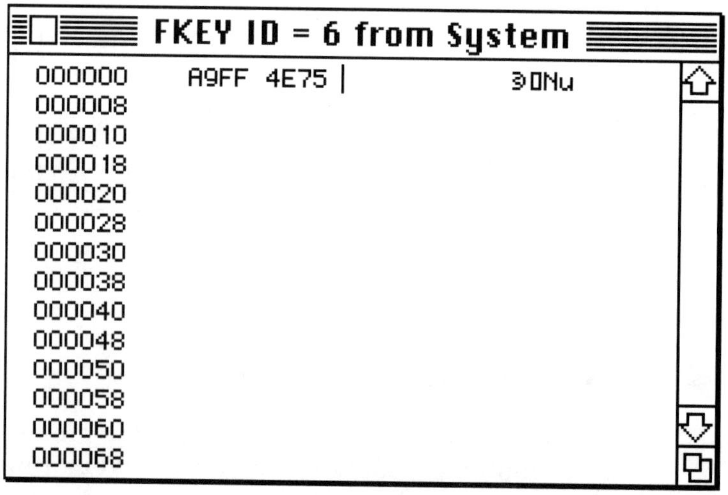

```
▤▢▤▤ FKEY ID = 6 from System ▤▤▤
 000000    A9FF  4E75 |              ꜱ⊡Nu        ⇧
 000008
 000010
 000018
 000020
 000028
 000030
 000038
 000040
 000048
 000050
 000058
 000060                                           ⇩
 000068                                           ◳
```

Figure 13-15. Fill in an 'FKEY' resource with these values to break into MacsBug.

5. Select Get Resource Info from the Resource menu. Change the resource ID of your new 'FKEY' to 6 (or any other unused number between 0 and 9). Also check the Purgeable check box to help with the System's memory management.

6. Close and save the System file. Now, when you press Command-Shift-6, you will immediately enter MacsBug (or see a bomb displayed if you don't have MacsBug installed).

▶ Changing the Names of Fonts

You might want to change the names of some of your screen fonts for several reasons. You might want to group your fonts so you can easily find the particular font you're looking for. For example, you might want all your text fonts at the top of the menu, followed by your display fonts. Or you might not want to list the bold and italic versions of the fonts in your Font menu. Or, maybe you just don't like the name the manufacturer gave the font. Whatever the reason, it's easy to change the name of any font. If you use PostScript fonts with a LaserWriter printer, you don't need to worry about confusing the LaserWriter. No matter what name the screen font has, the LaserWriter still knows it by its original name.

| Warning ▶ |

Before you dive into changing the names of all your fonts, you should know that you'll have to set the fonts again in all your documents because applications keep track of fonts by their names. For example, if you change the Los Angeles font to "Siberia," you'll have to change every document that used Los Angeles to use Siberia instead. Also, if you've changed the names of your fonts, your document won't look the way you expect when you take it to someone else's Macintosh. We recommend that you don't change the names of the standard fonts.

Here are the steps you should follow to change the name of a font.

1. Use ResEdit to open the System file (or a copy) or the suitcase file that contains the font you want to change.
2. Open the 'FONT' picker (double-click the 'FONT' type). You should see a window similar to the one shown in Figure 13-16.

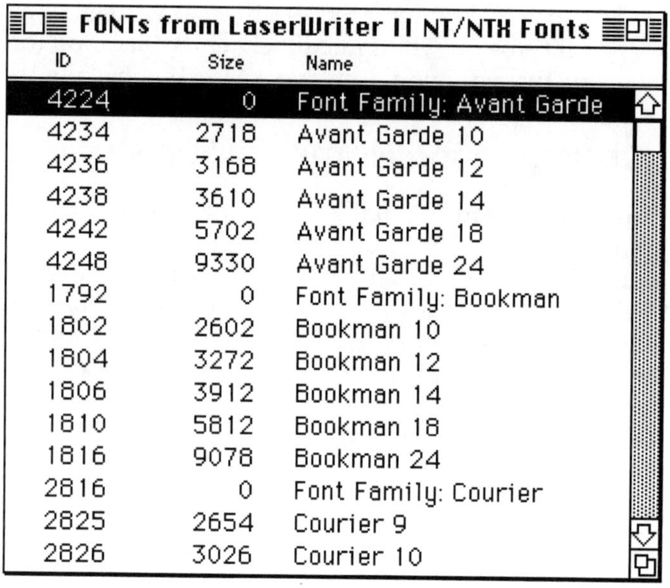

Figure 13-16. The 'FONT' picker shows fonts and font family resources (view by 'FONT').

3. Select the item in the list that starts with Font Family: followed by the name of the font you want to change. For example, to change the name of the Avant Garde font, select the first item in the window shown in Figure 13-16. Choose Get Resource Info from the Resource menu.

4. In the Resource Info window, change the name to anything you like.

5. Close the Resource Info window and the 'FONT' window.

6. Open the 'FOND' picker (double-click the 'FOND' type).

7. Select the 'FOND' resource with the name of the 'FONT' you want to change, and then choose Get Resource Info from the Resource menu.

8. Change the name of the 'FOND' to be exactly the same as the new name you specified for the 'FONT' in step 4.

9. Close and save the file. (Reinstall the System file if you modified a copy.) The next time you pull down an application's Font menu, you should see your new font name.

Hint ▶	If you use MultiFinder, be sure you don't have any applications open when you use ResEdit to change the names of your fonts. If an application is using a font when you change its name, you might be in for trouble.

▶ Hiding Styled Fonts

If you have styled versions of some of your screen fonts, you've probably been annoyed that the font and all its styles appear in the font menu. For example, if you have an Apple LaserWriter, you might have screen fonts called Helvetica, B Helvetica Bold, BI Helvetica Bold Oblique, and I Helvetica Oblique. Good news: If you insert a period as the first character of the stylistic variations of the font name, those names are hidden. Whether the font is hidden or not, the Macintosh uses the appropriate styled version of the font when it needs to draw a character. A few applications use their own methods for displaying the Font menu and display the styled fonts even if you make them invisible. In most cases, however, you'll no longer have to wade through all the fonts and their styles just to find the font you want. Follow the steps outlined in the previous section to add a period to the start of your fonts' names.

▶ Changing the Creation Date of a File

Have you ever been really annoyed when you discover that your Mac's clock has been set to the year 1999 for the last three months? You cringe, realizing you have dozens of files with weird creation and last modified dates. Now there's something you can do about it. ResEdit lets you change the creation date and last modified dates for your files to anything you want. Of course, you may have other reasons to change the dates. For example, Apple always sets the time part of both the creation date and the last modified date to exactly 12:00 PM on the day a product is released. Whatever the reason, here's what to do.

1. Start ResEdit, and select the Get File/Folder Info command from the File menu.
2. Choose the file whose date you want to change from the standard file directory dialog that appears.
3. A window similar to the one shown in Figure 13-17 should appear. You can enter any dates you want in the Created and Modified fields. Be careful to enter the dates in exactly the format you see in

the window. No matter what language you're using, you must enter the dates as month/day/year hour:minute:second PM (or AM). All the numbers must be one- or two-digit numbers. You can find further details about the File Info window in Chapter 23.

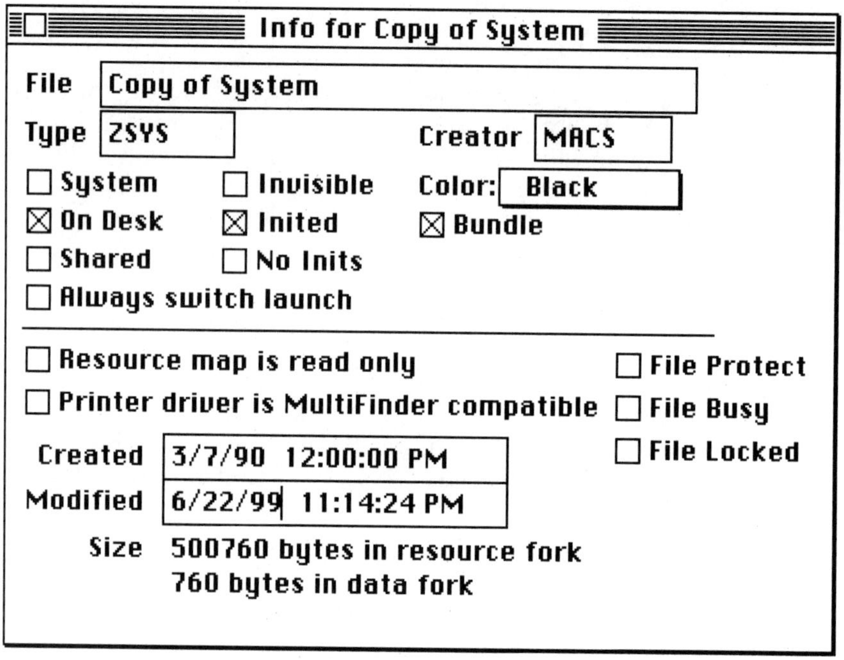

```
╒════════════ Info for Copy of System ════════════╕

  File │ Copy of System                            │

  Type │ ZSYS    │           Creator │ MACS    │

  ☐ System      ☐ Invisible    Color: │ Black     │
  ☒ On Desk     ☒ Inited       ☒ Bundle
  ☐ Shared      ☐ No Inits
  ☐ Always switch launch
  ─────────────────────────────────────────────────
  ☐ Resource map is read only              ☐ File Protect
  ☐ Printer driver is MultiFinder compatible ☐ File Busy
                                           ☐ File Locked
  Created  │ 3/7/90  12:00:00 PM │
  Modified │ 6/22/99  11:14:24 PM │
     Size   500760 bytes in resource fork
            760 bytes in data fork
```

Figure 13-17. Change the Created and Modified dates to anything you want.

▶ Making a File's Name Unchangeable

Let's say an office busybody changed the name of that important document you've been slaving over for weeks. Not only did you lose precious time trying to find it, but once you set to work, you realized the macros you set up didn't work. Now you've got to go back to the Finder to change the file name back. When you got home, you discovered that your kids thought "MacPaint" lacked originality, so they renamed it "Blotzo," then moved it to a different folder. Not even Find File can help you now! Why not prevent such problems? Locking files using the Finder's Get Info command may foil your kids, but determined name changers can easily unlock the file. There's another, more foolproof way. Follow these steps to use the mechanism that makes the System file's name unchangeable.

1. As long as you have a backup (just in case there's a power failure or other disaster), you don't have to make a copy of the file you want to protect. Just be careful to follow these instructions exactly and don't do anything else to the file.
2. Make sure the file you want to change is in a folder, not on the desktop.
3. Start ResEdit and choose Get File/Folder Info from the File menu.
4. Find your file in the standard file directory dialog that appears, and click the Get Info button. You see a File Info window similar to the one in Figure 13-17.
5. Click the first check box in the top left, labeled System. This sets the System bit, which tells the Finder not to let the file's name change.
6. Quit ResEdit, saving your changes.

You can follow these steps for any file whose name you want to protect. Note that if you duplicate the file in the Finder, the copy won't have the System bit set. Also, even though people can't change the file's name, they can still throw it out. With the next tip, you can go one step further to protect your files.

▶ Making Files or Folders Invisible

The previous tip showed you how to foil the office busybody who changed the names of your files—but what if someone took it one step further and deleted some files from your System Folder? Or, what if you have a Mac that kids use, and they keep throwing away important files? Either way, wouldn't it be great to make your important files and folders invisible? Just follow the steps outlined in the preceding tip, checking the Invisible check box (the first check box in the second column) rather than the System check box. One of the most useful changes you can make to protect your Mac is to make the entire System folder invisible. If you're using MultiFinder and the file or folder is on the desktop, you'll need to restart your Macintosh before the file will disappear. If the file or folder is in an open Finder window, you'll have to close and reopen the folder before it will disappear. (Now all you have to do is keep this trick a secret from your coworkers and kids!)

▶ Sharing an Application

Have you ever wished you could put one copy of an application onto a file server and have several users share it? This is especially useful if your Macs don't have hard disks but are connected to a network. You can keep your data on a floppy disk and run the application over the network. (Since HyperCard is provided free with each Macintosh, it's a perfect candidate for sharing.)

Before we divulge the secret to sharing an application, we need to pass on a few reminders and warnings. First, remember that you still need to purchase a copy of the application for each user. Sharing an application when you've only paid for one copy is stealing from the manufacturer. If a large number of people will be sharing an application, contact the manufacturer about obtaining a site license. You should also be aware that an application shared over a network will run more slowly than if it were on a hard disk (unless you have a fast network, such as EtherNet). Last but not least, keep in mind that some applications may not work in a shared environment. The safest approach is to contact the application's manufacturer and ask whether the application can be shared.

Now that you've been properly informed, we can tell you how to share your applications. All that's necessary is to check the Shared check box in the File Info window, like the one shown in Figure 13-17. Follow the steps outlined previously in "Making a File's Name Unchangeable," except check the Shared check box rather than the System check box. After you've checked the Shared check box, just put a copy of the application on your file server. Anyone connected to the file server can then start the application just as if it were located on a floppy or hard disk.

▶ Playing Sounds

Sounds are one of the most fun aspects of the Mac. You've undoubtedly run across them—one example is the beep you hear when an alert is displayed (you set this in the Sound Control Panel). You may have also encountered sounds in HyperCard and many other applications and accessories (many of them available as shareware from user groups and bulletin boards). Apple has defined the 'snd ' resource to contain all kinds of sound information, but some applications use their own sound resource formats.

▶ Sounding Off

ResEdit's 'snd ' picker has a 'snd ' menu that lets you try out a sound in three different ways. The first command, Try Sound, just plays the 'snd ' resource. The second command, Try as HyperCard Sound, adjusts the sound to middle C before it's played. This is what HyperCard does if a specific note isn't specified in the PLAY command. You'll notice that some 'snd 's sound the same when played normally and as a HyperCard sound. Sounds don't have to be adjusted if they were recorded with a base note of middle C. The last command, Try Scale With Sound, plays the sound adjusted to the notes of a major scale. This command can produce some pretty humorous results when a sampled sound (such as a grunt or a dog barking) is played with a scale.

By the Way ▶	Some sampled sounds (sounds that have been digitally recorded for use with the Mac) won't work with the Try Scale With Sound command. If you try a sound with the scale and get only silence for your trouble, you'll know the sound can't be adjusted to be played with different notes.

▶ Adding Beep Sounds to Your System

It's easy to add sounds to the list that appears in the Sound Control Panel—all you have to do is add the sound to your System file! The hardest part is finding good sounds to use. If you don't own Mac-Recorder from Farallon Computing (which lets you record any sound you want), you'll need to find a file that contains some fun sounds. Bulletin boards and user groups often have files of sounds available for free. Once you've found some sounds, follow these steps to make them available from the list in the Sound Control Panel.

Hint ▶	Sound resources can be very large, so you have to be careful not to run out of memory in ResEdit. If you use MultiFinder, are going to be copying lots of 'snd ' resources, and have more than one megabyte of memory in your Macintosh, the first thing to do is increase the memory available to ResEdit. You can do this from the Finder by selecting ResEdit and then selecting the Get Info command from the File menu. Put a larger number into the Application Memory Size field at the bottom of the Get Info window. Changing the size to 750K should be enough, but no matter how much memory you give ResEdit, it might still run out if you copy a lot of large resources. Resources you paste into a file remain in memory until you save the file, so if you paste lots of big 'snd 's, they'll take up lots of room in memory. The solution to this problem is easy, though. Just save the file occasionally.

1. Use ResEdit to open the file containing the sounds.
2. Open the 'snd ' picker.
3. Use ResEdit to open the System file (or a copy).
4. Select and copy the sounds from the first file. You can play them first using the 'snd ' menu to see which ones you want to copy.
5. Paste them into the System file.
6. Close and save the System file. (If you modified a copy, you'll have to install it and restart.)
7. Open the Control Panel desk accessory, and select the Sound Control Panel.

Your new sounds should be in the list of sounds you find there.

▶ Adding Sounds to HyperCard

If you want to use a new sound in HyperCard, all you have to do is copy the 'snd ' resource into HyperCard or a stack. If you want to use the sound only in one stack, just add it to the stack itself. If, on the other hand, you want to be able to play the sound from any stack, you might want to add it to the Home stack. Either way, you can follow the steps outlined in the previous tip, substituting Home or your stack for the System file.

Hint ▶	When you use ResEdit to open a HyperCard stack, you might see an alert warning you that the file doesn't contain a resource fork. This simply means that you haven't added any special functionality to your stack yet. It's OK to let ResEdit add a resource fork.

▶ File Verification's Hidden Diagnostic Window

If you press the Option key while choosing Verify File from the File menu or while opening a file (if you have file verification turned on in ResEdit's Preferences dialog), a diagnostic window appears that shows the details of the resource verification operation. Although this feature probably won't help most users, some technical support engineers and developers might find it useful. Progress through the verification procedure is indicated by a series of status and error messages. A diagnostic window for a damaged file is shown in Figure 13-18.

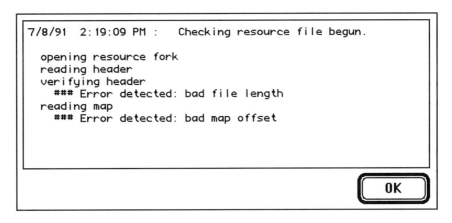

```
7/8/91  2:19:09 PM :    Checking resource file begun.

  opening resource fork
  reading header
  verifying header
    ### Error detected: bad file length
  reading map
    ### Error detected: bad map offset
```

OK

Figure 13-18. A hidden window that gives you details about the health of your files.

▶ Copying Files in the Background

Yes, if you use MultiFinder, it really is possible to make the Finder copy files while you do something else in a different application! Don't get too excited yet, though. You're limited in what you can do while the Finder is copying files and, since the Finder is pretty busy, your Mac's responsiveness to the mouse and keyboard is reduced. This isn't to say it's not useful, however. Even if you can only read a document, it's still better than staring at the Finder's thermometer dialog until it's done copying files.

Before we tell you how to work this miracle, a few warnings are in order. The Finder isn't designed to copy files in the background, which means it won't be quite as diligent in its effort to keep you out of trouble. Using common sense should keep you away from danger, however. When files are being copied in the background, don't mess with them in another application. If the Finder is copying a file and you're saving it at the same time, the results are bound to surprise you. Don't quit from an application. If you do, you'll be stuck waiting for the Finder to finish. It's best to avoid opening and closing files.

Enough of what you can't do. The most effective way to use this tip is to start an application and open a file you want to browse, then switch back to the Finder and start your copy. Before you start the copy, make sure a window of your application is visible. Once the Finder is copying files, you won't be able to use the menu bar to switch to your application—you'll have to click one of its windows. Once your application is the front window, you'll be able to browse your document. You'll occasionally notice some long delays between when you do something (like click the mouse or type a character) and when your Mac follows through on your action. Because the Finder is busy copying the files it doesn't give your application any time to pay attention to you.

Follow these steps to allow you to work while the Finder copies files.

1. Use ResEdit to open a copy of your Finder.
2. Open the 'DLOG' picker.
3. Open the 'DLOG' resource that contains the copy files thermometer. It's 'DLOG' ID 10241 in version 6.1.5 of the Finder (version 6.0.5 of the System). The window should look like the one shown in Figure 13-19.

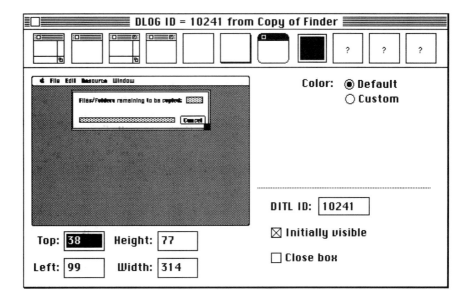

Figure 13-19. The Finder's file copy dialog can be changed to allow copying in the background.

4. At the top of the editor window, click any of the miniature windows that includes a close box. MultiFinder decides whether it's OK to switch to another window based on the window type of the frontmost window. By changing the dialog to a window type that includes a close box, you fool MultiFinder into believing it's OK to let you switch to another application. The window doesn't actually have to have a close box. It just has to be a window type that *allows* a close box. You can prevent a close box from appearing by making sure the Close Box check box isn't checked in the 'DLOG' editor window, as shown in Figure 13-19.

6. Close and save the copy of the Finder.

7. Install your new Finder and restart your Mac. The next time you copy a file, the Finder's dialog should look similar to the one shown in Figure 13-20.

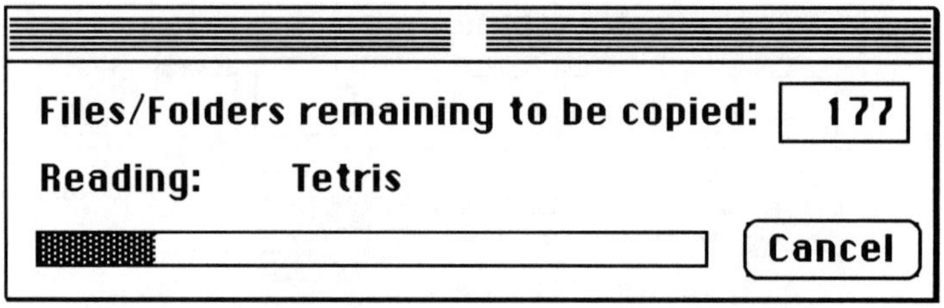

Files/Folders remaining to be copied: | 177 |

Reading: Tetris

[Cancel]

Figure 13-20. The Finder's new copy dialog.

▶ Summary

In this chapter we show you a variety of tips and tricks to personalize your Mac. On the silly side, you saw how to customize the graphical elements HyperCard uses, how to display a color picture when your Mac starts up, and how to play and move sound resources. On a more serious note, we describe how to protect or hide files and folders, how to reorder your Apple and Font menus, and how to share applications on a network. This chapter contains just a few examples of the zillion customizations you can make with ResEdit. You'll find more projects in Chapter 16, and you'll discover even more as you use ResEdit to explore your Macintosh.

PART THREE

▶ Templates: Keys to Dozens of Resources

14 ▶ Using Templates

Although ResEdit has built-in special editors for many resource types, there are numerous others you might want to edit. ResEdit allows you to edit a variety of resource types in dialog box-like windows called *templates*. ResEdit comes with over 60 templates, each allowing you to edit a different resource type. Some of these resource types are obscure, and you'll probably never need to edit them. Others, however, affect a variety of fun or useful Macintosh characteristics. For example, Chapter 6 has already shown you how to use the 'acur' resource to change animated cursors. Other resources edited with templates include 'PREC' resources, which define the defaults for your print dialogs; 'FOND' resources, which contain information about your fonts; and 'STR ' and 'STR#' resources, which contain text strings that can be fun to change. The template editor uses the templates stored within ResEdit to set up the window differently for each resource type. These windows can contain a variety of editable fields and radio buttons. Even though you can modify numerous different resource types with the template editor, you use the same editing techniques for all of them.

This chapter begins with an overview of what templates are and a list of the resource types that you can edit with templates, and finishes up with details of how the various template fields work. If you're interested in creating your own templates, Chapter 24 leads you through the necessary steps.

▶ What Is a Template?

Let's start with an example using a hypothetical desk resource type ('DESK'). A simple 'DESK' template would contain fields for defining four legs, a top, and some drawers—the parts that define a desk. The templates for other furniture resource types would contain different fields. But a 'DESK' template isn't a desk. Only when the fields contain valid values is a 'DESK' resource specified ('DESK' ID 128, for example). The same 'DESK' template allows you to see or enter values that specify other desk resources, too.

More realistically, a template stores a list of instructions that define what fields a window should contain to edit a particular resource type. As illustrated in Figure 14-1, the template editor resembles a special decoder that employs a variety of templates to let you see and edit existing resources or create new ones.

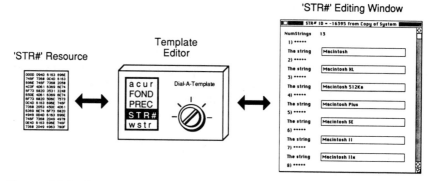

Figure 14-1. The template editor is like a special decoder that uses templates to let you edit resources.

A template displays the contents of a resource as a list of fields. Each field is identified by a label on the left and has a way of changing the field's contents on the right, perhaps an editable field or a pair of radio buttons. For example, the window shown in Figure 14-2 contains a resource displayed using a simple template made up of fields called Value and Title.

To edit this resource, you could enter a number into the Value field and a string of characters into the Title field. Fields that contain different kinds of data are described later in this chapter. The kind of data you're expected to enter is usually obvious, but even if you enter the wrong kind of data (for example, text where a number is required), ResEdit tells you what you've done wrong when you try to close the window.

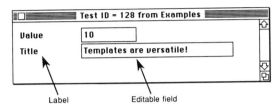

Figure 14-2. A window showing a resource displayed using a simple template.

▶ Available Templates

ResEdit comes with built-in templates for editing many different resource types, as shown in Table 14-1. Appendix B contains a short explanation of these and other resource types.

Table 14-1. ResEdit's Built-in Templates

actb	FREF	nrct
acur	FRSV	PAPA
ALRT	fval	PICK
APPL	FWID	PICT
BNDL	GNRL	pltt
cctb	hwin	POST
clut	icmt	ppat
CMDK	inbb	PRC0
cmnu	indm	PRC3
CMNU	infa	PSAP
CNTL	infs	qrsc
CTY#	inpk	resf
dctb	inra	RMAP
DITL	insc	ROv#
DLOG	itlb	RVEW
DRVR	itlc	scrn
FBTN	itlk	SIGN
FCMT	LAYO	SIZE
fctb	MACS	STR
FDIR	MBAR	STR#
finf	mcky	TEXT
fld#	mctb	TMPL
FOND	MENU	TOOL
FONT	minf	wctr
		WIND

▶ Filling in Templates

First, let's look at an example of a 'CNTL' resource. The template for this resource type is one of the simplest you'll find. 'CNTL' resources are used to define controls, such as buttons and scroll bars, that can appear in windows. The template contains all the information necessary to define a 'CNTL' resource.

The window shown in Figure 14-3 contains a template that looks and acts like a normal dialog box, except for a couple of differences. Unlike many dialogs boxes, templates windows aren't modal, so you can switch to other windows and use the menus while the template window is open. Also, notice that there's a scroll bar and a size box on the right side of the window. Because many (in fact, most) templates are much larger than the window in which they're displayed, you'll need to scroll to see all the information contained in the resource.

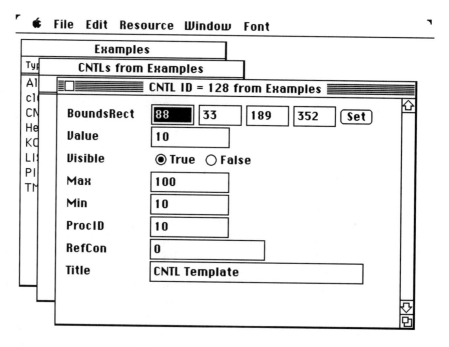

Figure 14-3. A 'CNTL' resource displayed by the template editor.

▶ Moving from Field to Field

The Tab key allows you to move between editable fields while skipping other field types, such as radio buttons. Shift-Tab performs a similar function in reverse, moving to the previous field (it'll move from the first field to the last field).

▶ Number Fields

You can enter either decimal or hexadecimal values (see Appendix C for details about hexadecimal numbers) into a numeric field. To enter a number in hexadecimal, simply precede it with a $ character. The length of the field tells you how big a number you can enter. Figure 14-4 shows the different field lengths and the maximum numbers they can contain. The smallest field can contain numbers between 0 and 255, the middle-sized field between -32,768 and 32,767, and the biggest field between -2,147,483,648 and 2,147,483,647.

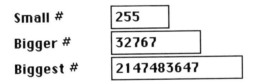

Figure 14-4. Number fields and the biggest numbers they can contain.

▶ String Fields

String fields contain simple strings of characters or numbers, as shown in Figure 14-5. They're often used for titles or text that might change when the application is translated to a different language. Strings can have different maximum lengths: Some strings are limited to 255 characters, while others allow up to 32,767. You usually only need to type a few characters, but when you need to enter a long string, the field grows, adding lines as necessary.

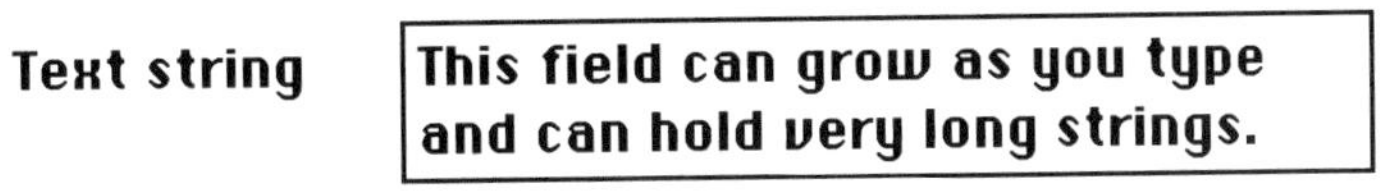

Text string | This field can grow as you type and can hold very long strings. |

Figure 14-5. A typical string field.

▶ True/False Fields

A true/false field consists of a pair of radio buttons, as shown in Figure 14-6. Click the one you want to set.

This is fun.   ⊙ **True**   ○ **False**

Figure 14-6. A true/false field.

▶ Bit Fields

Bit fields—which always come in multiples of eight— allow you to set a series of on or off values. As shown in Figure 14-7, there's a pair of radio buttons for each bit that can be set to either 0 (off) or 1 (on). Since all eight bits must always be defined in the template but aren't always needed by the resource, you'll often see labels like "Undefined 1" or "Reserved 1" for some of the bits. It's usually safest to leave these undefined bits set to 0 for compatibility with future versions of the resource.

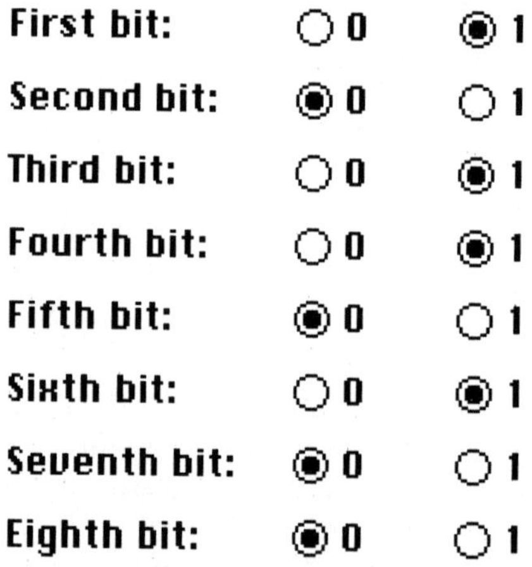

First bit: ○ 0   ⊙ 1

Second bit: ⊙ 0   ○ 1

Third bit: ○ 0   ⊙ 1

Fourth bit: ○ 0   ⊙ 1

Fifth bit: ⊙ 0   ○ 1

Sixth bit: ○ 0   ⊙ 1

Seventh bit: ⊙ 0   ○ 1

Eighth bit: ⊙ 0   ○ 1

Figure 14-7. Each pair of radio buttons represents one bit of a byte.

▶ Resource Type Fields

In many cases a resource needs to know the resource type of another resource so they can work together. This information is stored in a resource type field, as shown in Figure 14-8. For example, the 'ROv#'

(ROM override) resource contains the resource type of the resource being overridden. (Remember, resource types are always four characters long.)

Type name   `ICON`

Figure 14-8. A resource type field.

▶ Rectangle Fields

The rectangle is a special field in a template usually used to define the size and location (in pixels) of screen elements, such as dialogs and their contents. It consists of four small, editable fields containing the coordinates of the rectangle. (For example, in the 'CNTL' template in Figure 14-3, you can set the rectangle that defines the location of the control.) The first two fields contain the values for the top and left corners of the rectangle, and the last two fields contain the bottom and right values, as shown in Figure 14-9.

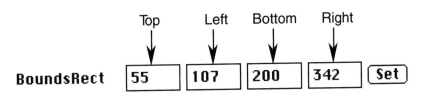

Figure 14-9. A rectangle field.

Using the Set Button With Rectangle Fields

The Set button lets you drag an outline of the rectangle you want to define. When you click the Set button, it becomes highlighted until you're done defining the new rectangle. Clicking the Set button again cancels the operation. After you click the Set button you can click and drag anywhere on the screen to draw a gray outline rectangle, and the values in the fields are updated, as shown in Figure 14-10. Since the rectangle you drag is relative to the entire screen, not to the window containing the template, the (0,0) location is in the upper left corner of the screen.

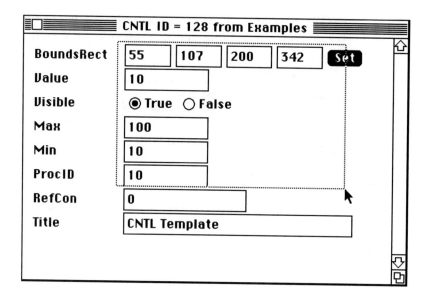

Figure 14-10. Using the Set button to define a rectangle.

Using the Set Button With MultiFinder

When you want to use the Set button to define a rectangle, all you have to do is click and drag. Simple, right? But what if you're using Multi-Finder and the place you want to click happens to be over a window of another application? You guessed it: MultiFinder switches you to that other application instead of letting you define your rectangle. There are two ways around this problem. One way is to simply restart without MultiFinder; if you're using a System before version 7.0, you can do this by holding down the Command key while you restart. The second way is to move the template window so that it covers the location where you want to start your rectangle.

Restarting without MultiFinder isn't possible if you're using System 7. However, the System 7 Finder contains a Show Application Only command on the Finder menu (the small icon at the right end of the menu bar) that lets you hide the windows of other applications. With other windows out of the way, you'll be able to start your rectangle anywhere you like, except over an icon on your desktop.

▶ Hexadecimal Fields

There are two kinds of hexadecimal (or hex) fields; fixed-length and variable-length. Both kinds have a $ character outside the field to indicate that data entered or displayed in the fields is always in hex format. (Remember that hexadecimal is base 16. You can find more details in Appendix C.) The numbers are formatted in pairs, with a space between each pair. Each pair of numbers represents one byte in the resource (since FF hex is 255 decimal and is the largest number that fits in a byte). Since the numbers are formatted only when you open the window, things get pretty messy as you enter new numbers. No matter how you format the numbers you enter, ResEdit assumes that each pair of hex digits represents a byte and ignores all spaces. A fixed-length field like the one in Figure 14-11 can appear anywhere in a template and is truncated if you enter too many digits.

10 Bytes $\$\boxed{\begin{array}{l} \text{01 23 45 67 \quad 89 AB CD EF} \\ \text{01 23} \end{array}}$

Figure 14-11. A fixed-length hex field.

Variable-length hex fields appear only at the ends of resources and contain all the rest of the data in the resource, as shown in Figure 14-12. In many cases, a resource contains some information at the beginning that you might want to modify and a lot of other information at the end that you should not modify. The data at the bottom is simply shown as a large hex field. If you do need to add to such a field, it grows as you enter more digits.

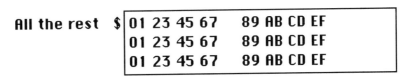

All the rest $\$\boxed{\begin{array}{ll} \text{01 23 45 67} & \text{89 AB CD EF} \\ \text{01 23 45 67} & \text{89 AB CD EF} \\ \text{01 23 45 67} & \text{89 AB CD EF} \end{array}}$

Figure 14-12. A variable-length hex field.

As you're modifying a hex field, it might look something like Figure 14-13, but after you close and reopen the window, ResEdit formats it, as shown in Figure 14-12.

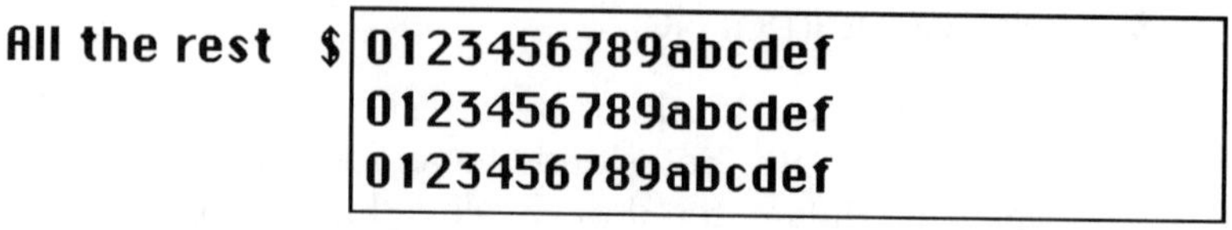
All the rest $
0123456789abcdef
0123456789abcdef
0123456789abcdef

Figure 14-13. A hex field that you just filled in.

Repeating Lists

Most resources contain a few general fields at the beginning followed by a variable-length list of information. For example, an animated cursor resource ('acur') contains two numeric fields followed by a list of cursor IDs. When a new 'acur' is created, it contains only the two numeric fields, as shown in Figure 14-14.

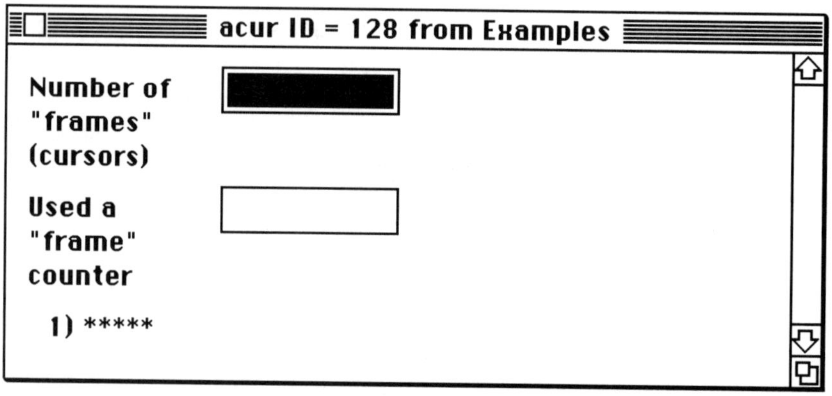
acur ID = 128 from Examples
Number of "frames" (cursors)
Used a "frame" counter
1) *****

Figure 14-14. A new empty 'acur' resource.

To add a cursor to the list, select the row of asterisks by clicking them, then choose Insert New Field(s) from the Resource menu. This command adds one set of fields, as shown in Figure 14-15. You can repeat this process as many times as necessary to get the number of fields you need.

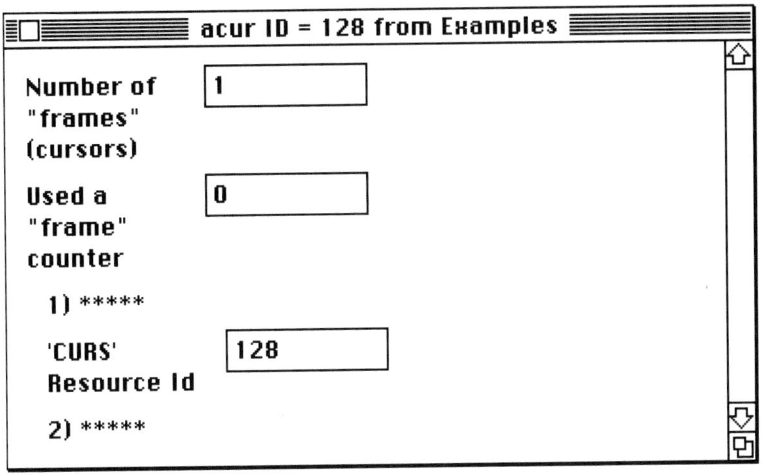

Figure 14-15. An 'acur' with one cursor ID.

By convention, the label used to indicate the start of a list is a row of five asterisks, but you might encounter other characters. Though lists may contain other lists, each nested list is indented, so you can see where it starts. For example, Figure 14-16 contains a list within a list: one identified by the ***** label and one identified by the ----- label.

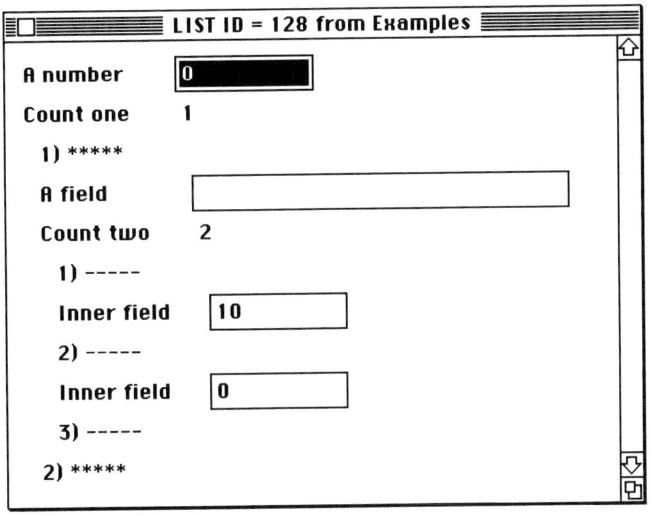

Figure 14-16. A template with two nested lists.

There's also usually a field just above a list that indicates how many sets of fields are contained in that list. Depending on the kind of list, this count can start at zero or one, or not be present at all. If the count is -1 before you add any fields to the resource, you'll know it starts with zero instead of one. You can always tell how many sets are in the list by looking at the number in front of the last list separator (usually a "*****" label). The number of sets is one less than this last number. For example, the last number in the list in Figure 14-17 is nine, so the list repeats eight times.

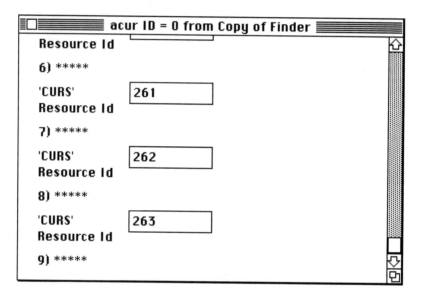

Figure 14-17. An 'acur' resource containing eight cursors.

▶ Adding and Removing Fields

The Insert New Field(s) command on the Resource menu is used to insert a new set of fields before the selected list separator. Selecting a separator selects all the fields between that and the next separator. The Edit menu commands work on these selected fields. For example, you could move a set of fields within a list by selecting the separator just above the fields, cutting the fields, selecting the separator just above where you want them to be moved, and pasting. Removing a set of fields is as easy as selecting a list separator and choosing Cut from the Edit menu or pressing the Delete key.

▶ Using Templates When There's a Custom Editor

There are a few cases where you'll want to use a template rather than the custom editor for a resource. For example, the 'PICT' editor simply shows the 'PICT' resource at full size, whereas the 'PICT' template lets you change the rectangle that defines the location and size of the 'PICT'. You can follow these steps to edit a 'PICT' resource with a template instead of with the custom editor.

1. Choose Open Using Template from the Resource menu or hold down both the Option and Command keys while you double-click the resource.
2. You see the dialog shown in Figure 14-18. Since 'PICT' is already filled in, just click the OK button. (If you wanted to use a different template, you could select it from the list or type it into the field.)
3. A window appears containing the 'PICT' resource in the specified template.

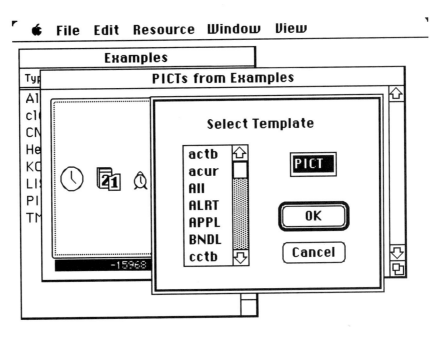

Figure 14-18. This dialog lets you select which template you want to use.

▶ Summary

This chapter describes how ResEdit uses templates to let you edit over 60 different resource types. You use templates by filling in a scrollable list of editable fields and radio buttons. The window for each resource type presents a different set of fields. We describe each possible field type and show you how to add and remove sets of fields from variable length field lists. In Chapter 24 we show you how to design your own templates.

15 ▶ Customizing the Finder's Layout

The Finder contains a 'LAYO' resource that controls a surprising number of operations. By changing certain settings in this resource you can customize the way the Finder draws files, folders, text, and icons. (You won't find this resource in Finder versions 7.0 or later, but you can make many of the same changes from the Finder itself.) You may be familiar with the Layout application (available as shareware from many user groups and bulletin boards), which also allows you to customize the Finder's layout. Layout is more convenient for some aspects of customizing the Finder because it gives you an idea of what your changes will look like, but it doesn't let you change other useful settings. An advantage of using ResEdit is that it lets you set the layout by specifying numerical values for locations and offsets. If you write these numbers down (or, better yet, keep a copy of your 'LAYO' resource in a separate file), you can use them each time you upgrade to a new Finder or create a new startup disk.

Remember, you can't edit the Finder directly if you're using Multi-Finder. As always, the most conservative approach is to edit a copy of the Finder and install it only after you're through making changes. However, since you're probably going to repeatedly make changes, try them out, and make more changes, you might want to edit your Finder directly. If you're careful to change only the fields we talk about, and enter only valid values, you shouldn't have any problems, especially if you keep a copy of your original Finder just in case. (You should have the rescue disk discussed in Chapter 4 available for starting up your Mac in an emergency.) To turn off MultiFinder, use the Set Startup command on the Finder's Special menu, and then restart your Mac. Conveniently, when you quit from ResEdit, the Finder will restart using your new 'LAYO' resource, so you can immediately see the results of the changes you've made.

Even if you don't decide to edit your Finder directly, we strongly recommend that you save a copy of the Finder's original 'LAYO' resource by duplicating it before you modify it. If you don't like some of your changes, you can always look in this backup copy to find out what the fields originally contained.

The 'LAYO' resource is pretty big, so we'll show you the basics of how to find the resource, and then go through the fields and what they're used for.

1. Use ResEdit to open the Finder or a copy.

2. Open the 'LAYO' type picker.

3. Select the 'LAYO' resource you find. There should be only one and its resource ID should be 128.

4. Choose Duplicate from the Edit menu. This makes a duplicate of the resource so you can refer to it later to find out what the original values were.

5. Open the original 'LAYO' resource with resource ID 128 which should look something like Figure 15-1.

6. Follow the instructions provided later in this chapter to make your changes.

7. Close and save the file.

8. Quit from ResEdit.

9. If you opened a copy of the Finder, install it in your System Folder and restart your computer. If you opened the Finder directly, your changes are already in effect.

10. Repeat steps 5 through 9 until you have the layout the way you want it.

Now for the interesting part: What do all the fields of the 'LAYO' resource do for you?

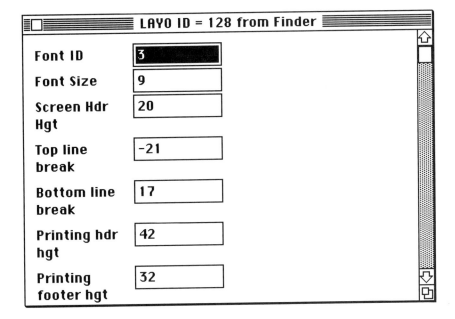

Figure 15-1. The Finder's 'LAYO' resource.

▶ Changing the Finder's Font

The Font ID and Font Size fields of the 'LAYO' resource tell the Finder which font to use whenever it draws text. This includes:

- Names under icons, both in folders and on the desktop
- File names and information shown in name, date, size, and kind views of folders
- Text in the heading area of windows (where the name, size, kind, and last modified headings are drawn)
- Text in the Finder's Get Info windows
- Text printed when you select the Print Directory command from the File menu

The Finder normally uses 9-point Geneva, but you can change it to any font you have installed in your System file. Changing the Finder's font doesn't affect any other application's font. Unfortunately, you can't select the font and size from menus. Instead, you have to type in the font number along with its point size. If you inadvertently enter a font number or size that doesn't exist in your System file, the normal default font (usually Geneva) or size (usually 9 point) will be used. Table 15-1 can help you determine the number to put into the Font ID field.

By the Way ▶	The Finder expects the font it's using to contain certain characters, such as the ellipsis (…). If you pick a font that doesn't contain these characters, you may want to add them. See Chapter 12 for more information about changing fonts.

Table 15-1. Some Common Font Numbers

Font Number	Font Name
0	System font (Chicago)
1	Default application font (usually Geneva)
2	New York
3	Geneva
4	Monaco
5	Venice
6	London
7	Athens
8	San Francisco
9	Toronto
11	Cairo
12	Los Angeles
13	Zapf Dingbats
14	Bookman
15	N Helvetica Narrow
16	Palatino
18	Zapf Chancery
20	Times
21	Helvetica
22	Courier
23	Symbol
33	Avant Garde
34	New Century Schlbk

Warning ▶	Before setting your Finder's font to something fun like Cairo, Zapf Dingbats, or Symbol, be sure to plan ahead for how you're going to restore the font so it's readable. Identifying the Finder in your System Folder is difficult when its name looks like ◆❋■❋❋▢!

Warning ▶	The font numbers shown in Table 15-1 are only the standard numbers. When you move fonts around with the Font/DA Mover, it may change the font numbers to make sure no two fonts have the same number. The safest way to determine the number of the font you want to use is to follow these steps.

1. Use ResEdit to open a copy of your System file.
2. Open the 'FONT' picker.
3. Find the 'FONT' resource that has a name of Font Family: followed by the name of the font you want to use (for example, Font Family: New York). This resource will have a size of zero.
4. Divide the resource number of this 'FONT' resource by 128.
5. This is the font number you should use.

For example, the Times font normally has a resource ID of 2560. Dividing this by 128 gives you a font number of 20, which is the same as the number found in Table 15-1.

▶ Using a Large Font with the Finder

It's sometimes useful to set up your Finder to use a large point size for the text it draws. You might be giving a presentation and want to make sure everyone can see what's on your screen, or you might just be slightly farsighted. Whatever the reason, you can make such changes in the 'LAYO' resource. Using a large point size involves a few more steps than just changing the font the Finder uses. You also need to allow more room for the headings and more room for each row in the list of files. You can follow these steps to change your Finder's font to Athens 18. (If you don't like Athens, just substitute the font of your choice.) Most of the fields you'll be changing are shown in Figure 15-1, and the Finder's new look is shown in Figure 15-2.

1. Open the 'LAYO' resource, as described previously.

2. Change the font to Athens by setting the value in the Font ID field to 7.

3. Change the point size to 18 by setting the value in the Font Size field to 18.

4. Change the value in the Screen Hdr Hgt field to 26 to make sure there's room for the window heading (the area just below the title bar where the number of items and disk usage is shown in icon view).

5. Change the value in the Bottom Line Break field to 23 to move the double line that separates the heading from the file information to the appropriate place.

6. Change the value in the Printing Hdr Hgt field to 48 and the value in the Printing Footer Hgt field to 38 to make sure your printed directories look OK.

7. Change the value in the Line Spacing field to 23 to make sure each line has enough room for the bigger characters. You have to scroll (or Tab) down in the template to find this field.

8. Add 20 to the values in the Tab stop 3 through Tab stop 7 fields to make sure you have enough room for the names of your files. (You'll learn more details about these fields later.)

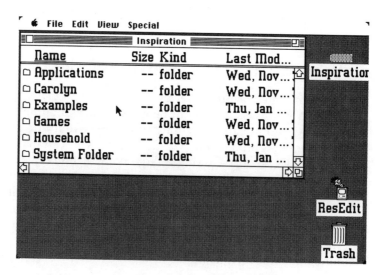

Figure 15-2. The desktop using Athens 18.

▶ Changing the View Used for New Disks

If you like to use a view other than by Icon in your Finder windows, you're probably pretty tired of changing the view every time you initialize a disk. You can easily make any view the default by changing the Default view field of the 'LAYO' resource (it's about halfway down the template). Find the appropriate number in Table 15-2, put it into the template, close and save the Finder, and the next time you initialize a disk, the view will be the way you like it.

Table 15-2. Numbers to Use to Change the Default View

If You Want	Use
by Small Icon	0
by Icon	1
by Name	2
by Date	3
by Size	4
by Kind	5

▶ Changing the Size and Location of New Windows

Now that your new windows have the view set to what you want, why not make them appear where you want on the screen and in the right size? The 'LAYO' resource contains a rectangle defining the size and location of new windows the Finder creates. Look for the rectangle (a set of four fields and a Set button all on the same line) named Window Rect. The first two fields of the rectangle determine the location of the window's top left corner, and the last two fields determine its bottom right corner.

There are a few things to keep in mind when you're changing these fields. When you set the location of the top of the window (the first field), remember you're setting the top of the content part of the window, not the top of the title bar. If you want your window to appear just under the menu bar, set the Top value to 39 (allowing 20 for the menu bar and 19 for the window's title bar). If you inadvertently create a window that has its close box under the menu bar or someplace equally invisible, don't forget you can always choose Close from the File menu to close the window. Setting the left side (the second field) is more straightforward. To make the window appear at the left side of the screen, simply set the Left value to 0. If you want the window to start partially off the screen, use a negative number in the Left field.

To set the size of the window, just add the height and width you want to the values already set for the top and left. For example, if you want your window to be 100 pixels tall, 200 pixels wide (remember, there's usually about 72 pixels per inch), and appear in the upper left corner of the screen, you should set your rectangle to 39, 0, 139, 200.

Setting up your window is an ideal time to use the Set button. Remember, all you have to do is click the button then drag out the rectangle in the location and size you want for your window. Another reminder: When you use the Set button, you need to start lower than you might think, because the window's title bar isn't included in the rectangle. If you start with a top value of 39 or more, the top of your window will be visible.

▶ Changing the Layout of Text Views

You can change a number of different aspects of the Finder's text views. You might want to make changes simply to suit your style, or because you're using a larger font and can't see all the information you need. Any changes you make will affect all four text views (by Name, by Date, by Size, and by Kind). Probably the most useful change is to scrunch things together a bit so you can see more useful information in a smaller window. To complement this change, you might also want to use a more abbreviated format for the date. We'll show you an example below, but don't hesitate to fiddle with the numbers until you get exactly the layout you want.

▶ The Text View Date Field

The Finder uses the Text View Date field to decide what format to use when it draws a file's last modified date. It normally uses the abbreviated long date format (something like Fri, Jan 25, 1991 in the United States), but you can change it to display either more or less detail. The field can contain three values: 0 for the short date format (something like 1/25/91); $0100 for the long date format (something like Friday, January 25, 1991) and $0200 for the abbreviated long date format. (Remember to include the $ character in front of the number to indicate that it's hexadecimal.) You can find all the details of how you can make these date formats look any way you want (almost) in Chapter 11, which discusses the 'itl0' and 'itl1' resources.

▶ The Tab Stop Fields

The Finder uses the Tab stop fields, shown in Figure 15-3, to determine where to draw the various kinds of information shown in text views. The Finder's normal default values are shown in the figure. Each Tab stop indicates the number of pixels from the left edge of the window to one of the parts of the text view.

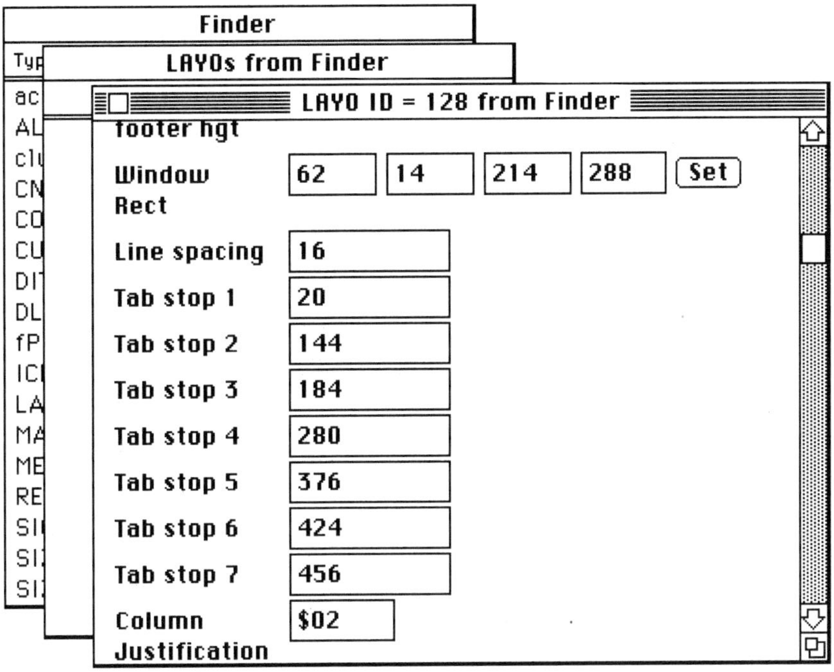

Figure 15-3. The Tab stop fields in the Finder's 'LAYO' resource.

As you can see from Figure 15-4, Tab stop 1 locates the start of the Name field, Tab stop 2 locates the Size field, and Tab stop 3 locates the Kind field. Tab stops 4 and 5 indicate the date and time the file was last modified. Tab stop 6 indicates the end of the information.

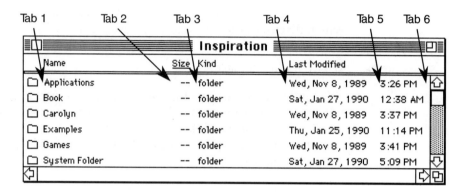

Figure 15-4. Tab stop locations in a Finder window.

▶ Changing the Text Views: An Example

So, let's change the text views to make more information visible in a smaller window. To do this, we'll change the Tab stops that control where the Finder puts information and change the date to a more compact format.

1. Open the Finder's 'LAYO' resource, as described previously.

2. Scroll the template until the Text View Date field is visible (it's slightly more than halfway down the template). For our purposes, we'll use the short date format, so enter zero into the Text View Date field.

3. Scroll the template until you can see all seven Tab stop fields, as shown in Figure 15-3.

4. Since the idea is to pack more information into a smaller window, the first job is to make the space available for the name smaller. If you regularly use names 27- to 30-characters long, you might want to skip this step. If you're using Geneva 9 (the standard Finder font), normal characters are no more than eight pixels wide. (You can find out the width of characters in other fonts with ResEdit's 'FONT' editor. The character width is shown in the lower left part of the window. For more information, see Chapter 12.) So, if you want to allow three fewer eight-bit-wide characters (like *W*) or four fewer six-bit-wide characters (like numbers) to show, you can subtract 24 from Tab stops 2 through 7.

5. You can also reduce Tab stops 4 through 7 if you can get by with less room for the file's type (there's normally room for about 17 or 18 characters). You don't want to lose too much information here, so just subtract 15 pixels.

6. Finally, since you set up a shorter date format in Step 1, you can move in Tab stops 5, 6, and 7 by subtracting 30 from each one. If you started with the default values shown in Figure 15-3, your new Tab stop values should be those shown in Table 15-3.

7. That's it. Now close and save your Finder and see if you like the new layout. It should look like Figure 15-5.

Table 15-3. New Tab Stop Values

Tab Stop	Location
1	20
2	120
3	160
4	241
5	337
6	355
7	387

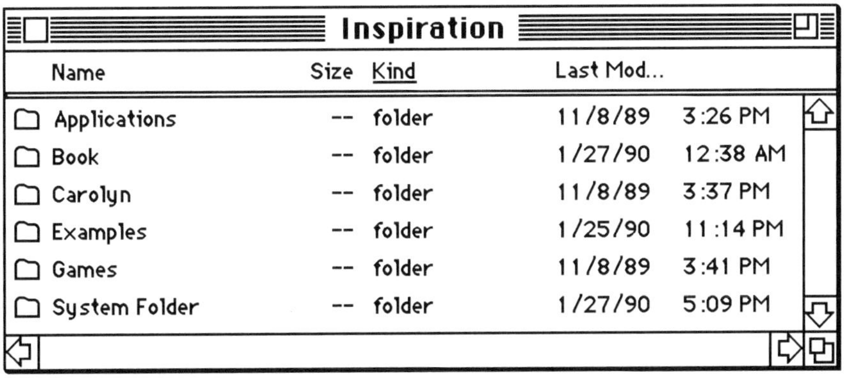

Inspiration				
Name	Size	Kind	Last Mod...	
🗀 Applications	--	folder	11/8/89	3:26 PM
🗀 Book	--	folder	1/27/90	12:38 AM
🗀 Carolyn	--	folder	11/8/89	3:37 PM
🗀 Examples	--	folder	1/25/90	11:14 PM
🗀 Games	--	folder	11/8/89	3:41 PM
🗀 System Folder	--	folder	1/27/90	5:09 PM

Figure 15-5. The same information in a lot less space.

▶ Changing the View Indication

Have you ever wondered why one of the headings in the Finder's text views is underlined? That's the Finder's way of letting you know which Sort method it used for the window. If the Kind heading is underlined, you know you've chosen by Kind from the Finder's View menu. If the underline is a bit too subtle for you, here's a way to make the heading really stand out.

1. Open the Finder's 'LAYO' resource.
2. Scroll down until you find the Sort Style field (it's about 3/4 of the way down the template).
3. This field contains the text style used for the heading. Each of the first seven bits of the field identifies a different style. If you want, you can use several styles in combination to make the heading really stand out. Be careful, though: Some styles (such as outline and shadow) can make the heading take up more room, and it might no longer fit in the space allotted. (An earlier example showed you how to make more room for the heading by changing the location of the Tab stops.)
4. You can use Table 15-4 to figure out what value to enter into the field. To add a single style, simply enter the number specified (enter 1 for bold, for example). If you want to combine several styles, just add up the numbers for each style you want to use. For example, if you want to combine bold and shadow you would add 16 and 1 and enter 17 into the style field. Figure 15-6 shows an example of the mess you can make if you combine all the styles.

Table 15-4. Style Values to Use in the Sort Style Field

Style	Value
bold	1
italic	2
underline	4
outline	8
shadow	16
condense	32
expanded	64

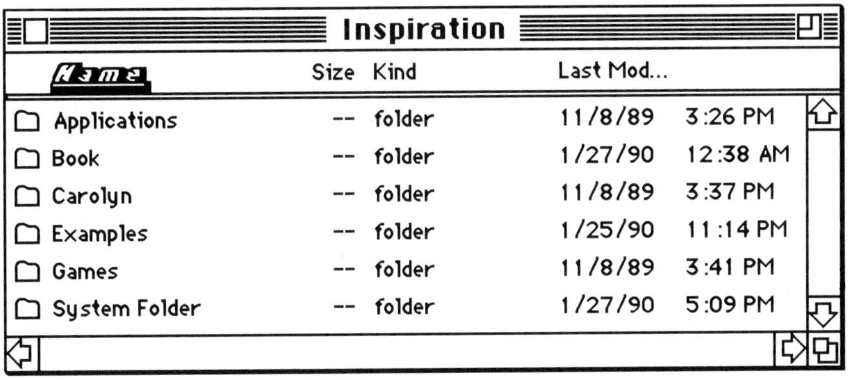

	Inspiration			
Name	Size	Kind	Last Mod...	
📁 Applications	--	folder	11/8/89	3:26 PM
📁 Book	--	folder	1/27/90	12:38 AM
📁 Carolyn	--	folder	11/8/89	3:37 PM
📁 Examples	--	folder	1/25/90	11:14 PM
📁 Games	--	folder	11/8/89	3:41 PM
📁 System Folder	--	folder	1/27/90	5:09 PM

Figure 15-6. A heading that really stands out.

▶ Turning Off the Zoom Rectangles

When the Finder opens or closes a window, it draws a series of "zoom" rectangles to show where the window is coming from or going to. If you'd like your windows to open a little faster, you can turn these rectangles off. Just look in the Finder's 'LAYO' resource for a pair of radio buttons labeled Use Zoom Rects (it's near the middle of the template). Click the 0 button to turn off the zoom rectangles; click the 1 button to turn them back on.

▶ Lining Up Your Icons with a Grid

Some people like icons to stay exactly where they put them, and other people always use the Clean Up Window command to make sure their windows look neatly organized. If you fall into the latter category, there's a field in the 'LAYO' resource that will make you very happy. By changing this field, you can make sure the Finder always lines up your icons with an invisible set of grid lines—the same grid lines the Clean Up Window command uses. The next two sections show you how to change the location of these grid lines. To turn this feature on, open the 'LAYO' resource, find the Always Grid Drags field (near the middle of the template), and click the 1 radio button. Once you've turned this feature on, whenever you let go of an icon after dragging it, the Finder auto*magically* moves it to the nearest grid line. This even happens with icons you've placed outside a window, directly on the desktop.

▶ Changing the Placement of Your Small Icons

If you use the small icon view for your folders but also use long file names, you may have been annoyed that the file name often overlaps the next small icon. The 'LAYO' resource contains a couple of fields that let you change the invisible grid used by the Clean Up Window command. Open the 'LAYO' resource and find the Sm Icon Horiz field (near the middle of the template). The contents of this field tell the Finder how far apart to put the small icons. The default is to place them 96 pixels apart. If you want more space, try adding 10 or 15 and see how it looks. If you want to add more space vertically between the icons, find the Sm Icon Vert field. This field tells the Finder how far apart vertically to place the small icons. Remember, after you've changed these fields and saved the Finder, you'll need to choose the Clean Up Window command from the Finder's Special menu to see the results of your changes.

▶ Changing the Placement of Your Normal Icons

As with small icons, the 'LAYO' resource allows you to change the spac-ing of your normal icons by changing the Icon Horiz spacing and Icon Vert spacing fields. Icons have two problems—their names are often so long they overlap, and the icons themselves are so big you can't see very many in a reasonably sized window. The Finder lets you specify what's called a *vertical phase* to help solve both these problems. After you've set the vertical phase, cleaning up alternates the icons, as shown in Figure 15-7.

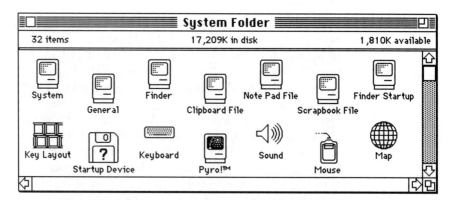

Figure 15-7. A Finder window with the vertical phase set to 15.

The vertical distance between the tops of adjacent icons is the vertical phase. Since the icons are offset from each other, you can also move them closer together horizontally without worrying that their titles will overlap. You can change your vertical phase by changing the Icon Vert phase field in the 'LAYO' resource. The layout shown in Figure 15-7 used a horizontal spacing of 60, a vertical spacing of 62, and a vertical phase of 15. If you have short file names, you may want to reduce the horizontal spacing even further. You can try these values or adjust them to whatever suits you. The standard default settings are 64 for both horizontal and vertical spacing, and 0 for vertical phase. These settings affect icons anywhere the Finder draws them, including the desktop. As with small icons described previously, you'll have to use the Clean Up Window command on a window before it will reflect your new spacing.

▶ Using the Title Click Field

The Finder has an interesting hidden feature you can enable by clicking the 1 radio button next to the Title Click label. You'll find the Title Click field near the bottom of the 'LAYO' template. Once enabled, this causes the Finder to open the current folder's parent folder (the folder containing a folder is its parent folder) whenever you double-click the title bar of a window. For example, in Figure 15-8, double-clicking the System Folder window's title bar would cause Inspiration, its parent folder window, to move to the front. If the parent folder window wasn't already open, it would be opened and brought to the front.

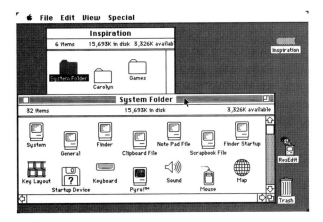

Figure 15-8. With Title Click turned on, double-clicking the title bar brings the parent window to the front.

▶ Showing Which Drive Your Floppy Disk Is in

Setting the Use Phys Icon (use physical icon) radio button (found near the bottom of the 'LAYO' template) to 1 causes the Finder to use a new kind of icon for floppy disks. Instead of the normal picture of a floppy disk, the Finder will use a picture of a Macintosh with an arrow indicating which drive contains the disk, as shown in Figure 15-9. If you have two floppy disk drives, and a disk in each drive, this icon reminds you which disk is in which drive.

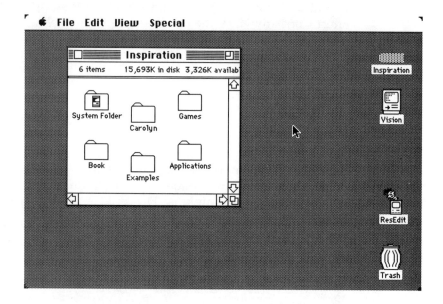

Figure 15-9. The floppy disk icon indicates which drive contains the disk.

▶ Changing the Maximum Number of Windows the Finder Can Open

If you have a hard disk that contains lots of folders, you've probably seen the Finder's "No more windows can be opened" alert. Increasing this limit is easy, as long as you have enough memory. The 'LAYO' resource has a Max # of windows field at the bottom of the template that contains a number one greater than the number of windows the Finder can open. This field normally contains 13, but you can increase it as much as you'd like. Increasing it to around 25 will probably be enough to let you open all the windows you'll ever need. Keep in mind, however, the more windows you allow the Finder to open, the more memory it uses. Even if you don't open the maximum number of windows, the Finder still uses about 200 bytes more for each extra window that it *could* open. For example, if you increase the maximum windows to 25, the Finder will use about 2500 more bytes even when no windows are open. Of course, if you really open 25 windows, the Finder will use much more memory. If you use MultiFinder and increase the Max # of windows, it would be a good idea to increase the amount of memory available to the Finder. You can do this by using the Finder's Get Info command to increase the Finder's Application Memory Size field. If you have enough memory available, increasing the Finder's memory to 350K should take care of the additional memory requirements.

▶ A Few Other Fields

The 'LAYO' resource contains a few other fields you can change. These fields are useful in certain special circumstances and are described only briefly here.

▶ Skip Trash Warnings

When you throw away an application or System file, the ever-vigilant Finder politely asks if that's really what you meant to do. Many people find this annoying since you just told the Finder you did, indeed, want to throw the file away. Even though it may seem tempting, we recommend against turning off these warnings. You would only have to throw away a valuable application once to make you wish you had put up with the warnings all those other times. And, besides, if you know for sure that it's OK to throw away a file, just hold down the Option key while you drag the file to the Trash and you won't be warned.

If you insist on turning off the warnings and know you never ever accidentally toss files you want to keep (possibly buried in a folder you thought you didn't need), you can follow these instructions. Just look in the 'LAYO' resource for the Skip Trash Warnings field (near the middle of the template) and click the 1 radio button. You can turn the warnings back on by clicking the 0 button.

▶ Column Justification

Each field of the file information shown in any of the text views can be either right or left justified. There isn't much advantage to changing this, but the point of customization is to make your Mac work the way that feels good for you. So, if you want your fields justified differently, here's how to do it. Open the Finder's 'LAYO' resource as described previously. Scroll to the Column Justification field (about a third of the way down the template). This field contains a number that tells the Finder what justification to use. Table 15-5 lists the numbers you need to calculate a new justification.

Table 15-5. Numbers to Use in the Column Justification Field

Column	Number
Name	1
Size	2
Kind	4
Date	8
Time	16

To set up your new justification, just add up the numbers from the table for each field you want right justified and enter it into the Column Justification field of the template. For example, if you want to make the name and size fields right justified, enter 3 into the template.

▶ Watch Thresh

The watch threshold field specifies the number of ticks (60ths of a second) the Finder waits before displaying the watch cursor when it's performing a time-consuming operation, such as copying files.

▶ Copy Inherit and New Fold Inherit

If you use an AppleTalk server network, the Copy Inherit and New Fold Inherit fields might be useful. If New Fold Inherit is set to 1, whenever you create a new folder on a server, the access privileges will be copied from the parent folder (the one that contains the new folder) to the new folder. Copy Inherit behaves similarly when you duplicate an existing folder.

▶ Icon-Text Gap

All text the Finder draws moves down by the amount specified in this field. The Finder applies this to all views (yes, even the text views, such as by Size). As you can imagine, this looks pretty ugly in most cases. The headings drawn at the top of the windows also move down, so they don't fit in the allocated space.

▶ Color Style

The Color Style field determines how the Finder applies the color specified in the Color menu. By default, Color Style contains 0, and the Finder draws icons with a colored frame and a white interior. When an icon is selected, the frame is white and the interior is drawn in the color selected from the Color menu. You can change this to more vividly identify files that aren't open. If you change Color Style to 1, the Finder will draw icons with a black border and filled with the color. Selected icons will be framed with the color and filled with black. As you can imagine, your icons will really stand out if they're filled with a bright color instead of white.

| Hint ▶ |

The Finder uses a 'clut' resource to determine which colors should be on its Color menu. When you change the Color Style field of the 'LAYO' resource to 1, you had better also change the black color in the Finder's 'clut' resource to white. If you don't, all of the icons that haven't been assigned a color will appear black—not a very appealing result. You can find out more about 'clut' resources and changing the Finder's colors in Chapter 17.

▶ Summary

This chapter shows you a number of ways to spruce up your desktop by changing the Finder's 'LAYO' resource. Detailed instructions are included to help you change everything from the font used in the Finder's windows to the maximum number of windows the Finder can open. In the next chapter, we'll show you several changes you can make using other templates included with ResEdit.

16 ▶ Template Projects

This chapter contains a collection of changes you can make using the template editor.

▶ Writing PostScript Code to a File

Have you ever wondered what PostScript—the page description language LaserWriters use—really looks like? Have you ever needed a PostScript file to take to your typesetting service? If so, you may already know that you can make the LaserWriter driver write the PostScript code to a file instead of to the LaserWriter by pressing Command-F just after you OK the Print dialog. (Hold down Command-K instead if you want to also include Apple's PostScript dictionary from the Laser Prep file.) The problem with this technique is that many applications intercept Command keys before they get to the LaserWriter driver, and it doesn't work at all under MultiFinder.

Fortunately, the authors of the LaserWriter driver have given you a way out of this dilemma. In LaserWriter versions between 5.2 and 7.0 there's a secret check box that causes the driver to write the PostScript to a file instead of the printer. Here's how to make the check box accessible. (In the LaserWriter driver that comes with System 7, the Print dialog already contains radio buttons to allow the PostScript to be sent to a file.)

1. Make a copy of your LaserWriter driver (a file named LaserWriter in your System Folder) and give it a new name such as LWToDisk or whatever makes sense to you. Leave the copy in the System Folder so you can use it later.
2. Use ResEdit to open the copy of your LaserWriter driver.
3. Open the 'DITL' picker so you see the list of 'DITL's in the driver.
4. Select 'DITL' ID -8191.
5. Choose Open Using Template from the Resource menu.
6. Click the OK button to say you want to use the 'DITL' template.
7. Scroll until item number 22 is visible. You should see a window similar to the one shown in Figure 16-1.

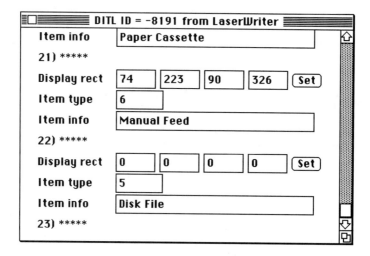

Figure 16-1. Change the Display rect field to make the Disk File check box visible.

8. You want to make the check box named Disk File visible (note that its Display rect[angle] is all zeros), so change the Display rect fields to 49, 315, 65, 390.
9. Close and save the file.
10. Now open the Chooser desk accessory and choose your modified LaserWriter driver (it must be in the System Folder for this to work). Since the Chooser shows you both the original LaserWriter driver and your modified version, you can easily switch between them.

From now on, when you print you'll see a dialog similar to the one shown in Figure 16-2. (If you're using LaserWriter version 6.0, you'll see a slightly different dialog.) If you check the Disk File check box the PostScript code will be sent to a file called PostScript0 (or 1 or 2, up to 9), which you can open with any word processing application. You can find the PostScript file in your System Folder or, if you're using MultiFinder, in the folder called Spool Folder in your System Folder. PostScript files can get pretty big, so don't forget to throw them away when you're finished with them.

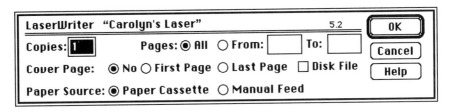

Figure 16-2. A new Print dialog with a Disk File check box.

▶ Speeding up Your Mouse

If you have a large screen monitor, you may have noticed how slowly the pointer seems to move when you have a long way to go, for instance, all the way between the Trash and the menu bar. Relief is at hand! With a few quick changes to a template, you can change any of the speed settings for the mouse Control Panel.

There are five 'mcky' mouse resources in your System file corresponding to the five possible mouse speeds in the Control Panel. The resource with ID 0 controls the speed of the Very Slow or Tablet setting, the resource with ID 4 controls the Fast setting, and the resources with IDs 1 to 3 control the speeds in between.

This is another time when you might want to edit the System file directly. If you just change the 'mcky' mouse resources and are careful not to touch any other resources, you shouldn't have any problems. Of course, it would be safer to work on a copy of the System file, but you'll see shortly why you might want to work on the original. If you do work on the active System file, be sure to make a backup copy first, just in case.

▶ Making a "Fast" Mouse into a "Very Fast" Mouse

1. Use ResEdit to open your System file.
2. Open the 'mcky' resource type.
3. Open 'mcky' ID 4. You'll see a window similar to the one shown in Figure 16-3.
4. Change the 8 Threshold fields to those shown in Figure 16-4.
5. Choose Save from the File menu to save your changes.
6. Choose the Control Panel from the Apple menu and select the Mouse icon.
7. Switch the speed from Fast to any other setting and then back to Fast (this activates your changes).

Move the mouse pointer about your screen. Is it moving too fast? Not fast enough? If it's moving too fast, you might try 1, 3, 4, 6, 8, 10, 13, 255. If it's moving too slowly, lay off the coffee for a few hours and check it again. If it's still too slow, try reducing some of the numbers a little. Small changes can have a big effect on your mouse speed so try subtracting 1 from each threshold value. Keep changing the numbers until you get a speed you like. It's generally a good idea to keep the smallest number in Threshold 1 and have the numbers increase to Threshold 8. Remember that after each change you must save the file and reset the speed in the Mouse Control Panel before you'll see the effect of your changes.

If you don't want to change your System file directly, trying out your changes will take a bit more work. Instead of saving the file and changing the setting in the Mouse Control Panel, you'll need to install your new copy of the System and restart your Macintosh. Each time you want to try a new set of values, you'll need to restart your computer. After you try this a few times, you'll understand why we recommend you take a deep breath and carefully edit your active System file.

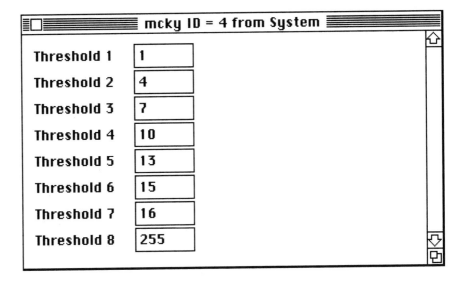

Figure 16-3. The 'mcky' resource controls the speed of your mouse.

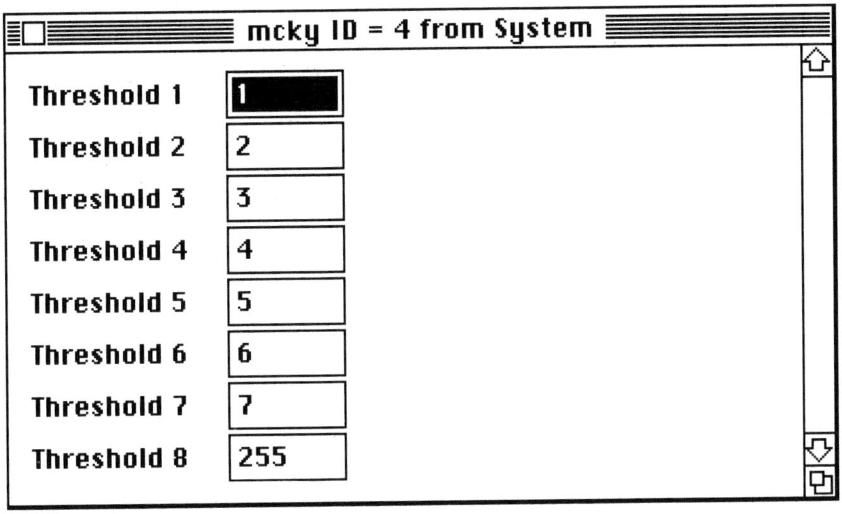

Figure 16-4. Threshold settings for a faster mouse.

▶ How Mouse Tracking Works

The easiest way to set the mouse speed is to use trial and error, but it may help to understand how the System uses each of the Threshold numbers. If the System moved the pointer one pixel for every pixel-equivalent you moved the mouse, you'd be surprised how slow that would seem. (The Tablet setting in the Mouse Control Panel roughly approximates such a one-to-one correspondence.) The Threshold values control acceleration of the pointer as you move the mouse faster and faster. (Remember, you move the mouse, the System moves the pointer on the screen.) Every sixtieth of a second (or tick of the System clock) the System checks the location of the mouse. The distance it has moved is compared with the values stored in the 'mcky' resource. Threshold 1 is checked first, followed by Threshold 2, up to Threshold 8. When a Threshold value is found that's greater than the distance moved (in pixel-equivalents), the distance is multiplied by the Threshold number (1 to 8) to determine how far the pointer moves.

An example will help you understand how the Thresholds work. Let's assume you've set your mouse to the Thresholds shown in Figure 16-3. With these settings, Table 16-1 shows how far the pointer moves for each movement of the mouse.

Table 16-1. Pointer Movement Based on Mouse Movement and Threshold Values

Mouse Moves*	Threshold Value*	Threshold Used	Pointer Moves*
1	1	1	1
2-4	4	2	2 x Distance moved
5-7	7	3	3 x Distance moved
8-10	10	4	4 x Distance moved
11-13	13	5	5 x Distance moved
14-15	15	6	6 x Distance moved
16	16	7	7 x Distance moved (16)
>16	255	8	8 x Distance moved

*Distances are measured in pixels or pixel-equivalents.

From the table, you can see that the smaller you make the Threshold values, the sooner the mouse accelerates. The slowest possible speed (the default for the Tablet setting) has all the Threshold values set to 255. This effectively eliminates any acceleration because you could never move the mouse that far in a 60th of a second so there's never any multiplication factor. The fastest mouse you could accurately position would use Threshold values something like 1, 2, 3, 3, 3, 3, 3, 3 (the absolute fastest would use Threshold values of 0, 0, 0, 0, 0, 0, 0, 1 and would cause every mouse movement to be multiplied by 8).

▶ Changing the ImageWriter's Paper Size

Most of the time, you probably use the ImageWriter's standard paper sizes, but wouldn't it be convenient to set up your own paper size for those occasions when you want to print on a different size paper? Maybe you'd like to print your own birthday card, use a preprinted form, an index card, or your own stationery. All of these would require careful planning unless you set up your own custom paper sizes. If you have an Apple ImageWriter, ImageWriter LQ, or LaserWriter IISC, you can change the paper size settings available in the Page Setup dialog.

Every printer driver contains a set of 'PREC' (Printer RECord) resources that control the behavior of the printer. The 'PREC' resource with ID 3 specifies the paper sizes displayed in the Page Setup dialog. You can specify up to six different paper sizes that correspond to the six possible radio buttons in the Page Setup dialog. Even better, you can override 'PREC' ID 3 by including a new 'PREC' resource with an ID of 4. In this way, you don't have to change your original resource, and you can easily restore it any time you want by deleting your custom resource.

| Hint ▶ | Some applications come with their own 'PREC' resource that contains what the manufacturer believes to be the best paper sizes for that application. These resources are ignored on version 2.7 of the ImageWriter driver that comes with System software version 6.0.5, but were used to override the defaults on earlier versions of the System. This is fine until you want to make your own custom paper sizes and the resource in the application overrides your custom resource. If your changes don't show up in one of your applications, check to see if it contains a 'PREC' resource with an ID of 4. If so, you'll have to either change its resource ID (so that it doesn't get used) or add your custom changes to it, also. Among the applications that contain their own 'PREC' resource are FileMaker II, Microsoft Word 4.0, and Microsoft Works 2.0. |

▶ How to Add Custom Paper Sizes

Here's how you can add custom paper sizes to your ImageWriter or LaserWriter IISC Page Setup dialog.

1. Make a copy of the printer driver file called ImageWriter (or AppleTalk ImageWriter, LQ AppleTalk ImageWriter, LQ ImageWriter, or LaserWriter IISC, depending on which type of printer you're using). Save this copy as a backup in case something goes wrong later on.

2. Use ResEdit to open your printer driver file (the file you made a copy of in Step 1).

3. Double-click the 'PREC' resource type to open the 'PREC' picker.

4. Select 'PREC' ID 3.

5. Choose the Duplicate command from the File menu.

6. Select the new resource (Duplicate probably gave it a resource ID of 128).

7. Choose the Get Resource Info command from the Resource menu.

8. Change the resource ID to 4 and close the Resource Info window.

9. Double-click the new resource to open an editing window like the one shown in Figure 16-5.

10. The first field (Number of Btns) contains a number between 1 and 6 that indicates how many radio buttons should appear in the Page Setup dialog. If you're going to add a paper size, be sure to update this field.

11. The next twelve fields contain the height and width for each of the six possible paper sizes. The height and width are specified in $1/120$-inch increments. For example, if you want to add an 8-inch-wide paper size, put 8 times 120, or 960, into the width field.

12. The next six fields contain the names to be displayed with the radio buttons. Change the field corresponding to the sizes you changed in Step 11. Be careful not to change the contents of the Data field at the end of the resource.

13. That's it. Now close and save the file, and select Page Setup from the File menu to see your changes. (If you don't see the results of your changes, check the Chooser desk accessory to make sure the correct printer is selected.) Figure 16-6 shows the ImageWriter's Page Setup dialog with three new paper sizes added.

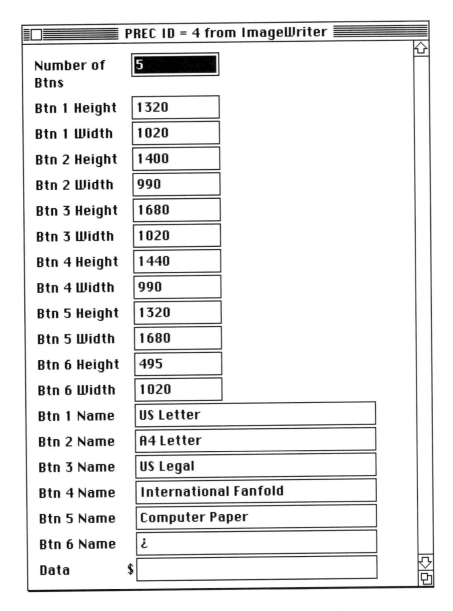

Figure 16-5. The 'PREC' resource from the ImageWriter file.

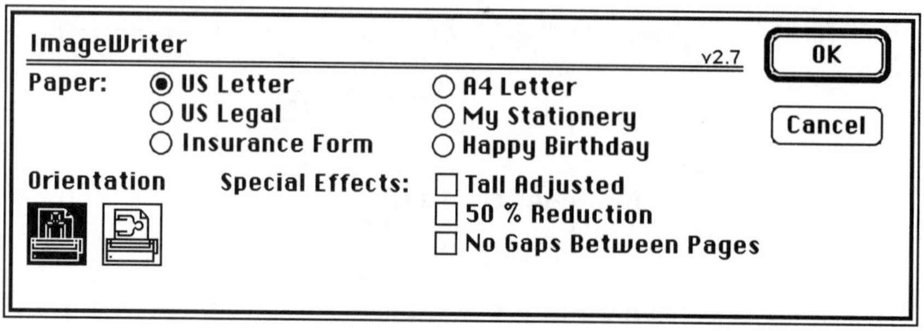

Figure 16-6. The ImageWriter's Page Setup dialog with a few new paper sizes.

By the Way ▶

Some applications may have problems with custom paper sizes, especially small sizes like you might use for index cards. Applications are generally tested only with the standard paper sizes, so, although most major applications should work, it's possible you'll find a few that don't (MacWrite 5.0 is the only one we know of that doesn't). Unfortunately, there's nothing you can do about this. Fortunately, you can still select the standard paper sizes from your customized Page Setup dialog, so you can use your custom paper sizes with other applications and use the standard sizes with these uncooperative applications. Microsoft Word 4.0 has a slightly different problem. Custom paper sizes only affect Word if you add them to the 'PREC' resource with ID 3 in the printer driver file. Word ignores 'PREC' resources with ID 4.

▶ Fun with Strings

Most applications, including the Finder and the System file, contain lots of text strings, which can be stored in either 'STR ' or 'STR#' (string list) resources. Unless you're localizing an application for another country, it's usually not important to change a string resource. You can't make your Mac behave in some neat new way by changing a word here and there. You can, however, buck convention and make the messages you see a lot more fun. We'll give you a few examples of strings to change, but we encourage you to explore. It's unlikely you could cause damage by changing a string, so just poke through your applications, the Finder, and the System file and see what you can find. Before you race off to customize what your applications have to say to you, here are a few tips.

- Don't make a string a lot longer than it was originally. If you do, it may no longer fit in the space provided for it. (If you really want a longer string in a dialog, you can find out how to change the size of a dialog item in Chapter 10).
- Be sure to save a copy of the file so you'll have the original strings to refer to later.
- Whatever you do, don't remove a string from an 'STR#' resource. Applications refer to strings by using an index into the list. If you delete the fourth string, thus making the fifth string the fourth, your messages will be very confused (you'll see the fifth string when you should have seen the fourth string, and so forth).
- If you see ^0, ^1, ^2, or ^3 in a string, that means the application is going to insert some more text before it uses the string (a file's name, for example). Even if you change the contents of the string, you should leave the ^0 characters alone.

Remember, applications should keep almost every piece of text you see on the screen in an 'STR ' or 'STR#' resource, so just look around for interesting things to change.

▶ Changing the Finder's Strings

Lots of strings in the Finder are fun to change. You'll find everything from error messages to the column titles shown when you view a folder by name. Here's an example of some changes you can make in the Finder (these strings are from version 6.1.5 of the Finder that came with version 6.0.5 of the System software).

1. Make a copy of your Finder so you can restore the strings later if you want.
2. Use ResEdit to open the copy of the Finder.
3. Open the 'STR#' picker.
4. Open resource ID 128. You'll find a lot of interesting strings here. Part of the resource is shown in Figure 16-7.
5. The third string contains the name given to new, empty folders (usually Empty Folder). Try changing it to New or Empty (you already know it's a folder).

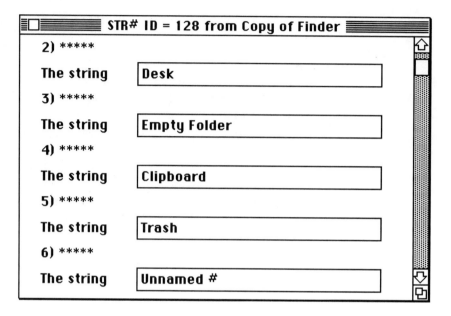

Figure 16-7. Some strings from the Finder.

6. The fifth string contains the name displayed under the Trash can. Try changing the name of your Trash to Slop or Refuse.

7. String 38 contains the text that's added to a file's name when it's duplicated. It's normally "Copy of ^0." Try changing it to "^0 Copy" or "^0 Clone" instead. This is the way System 7 names duplicates, and it keeps a file and its duplicate together when you view by name. Whatever you do, don't forget to leave the "^0" in the string, or the new name won't include the old name.

8. Close resource ID 128.

9. Open resource ID 7168.

10. String number 3 contains the names of the programmers who designed the Finder. These names are displayed in the About the Finder dialog box, shown in Figure 16-8. Since it's your Macintosh, why not put your name in the list in addition to, or instead of, theirs?

11. Close resource ID 7168.

12. Open resource ID 129.

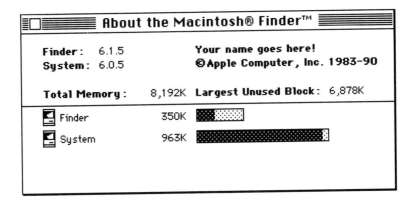

Figure 16-8. Add your name to the Finder's About box.

13. String number 3 in this resource contains the hated string, "the application is busy or missing." You see this string any time you try to open a file but you don't have the proper application. Why not change this to something a little more friendly, like "I can't find the application for that right now."

14. Close and save the Finder.

15. Keep your original Finder, install your new Finder, and restart your Mac to see all of your new strings.

▶ Changing the Frame for a 'PICT'

When you open ResEdit's 'PICT' picker, you see all the 'PICT' resources in a file shrunk down to fit in equal-size cells. When you double-click a 'PICT', a window appears showing you the 'PICT' at its normal size. This is convenient if you want to see what 'PICT's are available in a file, but not so convenient if you want to make changes to the 'PICT'. If you want to change the contents of a 'PICT', you should use a graphics program like MacDraw II or SuperPaint. ResEdit is the place to look if all you want to do is change the size or location of the 'PICT's frame. Here's how.

1. Use ResEdit to open the file containing the 'PICT' resource you want to change.

2. Open the 'PICT' picker.

3. Select the 'PICT' you want to change.

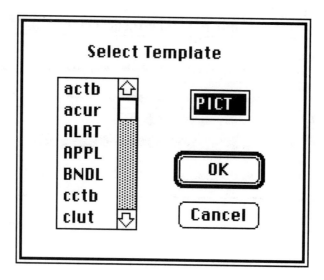

Figure 16-9. The template dialog defaults to 'PICT'.

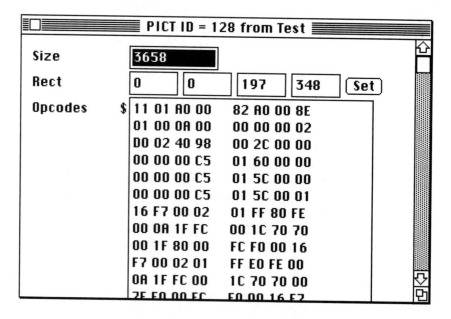

Figure 16-10. You can set the 'PICT' frame in the 'PICT' template.

4. Select Open Using Template from the Resource menu (or hold down the Command and Option keys while you double-click the 'PICT').

5. You'll see a dialog like the one shown in Figure 16-9. Since the 'PICT' type is already selected, just click the OK button.

6. Next you should see a 'PICT' template like the one shown in Figure 16-10. You can change the Rect field to anything you like. Don't change anything else in the template, or you'll more than likely ruin your 'PICT'.

7. Close the template window. You can see the effect of your changes by opening the 'PICT' editor (double-click the 'PICT').

8. Once you're satisfied with your changes, close and save your file.

Hint ▶

Changing the frame of a 'PICT' doesn't affect its contents in any way. Changing the frame only changes which part of the contents you'll see when the 'PICT' is drawn. By making the frame smaller, you can effectively hide parts of the 'PICT'. By making it larger, you can add white space around the 'PICT' or control the positioning of the 'PICT' when it's drawn.

▶ Changing Your System Font

Tired of using Chicago 12 for your System font? You can use any font you want, but you have to be careful. Once you've made this change, you won't have access to Chicago 12 at all—it will be as if the font doesn't exist anymore. (It still appears on your font menus but choosing it actually picks your new System font, not Chicago.) Since Chicago contains some special characters (the check mark used in menus and the apple used for the Apple menu, for example), you may need to make a few changes to any other font you want to use as the System font. Chapter 12 gives you details about how to edit a font. Keep in mind that the font you substitute will show up in many different places. The System font is used for menu titles and menu items, window titles, dialog boxes, and the text in many applications' windows. Because it's used in so many different places, you should keep the font size approximately the same as the size of Chicago 12. If you make the font bigger, the System will make the title bar of windows and the menu bar bigger to accommodate the new font, but most applications' dialogs won't resize themselves to hold the bigger characters. As you can see in Figure 16-11, a Finder window's title bar looks fine with a larger font. Figure 16-12 illustrates the problems you'll have with dialog boxes.

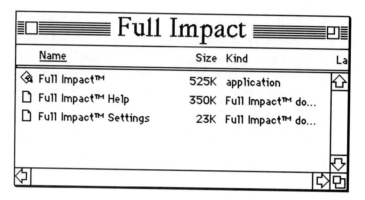

Figure 16-11. A Finder window using Times 24 for the System font.

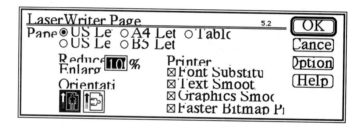

Figure 16-12. The Finder's Page Setup dialog doesn't look quite so good with Times 24.

Here's how to change your System font.

1. Using ResEdit, open a copy of your System file.
2. Open the 'FONT' picker.
3. Scan through the list of fonts until you find the 'FONT' you want to use for your System font. Make a note of its resource ID.
4. Switch back to the type picker window and open the 'FOND' picker.
5. Open the 'FOND' resource with ID 0.
6. Scroll to the bottom of the window (the Res ID field should be visible, as shown in Figure 16-13).

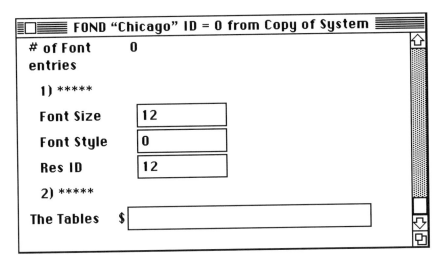

Figure 16-13. Change the Res ID field to the resource ID of any 'FONT' you want to use as your System font.

7. Change the Res ID field to the resource ID of the font you found in Step 3. For example, if you want to use Times 14 point, you can enter 2574 for the resource ID. (Times 14 works well as a substitute System font because it's approximately the same size as Chicago 12, although it's too thin to be readable when dimmed in menus.)

8. Close and save the file.

9. Install your modified System file and restart your Macintosh.

▶ Summary

This chapter shows you a number of projects you can do with tem-plates. Some examples show you how to customize specific resources. For instance, you can change the LaserWriter's 'DITL' resource to let you send PostScript data to a file instead of to a printer. You can also speed up your mouse by customizing the 'mcky' resource found in your System file. We also explore general techniques for customizing string ('STR ' or 'STR#') resources found in almost every application and include a few specific examples of fun changes you can make to the Finder's strings. The tips in this chapter are only a sampling of the many changes you can make with the more than 60 templates included with ResEdit.

PART FOUR

▶ Color, Color Everywhere

17 ▶ Color on the Mac

You've got a Macintosh II—a color Mac!—and you're just itching to customize with color. This chapter and the next two are for you. Those of you with monochrome monitors don't have to pout and flip to another chapter, because the grays your monitors display are "color," too. You don't need a color monitor to enjoy color resources. Whether you're working in color or grayscales, you'll complete your customization projects more smoothly and enjoyably if you have an understanding of how your Macintosh handles color. This chapter gives a brief overview of Macintosh color principles and describes two important color resource types that come into play. We also introduce features common to several color editors. The discussion of color resource editors assumes you're already familiar with ResEdit's fatbits editors (see Chapter 5 if you need a refresher). Similarly, the treatment of specific color resources assumes you're already familiar with the original black-and-white ones discussed in Part 2.

▶ Color Basics

The particular colors you see on your screen at a given moment result from complex interactions between software and hardware. Prior to the Mac II, you had no choice of displays. Mac screens were all black-and-white, built-in, and the same size. But Macintosh IIs support a variety of stand-alone monitors, which communicate with the computer via video cards. The number of possible colors a monitor can display is related to the amount of memory available to store screen images. Since the Mac II stores these images in memory chips (RAM) on the video card, the color capability of your Mac depends not just on the monitor, but also on the amount of memory on your video card.

To appreciate why memory is so important to color, you have to understand the difference between bits and pixels. On an SE, or on a Mac II set to the black-and-white mode, each dot on the screen, called a *pixel* (for picture element), requires one bit of memory. So when you're talking about black-and-white displays, bits and pixels amount to the same thing. Allocating more bits per pixel provides more information, allowing for shades of gray or various colors. The number of colors or grays a pixel can display is limited by the number of bits of memory dedicated to that pixel. The more bits per pixel an image or monitor has, the *deeper* it is said to be.

By the Way ▶	You've heard people tossing around terms like *two-bit color* and although you're not so naive as to assume they're referring to a monetary value, sometimes you wonder what they really mean. Here's the scoop. *Two-bit color* means you have enough memory to accommodate two bits per pixel. Because there are 2^2 or 4 ways to arrange those two bits per pixel (0,0; 0,1; 1,0; and 1,1), you can have four colors or grays. Here are the standard arrangements:

- 1 bit per pixel allows only white (0) or black (1)
- 2 bits per pixel (2-bit color) allows 2^2 or 4 colors or grays
- 4 bits per pixel (4-bit color) allows 2^4 or 16 colors or grays
- 8 bits per pixel (8-bit color) allows 2^8 or 256 colors or grays

You might also have 24-bit color, which works a little differently. ResEdit works just fine on 24-bit systems, but none of the resources we discuss take full advantage of all the colors.

▶ Colors by Numbers

You rarely get very far into a discussion about color on the Mac before people start throwing numbers around, and some of those numbers are impressively huge. You don't have to memorize the numbers, but

knowing where they come from and how they're related will help you
understand what your Mac is doing when you see colors or grays shift-
ing on your screen as you switch between windows. This understanding will also help you create and edit color resources intelligently. (As a
side benefit, you can spout off some numbers yourself next time the
conversation turns to color on the Mac.) Capsulized, the problem your
Mac must solve is as follows: At any given moment it can display only a
tiny fraction of a tremendous rainbow of possible colors (unless it's a 24-
bit system, which can display them all). How does it determine that
subset of colors?

Let's start with the monitor. Apple's RGB (red-green-blue) monitors
are capable of showing 2^8 colors for each of the three color beams—or
more than 16 million colors! (For math fans, that's $(2^8)^3$ or 2^{24}, which is
16,777,216.) But as we've already discussed, most video cards have only
enough memory to support 16 colors at a time, or 256 if you add the
memory expansion kit. Somehow your Mac has to tell the monitor
exactly which 256 colors to display.

Looking at the software side of the situation doesn't immediately solve
the problem. On the Macintosh, the red, green, and blue components of a
color are each specified by 16 bits, so each of the three components can
have values between 0 and 65,535. (That number may look familiar to
you if you've experimented with the standard Macintosh color picker.)
When all three RGB values are 0, none of the beams are turned on, so
you see black. When all three are set to the maximum, you see white.
Any time all three values are equal, you get shades of gray. (Of course,
on a monochrome monitor you get shades of gray from variations in
intensity, not from mixing three color beams.) The number of possible
RGB settings is humongous, meaning Color QuickDraw could theoret-
ically support the definition of as many as 2^{48} colors (that's $(2^{16})^3$ or
$65,535^3$)—more than 281 trillion! Because of limitations within Color
QuickDraw, however, it can actually display only 256 colors. Still, your
Mac has a problem. Out of the 281 trillion possible Color QuickDraw colors, and the 16 million possible monitor colors, how does the Mac determine which 256 colors you're going to get?

Hardware and software work together to decide which 256 (or which
16) colors to display. A streamlined description of the interaction follows. You don't have to remember the names of all the players, just the
end result. The application asks one of the Toolbox Managers or Color
QuickDraw for the colors it wants to use, choosing from the 281 trillion
possible Color QuickDraw colors. Color QuickDraw then asks the operating system's Color Manager for the colors that are actually available
on the monitor. For example, on a 16-color system, only 16 colors from

the monitor's possible 16 million are available. The Color Manager figures out how to translate what Color QuickDraw wants into what the monitor can actually provide, making the best match possible based on the monitor, video card, and Control Panel settings. This matching process is called *mapping*. The Color Manager then communicates with the monitor via the video card, which controls how the screen dots get turned on.

So if you try to draw in 256 colors or grays when your system is capable of displaying only 16, Color QuickDraw and the Color Manager map each of the 256 requested colors to one of the 16 colors available. (The frontmost window determines which specific colors are available on a monitor.) Exactly what's involved in color mapping is a complicated part of the Macintosh magic. For most purposes, you don't have to worry about it. But you should know something about two important resources that function as color collections your Mac can refer to when juggling colors.

Hint ▶	For best results with color, you should install 32-Bit QuickDraw. (This is an init that uses about 100K of RAM.) It's an improvement over Color QuickDraw, and also supports 24-bit color, which means your RGB monitor can display its entire 16-million-color repertoire—if you have a special video card. You can find 32-Bit QuickDraw in the Apple Color folder of System Software releases 6.0.5 and later. Just drag it into your System Folder. (Although the Macintosh IIci, IIfx, and up already have 32-Bit QuickDraw in their ROMs, we recommend IIci users install version 2.1 of 32-Bit QuickDraw anyway. The version in the IIci ROM has a few bugs that version 2.1 fixes.) System 7 already includes 32-Bit QuickDraw.

▶ Color Collections

When your Mac is figuring out how to map one color to another it needs a frame of reference; it needs to know exactly what colors are currently available. Similarly, when you create or edit a color resource, ResEdit needs to know which colors to make available. Color collections are stored in two types of resources. A 'clut' (Color Look-Up Table) is a collection of specific colors, or RGB values. This color roster resembles a list of recipes that tell the Mac exactly how to mix the red, green, and blue color beams. Mac II ROMs contain default 'clut's that provide a standard set of colors for each of the three standard pixel depths (4, 16, and 256 colors). ResEdit lets you choose these or other color collections, including your own custom collection. We'll talk more about this later in the chapter when we discuss the Color menu.

If necessary, a 'clut' can easily be converted into the second type of color collection, the 'pltt' (palette). A 'pltt' is similar to a 'clut', but includes additional color usage information that tells the system how to handle color conflicts. Another difference is that a 'pltt' can be associated with a window, to make sure that the window always has a certain specific set of colors available whenever it's active. In fact, that's why 'pltt's were invented. Windows without palettes are drawn by mapping the requested colors to whatever colors are currently available. But if a 'pltt' is associated with a window, the colors in the 'pltt' take top priority whenever the window is active. Using information in the 'pltt', your Mac changes the color environment in whatever way necessary to ensure that the specified set of colors is available to that window.

By the Way ▶	You may sometimes notice a screen flash and colors or grays shifting as you switch between windows while you're editing various color resources. Your Mac is simply switching from one subset of colors to another amongst the many it can display. Let's say you create a color icon using the standard 256 colors, and a color pattern using 256 grays. To make sure you see your resource in the colors you used to paint it, ResEdit associates a 'pltt' containing those colors with the editor window. Your Mac has no choice but to switch the color environment as you go from one window to the other because it can only display one set of 256 colors at a time.

Except for the people who want to change the eight colors the Finder offers on its Color menu, most users won't have much reason to edit 'clut's or 'pltt's. Programmers (and people interested in changing their Finders' colors) can find out how to edit these resources at the end of this chapter.

▶ Color Resources

ResEdit contains editors for numerous color resources, and several of its black-and-white resource editors allow you to colorize resource components. Table 17-1 lists the resource types that have their own editors. We've already introduced the first two resource types, 'clut' and 'pltt'.

You edit the remaining resource types in fatbits (or more correctly, fat-pixels) editors. We discuss color icons in Chapter 18 and color patterns in Chapter 19.

Table 17-1. Color Resource Types Having Their Own Editors

Resource Type	Description
'clut'	Color look-up table
'pltt'	Palette
'ppat'	Pixel pattern
'ppt#'	Pixel pattern list
'crsr'	Color cursor
'cicn'	Color icon
'icl4'	Icon large (32-by-32 pixels), 4-bit (16 colors), System 7
'icl8'	Icon large (32-by-32 pixels), 8-bit (256 colors), System 7
'ics4'	Icon small (16-by-16 pixels), 4-bit (16 colors), System 7
'ics8'	Icon small (16-by-16 pixels), 8-bit (256 colors), System 7

Table 17-2 lists color resources that are created when you colorize a black-and-white resource. You edit these color table resources via the editor for the resource with which they're associated. In other words, the 'MENU' editor creates an 'mctb' when you add color to a 'MENU' resource, and you also edit those colors via the 'MENU' editor. (You can also edit them in templates.) In Chapter 19, we talk more about editing these types of resources.

Table 17-2. Color Resource Types Edited Via Associated Editors

Resource Type	Description	Editor
'actb'	Alert color table	'ALRT'
'dctb'	Dialog color table	'DLOG'
'wctb'	Window color table	'WIND'
'mctb'	Menu color table	'MENU'
'cctb'	Control color table	'cctb' template

There are two additional color resource types. We mention them solely for the sake of completeness, because ResEdit doesn't have editors for them: 'ictb' (color dialog item list) and 'fctb' (font color table).

▶ Using the Fatpixels Editors

ResEdit's color resource editors aren't mysterious. They work just like comparable black-and-white editors, except they also have the ability to handle color. Figure 17-1 shows one of the fatpixels editors. Because color resources have common characteristics, the color resource editors share several features. For instance, three types of color resources ('ppat', 'ppt#', and 'cicn') differ from their original black-and-white counterparts in that they are not limited to a certain number of pixels; individual resources of these types can have different sizes. Consequently, these editors provide a way to let you adjust the size of the resources. Most of the fatpixels editors have a provision to include a black-and-white version. You can create this optional black-and-white version as easily as you can create a mask for an icon or pointer, by simply dragging the image to the appropriate part of the editor.

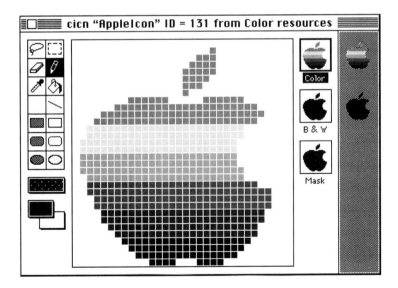

Figure 17-1. The 'cicn' editor is a prototypical fatpixels editor.

The fatpixels editors behave similarly to the black-and-white fatbits editors introduced in Chapter 5, and they use the same Transform menu. You click the swatch under the tool palette to see a tear-off pattern palette, just as in the black-and-white editors. But now you can change the colors of those patterns. Beneath the pattern swatch are two new swatches that show the current colors.

▶ ## Foreground and Background Colors

In the pair of color swatches, the swatch that's above and to the left, or on top, shows the foreground color. The partially covered swatch shows the background color. You set these colors independently. Click either swatch and ResEdit displays the pop-up color palette filled with the color collection chosen from the Colors menu. (More on that in a moment.) Like the pattern palette, you can tear off the color palette, but only from the foreground color swatch. Working with the foreground color is exactly like working with black bits in a black-and-white fatbits editor, and the background color acts just like white. For instance, clicking the pencil tool toggles pixels back and forth between the foreground and background colors.

Let's say your foreground color is orange (or dark gray) and your background color is yellow (or light gray). The first thing you might notice, especially if you've torn off the pattern palette, is that some patterns are now orange on yellow. (If you set your foreground and background colors to the same thing, you won't be able to see some patterns because you no longer have any contrast.) Most tools work only with the foreground color. But the pencil, eraser, and selection tools bring the background color into the picture. If you click the pencil once you place an orange pixel, but if you click it again in the same place, you remove the orange pixel and expose a yellow background pixel. The eraser removes all colors of pixels and uncovers the background color—effectively painting in the background color. Similarly, if you make a selection then move or delete it, you reveal the background color.

▶ ## The Eyedropper

The tool palette has an additional tool just below the eraser that's indispensable for manipulating color—the eyedropper. When you position it over a fatpixel and click, it "sucks up" a color from your resource and automatically sets that color in the foreground color swatch. Imagine trying to match a particular shade in a 256-color palette without the aid of the eyedropper!

Hint ▶	You can sometimes save yourself a trip to the tool and color palettes when you're working with the drawing tools. Simply press the Option key and the current tool (unless it's the eraser or one of the selection tools) transmogrifies into the eyedropper. While still pressing the Option key, use the eyedropper to click a pixel in your resource that's the color you want to switch to. When you release the Option key, the eyedropper changes back into the drawing tool that's now ready to draw in the new color.

Hint ▶	Here's another trick that can save you a lot of work—you can change every occurrence of one color to another color. Let's say you change your mind about a color you used in your resource. All the other colors are fine, but you're having second thoughts about chartreuse. You know that the paint bucket can change all the contiguous occurrences of a color, but because you used the chartreuse in a pattern, the paint bucket is no more useful than the pencil. Here's how to change every pixel of chartreuse to hot pink. Option-click a pixel of chartreuse to get the eyedropper to set that color in the color swatch. Now press the Command key as you click hot pink in the color palette. The color swatch momentarily shows both colors, but as soon as you release the mouse button, every pixel of chartreuse changes to hot pink.

▶ The Color Menu

All the color resource editors have a Color menu, shown in Figure 17-2. This menu allows you to control the color palette you see when you click the color swatches.

The first item, Apple Icon Colors, displays colors Apple recommends for desktop icons. This color collection, which is a subset of the standard 256 and contains close matches to most of the standard 16 colors, is stored in ResEdit. These are the colors used to design Apple's System 7 Finder icons.

The next item, Recent Colors, shows only the subset of colors used in the resource plus the ones you've selected while editing. As you select your favorite colors from one of the available color collections, ResEdit adds them to the color table that's part of the resource. Choosing Recent Colors tells ResEdit to display those colors. When you close the editor window after creating your color masterpiece, ResEdit deletes from the resource's color table any colors you didn't actually use. Thus, when you open an existing resource, the Recent Colors command displays only the actual colors used in the resource. (Black and white are always shown as recent colors even if you didn't use them. They're only saved in the resource if actually used.)

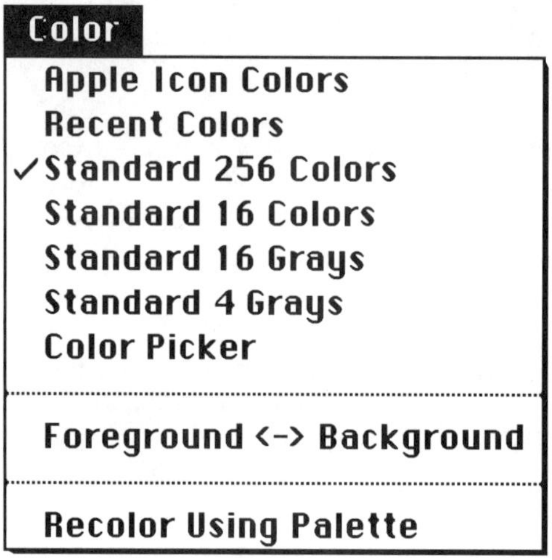

Color

Apple Icon Colors
Recent Colors
✓**Standard 256 Colors**
Standard 16 Colors
Standard 16 Grays
Standard 4 Grays
Color Picker

Foreground <-> Background

Recolor Using Palette

Figure 17-2. The Color menu helps you manipulate the colors you use in color resources.

The next four items on the Color menu allow you to choose standard color collections. Three come from ROM and one is stored in ResEdit. There's at least one collection for each of the three standard pixel depths, and they all include black and white. The standard four grays make up the two-bit collection, the standard 16 colors make up the four-bit collection, and the standard 256 make up the eight-bit collection. An important advantage of using these ROM standards is that every Mac II has these colors. The standard 16 grays are stored in ResEdit. Figure 17-3 gives you a rough, black-and-white idea of what these standard palettes look like.

The Standard 4 Colors

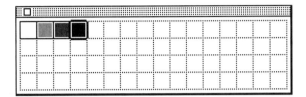

The Standard 16 Colors

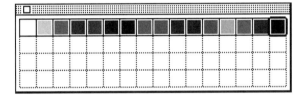

The Standard 16 Grays

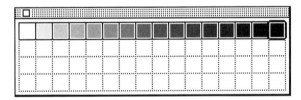

The Standard 256 Colors

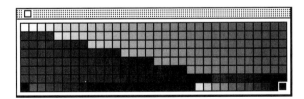

Figure 17-3. The Color menu offers four standard color palettes. Although these monochrome renderings can't do them justice, they give you an idea of the possibilities.

Hint ▶	Each time you add a color to a resource, the resource's color table gets six bytes larger. So, to keep your color resources compact, use the eyedropper or choose from the Recent Colors palette when you want to use the same color in two places. That way you can make sure you use the same colors, instead of ones that are similar.

Also, keep in mind that any time adding a color causes your resource to cross one of the "pixel-depth boundaries," it doubles in size. For example, the pixels in a 32-by-32-pixel icon occupy 128 bytes in black and white, 256 bytes in four colors, 512 bytes in 16 colors, and 1024 bytes—1 K—in 256 colors. Adding *one* color to a four-color icon doubles its size to 512 bytes (plus six more bytes for the additional color table entry). Similarly, a 17-color icon takes up as much room as if it contained 256 colors.

By the Way ▶	The standard 256 colors don't include the standard 16 colors, and only one of the standard four grays comes from one of these larger collections. That's right—they're non-overlapping sets! Fortunately, although exact color matches don't exist, the close approximations are good enough for most purposes.

The last item in this section of the menu, Color Picker, provides a way to add custom colors to a resource. When this item is selected, clicking one of the color swatches displays the Macintosh Color Picker instead of a color palette. However, you should generally stick with the standard colors because spending hours and hours to get your colors "just right" could be a waste of time. If you invest a lot of time chasing the perfect hue you should have a very good reason, and a good understanding of how color works on the Macintosh. The problem is that you can pick any color you want while you're creating your resource, but if that color isn't available later in the window where the resource is displayed, your Mac maps it to the closest available color. Fussing over subtle shadings could be a waste of time because unless the window the resource is going to be displayed in has an associated 'pltt' containing the custom colors, they may all end up mapped to another color anyway. ('pltt' resources are covered at the end of this chapter.) If you can stick with the standard 4, 16, or 256 colors, they should always be available, unless an application specifically requests a different collection of colors.

Foreground <-> Background simply swaps the colors in the foreground and background color swatches. The last command, Recolor Using Palette, lets you easily replace colors in your resource with those in the selected palette. If you choose the palette you want to use, then choose this item, all the colors in the resource get mapped to the closest match in the selected palette.

▶ Guidelines for Using Color

Apple's intent when adding color to the Desktop Interface is to add meaning, not just to jazz things up so they look spiffy. Of course, it's your Mac, and we're not saying you have to follow their advice. If you want your Mac to look like a video arcade game, that's your privilege. But Apple's Human Interface people put a lot of effort into thinking about how to use color effectively, so it wouldn't hurt to at least be aware of some of the principles involved. The principles may very well apply differently if you have your own Mac, and you're customizing resources just for yourself. Still, you might gain some insight into why color applications use color the way they do.

When handled properly, color can convey additional information, but if used carelessly, it can confuse and overwhelm. Generally, you should design your resource in black and white, making color supplementary. If you want to avoid a garish look, try to use as few colors as possible. A little bit of color goes a long way. Use light or subtle colors for large areas and reserve bright, distracting colors for small areas or accents. Keeping the outlines of color icons black can help prevent a fuzzy appearance and possible eyestrain.

Remember that colors often have associated effects and meanings. For instance, bright colors, such as reds and oranges are good at attracting attention, but reds also connote "warning" or "danger." This can be a tricky combination. For instance, if you color a "dangerous" menu item red, your eyes might be more attracted to it, and you might be more likely to select the item by mistake.

By the Way ▶	There are several general uses for color. You can use color to discriminate between areas on the screen, show functionally related items, show relationships among things, and identify crucial features. However, most people can effectively follow only four to seven color assignments on a screen at once, so there's probably not much point in getting carried away with complicated color relationship schemes.

For more information, see Apple's *Human Interface Guidelines: The Apple Desktop Interface* (Addison-Wesley, 1987).

▶ ## The 'clut' and 'pltt' Editors

The 'clut' editor and the 'pltt' editor look and act exactly the same. The only difference is that the 'pltt' editor provides a menu command that lets you assign usage information to the colors. As the 'clut' editor in Figure 17-4 illustrates, these editors can hold up to 256 colors. To select a color, simply click it. To select more than one color, click the first color, press the Shift key, and click the second color. All the colors in between also become selected, and you can cut, copy, or perform other operations on them. (The editors don't allow discontinuous color selections.) If you want to add colors to color collections having less than 256 colors, just choose Insert New Color from the Resource menu. This command adds one new color right in front of the currently selected color (or at the end if nothing is selected). The new color is always black, but you can change it just as you can any color.

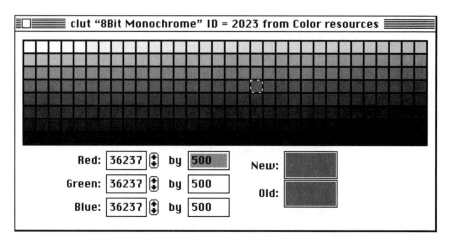

Figure 17-4. The 'clut' and 'pltt' editors, which are nearly identical, allow you to edit collections of 2 to 256 colors.

You can change an individual color by double-clicking, which causes the color picker to be displayed. You can also directly change the color values in the fields in the lower left corner of the editor, just as you would in the color picker. The small arrow control buttons increment or decrement the color values by the amounts you specify in the fields to the right.

The New box in the lower right corner of the editor shows you a larger swatch of the color you're experimenting with. The Old box shows you the original color. Clicking the old box restores the original color.

To fully appreciate what these editors can do with colors, you have to look at the menus.

▶ The Menus

The 'clut' and 'pltt' editors add three menus to the menu bar. The first two menus are shown in Figure 17-5. The bottom half of the 'clut' or 'pltt' menu lists four standard color models, and the model you choose determines your options on the Sort menu. It also changes the color value fields in the lower left corner of the editor window. (You're already familiar with two of the models. The color picker uses RGB and HSB.) The third menu, the Background menu, lets you choose the background against which the colors are displayed. Your choices are white, gray, or black.

The Blend command works on a selection of three or more colors, blending them into a smooth color gradient. Obviously, the more colors you blend, the smoother the gradient you get. The Complement command changes the selected color into its complement, which is the color directly across the color wheel.

A good way to create new color collections is to load the standard colors from ROM (so you're using colors that are generally available), then remove any colors you don't need or want. The Load Colors command and dialog help you with the first part of that process. The Load Colors dialog, shown in Figure 17-6, displays a list of all the color collections ResEdit can find in any file that's open. You can choose between 'clut's and 'pltt's by clicking the radio buttons at the top of the window. The selected color collection is displayed to give you a chance to look it over. When you click OK, the color collection you just selected completely replaces the colors in the editor.

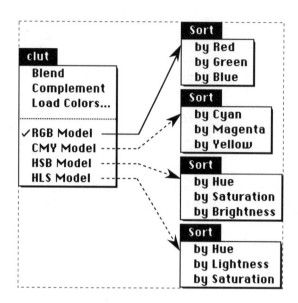

Figure 17-5. The 'clut' and 'pltt' editors give you a different Sort menu, depending on which color model you choose from the 'clut' (or 'pltt') menu.

By the Way ▶

If you compare a few 'pltt's and 'clut's in the Load Colors dialog, you might notice that the first two colors in 'pltt's are always white and black. That's just as it should be —something to remember when you're creating your own 'pltt's. (In fact, ResEdit doesn't let you change the first two colors.) Similarly, the first 16 entries in a 'pltt' should generally be the colors you want used on 4-bit systems. This way, the same 'pltt' can be used on 2-, 4-, and 8-bit systems. If you create a 'pltt' with 16 shades of yellow at the beginning, you'll get only those colors on a 16-color monitor—not a very useful collection. The palette ResEdit uses for all its windows provides a good example. The first two colors are black and white, the first four are grays, the first 16 are the standard 16, and the remaining colors come from the standard 256 color palette. (To see for yourself, open a copy of ResEdit and open the 'pltt' with ID 0, named "ResEdit Standard Colors.")

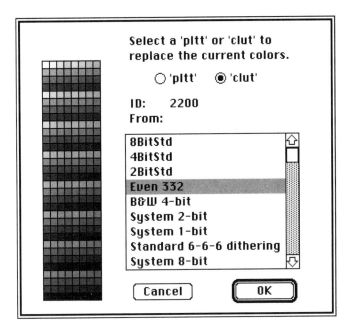

Figure 17-6. The Load Colors dialog lets you choose a color collection to replace the 'clut' or 'pltt' you're editing.

Hint ▶

If you have a color collection that you use frequently, you should add it to ResEdit's Preferences file so you can choose your own collection from the Color menu. Give your 'clut' a short, obvious name (with the Get Resource Info command) because that's how it will be listed in the Color menu.

As we've already mentioned, 'pltt's are associated with windows to provide color usage information to help the system deal with color conflicts. The 'pltt' editor's Usage command on the 'pltt' menu lets you determine usage parameters for selected colors, but setting color usage can be a pretty esoteric project. For more information about color usage, see the "Palette Manager" chapter of *Inside Macintosh*, Volume V.

Hint ▶	If you're creating a resource that has to look good in either 16 or 256 colors, create it using the Standard 16. You get better color matches mapping from 16 to 256 colors than you do the other way around.

▶ Changing the Finder's Colors

If you don't like the colors the Finder gives you on its Color menu, you can change them. For instance, you may have wondered why there are two blues but no purple. You can change either the light or dark blue to a medium blue, then change the remaining blue to purple. You can change all eight colors if you're so inclined. (If you need a refresher on how to edit the Finder, now would be a good time to flip back to Chapter 4.)

1. Use ResEdit to open a copy of your Finder. Open the 'clut' type. You should see one resource in the 'clut' picker; double-click it.
2. When the resource opens in the 'clut' editor, you should see the Finder's familiar eight colors. Change them into the eight colors you prefer.
3. Close the file and save it. Quit ResEdit.
4. Drag your Finder out of your System file onto your desktop, then rename your copy of Finder to "Finder."
5. Restart, and you should see your own colors in the Finder's Color menu.

▶ Summary

This chapter briefly describes how Macintosh IIs handle color. Your Mac can display only a limited number of colors at a time. How many colors it can show depends on the monitor, video card, and Control Panel settings. If an application asks the Mac for a color not available in the current color environment, the Mac maps the color to the nearest currently available color. Color collections are stored in two resource types: 'clut' (color look-up table) and 'pltt' (palette). Several standard 'clut's are stored in ROM, and the advantage of using these standard colors is that they're usually available. If you need to guarantee that certain custom colors are available to a window, you can associate it with a 'pltt' containing the necessary colors.

ResEdit's fatpixels editors work like their fatbits counterparts, except they can handle color. This chapter describes features common to all the fatpixels editors, such as the options on the Color menu, the foreground and background color swatches, and the eyedropper tool. Most users won't need to edit 'clut's or 'pltt's, but for programmers and people interested in changing the colors on the Finder's Color menu, the chapter concludes with a brief description of the 'clut' and 'pltt' editors.

18 ▶ Editing Color Icons

Although color has been available on the Mac for years now, people have been slow to take advantage of it for coloring icons, and in fact, many applications don't have any color icons. This lack is probably due, at least in part, to the fact that ResEdit didn't supply a way to create or edit color icons until version 2.0. But if you have a color monitor, you can use ResEdit to colorize icons to brighten up your working environment. (Remember, "color" includes gray tones.)

ResEdit has two color icon editors. One works on 'cicn' (Color ICoN) resources, the color equivalent of 'ICON' resources. The other, the icon family editor, handles System 7 icons, and we'll discuss it later in the chapter.

▶ 'cicn' Resources

Like 'ICON' resources, you can put 'cicn's in dialogs alerts and menus. Although 'cicn's can act as color stand-ins for 'ICON's, they differ in a few important ways.

- The size of a 'cicn' image is flexible. 'ICON' images are a defined size (32-by-32 bits), whereas 'cicn's can have almost any size. However, ResEdit only creates 'cicn's that vary from a lower limit

of 8-by-8 pixels to an upper limit of 64-by-64 pixels. They don't
have to be square, either.

- An 'ICON' resource always occupies the same amount of storage
  space. A 'cicn' resource can gobble a lot of space, depending on the
  size of the image and how many colors it uses. (Remember, in
  black and white, one pixel takes up one bit. But a color pixel can
  require two, four, or eight bits, depending on whether you have 4,
  16, or 256 colors.)

- A 'cicn' resource includes a mask and an optional black-and-white
  version of the icon; it's like a three-in-one package. An 'ICON'
  resource contains only one image.

Now that you have an idea what kind of creatures 'cicn's are, you're
ready to learn how to create and edit them.

▶ The 'cicn' Editor

With all the colors, tools, and patterns available, you can have a lot of
fun in the 'cicn' editor, even if you never come up with an icon you like.
Because so few applications have 'cicn's, you'll probably have to start
by creating the new resource type in your file. (From the type picker,
choose Create New Resource from the Resource menu. You have two
choices in the dialog that appears: You can scroll until you can double-
click 'cicn', or you can just type it.) ResEdit opens the 'cicn' picker,
(which, of course, is empty), and then the 'cicn' editor, which should
look something like Figure 18-1 (except empty, of course). By now, the
tool palette, pattern swatch, and color swatches probably look familiar
to you. (If not, you should review "Using the Fatbits Editors" in Chapter
5 and "Using the Fatpixels Editors" in Chapter 17.)

The right side of the window displays several actual-size views of the
icon. The three next to the editing panel are labeled "Color" (the color
version of the icon), "B&W" (the black-and-white version, if there is
one), and "Mask" (more on the mask in a moment). To switch between
views, simply click the one you want. A heavy box surrounds the
selected view, and its label is highlighted. The two views on the far right
show you the color and B&W icons combined with the mask and drawn
on one of several possible backgrounds.

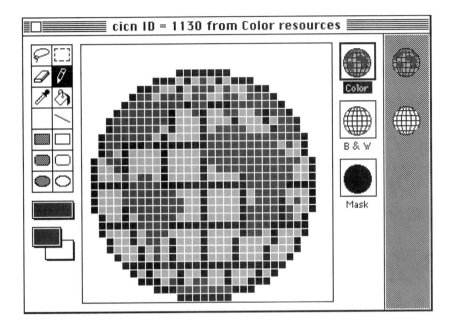

Figure 18-1. The 'cicn' editor is a full-featured editor.

If you want to include a black-and-white version of your icon, it's easiest to let ResEdit create it for you. Simply drag the Color view straight down onto the B&W view. Depending on the colors or grays you used in your color icon, you may want to touch up the B&W version, because some parts of the image may disappear. When you drag the Color icon onto the B&W one, your Macintosh has to map every color to either black or white. Light colors may map to white and disappear.

▶ Creating and Editing the Mask

As you may remember from the section on 'ICN#' resources in Chapter 7, a mask determines how an icon is drawn (and therefore how it looks) on various backgrounds. Although the general principle seems the same for color icons, the implementation is not. The mask for a 'cicn' works differently. (And you thought you could skip this section.) An 'ICN#' resource without a mask would be crippled, but you would be able to see the icon at least some of the time. A 'cicn' resource without a mask would give you an invisible icon, because you can't see any given pixel in a color icon unless there's a corresponding black pixel in the mask.

The same general rule for creating a mask applies to both types of icon resources: The safest mask is a filled-in version of the icon.

When ResEdit creates a 'cicn' resource, it also creates a mask that completely fills the available area. You can keep that one if you want to, and for many icons that's the best mask. Sometimes, however, you'll need a more form-fitting mask so your icon can blend into the background. Let's say your icon consists of an exquisite arrangement of attractively patterned ovals, circles, and rounded rectangles. When such an icon is displayed on a non-white background, it will appear in a square of white if you use the original square mask. Wherever there's a black pixel in the mask, the background is erased. Anywhere no colored pixels are drawn in, the white shows through. That's fine if that's the effect you want; if not, you need a different mask. You can easily have ResEdit make a more form-fitting mask. Simply click the Color icon view, then drag it down onto the Mask view. *Voila*—an instant, shapely mask!

Hint ▶	Creating the mask from the color icon is usually your best bet. You can also use the B&W icon to create the mask, but depending on the colors you've used, you may get a different mask. It all boils down to color mapping. When you drag the Color icon to the B&W icon, every color is mapped to either black or white. Some light colors may map to white, and those parts of the icon disappear. If you then use the B&W icon to make the mask, you won't see those light colors in the color icon either, because the mask won't allow for them. But when you drag the Color icon to the Mask, any non-white pixel is treated as black before the mask is filled in, so you get a better mask.
	If you create or edit a mask that doesn't work the way you want it to, and you want to go back to the filled-in square, do it the easy way. Click the Mask view and make sure you see solid black in the pattern swatch. Then use the filled rectangle tool or paint bucket to make a black rectangle the same size as the icon.

▶ The 'cicn' Menu

The 'cicn' editor has a resource-specific menu with commands that help you work with color icons and the 'cicn' editor. The first four items let you choose the background upon which the editor displays the icon. You can choose white, gray, black, or your current desktop pattern. The next command, Icon Size, displays the dialog shown in Figure 18-2. Res-

Edit defaults to a 32-by-32 (pixel) size when it creates 'cicn's, but as we mentioned previously, they can range from 8-by-8 to 64-by-64. Here is where you change the size. ResEdit assumes you would usually choose to scale an icon when changing its size, so the Scale to New Size check box is automatically checked. When scaling, ResEdit adds or removes pixels wherever necessary to stretch or shrink the icon image proportionally so it looks roughly the same in its new dimensions. If you shrink an icon without scaling, ResEdit simply truncates pixels from the bottom and right side. Similarly, if you enlarge an icon without scaling, ResEdit simply tacks on extra pixels, leaving them white. ResEdit also shrinks or enlarges the actual-size view and adjusts the editing area (in fact, the entire editor window) accordingly. Figuring out how you want to scale your icons may take some practice, so remember you can undo or revert any unsettling changes.

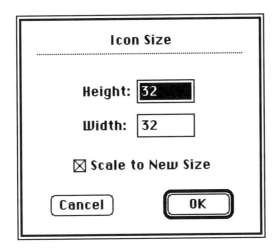

Figure 18-2. This dialog, which appears when you choose Icon Size from the 'cicn' menu, lets you change the icon's size.

Deleting the black-and-white version of the icon from your 'cicn' resource saves space, so the Delete B&W Icon command lets you do just that. For example, if the application displaying the icon requires color, a black-and-white icon would never be used. This item only becomes available when the B&W icon is selected. If one doesn't exist, ResEdit fills the actual-size view of the black-and-white icon with a gray pattern so you'll know that it's non-existent, not merely empty.

Now that you know how to create and edit 'cicn's, you're ready to start using them. You can substitute 'cicn's in most places where applications use 'ICON's.

▶ Customizing Dialog and Alert Boxes with Color Icons

You can turn many of the same icons you altered in the 'ICON' section of Chapter 7 into color icons. Figure 18-3 shows one possibility. Your Macintosh automatically substitutes color icons if they're present, so you can have a red Stop alert icon, or a light gray or yellow Caution alert icon. All you have to do is create a 'cicn' with the same resource ID as the corresponding 'ICON', and you'll have colored icons in your dialogs and alerts.

Figure 18-3. With a few shades of gray, it becomes obvious that the talking head in alerts is tall, dark, but still inarticulate.

1. Use ResEdit to open a copy of your System file.
2. Open the 'ICON' type, find the icon you want to colorize, and jot down its ID number. (The talking head's ID is 1.)
3. Copy the icon. You can't copy from the picker. You have to open the icon and copy its bits from within the editor. (Double-clicking the selection rectangle automatically selects the whole image.)
4. Open the 'cicn' type picker. (If there aren't any 'cicn's in the file, use the Create Resource Type command on the Resource menu. ResEdit creates a new 'cicn' and opens it in the editor for you, so you can skip to Step 6.)
5. Create a new 'cicn' with the Create Resource command.
6. Paste to get a black-and-white start for your color icon.

7. Colorize, modify, and otherwise edit your icon. (If you click the paint bucket in the black pixels, you can change all contiguous pixels to the selected color.)

8. Choose Get Resource Info from the Resource menu, and set the resource ID to the number you noted in Step 2.

9. Close and save the file.

10. Reinstall your System file.

The next time a dialog or alert appears that uses your icon, it should appear in color.

Hint ▶	You can't necessarily stuff any size icon into dialogs and alert boxes, so you may be better off staying with a 32-by-32 'cicn'. Your Mac scales inappropriately sized icons, and the result might not be just what you'd like. If you want to use odd-sized icons, you can change the size of the icon item in the associated dialog item list ('DITL') resource. See Chapter 10 for more details about resizing dialog items so you can work around potential size constraints. Remember, though, that alerts don't have icon items—the icons are inserted automatically. So for alerts, you're stuck with a 32-by-32 icon size.

▶ Adding a Color Icon to a Menu

A 'cicn' can be substituted for an 'ICON' in a menu, too. In fact, you can't just add a 'cicn'; you have to add an 'ICON' first, then substitute a 'cicn' that has the same ID number. See Chapter 8 to find out how to add an 'ICON' to a menu. If you've already created the 'cicn' you want to use, you can just copy the bits from the B&W version and use them to create a new 'ICON'. Remember, icons in menus must have IDs between 257 and 511, so give both your 'ICON' and your 'cicn' the same appropriate ID.

You can substitute 'cicn's for 'SICN's, too, You still need to add a 32-by-32 pixel 'cicn', which your Mac shrinks to 16 by 16.

By the Way ▶	The System file has two 'cicn's you might want to play with. One is the little striped apple you see above your Apple menu, and the other is the abstract Macintosh you see when your Mac starts up.

▶ System 7 Icons

Part of the System 7 revolution is that it finally brings color icons to the Desktop. To allow for standard screen depths, as well as large and small icon sizes, five new icon resource types were created:

- 'icl8'—(ICon Large, 8-bit) A 32-by-32-pixel, 256-color icon
- 'ics8'—(ICon Small, 8-bit) A 16-by-16-pixel, 256-color icon
- 'icl4'—(ICon Large, 4-bit) A 32-by-32-pixel, 16-color icon
- 'ics4'—(ICon Small, 4-bit) A 16-by-16-pixel, 16-color icon
- 'ics#'—(ICon Small, list) A 16-by-16-bit, black-and-white icon, with mask

Along with the familiar 'ICN#' resource type, these five new resource types make up a Finder icon family. The 'ics#' resource is a small version of the black-and-white Finder icon ('ICN#') resource you learned about in Chapter 7. When an 'ics#' is present, the Finder doesn't have to shrink the 'ICN#' for a black-and-white small icon view, or for use as the Multi-Finder icon. (Shrunken 'ICN#'s often look clogged or clumpy or both.) The System 7 Finder chooses one of these six icons based on the number of colors available on the screen and the size of icon it needs. You link all six types of related icons by giving them the same resource ID, and you can edit them all in the icon family editor.

▶ The Icon Family Editor

The icon family editor, shown in Figure 18-4, lets you edit six related resources all in the same place, essentially at the same time. The tool palette, patterns swatch, and color swatches on the left side of the window and the fatpixels editing area behave exactly the same as in the 'cicn' editor. To the right of the fatpixel editing area you see the actual-size views of the related icon resource types and their masks. (All icons of the same size share the same mask.) Simply click the icon type you want to edit. Just as in the 'cicn' editor, the selected view has a dark outline around it, and the label underneath is highlighted.

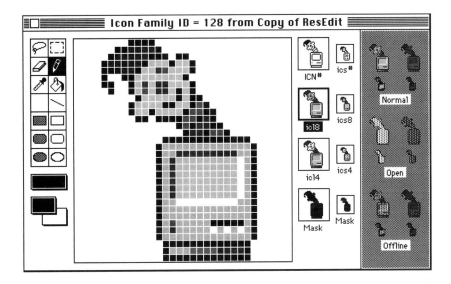

Figure 18-4. The icon family editor lets you edit up to six related resources at the same time.

On the right side of the window you see the icon you're editing as the Finder would draw it in several different states. As the labels indicate, the top views show the icon in its normal state (closed), the middle views show it open, and the bottom views show it offline (ejected but still mounted). In each case, the left side shows the icon unselected and the right side shows it selected. For large icons, you see the shrunken version of it underneath—even if the corresponding small resource type exists, you still see the reduced version of the selected large icon. (For small icons you see only the small icon.) You can change the background on which the samples are drawn with the aid of the Icons menu.

▶ The Icons Menu

The Icons menu, shown in Figure 18-5, lets you do two things. You can change the background color in the right side of the editor window between the four choices shown. The fourth choice, Desktop Background, uses your current desktop pattern or color. The last item, Delete <type> Resource, lets you delete the currently selected icon type, saving you a trip to the corresponding picker. (Remember, selecting and deleting the pixels empties the resource, but doesn't get rid of it. You have to use this command or go to the picker to delete.)

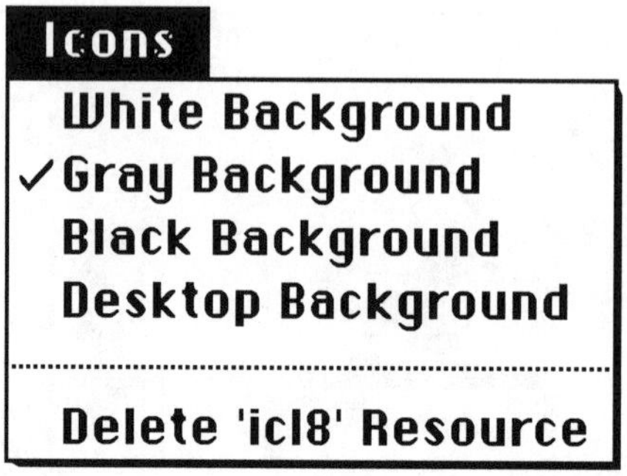

```
┌─────────────────────────────────┐
│ Icons                           │
├─────────────────────────────────┤
│  White Background               │
│ ✓Gray Background                │
│  Black Background               │
│  Desktop Background             │
│ ............................... │
│  Delete 'icl8' Resource         │
└─────────────────────────────────┘
```

Figure 18-5. The Icons menu lets you change sample backgrounds and delete unwanted icon family members.

▶ The Color Menu

We discussed the Color menu in the previous chapter, but we mention it again because the icon family editor uses a slightly different version. Your choice of color palettes is restricted to either a collection of standard colors or the Apple Icon Colors, the colors Apple recommends for Finder icons. You can't fool around with the colors the Finder uses for these icons. The standard collection is the set of ROM colors that corresponds to the selected icon's pixel depth. So you get the standard 256 for 'icl8' and 'ics8', and you get the standard 16 for 'icl4' and 'ics4'.

By the Way ▶

Unlike 'cicn's, System 7 icons occupy a fixed amount of memory because they have fixed sizes and pixel depths. Even if you use only four colors in an 'icl8', it takes up as much space as if you used the full rainbow of 256 colors.

▶ Creating New Icon Family Members

Creating new icon family members is as easy as creating a mask. Simply drag one of the existing icons onto the type you want to create, and ResEdit automatically scales the icon and maps its colors to the nearest colors in the appropriate pixel depth. Because of the level of detail you'll usually get better results if you make a small icon from a large one, rather than the other way around. Creating icons this way gives you the basic shape and a good start on the colors, but most likely you'll need or want to fine tune any icons you create by dragging. If you create black-

and-white icons from color ones they can sometimes look odd or ghostly, so you pretty much have to touch them up. You're better off going the other direction, creating System 7 icons from existing 'ICN#' resources. We talk about that next.

By the Way ▶ | Apple recommends creating the black-and-white icon first, the 8-bit icons next, and then the 4-bit icons. This is the top-to-bottom order shown in the editor. To aid creation of 4-bit icons from 8-bit icons, the color pattern palette contains a few dithered patterns you can use to approximate commonly used colors in the Apple Icon Colors palette (for example, fleshtone). Of course, you can create your own dithered colors with patterns that use the foreground and background colors. For example, if the foreground is red and the background is blue, an every-other-pixel pattern looks purple.

▶ Updating an Application's Icons to System 7

If you use System 7 but your applications don't have the icons you want or need, you might want to create some, starting with the 'ICN#' resources already present in the file. Remember, besides the application icon, there might be several document icons, so you need to repeat these steps for each kind of icon.

1. Use ResEdit to open a copy of the application, then open the 'ICN#' picker.
2. When the 'ICN#' picker opens, you'll see your application's black-and-white Finder icons. Double-click the one you want to update.
3. The 'ICN#' opens in the icon family editor, and you're ready to create other family members. Drag it to the 'icl4' or 'icl8' spot to give yourself a black-and-white start for your new icon. Now you can color and draw and fiddle to your heart's content.
5. If you think you're satisfied, go to the Icons menu and try out different backgrounds with your icon. You may want to make a new, more form-fitting mask. (See "Creating and Editing the Mask" in the 'cicn' section earlier in this chapter if you need more information.)
6. When you're happy with your work, you can use this new icon to create other new icon types. You might want to have an 'ics4' to go

with an 'icl4'. Simply drag the 'icl4' to the 'ics4' spot, then touch up the new icon to suit yourself.

7. After you're finished, quit ResEdit, saving your changes.

The Finder won't use your new icons unless it knows they exist, so you've got to update your Desktop. (See Chapter 7 for a refresher on how the Finder keeps track of icons.) Under System 7, the Finder stores icons in a Desktop database, which doesn't use resources—it's in the *data* fork of the file—so ResEdit can't get to them. That means there's only one way to rebuild your Desktop.

1. You don't want to confuse the Finder with two copies of the same file, so the easiest way to avoid that is to move the original version of the file to a floppy.
2. Restart your Mac while pressing the Command and Option keys. This makes the Finder automatically rebuild its desktop database—which may take a while if you have a hard disk storing lots of files.
3. When the Finder is done, you should see your new System 7 icons.

▶ Summary

The Macintosh uses several types of color icons, and this chapter describes them and the two editors that work on them. The 'cicn' (Color ICoN) resource type is the color equivalent of the 'ICON' resource type; it's used in dialogs, alert boxes, and menus. Unlike 'ICON's, 'cicn's can vary in the amount of space they occupy because they can vary in number of pixels, and in number of colors, or pixel depth. More and more applications are taking advantage of the 'cicn' resource type, but you don't have to wait—you can create your own. In dialogs, alerts, and menus your Mac automatically substitutes a 'cicn' for an 'ICON' having the same resource ID.

Five new icon resource types came along with System 7, and together with the 'ICN#' type, they make up icon families. Icons in a family are linked by their common resource ID, and you can edit all six types in the icon family editor.

19 ▶ Adding Color to the User Interface

Color icons may be what people think of first when they contemplate adding color to their work environment, but the Macintosh offers several other opportunities to brighten up the user interface. Why not add color to menus to help you find your way around? If you frequently forget Command keys, you can make them a bright color so you can quickly find them to remind yourself. Windows, dialogs, and alerts might also benefit from a touch of color. You decide. If you like color desktop patterns, you may find the Control Panel's limitations frustrating. You can create your own permanent repertoire of color desktop patterns once you know how to use ResEdit's color pattern editors.

▶ Color Patterns

The two kinds of color pattern resources ('ppat' and 'ppt#') are analogous to the two black-and-white pattern resources ('PAT ' and 'PAT#') introduced in Chapter 5. (If you need a refresher, now would be a good time to flip back.) The editors, shown in Figure 19-1, are quite similar, too. In this section we focus mostly on the color aspects of the 'ppt#' editor, because if you understand it, you can understand the 'ppat' editor. You should already be familiar with the features shared with the black-and-white editors. (For instance, just as in the 'PAT#' editor, when the scrollable list part of the 'ppt#' editor is active, you can drag individual patterns to move them in the list, and the Edit menu commands work on selections of one or more patterns.)

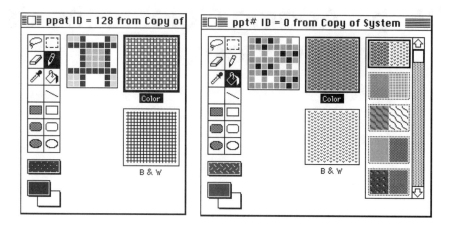

Figure 19-1. The color pattern editors: 'ppat' (left) and 'ppt#' (right).

Color patterns differ from their black-and-white counterparts in two ways, so the color editors have to support these differences. First, color patterns must include some sort of black-and-white version. They're really two-in-one resources. Second, whereas black-and-white patterns are defined as 8-by-8 bits, color patterns can vary in size (by powers of two), and they don't have to be square. However, ResEdit's pattern editors cannot work on patterns smaller than 8-by-8 nor larger than 64-by-64.

Hint ▶

Pressing the Option key when you create a color pattern (from the 'ppat' picker or the 'ppt#' editor) creates a *relative pattern.* Think of relative patterns, like the ones in ResEdit's pattern palette, as black-and-white patterns that can change color with the choice of foreground and background colors. The black pixels take on the foreground color, and the white pixels become the background color. Keep this in mind if you want to add patterns to ResEdit's pattern palette.

The black-and-white part of a color pattern exists even if you never click any bits in it; it's just all white. It doesn't have to correspond in any way to the color pattern, either. If you look at Figure 19-1 again, you notice that the patterns in the scrollable list box are split in half. The left half shows the color version, and the right half shows the black-and-white version. The bottom two patterns in the scrollable list have just the standard gray desktop pattern for their black-and-white half. The top patterns have matching black-and-white versions. To create a matching black-and-white pattern, click the sample of the pattern labeled "Color" and drag it straight down into the box labeled "B&W." Any time you want to touch up the B&W pattern (some light colors or grays may drop out when you drag to create the B&W version), simply click it and it appears in the fatpixels editing panel.

If an 8-by-8 color pattern feels cramped, you can enlarge it. (The black-and-white version must remain 8-by-8, however.) To adjust a pattern's size, you have to go to the editor's pattern menu. (The 'ppat' and 'ppt#' menus are essentially the same.)

▶ The 'ppat' and 'ppt#' Menus

The pattern editors' menus have only two items, and the first is the Pattern Size command, which displays the dialog shown in Figure 19-2. The dialog shows the possible sizes for a pattern; simply click your choice. ResEdit either repeats the pattern to make it larger or truncates it (from the bottom and/or right) to make it smaller. The pattern is not scaled.

| Hint ▶ |

If you want to scale up a pattern (perhaps to add detail), it's easy. Double-click the selection rectangle to select all the pixels in the editing panel, then copy. Next, change the size in the pattern Size dialog. Select all, just as before, and paste. The pattern is automatically scaled to the new size.

If you want to see your new pattern fill a larger expanse, choose the second and last item on the pattern editors' menus, Try Pattern. Just as in the black-and-white pattern editors, this command temporarily spreads your pattern over the entire desktop, and updates it as you make changes.

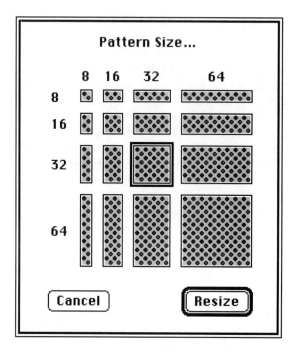

Figure 19-2. The Pattern Size dialog lets you adjust the dimensions of a pattern.

▶ Customizing ResEdit's Pattern Palette

You might want to customize ResEdit's pattern palette for a variety of reasons. You can remove patterns you never use, add custom patterns you frequently use, or just change the ones already present. (If you increase the number of patterns, the tear-off palette window grows to accommodate them.) Before we list the steps, here are a few things to keep in mind. For consistency, your black-and-white patterns ('PAT#') should match your color ones ('ppt#'). Also, within your color patterns the black-and white version of the pattern should match the color version. (Remember, you can press the Option key if you want to create a relative pattern.)

1. Use ResEdit to open ResEdit. (You're just going to copy a resource, so you don't need to work on a copy of the application.)

2. Open the 'ppt#' resource type, then copy the pattern list containing all the familiar pattern palette patterns. (The first several patterns are relative patterns, so they appear black-and-white.)

3. Close ResEdit, then open the ResEdit Preferences file (it's in your System Folder). Paste the 'ppt#' resource into the type picker.

4. Open the 'ppt#' resource you just pasted. Now you can add, subtract, and modify patterns as you please.

5. When you're through, close the Preferences file. Now ResEdit will use your custom patterns in its pattern palette.

▶ Adding Color Desktop Patterns to the Control Panel

You can create snazzy new desktop patterns in the Control Panel, but you can't switch between them. As soon as you switch to a new pattern, your old original is lost, just as in the black-and-white case mentioned in Chapter 5. The problem is somewhat more acute in the color case, however, because the Control Panel includes so few color patterns— even though color patterns give you a zillion more options. The bad news is that the Control Panel can't accommodate all the possibilities the color pattern resources offer. It can only handle 8-by-8 patterns in no more than eight colors. To protect you from the frustrating results of giving the Control Panel larger patterns having the wrong number of colors, ResEdit scans 'ppt#' resources when you open them. If all the patterns are 8-by-8 with eight colors, ResEdit makes sure any patterns you add follow suit.

1. Open a copy of your System file with ResEdit, and open the 'ppt#' resource type.

2. Double-click anywhere on the patterns list (the bar of patterns) in the 'ppt#' picker to open the 'ppt#' editor.

3. Scroll to the end of the pattern list, and choose Insert New Pattern from the Resource menu.

4. Now you're ready to create a new pattern by clicking fatpixels, or touching up a pattern copied from somewhere else. Don't use more than eight colors, and keep the pattern 8-by-8 pixels. Remember that dragging a selection can create new patterns and visual effects.

5. Once you're satisfied with your results, save the file, quit ResEdit, and reinstall the copy of your System file.

▶ Color Pointers

Another resource type added when the Mac II was introduced is the 'crsr' resource used to store color pointers (or cursors). Since there was no editor available to create these resources until ResEdit 2.1 was released, few applications use color pointers. Unfortunately, it's not possible to simply substitute a color pointer for a black-and-white pointer as you can with color icons. For these reasons, you won't find many color pointers to customize, and we can't pass on any fun tips.

The color pointer editor shown in Figure 19-3 should seem familiar to you. It works almost the same as the black-and-white 'CURS' editor described in Chapter 6. The only additions are the foreground and background color swatches and the eyedropper tool. The color aspects of this editor work just as they do in other fatpixels editors.

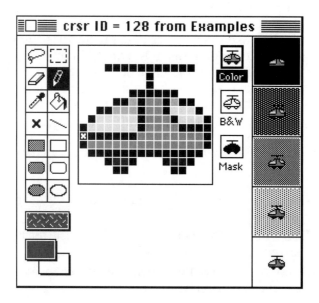

Figure 19-3. The 'crsr' editor lets you edit color pointers.

▶ Customizing Menus with Color

ResEdit gives you a variety of ways to add color to menus, which can make them more effective and easier to use. Of course, if you take advantage of *every* option on any one menu, you risk creating something jarringly garish. To avoid gaudy menus, try to have a plan or design in mind. Try not to splash everything with color just because you can. This section assumes you're familiar with the 'MENU' editor, which we describe in Chapter 8. Here we discuss only the editor's color fields.

When the 'MENU' editor opens, the title is automatically selected, and you see the first three color options, two of which apply to the entire menu. The first field allows you to set the color for that menu's title. The second field lets you set the default color for all the menu item text. The last field lets you set the menu's background color. In each case, simply press the mouse button with the pointer in the field of your choice and a standard palette pops down. (You get the standard palette that corresponds to your screen depth.) Release the mouse button to select the color of your choice. Figure 19-4 shows this palette displayed for the last field. As you make your selections, the 'MENU' editor applies the colors appropriately in the editor window and the test menu so you can see how the menu will look.

Once you select one of the menu's items, you see the next three color options. The first field lets you set the color for the selected item's text, thus overriding the default color. The next field lets you set the color for the Command key, which doesn't have to match the item text. The last field lets you set the color for any marks (such as checkmarks or diamonds) a menu item might have.

The first time you click one of the color fields, ResEdit alerts you that it's about to create an 'mctb' (Menu Color TaBle). That's where the colors you choose for your menu are stored, and when you edit your menu's colors, you're editing the 'mctb'. (A 'MENU' and its 'mctb' have the same resource ID. If you try to open an 'mctb', ResEdit opens the 'MENU' editor and the 'MENU' resource having the same ID.) If you copy or delete the 'MENU' resource, remember that you have to do the same for the associated 'mctb'. If you'd like all the menus in an application to have the same overall appearance, you don't have to set the colors for each one, which clutters up the file with duplicate 'mctb's. You can make one default 'mctb' do the job for all the menus in the file. We talk about that next.

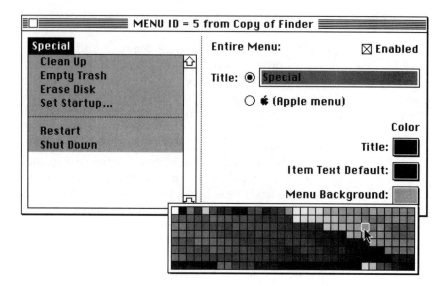

Figure 19-4. To pick a color for any of the fields, simply click the field and drag the mouse pointer onto the pop-up color palette that appears.

▶ Giving an Application's Menus a Uniform Color Scheme

You can set the default colors for the title, background, and item text for one menu in an application, then make those color selections apply to every other menu in the file. (You can't set default Command Key or Mask colors, however. They use the item text color unless you specify colors for them on individual menus.)

1. Use ResEdit to open a copy of the file. Open the 'MENU' type, choose a menu to color, and double-click it. (It doesn't matter which menu you pick.)

2. When the menu opens in the 'MENU' editor, the title is selected and the color fields apply to the whole menu—that's just what you want. Make your color selections for the title, menu background, and default item text.

3. Close the 'MENU' editor and 'MENU' picker and go back to the type picker. Double-click the 'mctb' type. In the 'mctb' picker, you should see an 'mctb' with the same ID and name as the 'MENU' resource you just edited. (ResEdit uses the menu's title to give the

'mctb' a name.) Click it, then choose Get Resource Info from the Resource menu. In the dialog that appears, change the ID to 0. Because the name is no longer accurate, you should change that, too. "Default" might be a good name. Close the Resource Info window.

4. Open the 'mctb'. You should see a template that looks something like the one in Figure 19-5. (When the resource ID of an 'mctb' doesn't match the ID of a 'MENU' resource in the file, it's opened in a template. If you need information about using templates, see Chapter 14.) Change the first two fields (Menu ID and Item No.) to 0.

5. Now you have to swap the second and fourth set of RGB values, which are expressed in hexadecimal. Copy the value in Red 2 to Red 4, and vice versa. (You may need to jot down some notes.) Do the same for Green 2 and Green 4, and Blue 2 and Blue 4. The example in the figure shows values for grays, so the RGB values in each set are the same. Yours may be different. (Hint: $0000 is black and $FFFF is white.)

6. Close all the windows, save the file, and quit ResEdit. When you start up your application, all the menus should have the same colors.

By the Way ▶	You may be wondering why you had to swap values in the 'mctb'. It's because you created the 'mctb' for one situation (for use with a single menu), but you're using it in a different situation (for use with many menus). Your Mac looks at 'mctb's differently in these two situations—the second and fourth sets of RGB values are swapped— so you have to put your color values where the Mac expects to see them. (Otherwise, the color you chose for your menu background shows up in your menu bar!)

Hint ▶	If you want your menu color scheme to apply system-wide, instead of just application-wide, copy the 'mctb' you just modified into your System file, leaving the ID set to 0. After you restart, most applications will use your menu color scheme.

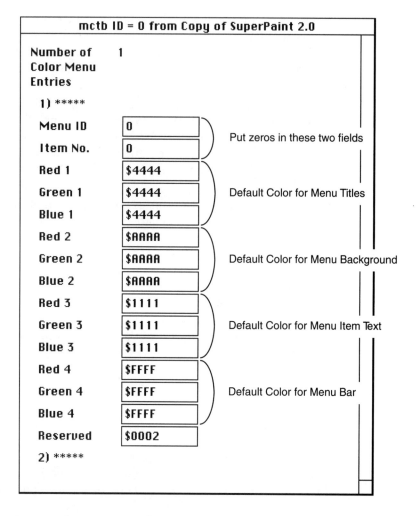

Figure 19-5. An 'mctb' template.

▶ Colorizing Windows, Dialogs, and Alerts

If you read Chapter 10, you probably remember that window ('WIND'), dialog ('DLOG'), and alert ('ALRT') resources are closely related. (If you haven't read Chapter 10, now might be a good time to do so. This section assumes you're already familiar with these editors, which are described in that chapter.) So it probably comes as no surprise that adding color works the same way for these three resources.

You can add color to two parts of alerts, and five parts of windows and dialogs. The first step is to click the Custom radio button beside the Color: label in the upper right corner of these editors, which causes the five color fields shown in Figure 19-6 to appear. Clicking the color fields causes a standard color palette to appear, just as in the 'MENU' editor discussed previously. As you make your selections, the editors apply the colors appropriately to the sample resource in the MiniScreen so you can see what they'll look like.

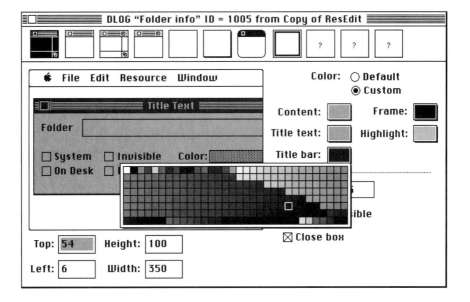

Figure 19-6. You can choose different colors for five areas of windows and dialogs, and two areas of alerts.

In the Content field, you set the background color for the area defined by the resource's rectangle. You can make title text appear in a vibrant hue by setting the Title text field. Of course, dialogs and windows don't always have title text, and alerts never do. The Title bar field lets you set the background color for the title bar. In the Frame field, you can choose a color for the frame, the borderline that runs around the content area and title bar. Finally, the Highlight field lets you set the color of the horizontal lines in the title bar. Because alerts have no title bars, you can colorize only their content areas and their frames.

The first time you click one of the color fields, ResEdit alerts you that it's about to create an associated color table resource. (The resource types are 'actb', 'dctb', or 'wctb' for alert, dialog or window color table, respectively.) That's where the colors you choose are stored; for example, when you edit an alert's colors, you're editing the 'actb'. If you copy or delete one of these resources, remember that you have to do the same for the associated color table resource.

By the Way ▶

The Mac doesn't provide you with an easy way to make all the dialogs or alerts in an application have the same color scheme. It's possible to create a default 'wctb' that contains a set of colors you'd like to see, and the Mac can refer to this color table resource for *all* windows—which means document windows as well as dialogs and alerts. Unfortunately, the Mac can't faithfully apply all those "default" colors unless each dialog and alert has its own associated color table resource that lets the Mac know it's supposed to use color. (The frame and title bar text, highlight, and background colors come through OK, but the content, or background, color gets overridden.)

If you're an experienced ResEdit user and want to give it a try, here's a brief set of instructions. Your results may vary greatly with the application you try it on, so be sure to work on a copy. Create a 'WIND' resource; choose your default color scheme in the 'WIND' editor; delete the 'WIND'; and change the resource ID of the 'wctb' to 0. Now note the resource ID of each dialog or alert in which you'd like to see this color scheme. From the type picker, create an 'actb' or 'dctb' (this automatically opens the 'ALRT' or 'DLOG' editor, which you can just close), and make its resource ID match that of the dialog or alert. (You don't have to change anything in the color table template—in fact doing so would override the 'wctb'.)

Just for the record, if you really, really like the colors you chose when you made your 'wctb', you can make them apply system-wide, rather than just application-wide, by copying the 'wctb' you created to your System file. Leave the ID set to 0. Your System file already contains a 'wctb' with ID 0, so you might want to renumber it first, rather than override it. That way you can easily switch back to black and white just by switching resource IDs. Remember, you probably won't see your background color because you can't possibly create color look-up tables for every dialog and alert.

As you sit back and gaze at your colorful dialog or alert, you may think, "Wait. The text inside remains boring old black." Yup. Remember, the items inside dialogs and alerts are stored in dialog item lists, or 'DITL' resources. Unfortunately, the 'DITL' editor in ResEdit 2.1 can't help you with colorizing dialog items (although a future version may).

By the Way ▶	A freeware Control Panel device called Kolor also lets you set System-wide menu and window colors. It uses the Macintosh color picker instead of a standard color collection from ROM, so you may pick colors you can't have (but they'll be mapped to colors that are close). Kolor offers an advantage over ResEdit, however, because it lets you add color to controls such as buttons, check boxes, and scroll bars.

▶ Summary

You can add color to your Macintosh work environment in several ways. This chapter begins by describing color pattern resources and their editors. The color pattern resource types ('ppat' and 'ppt#') are analogous to the black-and-white pattern resource types ('PAT ' and 'PAT#'), but you can make color patterns in sizes other than 8-by-8. You can add color desktop patterns to the Control Panel by editing the System file's 'ppt#' resource. Menus can also appear in color. The title, background, item text, and Command keys can all appear in different colors. You can choose default colors for a whole menu, or color items individually. You can also make all the menus in an application use the same set of colors by making a few simple modifications to an 'mctb' (Menu Color TaBle) resource. Finally, you can add color to windows, dialogs, and alerts by altering their frame and content colors. For windows and dialogs, you can also color three aspects of the title bar: the title text, the background color, and the highlight or horizontal lines.

PART FIVE

▶ Programming with ResEdit

20 ▶ Creating Windows, Dialogs, and Alerts

When you're prototyping or implementing an application, one of your primary uses for ResEdit will be to lay out the windows, dialogs, and alerts that you'll use. Although not every application uses resources to store its window information, it's hard to imagine how an application could get by without dialog and alert resources. Dialogs and alerts are especially important because they provide the means for you to communicate with your users. If you need to inform them of a problem, you use an alert. If you need some information from them, only a dialog makes sense. Since dialogs and alerts are so crucial to an application, it's important to make them easy to use and understand. ResEdit provides the tools you need to lay out your windows, dialogs, and alerts and see what they'll look like on different size screens.

Windows, dialogs, and alerts are represented by eight resources and four editors, as shown in Table 20-1. In this chapter we assume you have a basic understanding of how the four editors ('WIND', 'DLOG', 'ALRT', and 'DITL') work. If you need a refresher, refer to Chapter 10 for information about the editors and Chapter 19 for information about using them with color.

Table 20-1. Window, Dialog, and Alert Resource Types.

Resource type	Editor	Description
'WIND'	'WIND'	Window resource
'wctb'	'WIND'	Window color table for 'WIND' resource
'DLOG'	'DLOG'	Dialog resource
'dctb'	'DLOG'	Dialog color table for 'DLOG' resource
'ALRT'	'ALRT'	Alert resource
'actb'	'ALRT'	Alert color table for 'ALRT' resource
'DITL'	'DITL'	Dialog item list for 'DLOG's and 'ALRT's
'ictb'	None	Item color table used for 'DITL' resource

Since 'WIND' resources are very similar to 'DLOG' resources, we won't discuss the 'WIND' editor in this chapter. If you want to create a 'WIND', just look at the discussion of the 'DLOG' editor and ignore the parts about the associated 'DITL' resource.

▶ The Dialog Editor

The dialog editor lets you create and edit 'DLOG' and 'dctb' resources. Its basic use was described in Chapter 10 so we focus here on the parts of interest only to someone writing an application. Figure 20-1 shows a typical 'DLOG' editor window.

In the lower right side of the window shown in the figure, you'll notice two check boxes labeled Initially visible and Close box. These two check boxes correspond to the *visible* and *goAwayFlag* boolean fields in the *DialogTemplate* data structure. If the Initially visible check box isn't checked, the dialog won't be drawn when it's initialized (it can be drawn later by calling the **ShowWindow** Toolbox procedure). If the Close box check box isn't checked, modeless dialog boxes are drawn with no close box. "What," you might ask, "is a modeless dialog box with no close box?" It's probably a dialog that lets you switch to other windows, but that requires you to click a button when you're done. (Of course, the application could treat it in a variety of different ways. For example, MacWrite II uses this method to implement move-able modal dialogs.)

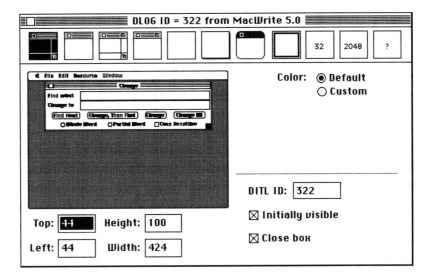

Figure 20-1. A typical dialog editor window showing a 'DLOG' from MacWrite.

▶ Picking a Window Definition ID

Across the top of the 'DLOG' editor window you see pictures of different kinds of windows. Just click the picture of the type of window you want to create. Table 20-2 shows each picture and the window definition ID it represents.

Table 20-2. Window Pictures and Their Corresponding Window Definition IDs

Picture	ID	Description
	0	Standard document window
	4	Document window without a size box

Table 20-2. Window Pictures and Their Corresponding Window
Definition IDs (continued)

Picture	ID	Description
	8	Document window with both zoom and size boxes
	12	Document window with zoom box but no size box
	2	Plain box
	3	Plain box with a drop shadow
	16	Rounded corner window with black title bar
	1	Standard alert or modal dialog box
?	-	Available for custom window definition ID

▶ Using Your Own 'WDEF'

If you have your own window definition procedure ('WDEF') that you
like to use for dialogs, you'll want to add it to the list of pictures at the
top of the window. You can do this by double-clicking one of the last
three pictures (the ones containing a "?" character). Figure 20-2 shows
the dialog that appears. You should enter the window definition ID,
not the 'WDEF' ID, into the dialog. You can calculate the window definition ID by multiplying the 'WDEF' ID by 16 and adding the variation
code. (Variation codes are explained in *Inside Macintosh*, Volume I.)

Using this method of calculation, you'll notice that all the window defi-nition IDs in Table 20-2 use the same 'WDEF' ID (with a resource ID of 0) except the rounded corner window. The different types of windows are just variations using the same basic 'WDEF'.

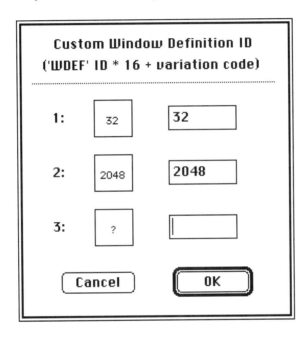

Figure 20-2. This dialog lets you define custom window definition IDs.

Once you've defined your own window definition IDs, why not add a mini-picture of the window? All you have to do is add a 'PICT' resource to the ResEdit Preferences file, and ResEdit will use that 'PICT' instead of just showing an empty rectangle with a number in the middle. Fol-low these steps to add your own 'PICT'.

1. Use ResEdit to open ResEdit (or a copy).
2. Open the 'PICT' picker and type 1808. (You can also use 1809 or 1810. These three 'PICT' resources correspond to the last three choices in the 'DLOG' editor window.) This moves you to the 'PICT' resource with ID 1808, which should be an empty rectangle.
3. Copy this 'PICT' resource.
4. Close ResEdit but don't quit (unless you're not using MultiFinder).

5. Open your favorite paint or draw program and paste the 'PICT' you copied. Make whatever changes you want inside the rectangle to make it look like a miniature version of a window that your 'WDEF' would draw.

6. Select just the rectangle containing your mini-window and copy it.

7. Go back to ResEdit and open the ResEdit Preferences file (it's in the System folder).

8. Paste the 'PICT' you copied from your paint or draw program.

9. Open the 'PICT' picker and select your new 'PICT'.

10. Choose the Get Resource Info command from the Resource menu. Change the resource ID to 1808, (or 1809 or 1810, depending on which of the three available window definition mini-pictures you're using). Also set the Purgeable attribute for the resource.

11. Close and save the Preferences file.

▶ Drawing with Your 'WDEF'

If you have a simple 'WDEF' that doesn't depend on any other part of your application's data when it draws the window, you're probably pretty happy with the way ResEdit handles custom 'WDEF's. If, on the other hand, you have a 'WDEF' that needs information provided by your application to correctly draw the window, you're probably not quite so happy. For 'WDEF's like these, having ResEdit use them to draw the miniature window may cause the System to crash since ResEdit isn't providing the environment they were written to expect (normally provided by the application). Fortunately, it's easy to get around this problem. Just choose the Never Use Custom 'WDEF' for Drawing command from the 'DLOG' menu. Once this menu item is checked, ResEdit always uses one of the standard System 'WDEF's to draw the miniature picture of the window.

▶ Dialog Characteristics

The Set 'DLOG' Characteristics command on the 'DLOG' menu displays the dialog shown in Figure 20-3. The Window title field simply contains the title that will be used in the title bar when the dialog is displayed (assuming there is a title bar for the specified ProcID). You probably won't want to store anything in the refCon field. It's typically filled in with a handle to an important data structure when the dialog is about to be used. This field can, however, contain anything you like, so if you have four bytes of information you'd like to store there, go right ahead.

The ProcID field contains the window definition ID (or window PROCedure ID). This is the same value that's specified by selecting one of the mini-windows at the top of the main 'DLOG' window. This field can, however, contain a value that's not available from the main window. In this case, none of the mini-window pictures is highlighted. Since this is a little confusing, it's best to add any special window definition IDs you'll be using to the main window. Of course, if you use more than three custom 'WDEF's, you have to assign them here since you can add only three to the main window.

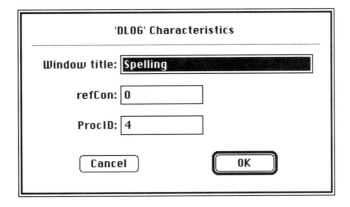

Figure 20-3. The 'DLOG' Characteristics window for one of MacWrite II's dialogs.

▶ The Alert Editor

The 'ALRT' editor is similar to the dialog editor because alerts are similar to dialogs. In fact, alerts are really just special cases of dialogs that are used to give information to the user. As you can see in Figure 20-4, the alert editor doesn't include the list of window types across the top of the window since alerts are always modal. The Initially visible and Close box check boxes found in the dialog editor's window are also missing since they have no meaning for alerts.

Although alert resources use 'DITL' resources to specify their contents just as dialogs do, the 'DITL's for alerts shouldn't contain fields for entering data. In fact, alerts should only contain static text, 'ICON's, 'PICT's, and buttons. Alerts come in four varieties, explained in Table

20-3.

| Hint ▶ | You don't have to add the icons shown in Table 20-3 to your alerts. In fact, you shouldn't. All you need to do is leave room in an alert's 'DITL' resource so the System can add the icon for you. The type of icon added depends on the Toolbox procedure you call: **StopAlert**, **CautionAlert**, **NoteAlert**, or just **Alert**. |

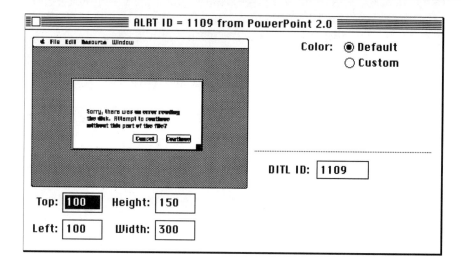

Figure 20-4. A typical alert editor window showing an 'ALRT' from PowerPoint.

Table 20-3. The Four Kinds of Alerts.

Icon	Description
	Stop alert. Used when a serious problem has occurred. Contains one button, labeled OK.

Caution alert. Usually contains a warning about an operation that could have an undesirable side effect. Always provides a way for the user to cancel the operation (such as with a Cancel or No button).

 Note alert. Contains information the user needs to know but that isn't critical to the performance of the application. For example, the results of an operation could be displayed in a note alert. Contains one button, labeled OK.

none   Plain alert. These are usually equivalent to Note alerts.

▶ Standard Layout

Since alerts always have a similar layout, Apple has defined some standards to make them as consistent as possible. Figure 20-5 shows a typical "correct" alert. When deciding on the wording for your alerts, be sure to phrase them so users know which button to press. It's all too easy to phrase a question in a Caution alert so users have to guess which button does what they want. Make the question simple, and use words in the buttons that really answer the question. "Yes" and "No" are often better than "OK" and "Cancel." The book *Human Interface Guidelines: The Apple Desktop Interface* can give you more hints for creating clear and effective alerts.

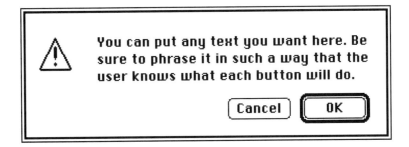

Figure 20-5. An alert that follows Apple's guidelines for item placement.

▶ Alert Stages

The Set 'ALRT' Stage Info command on the 'ALRT' menu lets you set up the stages of your alert. Each stage of an alert represents an occurrence of the problem that triggers the alert. For example, if the user makes an invalid entry, a Stage 1 alert is triggered. If the user makes the same mistake again (without doing something else first), a Stage 2 alert occurs. Choosing the Set 'ALRT' Stage Info command displays the dialog shown in Figure 20-6. Most applications configure their alerts with all the stages the same—usually visible, with one sound, as shown in the figure. Set the Default radio button to OK if button number 1 should be the default (shown with a dark outline), and to Cancel if button number 2 should be the default. You can find more information about alert stages in the "Dialog Manager" chapter of *Inside Macintosh*, Volume I.

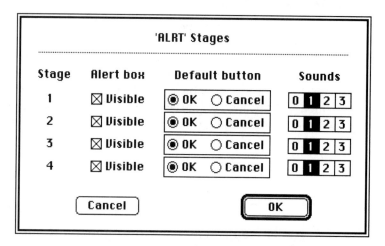

Figure 20-6. The 'ALRT' Stage dialog containing typical settings.

▶ **The 'DITL' Editor**

When you're designing a dialog or alert, you'll spend most of your time in the 'DITL' editor. This is where you'll design the contents of your dialogs or alerts, adding and arranging fields as necessary. Chapter 10 described how to use the 'DITL' editor to customize dialogs and alerts; here we show you how to create your own 'DITL's.

You can create a new 'DITL' from the 'DLOG' or 'ALRT' editor by opening the 'DITL' using any of the methods described in Chapter 10 (press the Return key, for example). Of course, you can also create a 'DITL' from the 'DITL' picker. Either way, you'll end up with a new window like the one shown in Figure 20-7. On the right side of the figure, you see the floating item palette, which you can use to add items to your new 'DITL'—just drag the type of item you'd like to add to where you want it to appear in the 'DITL' window. Repeat this process until you have defined all the item fields you want.

The size of the 'DITL' editor window is determined by the size specified for the associated 'DLOG' or 'ALRT'. You don't have to go back to the 'DLOG' or 'ALRT' editor to change the size, however. Just grab the size box in the lower right corner of the 'DITL' editor's window and change the size to whatever you want. The size saved in the 'DLOG' or 'ALRT' resource is changed to match the new size of your 'DITL' window.

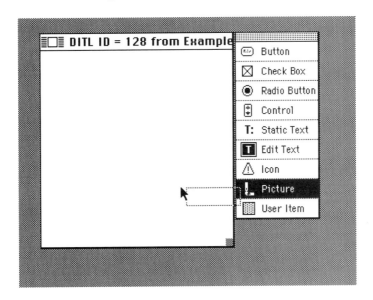

Figure 20-7. You can add items to a 'DITL' by dragging them from the floating palette.

▶ The Dialog Item Editor

You can arrange dialog items right in the 'DITL' editor window, but sometimes you need to change characteristics of an individual item. You can do this by double-clicking an item to open a dialog item editor window like the one shown in Figure 20-8. Dialog item editor windows are modeless windows—you can have as many of them open as you like. As you can see in the figure, there are four parts to the item editor window. You can use the pop-up menu to change an item to any of the other item types. The Enabled check box determines whether the item will be active (whether the user can interact with the item by clicking or typing) when the 'DITL' is used. Remember, though, a disabled control item can still be active—you must use the **HiliteControl** Toolbox procedure to make a control inactive. The editable field in the upper right part of the window is used to specify the title for buttons, check boxes, and radio buttons, the text for static text and edit text items, and the resource ID for icons, controls, and pictures. Lastly, the four fields at the bottom right of the window set the size and location of the item. The Item menu lets you choose between showing the Bottom and Right or the Height and Width of the item. Any changes you make in the item editor window (such as changing the item's location or title) are reflected immediately in the 'DITL' editor window so you can see the effect of your change.

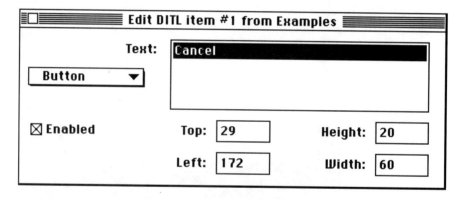

Figure 20-8. A typical dialog item editor window.

▶ Dialog Item Tips

Most of the item types in the floating item palette are probably familiar to you, so we won't go into much detail about them. A few, though, can be a little tricky, so we talk about them next. Complete details about dialog items can be found in the "Dialog Manager" chapters of *Inside Macintosh*, Volumes I and VI.

Resource Items

As you no doubt know, you can include 'ICON', 'CNTL', and 'PICT' resources as items in a 'DITL'. When you first drag a resource item off the palette, it appears in the 'DITL' window looking like one of the default resources shown in Table 20-4. To make the item show up using the resources you want, you need to set the item's resource ID. You can do this by double-clicking the item to open the dialog item editor, where you can enter the resource ID. You should then see the resource in the 'DITL' editor window. If you still don't see your resource, that means ResEdit couldn't find it, and you should go to the 'ICON', 'CNTL', or 'PICT' picker to verify the ID of the resource you want to use.

Table 20-4. The 'DITL' Editor's Default Resource Items

Resource Type	Default Appearance	Name in Palette
'ICON'	ICON	Icon
'CNTL'	◁ ▷	Control
'PICT'	PICT	Picture

What the Rectangles Really Mean. For most item types, such as static text and buttons, it's obvious what the item rectangle is used for—it defines the size of the item. For the resource items, however, it's less clear since the resources also either contain their own rectangles ('CNTL's and 'PICT's) or are a fixed size ('ICON's are always 32-by-32). If the item rectangle for an 'ICON' or 'PICT' is different from the size of the resource, the resource is scaled to fit the item rectangle. 'CNTL' resources behave differently, however. The top and left coordinates of the control are determined by the item rectangle, but the height and width are determined by the rectangle stored in the 'CNTL' resource. Whatever the item type, you'll more than likely want to use the size associated with the resource you're displaying. You can easily make the item rectangle the same as the resource's rectangle by selecting the item and choosing Use Item's Rectangle from the 'DITL' menu. For controls, this command will set only the height and width and won't change the top and left coordinates.

Editing Resource Item. As with any of the other item types, double-clicking a resource item opens an Item editor window. Many times, however, you'll want to edit the resource itself and not the dialog item using the resource. You can do this by using the two alternate Open commands on the Resource menu or their shortcuts. After selecting a resource item, the third item on the Resource menu changes to Open 'CNTL', Open 'ICON', or Open 'PICT', depending on the situation, and opens the appropriate editor. You can also use the Open Using Hex Editor item to open the resource using the hexadecimal editor. You can use the Command-Option double-click shortcut to open the resource editor and the Option double-click shortcut to edit the resource using the hexadecimal editor.

| By the Way ▶ | You can susbstitute a color icon in a dialog by including in the file a 'cicn' with the same ID as that of the 'ICON'. If the 'cicn' is not 32-by-32 pixels, you can change the item rectangle to match. Note, however, that the 'DITL' editor doesn't show 'cicn's. Also, opening the editor for an 'ICON' item always opens the 'ICON' editor, even if a 'cicn' will be substituted when the dialog is displayed. |

Adding System 7 Balloon Help Items

One of the new features provided by System 7 is Balloon help. An application can specify text to appear in balloons as the user moves the mouse over a document or menu. Each part of the screen—such as windows, menus, menu items, and dialogs—can have its own set of balloon messages. Several new resource types were introduced to support these balloon messages ('hmnu', 'hdlg', 'hwin', and 'hrct'). These resources aren't supported by ResEdit but are supported by a new application available for developers from Apple. One aspect of balloon help that ResEdit does support is the new balloon help dialog item that can be included in a 'DITL' resource. All this new dialog item does is direct the Help Manager to the proper help resource. Figure 20-9 shows the dialog displayed when you choose the Balloon Help command from the 'DITL' menu. You can enter the resource IDs of the associated help resources. The pop-up menu lets you choose the type of the associated resource. You normally won't need to use this feature since the application provided by Apple automatically adds the dialog items for you.

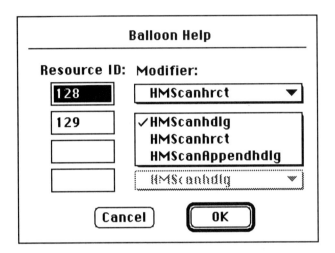

Figure 20-9. Adding help items to a 'DITL'.

What's on top of What?

Usually each dialog item occupies its own area of the dialog, but sometimes it's useful or necessary to have items that overlap. For example, you might want to put a user item over a button so you can draw a dark frame to show that it's the default, or you may want a picture in the background of the entire 'DITL'. In any case, you need to know the order in which the dialog items are drawn so you can know which items appear on top. You might expect that item 1 would be on the bottom and the last item would be on the top but, unfortunately, the Dialog Manager doesn't make it quite that easy. When drawing a 'DITL', the Dialog Manager first draws all buttons, check boxes, and radio buttons in *reverse* item number order. It then draws the rest of the items, this time in *ascending* order. You can never have a button, check box, or radio button on top of an item of one of the other types. User items are a little different since they're transparent—when they're on top of another item, you can still see through to the other item. You can tell that a user item is on top of another item if the entire user item is filled with gray (otherwise, you'll see the other item drawn across the user item). Because the 'DITL' editor uses the Dialog Manager to draw its window, the items are drawn in exactly the order they'll appear when you use the 'DITL'.

▶ The 'DITL' Menu

The 'DITL' menu contains items to help you design your 'DITL' and set up the 'DITL' editor the way you like to work. Except for the first group of commands, which pertains to item numbering, this menu's commands are discussed in Chapter 10.

Renumber Items

When you choose the Renumber Items command, the editor temporarily turns on the Show Item Numbers command (described shortly) and every item in the 'DITL' is displayed with its current item number. Then, as the small floating dialog window that appears tells you, all you have to do is press the Shift key while you select the items in the order you want them renumbered. As you Shift-click, a white-on-black number appears for each item you've renumbered. Figure 20-10 shows how all this looks. If you're satisfied with your new numbering scheme, click the Renumber button. (Shift-click also deselects an item already selected for renumbering. If you want to deselect all of them and start over, just click once without pressing the Shift key.)

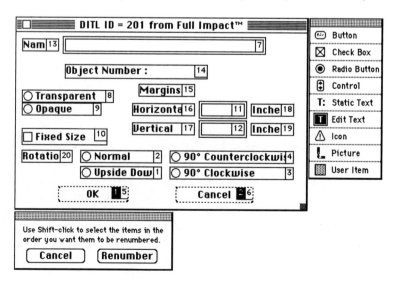

Figure 20-10. A 'DITL' in the process of being renumbered.

Set Item Number

The Set Item Number command lets you set the item number for a single item. (Other items are renumbered to avoid duplicate numbers.) Using this command is simpler than using the renumber command if you only want to change one item or you want to change the number of an item that's hiding behind another item.

Select Item Number

The Select Item Number command lets you specify the number of an item to be selected. This is especially useful for items that aren't visible (because they're outside the dialog's rectangle) or are under another item. Once the item is selected, you can use the Open as Dialog Item command on the Resource menu to open an Item editor window (even if the item isn't visible).

Show Item Numbers

Choose Show Item Numbers when you want to see the item numbers of all the items. A black-on-white numeral appears in the upper right corner of each item. This can be invaluable when you're designing a new dialog. Figure 20-10 shows a 'DITL' with the item numbers displayed.

Hint ▶

Holding down the Option key is a shortcut for choosing the Show Item Numbers command. If Show Item Numbers is off, pressing the Option key displays the item numbers until you release the key. If Show Item Numbers is on, pressing the Option key turns the numbers off until you release the key.

▶ The Alignment Menu

The Alignment menu contains commands that help you arrange the items in your dialog. The action performed by these commands is usually obvious from the name of the command. Chapter 10 has more details.

▶ Summary

In this chapter we cover details of the 'DLOG', 'ALRT', and 'DITL' editors. We show you how to design dialogs and alerts from scratch, including using your own window definition procedures ('WDEF's). We also show you how to set up the various kinds of alerts and the alert stages. Finally, we show you how to use the 'DITL' editor to create the contents for both alerts and dialogs. More information about all these editors can be found in Chapter 10.

21 ▶ Creating Menus

One of the editors you'll find most useful as you create an application is the 'MENU' editor. In Chapter 8 we showed you how to use the 'MENU' editor for updating an existing menu. This chapter fills in the remaining details about the 'MENU' editor by providing information that's useful only if you're writing the application that will use the menu. If you're not familiar with the 'MENU' editor, be sure to review Chapter 8 since we cover only new information here.

▶ The Basics

When you create a new 'MENU' resource, you see a window similar to the one shown in Figure 21-1. The menu initially has no items, and its title is simply "Title." The first change you'll want to make is to enter the menu's title. Selecting the Apple radio button is equivalent to entering the character into the Title field. The Enabled check box in the upper right corner of the window determines whether the entire menu is enabled or disabled when it's installed on the menu bar. ResEdit assumes the menu should be enabled and automatically checks the Enabled check box for you when you create a new menu.

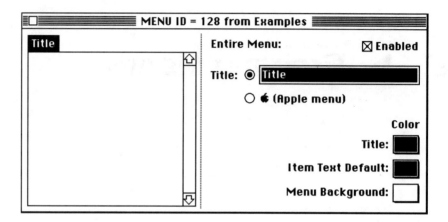

Figure 21-1. The 'MENU' editor showing a new resource.

▶ Adding New 'MENU' Items

Once you've entered the title, you're ready to start adding new menu items. As with many other operations in ResEdit, there's a menu command and a shortcut to add new items. You can choose the Create New Item command from the Resource menu or simply press the Return key. Either way, a new item is added at the end of the menu. (In a menu that already has items, pressing the Return key moves to the next item. If the last item is selected, Return creates a new item.) After you've added your first item, the window looks like the one shown in Figure 21-2. Notice that several new fields appear to let you set the characteristics of your new item. We'll talk more about the has Submenu and Mark fields later in this chapter. The Enabled check box in the upper right corner of the window indicates whether the selected item is enabled. If you want the item to appear as a gray separator line, just click the Separator line radio button (or type a hyphen into the Text field). You can continue pressing Return and entering item information until you've filled out your menu.

▶ Rearranging 'MENU' Items

Before you're finished with your menu, you'll probably want to move some items around, insert an item or two you forgot, or get rid of an item you don't really need. Most of these operations work just as you'd expect. You can cut, copy, paste, clear, or duplicate a menu item simply by selecting it and choosing the appropriate command from the Edit menu (or typing the Command-key equivalent). Here are a few things to keep in mind when using the Edit menu with 'MENU' resources.

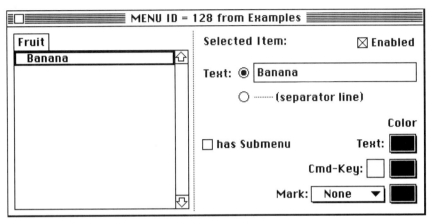

Figure 21-2. When you add a menu item, new fields appear in the 'MENU' editor window.

- If you want the Edit menu commands to affect an entire item, make sure the item is selected with a solid selection. A hollow selection in the list indicates that one of the text fields on the right side of the window is selected instead of the entire menu item.
- Since you can select only one item at a time, you can only copy and paste items one at a time.
- When you copy an item, all the information about that item (Command key, Mark, and so on), except the color information, is also copied. You'll have to reset any colors that you had set for the item you copied.
- Paste adds the new item after the currently selected item. If you want a new item to be at the top of the menu, you'll have to drag it there. (Dragging menu items is explained next.)

Hint ▶

If you need to create a menu that includes all the items in another menu, here's a shortcut. In the 'MENU' picker, select and cut or copy the menu whose items you want to include as part of another menu. Now open the other menu, select the item after which you want to add the new items, and paste. The entire menu you copied (except the title) will be inserted into your menu.

▶ Moving Items

You can move an item in a menu by selecting it and dragging it to a new location. You don't actually drag an item when you're moving it. Instead, the item remains in its original location (still selected) and you drag a black line which indicates the place where the menu item will end up when you release the mouse button, as shown in Figure 21-3.

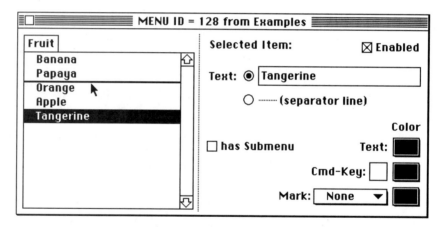

Figure 21-3. You can drag a menu item to a new location in the menu.

▶ **Creating Hierarchical Menus**

Creating hierarchical menus is as easy as clicking the has Submenu check box. When you check the check box, the Cmd-Key and Mark fields disappear and an ID field appears. You can enter the resource ID of the submenu in the ID field. Double-clicking an item with a submenu (or selecting Open Submenu from the Resource menu) opens the

'MENU' resource specified in the ID field. The 'MENU' resource is created for you if it doesn't exist. Submenus are not shown in the test menu to the right on the menubar.

▶ Using the Mark Menu

The Mark pop-up menu is easy enough to use if you like one of the marks on the menu—just select the mark. If the default set of marks doesn't fit your needs, however, you can add any character you want to the Mark menu. When you choose the Other item on the Mark menu, you see the dialog shown in Figure 21-4. Any character you enter in the dialog appears in the Mark menu. If you check the Remember in Preferences check box, the new mark is saved in ResEdit's Preferences file and appears on your Mark pop-up menu every time you use the 'MENU' editor.

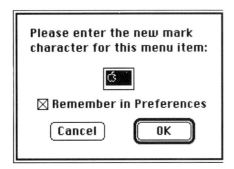

Figure 21-4. The 'MENU' editor's New Mark dialog.

▶ Removing Marks from the Mark Menu

You've added a few marks to your Mark menu that you don't need anymore—how do you get rid of them? Just follow these steps.

1. Use ResEdit to open the ResEdit Preferences file in your System folder.
2. Open the 'MENU' picker.
3. Find the 'MENU' resource with ID 1652 (it's probably the only 'MENU' in the file).
4. If you want to go back to the default Mark menu, just delete this resource.

5. If you want to remove one or more marks, open the resource in the 'MENU' editor and delete the items you no longer need.

6. Close and save the Preferences file.

▶ Changing the 'MENU' and 'MDEF' IDs

If your application includes a tool palette or tear-off menu, you'll need to write your own menu definition procedure ('MDEF'), and then set up a menu to use your 'MDEF' instead of the normal System 'MDEF'. You can set up a menu to use any 'MDEF' by selecting the Edit Menu & 'MDEF' ID command from the 'MENU' menu. The dialog that appears is shown in Figure 21-5. Put the resource ID of your 'MDEF' into the MDEF ID field.

In the same dialog shown in the figure, you'll see a field labeled "Menu ID." This field is a little confusing since it doesn't necessarily contain the resource ID of the 'MENU' resource being edited. Instead, it contains the number the Menu Manager returns to your application when you call the **MenuSelect** or **MenuKey** Toolbox procedures. By convention, this number should always be the same as the resource ID of the 'MENU' resource (although you can set it to any number you want). When you change the ID of the 'MENU' (with the Get Resource Info command on the Resource menu), ResEdit asks if you want to update this other, hidden 'MENU' ID as well.

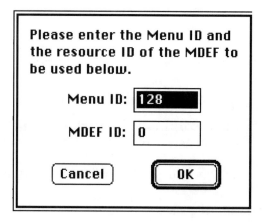

Figure 21-5. You can change the internal 'MENU' ID and the 'MDEF' ID with this dialog.

▶ Summary

In this chapter we show you how to create and update menus for your applications. We show you how to add items to menus, as well as how to move existing items. We also give you some tips on how to use marks and a custom 'MDEF'. Many other important parts of the 'MENU' editor are described in Chapter 8.

22 ▶ Editing 'BNDL', 'vers', and 'TEXT' Resources

In this chapter we describe the editors for several different resource types. These resources aren't related, but aren't complex enough to warrant chapters of their own. Every application has a 'BNDL' resource that tells the Finder what icons to use for the application and its document files. Most applications also have 'vers' resources. These resources provide the version information the Finder displays in its Get Info window. Last, but not least, we discuss the 'TEXT' resource and its associated 'styl' resource. These provide the ability to store styled text for use in your application.

▶ Editing 'BNDL' Resources

You may have heard about (or experienced) horror stories involving 'BNDL' resources, but ResEdit's 'BNDL' editor should quickly change the 'BNDL' resource's reputation. Every application needs a 'BNDL' resource if it's to display a custom icon for itself or its document files. The 'BNDL' resource describes a bundle of other resources. It associates a *signature* resource with file reference resources ('FREF's) and Finder icons ('ICN#', 'ics#', and so on) by using something called *local IDs*. With ResEdit's 'BNDL' editor you don't have to worry about any of these peripheral resources or the local IDs—they're all created for you. Figure 22-1 shows a typical 'BNDL' editor window.

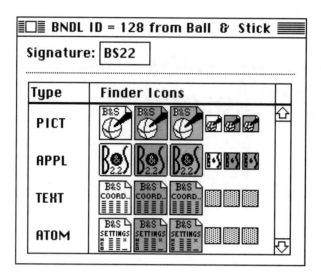

Figure 22-1. A typical 'BNDL' from Ball & Stick.

The right side of the 'BNDL' editor window shows the icons the Finder uses for the application's files with the file Types listed on the left side of the window. The 'APPL' Type associates an icon with the application itself. (If you need to refresh your memory, file Types and Creators are discussed in Chapter 7.) The other file Types can be anything you like. At the top of the window is a field to enter the application's signature resource. The signature is the same as the Creator for the application and its documents, and is used by the Finder to find a document's Creator. You can use the Create New File Type command on the Resource menu to add new file Types to the end of the list.

As you move the pointer across the window you'll notice that it can assume three shapes: the normal arrow, the I-beam, and the plus symbol. This changing pointer indicates that clicking the mouse selects different parts of the 'BNDL'. You see the arrow both when the pointer is over the icons and when it's in those parts of the window where there's nothing to select. You can double-click the icons to edit them. You see the I-beam when the pointer is over the signature field or one of the Type fields. When you see the plus symbol, clicking selects the entire row. Once a row is selected, you can cut, copy, clear, or duplicate it.

▶ Bundles of Icons

The right part of the 'BNDL' editor window shows the icons associated with the file Types shown on the left side of the window, but you may be wondering why there are so many icons. The first icon is the familiar 'ICN#' resource the Finder has always used to represent documents and applications. The other five icons are used by System 7 to give you more flexibility when creating your icons. These five icon types are (in order from left to right): 'icl4', 'icl8', 'ics#', 'ics4', and 'ics8'. The Finder uses the appropriate icon based on the number of colors available on the screen and the size of icon it needs. If one of the icons hasn't been defined, it's shown as a gray square. If a Type already has associated icons, you can edit them simply by double-clicking any of the icons. You can edit all of them in one editor—the icon family editor, shown in Figure 22-2. This editor is described in Chapter 18.

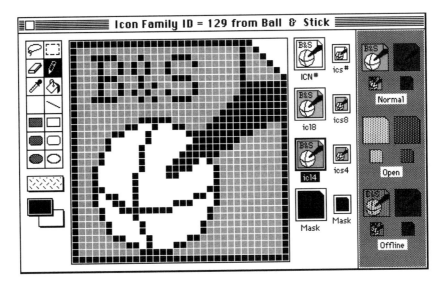

Figure 22-2. The icon family editor lets you create all the icons the Finder needs.

If no icons are associated with a file Type, double-clicking the gray squares displays the Choose Icon dialog, shown in Figure 22-3. If you already have an icon but you'd like to pick a different one, you can select Choose Icon from the 'BNDL' menu to see the same dialog. This dialog shows you all the 'ICN#' resources in the file being edited. You

can select one of these icons or you can click the New button to create a
new icon from scratch. If you like one of the icons but want to change it
a little before you add it to your 'BNDL', you can select the icon and
click the Edit button. (Editing the icon changes its appearance every
place it's used, not just in the 'BNDL'.)

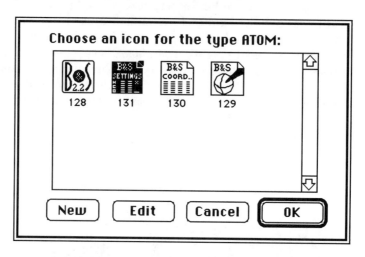

Figure 22-3. You can use the Choose Icon dialog to choose an icon
to add to your 'BNDL'.

Hint ▶

Once you've changed the icon for an application, you'll probably
want the Finder to use the new icon when it displays the application
or document files. Unfortunately, the Finder stores the icons in its
Desktop file and there's no easy way to tell the Finder that it should
look for a new icon. The most straightforward way to force it to use
your new icon is to rebuild the Desktop file from scratch. You can do
this by holding down the Command and Option keys when you
restart your Mac. If you make use of the Get Info comments that the
Finder saves for you, you won't want to rebuild your Desktop since
you'll lose all the Get Info comments. Chapter 7 discusses another,
more complex way to update your Desktop file that saves your Get
Info comments if you're using System software before System 7.

Hint ▶	If you've just created a 'BNDL' in a new application, don't forget to set the *bundle* attribute to let the Finder know it should look in the file for a 'BNDL' resource. Just check the Bundle check box in the file's File Info window (choose Get File/Folder Info from the File menu).

By the Way ▶	Five of the six icons are used only with System 7. If your application might be used with System 7, you should think about including at least some of the extra icons. At the least, you should include an 'ics#' resource so the Finder won't have to shrink your 'ICN#' to use for the MultiFinder icon in the upper right corner of the screen. Of course, your application will still work with System 7 even if you only include an 'ICN#'.

▶ The Extended View

If you miss the days when you had to figure out your own local IDs and set up your own 'BNDL' resource, the Extended View command on the 'BNDL' menu is for you. Selecting this command changes the display to look like Figure 22-4. If you really need to use this view of the 'BNDL', you can find details about the extra fields in *Inside Macintosh*, Volume III and in Macintosh Technical Note number 48.

Hint ▶	In versions of the Finder before version 6.1, the text shown in the extended view's String field was displayed in the Finder's Get Info window. More recent versions of the Finder, use a file's 'vers' resource (described next) instead if one's present. If your application might be used with very old versions of the System software, you might want to include a copyright string in the 'BNDL's String field.

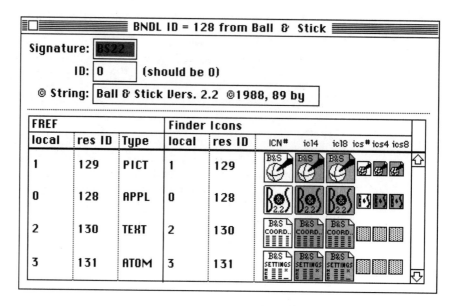

Figure 22-4. The extended view of a 'BNDL' resource.

▶ Editing 'vers' Resources

In version 6.1 of the Finder, the 'vers' resource type was introduced to hold an application's version information. The Finder uses this version information in its Get Info window. This method has several advantages over the older method of storing a version string inside the 'BNDL' resource.

- It stores more information, including a numeric form of the version number, rather than just a string of unformatted text.
- The 'vers' resource type can be used in any file, not just applications containing 'BNDL' resources.
- Applications can include two 'vers' resources: one to indicate the version number of the file itself, and one for the version number of a set of files that work together (for example, System files can have their own version number yet still indicate the System release they belong to).
- The structure of the 'vers' resource type helps standardize the release numbering scheme applications use. This helps users

understand how different versions of the same application are related.

The 'vers' resource editor is shown in Figure 22-5. Most of the information in the window is pretty standard and doesn't need much explanation. The most important information in this window is contained in the Long version string field since that text is displayed by the Finder in its Get Info window, as shown in Figure 22-6. As you can see in the figures, The Get Info window contains room for only one line of text from resource ID 2, and two lines from ID 1.

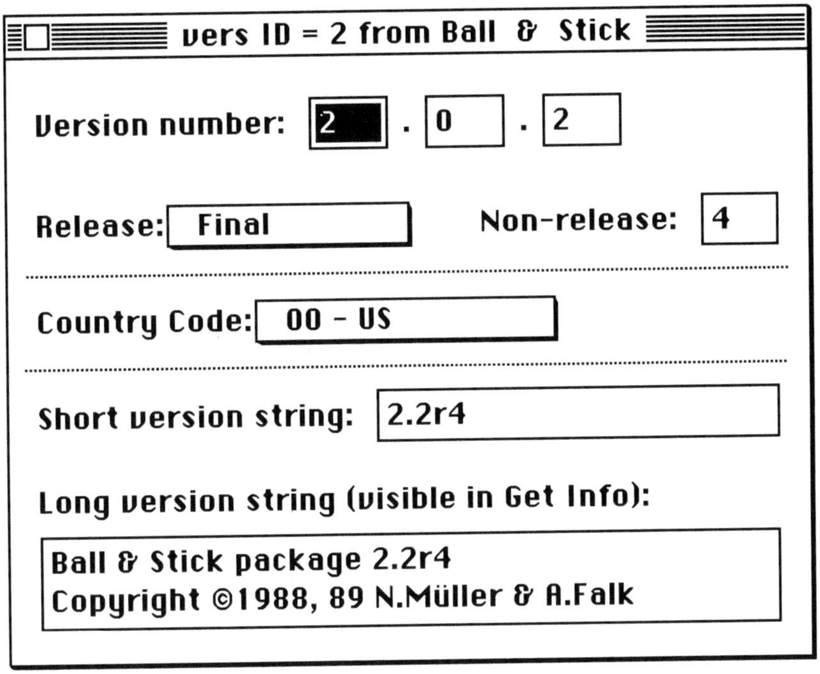

vers ID = 2 from Ball & Stick

Version number: [2] . [0] . [2]

Release: [Final]   Non-release: [4]

Country Code: [00 – US]

Short version string: [2.2r4]

Long version string (visible in Get Info):

Ball & Stick package 2.2r4
Copyright ©1988, 89 N.Müller & A.Falk

Figure 22-5. The 'vers' editor lets you set the information displayed in the Finder's Get Info window.

The version number displayed in three fields across the top of the 'vers' editor window is stored in the resource in BCD (Binary Coded Decimal) format and can be accessed for comparison purposes by utility applications. By convention the first field contains the major release number. For example, the first version of a product to ship would have a 1 in this field. The second number contains the minor revision number. The second version of an application that contains a few enhancements but no really significant changes might have a 1 in the second field. If the release was made strictly to fix a few bugs but had no other feature changes, it would increment the third field. Table 22-1 shows a few examples of this scheme.

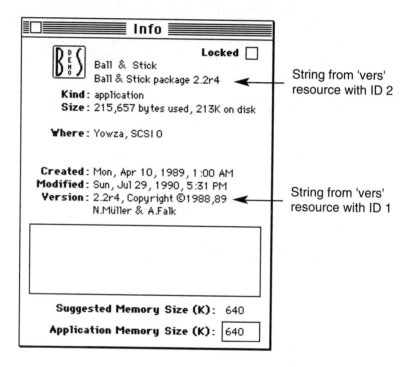

Figure 22-6. The Finder's Get Info window uses the strings from two 'vers' resources.

Table 22-1. Recommended Use of Version Number Fields

Version	Meaning
1.0.0	The first release
1.0.1	The first bug fix release of the file
1.1.0	The first minor update of the file
2.0.0	The second release

Hint ▶

Remember, you can put a 'vers' resource in any file. This is a better way to add comments to a file than by adding a Get Info comment since it won't be lost if you need to rebuild your Desktop file. See Chapter 13 for more details.

▶ Editing 'TEXT' and 'styl' Resources

When the Mac II and the SE were introduced, the Mac's built-in text editing capabilities were enhanced to include styled text. This styled text is stored in two resources. The 'TEXT' resource contains the characters, and the 'styl' resource contains the associated style information. Few applications have taken advantage of styled text because there was no way to create the resources. Now you can edit this styled text in the editor shown in Figure 22-7. As you can see, this is one of the simplest editors you're likely to encounter. You can use it like any other word processing application, although its capabilities are limited. You can enter up to 32,000 characters and change the font, size, or style as often as you like.

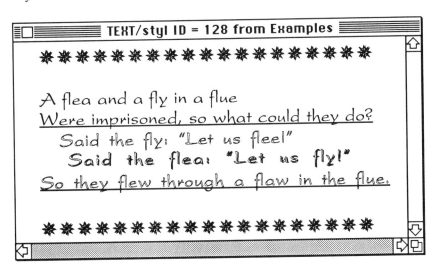

Figure 22-7. The 'TEXT' and 'styl' editor is a simple text editor.

▶ Summary

In this chapter we summarize the use of three editors that you'll find useful when you're programming with the Mac. The 'BNDL' editor lets you associate icons with your application and its documents. The 'vers' editor lets you enter the version information the Finder displays in its Get Info window. Finally, the 'TEXT' and 'styl' editor lets you save styled text for use by your application.

23 ▶ File, Folder, and Resource Info Windows

Files, folders, and resources all have various characteristics that control their use by the System and Finder. You can change these characteristics (or in some cases just observe them) in ResEdit's info windows. For example, by changing these characteristics you can modify the color of a folder, the last modified date of a file, or the ID of a resource. You can make a file or folder invisible, or change the Type and Creator of a file or the name of a resource. In this chapter we show you what each of the characteristics is used for and how to change it.

▶ The File Info Window

The File Info window lets you change file characteristics important to both the Finder and the operating system. When you choose the Get File/Folder Info command from the File menu, the dialog shown in Figure 23-1 is displayed. This dialog is slightly different from most other standard file directory dialogs because it allows you to select either a file or a folder. The only way to see the contents of a folder is to double-click the folder. Pressing the Return or Enter key when a folder is selected displays the Folder Info window (rather than showing the contents of the folder). Just remember: Double-click to open a folder and show its contents in the standard file directory dialog, click the Get Info button to show a file's or folder's info window. Of course, double-clicking a file is equivalent to clicking the Get Info button with the file selected.

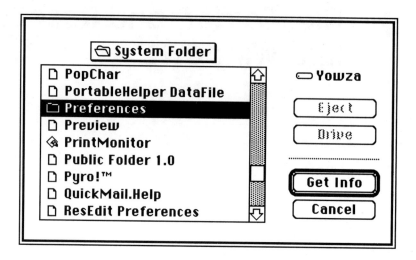

Figure 23-1. The standard file directory dialog for the Get File/Folder Info command.

After you've selected a file and clicked the Get Info button, you see a window similar to the one shown in Figure 23-2. The top half of the window contains the file name, Type, and Creator as well as a set of check boxes that let you change characteristics used by the Finder. The bottom half of the window contains some file system characteristics, the creation date, and last modified date of the file, and the size of its data fork and resource fork. Table 23-1 lists the use for each field in the File Info window. A few of the fields are too complex (or interesting) to capsulize in the table, so they're described in more detail after the table. These fields are marked with an asterisk in the table.

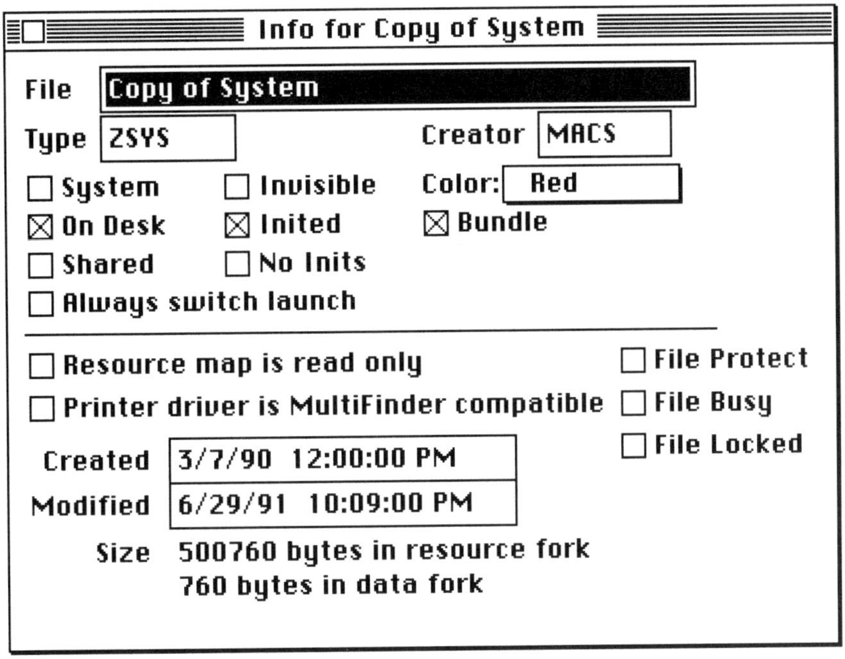

Figure 23-2. A File Info window.

| Hint ▶ | Sometimes after you change a file's characteristics, you won't see the change take effect right away. Usually closing and reopening the folder containing the file makes the change take effect. For example, if you make a file invisible by setting the Invisible characteristic, you need to close and reopen the folder containing the file before its icon disappears. |

Table 23-1. Fields of a File Info Window

Field Name	Description
File	The name of the file. You can enter any name up to 30 characters long.
Type*	A file's Type ('APPL' for applications, for example).
Creator*	A file's Creator. An application and its associated documents all have the same Creator.
System*	Checked if the file's name can't be changed from the Finder.
On Desk	Checked if the file is on the desktop, not in a folder (Pre-System 7).
Shared*	Checked if a file can be opened more than once.
Always switch launch*	When this is checked, the System and Finder on a disk containing an application become active when the application is started.
Invisible*	Checked if the file's icon is invisible in the Finder. You can always see invisible files in ResEdit's standard file directory dialogs.
Inited	The Finder checks this the first time it notices a file. The Finder saves certain information (such as the file's icon) when the file is inited.
No Inits	Checked if the file doesn't contain any 'INIT' resources. (Actually, the file can still contain 'INIT's, but they're ignored.)
Color	A pop-up menu containing the color the Finder uses when it displays the file's icon. This is the same color selected from the Finder's Color menu (the Label menu under System 7).
Bundle	Checked if the file contains a 'BNDL' resource. Any application that has its own desktop icon or opens document files must contain a 'BNDL' resource. Chapter 22 explains the use of 'BNDL' resources.
Resource map is read only	Checked if changes can't be made to the file's resources. You can't change this characteristic with ResEdit.
Printer driver is MultiFinder compatible	Checked if the file is a printer driver that can be used when MultiFinder is in use (in other words, if the printer driver can be shared by several applications at once).
File Protect	Checked if the Finder can't copy the file. File Protect can't be changed by ResEdit.
File Busy	Checked if the file is open (either the resource fork or data fork is open by ResEdit or another application). File Busy can't be changed by ResEdit.
File Locked	Checked if the file is locked and can't be thrown into the Trash. File Locked is the same as the locked check box in the Finder's Get Info window.
Created*	The time and date the file was created.
Modified*	The time and date the file was most recently modified.

* Indicates characteristics with more detailed explanations following this table.

▶ Type and Creator

Every file has a Type field and a Creator field which the Finder uses to establish the relationship between a document and the application that created it. The Type and Creator are both four characters long (just like a resource type). The Creator field of a document file is the same as the Creator of the application that created it. Applications must have unique Creators so the Finder will know which document files belong to which application. The Type field of a document file distinguishes between different document types of the same application. The Type field of an application is always set to 'APPL' so the Finder will know it's an application. Types and Creators are explained in more detail in Chapter 7.

Hint ▶	Sometimes the Type and Creator fields may contain non-printing characters. For example, you might see a Type field that looks like it's empty but, in fact, contains four null (0) characters. When you close the File Info window, ResEdit uses the first four characters it finds in the Type and Creator fields. If there are four null characters at the beginning of the field (which you can't see) and you enter four new characters, ResEdit blithely throws away your new characters, leaving the nulls. To avoid this problem, press the Backspace key four times before entering your new Type or Creator.

▶ System and Invisible

If other people use your computer and you want to protect yourself from their careless mistakes, you can turn on the System or Invisible characteristics for important files. For files whose names you don't want changed, just check the System characteristic. If you're worried that someone might inadvertently delete one of your important files, just make it invisible. You can even make your applications invisible, as long as you have a document to double-click when you want to start the application. (See Chapter 13 if you want step-by-step instructions.)

| By the Way ▶ | The System won't look for 'INIT' resources (code resources that are installed when the Mac starts up) in invisible files, so be careful not to make files in your System Folder invisible. Making your entire System folder invisible should be OK, though, and is a good way to keep other people from tampering with your System. |

▶ Shared

If you have a site-licensed application and a network, you can let a group of people share one copy of the application by checking its Shared characteristic. For example, you could put a copy of HyperCard into a locked folder on a server (be sure to lock it so the Home stack won't be changed), and everyone connected to the server could use it.

The Shared characteristic should only be checked for applications that several people share. Don't check the Shared characteristic for a file that you write to, though. With Shared checked you could, for example, use ResEdit to edit an application while it's running. This would more than likely result in a System crash and could possibly destroy your application. If you want to share an application, it's best to contact the application's developers and get their assurance that the application works properly in a shared environment.

▶ Always Switch Launch

Normally your Mac continues to use the System file and Finder on the disk you started up from until you start up from a different disk. Sometimes, however, switching to a System on a different disk is useful. Maybe you want to switch language script systems (everybody needs to use Kanji or Arabic occasionally, don't they?) or you have a hard disk but occasionally start your Mac from a floppy and are tired of having to constantly switch floppy disks. In any case, checking the Always Switch Launch characteristic for an application causes the System and Finder on the disk containing the application to become active when the application is started. Unfortunately, this won't work if you use MultiFinder (or System 7).

▶ Setting a File's Created and Last Modified Date

When you set a file's creation date or last modified date, you must enter the date and time in a very specific format. Both the date and time must be present and must be in the "month/date/year hour:minute:second AM" format. Month, date, and year should be one- or two-digit numbers. The time must be in the 12-hour format followed by AM or PM. If you type a new date and time in exactly the same format that you see in the field when you open the window, you should get the results you expect.

▶ System 7 Additions

When System software version 7.0 or later is in use, a few more check boxes appear in the File Info dialog. Figure 23-3 shows the new File Info window, and Table 23-2 tells you what each new check box is used for. Notice also that the Color pop-up menu no longer specifies specific colors. This is because in System 7 you can change the set of available colors.

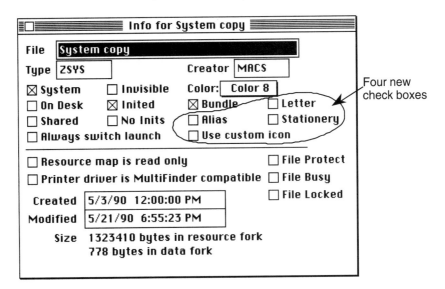

Figure 23-3. A File Info window gains a few more check boxes under System 7.

Table 23-2. New File Info Check Boxes for System 7

Field Name	Description
Alias	Checked if the file is an alias to another file.
Use custom icon	Checked if the file contains a custom icon that the Finder should use in place of the default icon provided by the application that created the file.
Letter	Checked if the file contains mail. Reserved for use with future electronic mail software.
Stationery	Checked if the file is a stationery file. Stationery files are copied before they are opened, so the original is never changed.

▶ The Folder Info Window

The Folder Info window is used to set the characteristics for a folder, and is shown in Figure 23-4. Characteristics for a folder are just a subset of the characteristics for a file, and are explained in Table 23-1.

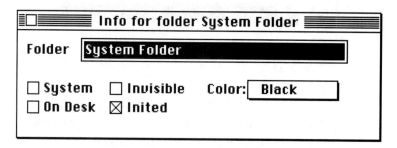

Figure 23-4. A Folder Info window.

▶ System 7 Additions

If you're using System 7 or later, you'll see the slightly different Folder Info window shown in Figure 23-5. The only differences are that a Use custom icon check box has been added and the Color pop-up menu has been changed to no longer specify the names of the colors.

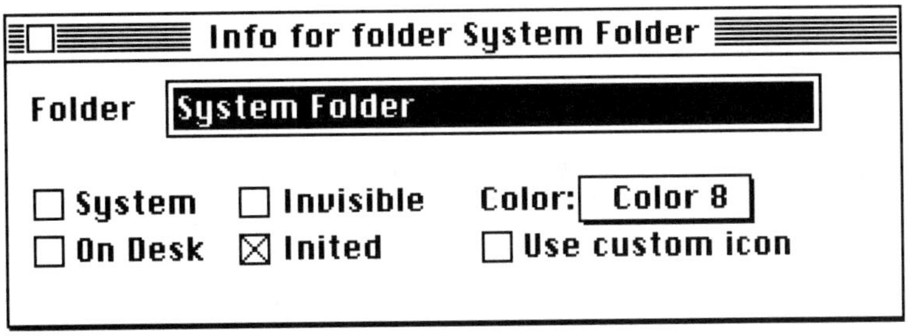

Figure 23-5. A Folder Info window under System 7.

▶ The Resource Info Window

Selecting the Get Resource Info command from the Resource menu (when a resource picker or editor is the frontmost window) opens a Resource Info window like the one shown in Figure 23-6. The Resource Info window lets you change characteristics that control how the System treats the resource. Two fields at the top of the window let you change the resource's ID and name. These two fields control how an application finds the resource it's looking for. It's usually not a good idea to change the resource ID of an existing resource since most applications locate their resources by looking up the resource ID. It's usually safe to add a name to a resource that doesn't have one. Just be careful not to use a name already taken by another resource of the same type. When you're creating a new resource, you should be sure to follow Apple's guidelines for allocating resource IDs. The guidelines are summarized in Table 23-3. Other restrictions may apply for some resource types. For example, icons used in menus must have IDs between 257 and 511.

Table 23-3. Guidelines for Allocating Resource IDs

Resource ID Range	Use
-32,768 to -16,385	Reserved by Apple
-16,384 to -1	Reserved for owned resources (explained shortly)
0 to 127	Used for System resources
128 to 32,767	Available for applications to use

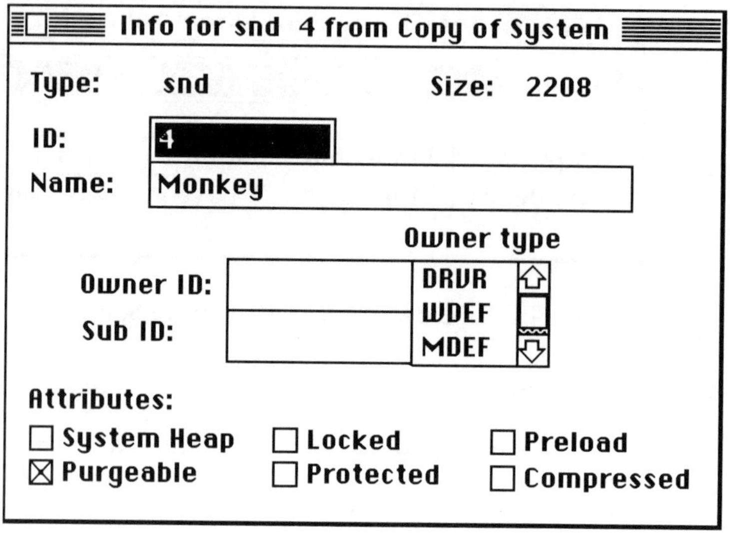

```
┌─────────────────────────────────────────────────────┐
│ ▤▢▦▬  Info for snd  4 from Copy of System ▬▬▬▬▬      │
├─────────────────────────────────────────────────────┤
│  Type:     snd              Size:   2208            │
│                                                      │
│  ID:      [ 4            ]                           │
│  Name:    [ Monkey                              ]   │
│                                                      │
│                              Owner type              │
│       Owner ID:  [          ]  DRUR  ⬆              │
│                                WDEF  ▯              │
│       Sub ID:    [          ]  MDEF  ⬇              │
│                                                      │
│  Attributes:                                         │
│  ☐ System Heap    ☐ Locked      ☐ Preload          │
│  ☒ Purgeable      ☐ Protected   ☐ Compressed       │
└─────────────────────────────────────────────────────┘
```

Figure 23-6. A typical Resource Info window.

▶ Resource Attributes

A resource's attributes control where it's loaded into memory and what happens to it after it's loaded. Whenever you create a new resource, it's important to make sure you set its attributes properly. The resource attributes are explained in Table 23-4.

| Hint ▶ | Whenever possible, be sure to check the Purgeable attribute. This helps avoid memory shortages by allowing the Memory Manager to remove the resource when memory starts getting full. However, don't set the Purgeable attribute unless you're sure the application can recover if the resource is purged from memory. For example, the Menu Manager doesn't recover purged 'MENU' resources. |

Table 23-4. Resource Attributes

Resource Attribute	Description
System Heap	Checked if the resource should always be loaded into the System heap. Use this only for resources that need to be shared by multiple applications. This should generally not be checked for an application's resources.
Purgeable	Checked if it's OK for the Memory Manager to remove the resource from memory if more space is needed.
Locked	Checked if the resource can't be moved in memory. The Locked attribute overrides the Purgeable attribute.
Protected	Checked if the resource and its ID and name can't be modified or deleted by an application.
Preload	Checked if the resource should be loaded when the file is opened.
Compressed	Checked if the resource is compressed. You'll probably only find this checked in ResEdit itself and in some System 7 files. You can't change this attribute.

Hint ▶

Be very cautious when you check the Locked attribute. A locked resource can't be moved when the Memory Manager needs to make room for new information. You can end up with plenty of unused memory but no way to make use of it because you have a locked resource right in the middle of the memory you need. If you need to use a locked resource, it's a good idea to also check the Preload attribute. This ensures that the resource is loaded into memory before any other memory is allocated, and keeps the resource out of the Memory Manager's way.

▶ Owned Resources

Since the System file is a collection of lots of resources (fonts and desk accessories, for instance) from many different places, there needs to be a way to determine which groups of resources belong together. This is especially important when a resource copying program (such as Font/DA

Mover or the Finder in System 7) tries to install a group of resources and the System file already contains resources with the same resource IDs. Font/DA Mover has to be able to renumber one of the groups of resources, which it can only do if it can figure out which resources belong together.

So, how does this work? It works by convention. Apple has reserved certain ranges of ID numbers for resource types that are likely to "own" other resource types. The System file can contain 64 resources of each of these special owner types before it runs out of unique resource IDs. Each owner can own up to 32 resources of any other type. Table 23-5 lists each possible owner type and the range of resource IDs it can own. The resource ID of the owning resource must be between 0 and 63 or it won't be recognized as a possible owner of other resources. Note that, because only certain resource IDs are valid for owned resources, some resource types having restricted ID ranges (such as 'FONT' and 'WDEF') can't be owned.

Table 23-5. Owned Resource ID Ranges

Owner Type	ID Range of Owned Resources
'DRVR'	-16,384 to -14,337
'WDEF'	-14,336 to -12,289
'MDEF'	-12,288 to -10,241
'CDEF'	-10,240 to -8193
'PDEF'	-8192 to -6145
'PACK'	-6144 to -4097
Reserved 1 (RSV1)	-4096 to -2049
Reserved 2 (RSV2)	-2048 to -1

In the middle of the Resource Info window are two fields and a list to help you figure out the correct resource ID for an owned resource. As you fill these in, ResEdit automatically calculates the proper resource ID for you. Figure 23-7 shows a Resource Info window for an owned 'DLOG' resource. The Owner ID field contains the resource ID of the owning resource. The Sub ID field contains a number to uniquely identify each resource of the same type owned by a given resource. For example, if a resource owns two 'DLOG' resources, the first one could have a Sub ID of 0 and the second one could have a Sub ID of 1. You can follow these steps to set up the resource ID of an owned resource.

1. In the Owner Type list, click the type of resource that will own your new resource.
2. Enter the resource ID of the owning resource in the Owner ID field (remember, it must be between 0 and 63).
3. Enter the Sub ID number. If this is the first resource of this type to be owned by this owner, enter 0. Otherwise enter the number equal to the count of all resources of the same type owned by the same owner. Sub ID numbers must be between 0 and 31, inclusive.

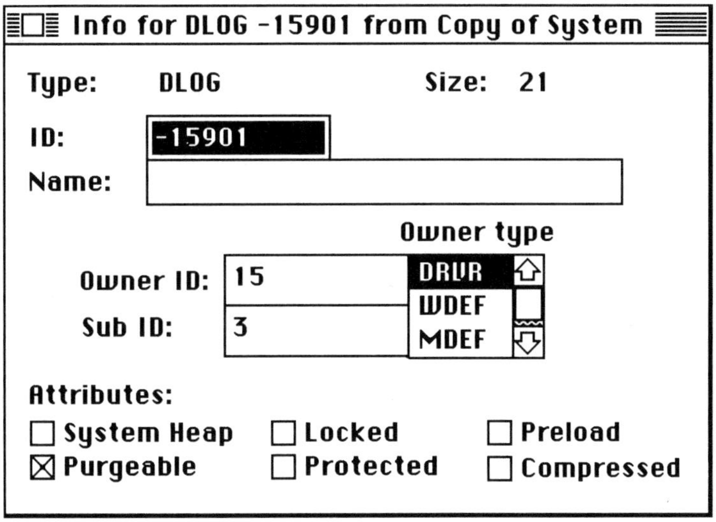

```
┌─────────────────────────────────────────────────┐
│▓□▓ Info for DLOG -15901 from Copy of System ▓▓▓▓│
├─────────────────────────────────────────────────┤
│  Type:     DLOG            Size:   21            │
│                                                  │
│  ID:     ┌────────────┐                          │
│          │ -15901     │                          │
│  Name:   ┌──────────────────────────────────┐    │
│          │                                  │    │
│          └──────────────────────────────────┘    │
│                           Owner type             │
│                          ┌─────────┐             │
│      Owner ID: │ 15  │   │ DRUR  ⬆ │             │
│                          │ WDEF    │             │
│      Sub ID:   │ 3   │   │ MDEF  ⬇ │             │
│                          └─────────┘             │
│  Attributes:                                     │
│  □ System Heap   □ Locked      □ Preload         │
│  ⊠ Purgeable     □ Protected   □ Compressed      │
└─────────────────────────────────────────────────┘
```

Figure 23-7. A Resource Info window using the Owner ID and Sub ID fields.

▶ Desk Accessories and Drivers

You may be wondering why desk accessories aren't among the resource types that can own other resources. In fact, they are. 'DRVR' resources can include both drivers (such as printer and network drivers) and desk accessories. The resource ID for a 'DRVR' resource that contains a desk accessory must be between 12 and 31 inclusive. The System uses the first character of a 'DRVR' resource's name to determine whether it's a desk accessory or a driver. For drivers the first character must be a period (.) and for desk accessories it must be a null (0). ResEdit helps make sure the name starts with the correct character by providing a pair of radio buttons in 'DRVR' Resource Info windows. A Resource Info window for a 'DRVR' is shown in Figure 23-8. When the resource info is saved, ResEdit sets the first character to the proper value depending on the state of the radio buttons.

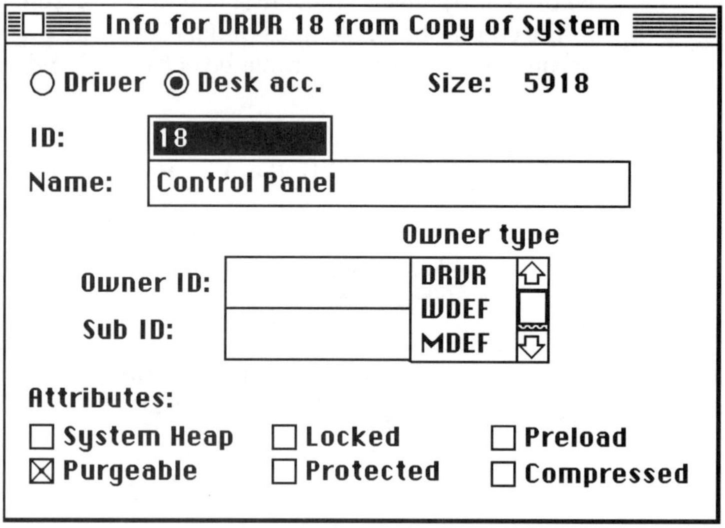

Figure 23-8. The Resource Info window for a 'DRVR' resource has two radio buttons at the top.

▶ Summary

This chapter begins with an introduction to the File Info window and all the interesting information it tells you about a file. You see how to change various characteristics the Finder stores for each file. You also see how the Finder uses a file's Type and Creator. Next, we explore the Folder Info window and its smaller set of Finder characteristics. We finish the chapter with a discussion of the Resource Info window. You see how to change various attributes of a resource as well as how to set up a resource ID for an owned resource.

24 ▶ Creating Templates for Your Resources

In Chapter 14 you learned how to use templates to edit a variety of resource types. But wouldn't it be nice if you could create custom templates for resource types you've defined? ResEdit's template editor lets you do just that. This chapter gives you all the information and examples you need to create templates for your own resources.

A template allows you to display in a dialog, a field for every field that occurs in your resource. Although templates can represent most types of data you're likely to have in your resource, a few constructs are just too complex. Understanding the limitations of templates before you design your resource's data structures helps assure that you can define your resource in such a way that you can create a suitable template.

ResEdit stores its templates in 'TMPL' resources. The name of the 'TMPL' resource determines which resource type it's used with. For example, the 'TMPL' resource named "CNTL" is used to define a window layout to edit 'CNTL' resources. One of the templates that comes with ResEdit is for the 'TMPL' resource, so you use the template editor itself to create your templates! If you're not familiar with the procedure for filling in templates (especially repeating lists), be sure to review Chapter 14.

The 'TMPL' resource contains a list of labels and field types that correspond to the data contained in your resource and to fields in a window when the template is used. Each field in the template tells ResEdit how to treat a certain part of your resource. One field may say to display the next two bytes as a decimal word, while the next field may say to skip four bytes.

Let's begin by taking a look at a simple template. The 'CNTL' template is shown in use in Figure 24-1.

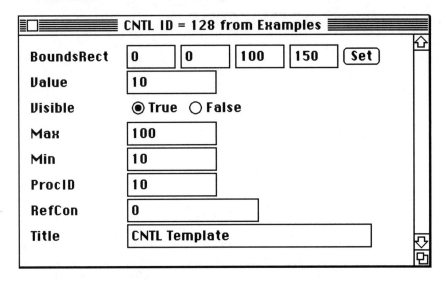

Figure 24-1. The 'CNTL' template is one of the simplest templates you'll see.

The 'TMPL' resource named "CNTL" that defines the window layout used to edit 'CNTL' resources is shown in Figure 24-2. Each label/type pair shown in Figure 24-2 corresponds to a label and field in Figure 24-1.

As you can see in Figure 24-2, the template is made up of a long list of labels and types. The types tell ResEdit how to format the data for a field. For example, the first field contains a rectangle (RECT) called "BoundsRect," while the second field contains a decimal word (DWRD). You can interpret the rest of the fields similarly.

ResEdit recognizes about 40 different field types. When you use these types, remember to enter them exactly as they're shown below. All the types must be entered in uppercase, and they're all four characters long. The types can be broken down into two groups: those that define single fields and those that define lists. We'll describe the single field types next, followed by a few examples, then we'll describe the list types.

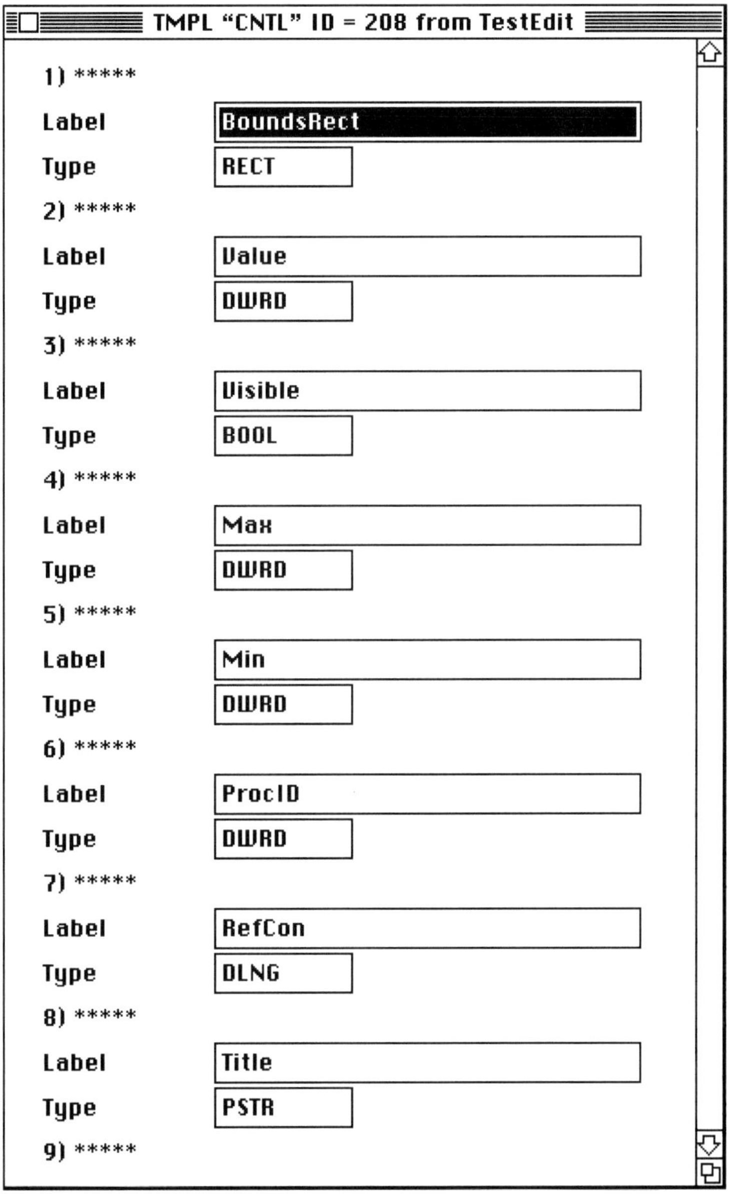

```
┌──────────────────────────────────────────────────────────┐
│▤□▤▤▤▤▤ TMPL "CNTL" ID = 208 from TestEdit ▤▤▤▤│⬆│
│ 1) *****                                                │
│ Label        │ BoundsRect                    │           │
│ Type         │ RECT  │                                   │
│ 2) *****                                                │
│ Label        │ Value                          │          │
│ Type         │ DWRD  │                                   │
│ 3) *****                                                │
│ Label        │ Visible                        │          │
│ Type         │ BOOL  │                                   │
│ 4) *****                                                │
│ Label        │ Max                            │          │
│ Type         │ DWRD  │                                   │
│ 5) *****                                                │
│ Label        │ Min                            │          │
│ Type         │ DWRD  │                                   │
│ 6) *****                                                │
│ Label        │ ProcID                         │          │
│ Type         │ DWRD  │                                   │
│ 7) *****                                                │
│ Label        │ RefCon                         │          │
│ Type         │ DLNG  │                                   │
│ 8) *****                                                │
│ Label        │ Title                          │          │
│ Type         │ PSTR  │                                   │
│ 9) *****                                              │⬇│
└──────────────────────────────────────────────────────────┘
```

Figure 24-2. The definition of the 'CNTL' template.

▶ Field Types

▶ Numeric Field Types

AWRD, ALNG

Align to word (AWRD) and align to long (ALNG) act like spacers and don't show up when ResEdit displays the template—they just make sure the template editor looks in the right place in the resource for the data. For example, you could have the following data structure in a Pascal module:

```
animal: RECORD
            isHuman: BOOLEAN;
            numberOfLegs: INTEGER;
        END;
```

The boolean occupies only one byte, but the integer must start on an even-word boundary, so Pascal puts an empty byte in between the two fields. The template for this data structure would contain:

DBYT   For the one-byte boolean field
AWRD   To skip the next byte
DWRD   For the decimal word

You need to use an AWRD field any time you have a single byte followed by a multi-byte field. Keep in mind, though, that compilers are smart enough to avoid adding spare bytes if you have two one-byte fields in a row. For example, if you changed your data structure to

```
animal: RECORD
            isHuman: BOOLEAN;
            hasHair: BOOLEAN;
            numberOfLegs: INTEGER;
        END;
```

you wouldn't need to include an AWRD field because the two booleans would occupy one word.

When you use an AWRD or ALNG field, you can leave the label field blank or add a label that will help you understand the template the next time you look at it. Anyone using the template never sees the label.

DBYT, DWRD, DLNG

Decimal fields come in three sizes, shown in Figure 24-3. The numbers shown in the fields in the figure are the largest numbers you can enter.

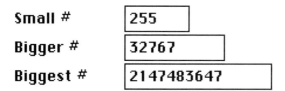

Figure 24-3. Decimal fields.

FBYT, FWRD, FLNG

Adding FBYT, FWRD, or FLNG to your template definition causes the byte, word, or long always to be filled with zero. The field acts like a spacer and does not appear when the template is used—the template user doesn't even know the field exists. These types are useful if you have unused or reserved fields you might want to use later. If you fill them with zero now, you can use them later and not worry that old versions of the resource might contain unknown values.

HBYT, HWRD, HLNG

HBYT, HWRD, and HLNG are hex versions of the decimal fields. The only real difference is that the numbers are formatted in hex ($1F02, for example) when the window opens.

▶ Pascal String Field Types

PSTR

A Pascal string field contains one byte containing the length of the string, followed by the text of the string, as shown in Figure 24-4. For example, if you have a field of type *STR255* in your data structure, you could use this template type if you want to save only the number of characters that are actually used in your string. That is, this type represents a variable amount of data in the resource—from one byte (an empty string) to 256 bytes.

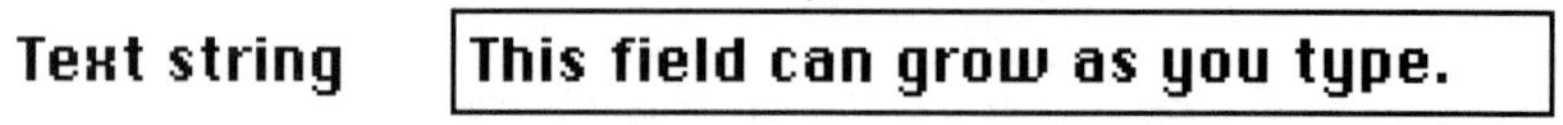

Text string | This field can grow as you type. |

Figure 24-4. All the string field types look like this.

WSTR

WSTR is similar to PSTR, except the length occupies a word (two bytes).

LSTR

LSTR is similar to PSTR, except the length occupies a long word (four bytes).

ESTR

ESTR is the same as PSTR, except the total length (including the length byte) must always be even. If the user enters an even number of characters (which, with the length byte would give the string an odd length), ResEdit adds a byte filled with zero to the end. For example, if the string contained the character *a*, the resource would contain $01 (length byte), $61 (*a*). If the string contained *ab*, the resource would contain $02 (length byte), $61, $62 (*ab*), $00 (a null pad byte) to make the total length even (four).

OSTR

OSTR is the same as ESTR except padded to an odd length. For example,
   a will be $01, $61, $00 (null pad byte) and
   ab will be $02, $61, $62.

P0nn

P0nn represents a Pascal fixed-length string. You should replace the "nn" with a hex number representing the maximum length of the string (not including the length byte). Since this is a Pascal string, it starts with a byte for the length and is limited to a maximum length of 255 characters (P0FF is the largest allowable string). The length byte indicates how much of the fixed-length string is actually being used. For example, P010 would represent a 16-byte string with a one-byte length.

This is the most commonly used of the fixed-length string types. For example, if you have an *STR64* field in your Pascal data structure, you could include a P040 in your template. This way, you wouldn't have a variable-length field in your resource as you would if you used a PSTR field to only save the part of the *STR64* that was actually used.

▶ C String Field Types

CSTR

CSTR is similar to PSTR, except it's used for C strings which have no length byte and end with a null ($00) byte.

ECST

ECST is similar to ESTR, except it's used for C strings. For example,
a will be $61, $00 (null termination byte) and
ab will be $61, $62, $00 (null termination byte), $00 (pad byte).

OCST

OCST is similar to OSTR, except it's used for C strings. For example,
a will be $61, $00 (null termination byte), $00 (pad byte) and
ab will be $61, $62, $00 (null termination byte).

Cnnn

Cnnn represents a C fixed-length string. You should replace the "nnn"with a hex number indicating the maximum size of the field. There's no length byte involved as there is for P0nn, so the length can be up to $FFF (4095 decimal). Since it's a C string, the characters are displayed up to the first null (0) byte. Unlike Pascal strings, no extra byte is added for C strings. For example, C010 would represent a 15-byte string plus a null byte. Don't forget to leave room for the extra byte used by the null terminator.

▶ Hex Dump Field Types

Hnnn

Hnnn represents a fixed-length hex list. Unlike the Cnnn and P0nn fields all "nnn" bytes in an Hnnn field are always shown. The length can be up to $FFF (4095 decimal) bytes. This type is especially useful if you have some structured data which doesn't match any of the other template types. For example, if you have a black-and-white pattern (*Pattern = PACKED ARRAY [0..7] of 0..255*) in your data structure, you could use an H008 template field to display it.

HEXD

HEXD represents a hexadecimal dump field. This type may be specified only as the last type in a template and displays the rest of the resource in a hex field. Many resources contain formatted information at the beginning that can be modified and constant, or complex information at the end that won't be modified. This situation is perfect for a HEXD field.

▶ Miscellaneous Field Types

BOOL

BOOL represents a two-byte boolean value as shown in Figure 24-5. It's displayed as a pair of radio buttons. A 0 value is interpreted as false and a 1 is true. Note the warning with the BBIT definition below.

This is fun ⦿ **True** ◯ **False**

Figure 24-5. True is 1 and false is 0 for boolean fields.

By the Way ▶ | This field type is not nearly as useful as you might think. You can't use this type for C or Pascal booleans since they only take up one byte.

BBIT

A BBIT field represents one bit of a byte as a pair of radio buttons. BBIT fields must come in sets of eight. If you're only using one bit of a byte, you must still include the other seven bits (you can label them as "Unused"). The first BBIT field represents the high-order bit of a byte. A few BBIT fields are shown in Figure 24-6.

Warning ▶	Be cautious in your use of these fields. If you have a lot of BBIT or BOOL fields (for example, if you use them in a repeating list), scrolling can become painfully slow.

First bit:	○ 0	◉ 1
Second bit:	◉ 0	○ 1
Third bit:	○ 0	◉ 1
Unused bit:	◉ 0	○ 1

Figure 24-6. Each pair of radio buttons represents one bit of a byte.

CHAR

CHAR fields are used for a single character (one byte).

RECT

RECT represents a rectangle made up of four words. As shown in Figure 24-7, it also includes a Set button used to set the values in the RECT fields. See Chapter 14 for more information about the Set button.

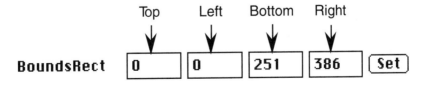

Figure 24-7. RECT fields can be filled in using the Set button.

TNAM

A TNAM field, like the one in Figure 24-8, contains a four-character type name. For example, the BNDL template uses a TNAM field for the application's signature resource, and the installer script templates use it to tell the installer which resources to install.

Type name | ICON |

Figure 24-8. TNAM fields can contain resource types.

▶ A Few Examples

That's all the different types of fields, so let's take a look at a few examples.

Defining a 'CNTL' template

Table 24-1 shows the definition of a 'CNTL' resource and the template types that would be used to make a 'CNTL' template. As you can see, for a simple data structure like this there's an easy one-to-one mapping between the Pascal data type and the template field type. This is a case where the BOOL type can be used because the visible field is not really saved as a Pascal boolean.

Table 24-1. Template Types for a 'CNTL' Resource

'CNTL' Field	Pascal Data Type	Template Field Type
boundsRect	Rectangle	RECT
value	Integer	DWRD
visible	Integer	BOOL
max	Integer	DWRD
min	Integer	DWRD
procId	Integer	DWRD
refCon	LongInt	DLNG
title	Str255	PSTR

Defining a 'ppat' Template

Now let's look at a slightly more complex example. The 'ppat' resource contains a pixel pattern that can vary in size and can contain up to 256 colors. As you can imagine, this is a complex data structure. The first part of the resource directly corresponds to the memory-resident data types PixPat and PixMap. This part of the resource contains lots of useful information, such as the size of the pattern and the bits per pixel (number of colors). The last part of the resource contains the pixel data itself and the table of colors that goes along with it. This last part of the resource would be much too difficult to edit in an unstructured way. (People have done it, but few survived unscathed.) Table 24-2 shows a way that a 'ppat' template could be designed.

Table 24-2. Designing a Template for a 'ppat' Resource.

'ppat' Field	Pascal Data Type	Template Field Type	Description
PixPat			
patType	Integer	DWRD	Type of pattern
patMap	PixMapHandle	DLNG	Offset to PixMap
patData	Handle	DLNG	Offset to pixel data
patXData	Handle	FLNG	0
patXValid	Integer	FWRD	-1
patXMap	Handle	FLNG	0
pat1Data	Pattern	H008	Old-style pattern
PixMap			
baseAddr	Ptr	FLNG	0
rowBytes	Integer	HWRD	Offset to next line
bounds	Rect	RECT	Boundary of image
pmVersion	Integer	DWRD	Version number
packType	Integer	DWRD	Packing format
packSize	LongInt	DLNG	Length of pixel data
hRes	Fixed	HLNG	Horizontal resolution
vRes	Fixed	HLNG	Vertical resolution
pixelType	Integer	DWRD	Pixel type
pixelSize	Integer	DWRD	Number of bits in pixel
cmpCount	Integer	DWRD	Number of components in pixel
cmpSize	Integer	DWRD	Number of bits per component
planeBytes	LongInt	DLNG	Offset to next plane
pmTable	CTabHandle	DLNG	Offset to color table
pmReserved	LongInt	FLNG	0
pixel data	—	HEXD	Data for pattern
color data	—	—	Data for color table

There are several things to note in this table.

- Since the resource's format is the same as the data structure in RAM, several fields in the resource are not used (they're mostly reserved for handles used when the pattern is loaded into RAM). These fields are represented by one of the fill types, so the user doesn't have to worry about them at all.
- The old-style pattern is represented by an 8-byte hex field since it's eight bytes of unformatted data.
- The last part of the resource is structured data that can't be edited using a template, so it's just listed in hex with the hex dump type.

▶ Using Lists in Templates

Now let's move on to some more complex resource types. Many resources contain a standard element repeated a variable number of times. For example, the 'FOND' resource contains a bunch of fixed information about a 'FONT' followed by the style and 'FONT' resource ID for every available size of the font. Since the resource has a variable number of fields, you can't use the field types described previously without some additional constructs. For this situation, ResEdit lets you define several kinds of repeating sequences. Any of the normal field types can appear within a repeating list (including other repeating lists).

By convention, the label for list-start and list-end fields is five asterisk (*) characters. Always using the same label makes it easy for users to know when they're editing a repeating list. Whenever you create a list, remember to include an LSTE field to mark the end of the list.

▶ LSTZ, LSTE

List zero, list end. These lists repeat until the first byte of the list entry contains zero. You probably won't find much use for this kind of list, but ResEdit uses it for both 'MENU' and 'cmnu' templates. The menu template definition is shown in Table 24-3. The fields between the ***** labels are repeated until the first byte of the "MenuItem" string contains a zero. This is especially convenient for 'MENU' resources since the zero would also indicate the MenuItem was a zero-length string.

Table 24-3. The 'MENU' Template

Label	Template Field Type
MenuID	DWRD
Width	FWRD
Height	FWRD
ProcID	DWRD
Filler	FWRD
EnableFlgs	HLNG
Title	PSTR
*****	LSTZ
MenuItem	PSTR
Icon#	DBYT
Key equiv	CHAR
Mark Char	CHAR
Style	HBYT
*****	LSTE

▶ ## ZCNT, LSTC, LSTE

Zero count, list count, list end. These lists are preceded by a zero-based count of the number of entries in the list. A ZCNT field must always be followed immediately by an LSTC field. This count occupies two bytes and contains -1 if there are no items in the list. The user can't modify the count field but sees it as a constant number maintained by ResEdit. For example, a 'clut' template is shown in Figure 24-9. The CtSize field shows how many colors (minus one, since the count is zero-based) are in the table and it can only be changed by adding or removing colors.

The 'clut' template definition is shown in Table 24-4. The fields between the ***** labels are repeated the number of times indicated by the ZCNT field, plus one. Note that the ZCNT field has a label and appears in the template but is not part of the list, as shown in Figure 24-9.

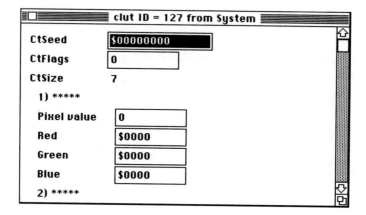

Figure 24-9. This 'clut' resource contains eight colors.

Table 24-4. The 'clut' Template Definition

Label	Template Field Type
CtSeed	HLNG
CtFlags	DWRD
CtSize	ZCNT
*****	LSTC
Pixel Value	DWRD
Red	HWRD
Green	HWRD
Blue	HWRD
*****	LSTE

▶ OCNT, LSTC, LSTE

One count, list count, list end. This type of list is identical to the ZCNT, LSTC, LSTE list just described, except the count that precedes the list is one-based rather than zero-based.

▶ LSTB, LSTE

List begin, list end. This list repeats until it reaches the end of the resource. For example, the 'pltt' template defined in Table 24-5 contains some information about the palette followed by a list of the colors making up the palette. Notice in this template that although there's a count of the number of palette entries, it's not immediately preceding the list, so an OCNT, LSTC, LSTE type of list can't be used. Using a template to edit 'pltt' resources would have been much more convenient if an OCNT, LSTC, LSTE list could have been used because the count would have been automatically updated when a color was added or removed. Try to avoid this kind of mistake when you design your data structures.

Table 24-5. The 'pltt' Template Definition

Label	Template Field Type
Color table count	DWRD
Reserved	FLNG
Reserved	FWRD
Reserved	FLNG
Reserved	FLNG
*****	LSTB
Red	HWRD
Green	HWRD
Blue	HWRD
Color usage	DWRD
Tolerance value	DWRD
Private flags	HWRD
Private	FLNG
*****	LSTB

▶ Creating Complex Templates

Now let's look at an example of creating a template for a more complex resource. This example illustrates techniques you can use to create templates for your own resource types.

When you add files to ResEdit's Open Special menu, your selections are stored in a resource of type 'FILE' in the ResEdit Preferences file. The data structure it uses contains some general information followed by a list of files.

```
FileListItem = RECORD
                    volName:  STR64;
                    dirID:    LONGINT;
                    cmdKey:   CHAR;
                    dupName:  BOOLEAN;
                    name:     STR64;
               END;
FileListRec = RECORD
                    count:    INTEGER;
                    unused:   INTEGER;
                    version:  INTEGER;
                    theFiles: ARRAY [1..5] OF FileListItem;
               END;
```

Here's an outline of what you could do to convert this data structure into a template so you could look at the Open Special menu data stored in the Preferences file.

- The first and third fields of the FileListRec are simple integer fields that can be represented by DWRD fields in the template.
- You can use an FWRD field for the unused integer.
- The rest of the resource contains an array of file information that ends at the end of the resource. Since there's no count field, you can use an LSTB, LSTE list to represent the array.
- The first field in the array is a 64-character Pascal string. Since all 64 bytes are saved in the resource, and not just the number of charac-ters used in the string, a P0nn field can be used in the template. The "nn" in P0nn is the number of characters in the string repre-sented in hexadecimal. The number 64 decimal is 40 hexadecimal, so you can use a P040 field.
- The length of the string is odd (64 characters plus the length byte), so an AWRD field is needed to make sure the next field starts on a word boundary.
- The dirID field is a long integer and can be represented by a DLNG template field.

- Since this is not a packed data structure, the Command key occupies two bytes. Characters always fit in a single byte, so the first byte has no meaning and can be represented by an FBYT field. The Command key itself can be a CHAR field.
- The dupName boolean only uses one byte, so you can't use a BOOL field type. Instead, use a DBYT field (a zero represents false and a one represents true).
- Since the boolean was only one byte, another AWRD field is needed to keep things lined up properly.
- The last field is another *STR64* and can once again be represented by a P040 field followed by another AWRD. The last AWRD is important to keep the next set of fields in the list in the right place.
- Finally, use an LSTE to mark the end of the list.

The finished template is shown in Table 24-6. If you want to give this a try, just create a template with the fields shown in the table. Use the Get Info Command on the Resource menu to give the template a name of "FILE". Now you can open the 'FILE' resource in the ResEdit Preferences file, and you'll see the contents of your Open Special menu, as shown in Figure 24-10.

Table 24-6. A Template for ResEdit's 'FILE' Resource Type

Label	Template Field Type
Count	DWRD
Unused	FWRD
Version	DWRD
*****	LSTB
Vol name	P040
(none)	AWRD
Dir ID	DLNG
(none)	FBYT
CMD Key	CHAR
Duplicate?	DBYT
(none)	AWRD
Name	P040
(none)	AWRD
*****	LSTE

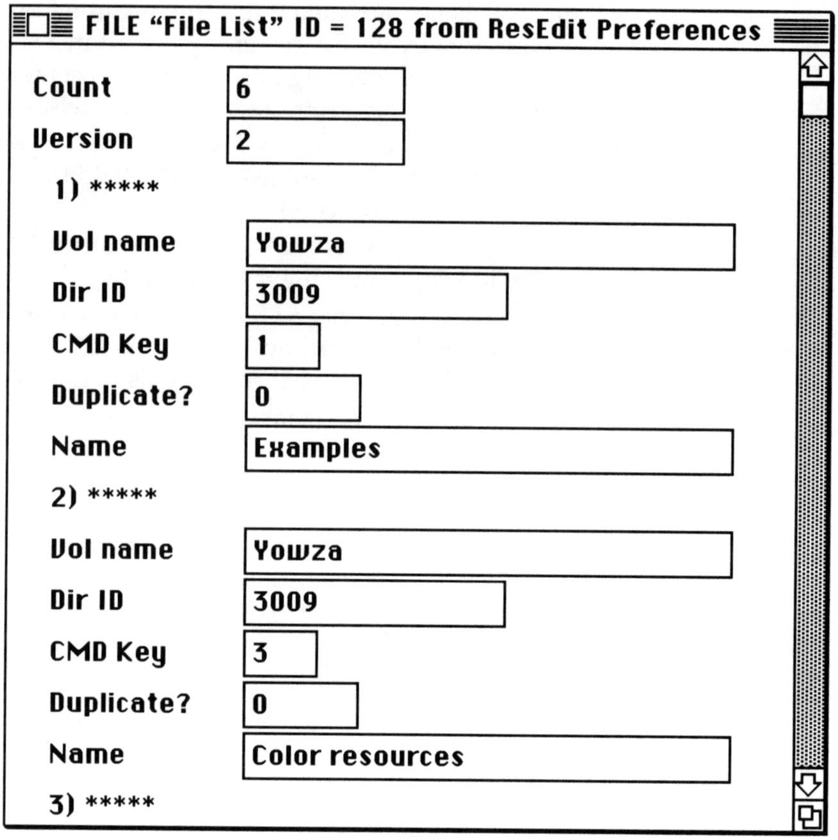

Figure 24-10. The 'FILE' template in use.

▶ What You Can't Do with Templates

As you have seen, you can create templates for most data structures you're likely to use in your resources. However, you could easily create a data structure that couldn't be edited with a template. The 'ictb' resource type (dialog item color table) is a good example of a resource type that can't be edited using a template. This resource type is used to set colors and styles for items in dialogs and alerts. Unfortunately, to make sense of the 'ictb', you have to simultaneously look in the corresponding 'DITL' (dialog item list) resource. For example, the 'ictb' resource starts with an array that contains two words for each item in the dialog, but there's no way of knowing how many items are in the dialog without looking in the 'DITL' resource.

Another technique that strikes terror into the hearts of template designers is the inclusion of pointers or offsets within a resource. The 'ppat' resource contains several offsets, including one to the color table, which is stored at the end of the resource. It would be useful to edit the color table, but there's no way to let the template know where the colors start. If the color table data had been stored before the pixel data at the end of the resource, and a count of the number of colors had been added, the table could have been edited.

The third bane of template designers is variable-length blocks of data. The 'cicn' resource contains several variable-length fields for things like the mask data and the color table. Since there's no way to know the size of these in advance (the size of these fields must be computed from other fields in the resource), there's no way to create a template to edit them.

The 'snd ' resource provides an example of another technique that's sure to ruin your template-designing dreams. Depending on the value in the first word of the resource, the structure of the rest of the resource changes! Making a template to deal with this situation isn't possible.

▶ Caring for Your Templates

▶ Name Your Templates

Be sure to give your template a name that's exactly the same as the resource type you designed it to edit. For example, if you want to edit an 'ABCD' resource, you need a 'TMPL' resource named "ABCD".

▶ Where to Keep Your Templates

ResEdit looks in all open files when it needs to find a template. If you'll only need to use your template with one file, you could put it into that file. This would guarantee it would always be available when you were using that file.

If you want to use your template on several files, the best place to put it is in the ResEdit Preferences file. ResEdit automatically opens this file, which is in your System Folder, and can use any template you put there.

▶ Make Them Purgeable

Don't forget to make your 'TMPL' resources purgeable. If you don't, memory will be wasted on resources you're no longer using. Here's how to do it.

1. Open your 'TMPL' resource.
2. Choose Get Resource Info from the Resource menu.
3. Check the Purgeable check box.
4. Close the info window and save the file.

▶ Template Limitations

Templates have a few limitations, but you shouldn't have to worry about running into them. In fact, if you even get close to these limits, you should think about writing your own editor (see Chapter 28) instead of using a template. For example, the 'pltt' template works only for very small palettes. Since the typical palette contains 256 entries and each entry contains six fields, a template would contain over 1500 data fields! You wouldn't want to wade through 1500 data fields to find the color you want to change.

Each field of a template can contain no more than 32,000 characters (this is a limit of the TextEdit routines in the Macintosh Toolbox). For fields containing just text, this limitation is straightforward. However, for fields that display the information in hex (such as HEXD), one character in the resource can translate into several characters in the field. For hex fields, you can display about 8770 bytes before you hit the 32,000-character limit.

There can be no more than 2048 total fields in a template. Needless to say, templates this big get a bit unwieldy. This field limitation is imposed by the Macintosh's Dialog Manager, so it includes all fields—not just data fields, as you might expect. Calculating the number of fields you're using can be tricky, but here is a formula that should work.

1. Count the number of fields outside of repeating lists and multiply by 2 (one for the data and one for the label). We'll call this number "Constant" in our formula.
2. Count the number of times your lists repeat. We'll call this "ListCount."

3. Count the number of fields inside one instance of your list. Call this "Fields."

Now, using these names, our formula would be:

TotalFields = Constant + (ListCount + 1) + (ListCount * Fields * 2)

In the formula, the (ListCount + 1) item accounts for the ***** labels and the (ListCount * Fields * 2) accounts for the labels and data fields inside the lists.

Here's an example. A 'pltt' resource has one visible field of constant information and six fields for each palette entry. If we have a 'pltt' resource with 157 palette entries, we can use the formula to figure out that:

2 + (157 + 1) + (157 * 6 * 2) = 2044 fields.

So, this resource could just barely be displayed. Adding one more palette entry would put it over the limit.

▶ Adding an Icon for Your Resource Type to ResEdit

When you select View by Icon from a type picker's View menu, you see a custom icon for each resource type that ResEdit can edit—except yours. This problem is easy to fix, however. All you have to do is add an 'ICON' resource and an 'icl4' resource (if you want to have a color icon) to your ResEdit Preferences file. The resource ID you use doesn't matter, just make sure the name of each resource is the same as the resource type it represents. For example, if you want to add an icon for the 'FOOB' resource type, just add an 'ICON' and an 'icl4' named "FOOB." On a color screen, ResEdit first looks for an 'icl4' but if it doesn't find one, it uses the 'ICON'.

▶ Data Type Reference

This section contains a partial list of Pascal and C data types and their corresponding template field types. Table 24-7 lists common Pascal types, and Table 24-8 lists C types. If you need to use a data type not in the list, just find out how many bytes it occupies and look for a template type that's the same size.

Remember, you need to use the AWRD type after a boolean or even-length string field (unless the data structure was not declared as *PACKED* in Pascal).

Table 24-7. Pascal Data Types and Their Corresponding Template Field Types.

Data Type	Size	Template Field Type
boolean	1 byte	DBYT
SignedByte	1 byte	DBYT
Byte	2 bytes	FBYT + DBYT, FBYT + HBYT
Char	2 bytes	FBYT + CHAR
Integer	2 bytes	DWRD
Longint	4 bytes	DLNG
Ptr	4 bytes	HLNG
Handle	4 bytes	HLNG
Real, Single	4 bytes	HLNG, H004
Double	8 bytes	H008
Comp	8 bytes	H008
Extended	10 bytes	H00A
ResType	4 bytes	TNAM
Rect	8 bytes	RECT
String[nn]	n+1 bytes	P0nn
STR255	256 bytes	P0FF

Table 24-8. C Data Types and Their Corresponding Template Types

Data Type	Size	Template Field Type
boolean	1 byte	DBYT
unsigned char	1 byte	DBYT, HBYT
char	1 byte	DBYT, CHAR
short	2 bytes	DWRD
unsigned short	2 bytes	DWRD, HWRD
int	4 bytes	DLNG
unsigned int	4 bytes	DLNG, HLNG
long	4 bytes	DLNG
enum	1-4 bytes	DBYT, DWRD, DLNG
Ptr	4 bytes	HLNG
Handle	4 bytes	HLNG
float, single	4 bytes	HLNG, H004
double	8 bytes	H008
comp	8 bytes	H008
extended	10 bytes	H00A
long double	10 bytes	H00A
ResType	4 bytes	TNAM
Rect	8 bytes	RECT
STR255	256 bytes	P0FF

▶ Template Field Type Summary

▶ Numeric Field Types

AWRD, ALNG	Align to word, align to long
DBYT, DWRD, DLNG	Decimal byte, decimal word, decimal long
FBYT, FWRD, FLNG	Fill byte, fill word, fill long with zero
HBYT, HWRD, HLNG	Hex byte, hex word, hex long

▶ String Field Types

Pascal string types

PSTR	Pascal string starting with length byte
WSTR	Pascal string starting with length word
LSTR	Pascal string starting with length long word
ESTR	Even-padded PSTR
OSTR	Odd-padded PSTR
P0nn	Fixed-length Pascal string "nn" characters long

C string types

CSTR	C string terminated by a null (0) byte
ECST	Even-padded CSTR
OCST	Odd-padded CSTR
Cnnn	Fixed-length C string "nnn" characters long

▶ Hex Dump Field Types

Hnnn	Hex dump of "nnn" bytes
HEXD	Hex dump of the rest of the resource

▶ Miscellaneous Field Types

BOOL	Two-byte boolean
BBIT	Binary bit—must use in sets of eight
CHAR	One-byte character
RECT	Rectangle made up of four words
TNAM	Four-character type name

▶ List Field Types

LSTB, LSTE	Repeat list to end of resource
LSTZ, LSTE	Repeat list until first byte of list is zero
OCNT, LSTC, LSTE	List starts with a one-based count
ZCNT, LSTC, LSTE	List starts with a zero-based count

▶ **Summary**

This chapter contains all the information you need to create your own templates. The detailed description of each field type will help you decide which types to use. We include several real-life examples of creating templates from scratch. A set of tips and suggestions finishes off the how-to part of the chapter. The chapter concludes with some reference tables that will be indispensable when you start creating your own templates. Now that you have all the information you need, the next step is up to you—go forth and create templates!

25 ▶ Mapping Resources

Occasionally you'll find that a resource type you've defined looks exactly like one that already has a template or editor in ResEdit (though it may even serve a very different purpose). There's a special type of resource you can create to tell ResEdit to pretend that a resource of one type is really a different type. This 'RMAP' resource must be located either in ResEdit itself or in the ResEdit Preferences file (located in your System Folder). For example, ResEdit uses an 'RMAP' resource to make sure the 'MENU' editor is started when an 'mctb' (menu color table) resource is opened. When you create a new 'RMAP', you fill out a template that tells ResEdit which two resource types to consider equivalent.

Warning ▶	Be very careful when you create 'RMAP' resources. Most editors simply won't work if you ask them to edit a resource containing data that's different from what they expect. Make sure the structure of the two resource types really is the same before you create an 'RMAP'.

▶ An 'RMAP' Example

Suppose you've defined a new resource type, 'ABCD', that has a structure just like the standard 'STR#' resource type. Instead of creating a new template, you can follow these steps to add an 'RMAP' to ResEdit's Preferences file.

1. Open the ResEdit Preferences file found in your System Folder.
2. Open the 'RMAP' resource type and create a new resource.
3. Type 'STR#' in the MapTo field of the window that appears.
4. Put a 0 in the Editor only field.
5. Choose Get Resource Info from the Resource menu.
6. Change the name of the resource to "ABCD," and click the Purgeable check box.
7. Close the Resource Info window. The window should now look like Figure 25-1.
8. Close and save the Preferences file.

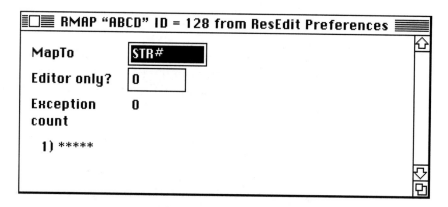

Figure 25-1. An 'RMAP' for 'ABCD' resources.

Now when you open an 'ABCD' resource, you'll see it displayed using the normal ResEdit 'STR#' template.

▶ Mapping by Resource ID

Sometimes it's convenient or desirable to have resources with different resource IDs, but the same resource type, contain different types of data. For example, the old 'INTL' international resource type always contained two resources. The 'INTL' resource with ID 0 contained the format for numbers, short dates, and times, while the 'INTL' resource with ID 1 contained the long date format. Because of the limitations of the template editor, it would be impossible to create an 'INTL' template that would satisfy the needs of both these data structures.

Creating an 'RMAP' resource to map individual resource IDs to different editors or templates solves this problem. For example, the 'RMAP' for the 'INTL' resource maps resources with ID 0 to the 'itl0' editor, and those with ID 1 to the 'itl1' editor, as you can see in Figure 25-2.

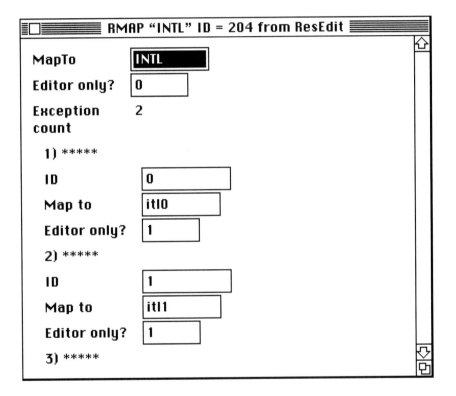

Figure 25-2. An 'RMAP' can map each resource ID to a different editor or template.

All resource IDs that aren't specified in the exception list will be mapped to the resource type specified in the MapTo field at the top of the 'RMAP' template. For example, in Figure 25-2, an 'INTL' resource with ID 6 would be edited as an 'INTL' resource—in other words, not mapped at all.

▶ What Does "Editor Only" Mean?

Set the Editor only field to true (1) if you're mapping a resource to an editor, and false (0) if you're mapping it to a template. For example, in Figure 25-2, the 'INTL' resource is being mapped to the 'itl0' and 'itl1' editors, so Editor only is true. However, when the 'FCMT' (Finder comment) resource is mapped to the 'STR#' resource, Editor only is false because the resource is being mapped to a template.

Here are the sordid details behind this obscure mechanism. One of the most important jobs of the 'RMAP' resource is to map resources (such as 'mctb's) to editors (such as the 'MENU' editor) that can understand more than one resource type. The problem arises when an editor decides that it can't really edit the resource for some reason (for example, the 'mctb' doesn't have an associated 'MENU' resource, so the 'MENU' editor can't edit it). When an editor detects this situation, it tells ResEdit to start up the template editor for the resource (for example, launch the template editor with the 'mctb' resource). The template editor looks through the 'RMAP' resources and sees that the resource should be mapped ('mctb' is mapped to 'MENU'). It then uses the template for the *mapped to* resource to open the *mapped* resource (for example, it opens the 'mctb' resource using the 'MENU' template), giving you really screwy results since the resource won't match the template. So, to prevent such a mess, if the template editor is looking for a template, it will not use the 'RMAP' resource if Editor only is true.

▶ Summary

This chapter shows you how to set up an 'RMAP' resource to allow more than one resource type to be edited by the same editor. This can be useful if ResEdit already contains an editor or template for a resource type that's just like the one you're creating. Use this feature with caution, however—make sure the resource types really are identical before you proceed.

PART SIX

▶ Customizing ResEdit

26 ▶ Overview for Writing Pickers and Editors

If you've created your own resource type for your application, wouldn't it be nice to be able to edit it in your own custom editor? Or maybe you've created a graphical resource type, and you have a hard time telling the resources apart just using ResEdit's built-in picker. A resource picker that draws the resources and lets you select the one you want might be just what you need. This chapter can help you decide whether it makes sense to go to all the effort required to write your own editor or picker. It also gives you an overview of what you need to know before you start crunching out code. Chapters 27 through 29 give you more explicit details about creating editors and pickers.

▶ Writing Your Own Picker or Editor

Writing your own editor or picker doesn't have to be a big deal. In most cases, writing your own picker is quite straightforward. In fact, if you use the example code that comes with ResEdit, you probably won't have to do much more than provide a procedure to draw your resource. Writing your own editor is usually more complex, but if you have a simple resource and you want to do only simple editing, your job won't be too hard. If, on the other hand, you have a complex resource, it may take you significantly longer to write an editor. In any case, ResEdit provides lots of help.

▶ Writing a Picker

Most of the time, you won't need to bother creating your own picker since ResEdit's built-in pickers are usually sufficient. There are, however, a few cases where you could make your life as a developer significantly easier by spending a day setting up your own picker.

Why Write a Picker?

Here are some situations where you might want to write your own picker.

- If you have a graphical resource type and you want to draw it in the picker window, you can add a new list definition procedure. Most of the pickers in ResEdit were implemented solely to display resources in the appropriate format. (For example, the 'ICON' picker draws 'ICON' resources.)

- If you want to initialize a new resource with certain default values, you can modify the example code and simply intercept the Create command.

- If you want to perform an operation on a set of resources, you'll need your own picker. For example, the 'snd ' picker allows 'snd ' resources to be played.

- If you want to display additional information about your resources, you can customize the list definition procedure. The 'DRVR' picker does this to include "Driver:" or "Desk Acc:" in front of the resource's name.

- If you want to sort your resources in a special way, you can do this in your picker. The 'FONT' picker does this to group fonts by family.

- If you want to do something special when one of your resources is cut, copied, pasted, cleared, or reverted, you can add your own event-processing code. The 'FONT' picker uses this technique to add and remove font family resources.

- If you want to let your users pick from a list of possibilities when a new resource is created, you can intercept the Create command and add your own dialog. Again, the 'FONT' picker does this to allow users to pick from a list of fonts already installed in their System file.

▶ Writing an Editor

If you've defined a new resource type and need to create lots of different resources of that type, you may want to write an editor. Writing an editor can be difficult, but the payoff can also be large. If possible, you should try to define your resource type so you can use a template instead of writing your own editor, because you would surely rather spend your time working on your application than writing an editor for your resources. Chapter 24 contains details about creating templates and the pitfalls to watch out for when defining the structure of your resources.

Why Write an Editor?

Here are some situations where you might want to write your own editor.

- If you have a graphical resource type, you'll probably want to write your own editor so you can conveniently edit it. Imagine trying to create an 'ICON' using the hexadecimal editor!
- If you have a structured resource type with fields that can only take certain values, you may want to write an editor. Resources such as 'MENU's could be edited with a template, but it would be tedious (as you already know if you used ResEdit before version 2.0).
- If you have a set of interrelated resource types, you'll probably want to write an editor that will help maintain the proper relationships. Before ResEdit included a 'BNDL' editor, people had trouble creating the set of resources that make up the bundle because of the difficulty of getting that many resources to work together properly.
- If you have a resource that contains a fixed number of fields, you may want to write an editor that simply displays a dialog box. The 'itl0' and 'itl1' resources could be edited with a template, but editing them is much easier in a dialog box that doesn't have to scroll and that contains useful fields such as pop-up menus and check boxes.

▶ How Pickers and Editors Work

Pickers and editors are stored within ResEdit in 'RSSC' (named for Rony Sebok and Steve Capps, the creators of the first ResEdit) and 'PICK' resources. The names of these resources tell ResEdit what each 'RSSC' or 'PICK' resource should be used for. 'PICK' resources are used to create simple pickers that don't need to do any of their own event processing. There are three categories of 'RSSC' resources: editors, pickers, and subeditors (we'll explain subeditors shortly). The format of the name distinguishes these types of resources. If the name of an 'RSSC' resource is the same as a resource type, then the 'RSSC' resource contains a picker for that resource type. If the name of the 'RSSC' resource starts with an @ character, it's an editor. If the name starts with a dollar sign character ($), it's a subeditor. Table 26-1 illustrates this relationship. To see more examples, use ResEdit to open itself, open the 'RSSC' resource picker, and you'll see all the editors and pickers that come with ResEdit.

Table 26-1. 'RSSC' Resource Name Formats.

'RSSC' Name	What It Does
FONT	Picker for 'FONT' resources
@FONT	Editor for 'FONT' resources
@KCHR	Editor for 'KCHR' resources
$KCHR	Subeditor for 'KCHR' resources

When ResEdit needs to find a picker, editor, or subeditor for a particular resource type, it adds the appropriate character (nothing, @, or $) to the type of the resource it's looking for, then tries to find an 'RSSC' resource with that name inside ResEdit. If it's looking for a picker, it first checks for a 'PICK' resource before it looks for an 'RSSC'. If it doesn't find either a 'PICK' or an 'RSSC', it uses the general picker (stored in a 'PICK' resource named "GNRL") which displays a text list of the resources. If it's looking for an editor and doesn't find one, it uses the general editor (an 'RSSC' resource named "GNRL") which is the template editor. The template editor looks in all open files for a template ('TMPL' resource) with a resource name the same as the type of the resource to be edited. If it doesn't find a template, the template editor starts the hexadecimal editor (an 'RSSC' named "HEXA") which can edit resources of any type.

We've mentioned subeditors several times, so we had better let you know what they are and how they're used. A subeditor is just a part of another editor. It allows the editor to open non-modal windows to edit parts of a resource. For example, the 'DITL' editor uses a subeditor to edit the characteristics of individual dialog items and the 'KCHR' editor uses a subeditor to edit dead keys (dead keys are explained in Chapter 9). Subeditors are particularly convenient when your resource type contains a variable number of similar components (such as dialog items in the 'DITL' resource type). An editor can have only one subeditor.

▶ Using the Example Code

ResEdit comes with a set of code examples that can help you write your own pickers and editors. In fact, you can usually just make a few changes and have your own picker or editor up and running in no time. Before you can use the example code, however, you need to understand how the files are organized and how you can build the examples.

The examples are set up to use Apple's Macintosh Programmer's Workshop (MPW) development environment (version 3.2 or later), which is available from APDA (Apple's mail-order source for programming tools). We highly recommend that you use MPW, since we don't know of anyone who has successfully created an editor or picker in a different development environment. (It may be possible, we just don't know of anyone who has done it.)

A sample resource picker, editor, and 'LDEF' (List DEFinition procedure used with pickers) are included with the examples. All of the examples are provided in both Pascal and C—you can pick your poison. A few assembly language modules that you won't need to modify are also included. You'll need to assemble them and use them when you link together your files.

A picker is made up of two parts: a list definition procedure stored in an 'LDEF' resource and either picker code stored in an 'RSSC' resource or a picker definition stored in a 'PICK' resource. The example picker code displays 'ICON' resources, but you may not need to use the picker code at all. You might be able to get by with creating a 'PICK' resource. We'll talk more about 'PICK' resources in the next chapter. Whether you write a picker or use a 'PICK' resource, you'll need to implement an 'LDEF' to draw the picture or text for each resource. You don't need to know too much about the List Manager, but reviewing Chapter 30 of *Inside Macintosh*, Volume IV before you make changes to the 'LDEF' would be a good idea.

The example editor displays a window and inverts its contents. This doesn't sound like much, but it does handle quite a bit of the overhead for you. You won't have to worry about decoding events or setting up your window. Of course, since only you know the details of editing your resource, it's up to you to fill in the code necessary to make this into a real editor.

▶ The Example Files

The Examples folder contains several other folders that help organize the example code. The layout of the folders is shown in Figure 26-1. The Examples folder contains a file with some basic instructions and three folders—one for C examples, one for Pascal examples, and one for the assembly language libraries you'll need to link with. The C and Pascal folders contain the same set of files, so we'll describe the files generically here instead of giving specific details for each language.

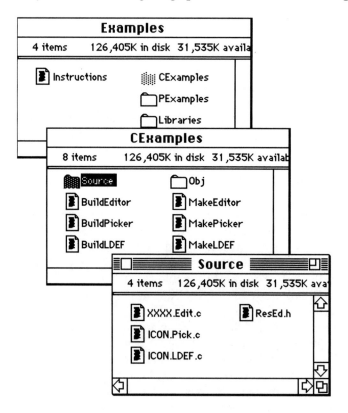

Figure 26-1. The files in the Examples folder.

Files Included in the CExamples and PExamples Folders

BuildEditor, BuildPicker, BuildLDEF. These files contain MPW scripts that compile, link, and install the editor, picker, or 'LDEF' example. BuildPicker builds both the picker and the 'LDEF' code and should be used if you're writing picker code. If you're using a 'PICK' resource, all you need is the 'LDEF', so you can use the BuildLDEF script. In the next section, we describe how to use these files to build the examples.

MakeEditor, MakePicker, MakeLDEF. These are the Make files used by the build scripts. They contain the dependencies that determine when the files are compiled and linked.

Files Included in the Source Folder

ResEd.h or ResEd.p. This is the interface file for the procedures in ResEdit that pickers and editors can use. The contents of this file are discussed in detail in Chapter 29.

XXXX.Edit.c or XXXX.Edit.p. This file contains the code to implement a simple editor for resources of type 'XXXX'. This is the file that will be the starting point for your editor. Chapter 28 analyzes this code in detail.

ICON.Pick.c or ICON.Pick.p. This file contains an 'ICON' picker. You can use this code as the starting point for creating your own picker. The details of the code are explained in the next chapter.

ICON.LDEF.c or ICON.LDEF.p. This file contains the list definition procedure the 'ICON' picker uses. The next chapter includes a detailed description of this code.

Files Included in the Libraries Folder

ResDisp.a. This is the file that "hooks" editors and pickers to the main part of ResEdit. Each of the procedures defined in the ResEd interface file has an entry point here (thus the name RESource DISPatch). You won't need to change this file, but you'll need to link it with your editors, pickers, and 'LDEF's.

RSSC.a. This file is similar to the ResDisp file, except that it provides the hooks for the main part of ResEdit to call your editor or picker. Each editor or picker must contain a few specific procedures (for initialization and event processing) that the main part of ResEdit can call. These procedures are described later in this chapter. You won't need to change this file either, but you must include it in your editor and picker links (but not your 'LDEF' link, since the Toolbox, not ResEdit, calls your 'LDEF').

LDEF.a. This file allows you to write your 'LDEF' in a high level language instead of assembly language. You won't need to change this file, but you should link it with your 'LDEF'.

▶ Building the Examples

The build scripts are already set up to build the examples for you. The scripts assume copies of ResEdit and the Examples folder are located in a folder named ResEdit at the root level of your boot volume. Before you can run the script, you need to set the directory to the Examples folder. You can do that with this MPW command

```
Directory {Boot}ResEdit:Examples:CExamples:
```

for the C examples or

```
Directory {Boot}ResEdit:Examples:PExamples:
```

for the Pascal examples. After setting the directory, just run the Build-Editor, BuildPicker, or BuildLDEF script.

The scripts will use the example Make files to build the examples and install them directly into ResEdit. After the scripts have successfully finished, just start up ResEdit and check out what you've built. It will be hard to tell that the picker example is installed since ResEdit normally uses a 'PICK' resource to implement the 'ICON' picker. (You can delete the 'PICK' resource named 'ICON' from ResEdit to try out your picker.) We'll talk more about 'PICK' resources in the next chapter. The example editor is a little easier to test. Just create a resource of type 'XXXX' and you should see a small window filled with black. That's all the 'XXXX' editor does—it's up to you to fill the window with something useful.

Don't forget to keep a backup copy of ResEdit just in case something goes wrong with the build. You should always have a spare copy to go back to if you need to start over.

▶ The Global Data Structures

Since pickers and editors aren't linked with the main part of ResEdit, they don't have access to global data. Instead of using global variables, they must store all their data in a handle which they allocate and save in the window's *refCon* field (this field is found in every window record and is available for use by applications). All pickers and editors use a variation of the *ParentRec* data type to hold their data. Every picker and editor will have different information in its *ParentRec*, but the first few fields must always be the same. Even though each editor and picker has its own version of the *ParentRec* data structure, we'll refer to them by the generic name *ParentRec* (or *ParentHandle*) unless we're referring to a specific type of *ParentRec*. The main part of ResEdit uses the first part of the *ParentRec* to get information about the editor or picker that owns a window. The version of the *ParentRec* used by pickers has a few additional required fields and is called a *PickRec*. Figure 26-2 illustrates the way *ParentRec*s and windows are linked together.

<table>
<tr><td>By the Way ▶</td><td>The name ParentRec is a little misleading. Each editor's or picker's ParentRec contains its own data, not its parent's data.</td></tr>
</table>

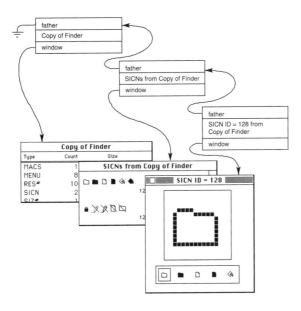

Figure 26-2. A linked list of parent records and their windows.

▶ The *ParentRec* Data Type

The *ParentRec* data structure (accessed via a *ParentHandle*) defined in the ResEd interface file defines only those fields that are required by Res-Edit. When you define your own version of this structure, you'll add other fields to the bottom. Here's the definition of the fields of a *Parent-Rec* that all editors and pickers must include.

```
typedef struct ParentRec {
        ParentHandle      father;
        Str255            name;
        WindowPeek        wind;
        Boolean           rebuild;
        Boolean           resWasntLoaded;
        unsigned char     windowType;
        ResType           theResType;
        short             theResFile;
        short             codeResID;
        Handle            theResToEdit;
        /* Editor or picker specific fields start here. */
} ParentRec;
typedef   ParentRec       *ParentPtr;
typedef   ParentPtr       *ParentHandle;
```

Each of the fields is explained in the following list.

- *father*—When a new window is opened, the new window's *ParentRec* is initialized to contain a handle to the *ParentRec* of the window that opened it. This field forms a linked list of *Parent-Handle*s so that ResEdit can find the windows in the order they were opened. For example, when a resource picker window is closed, ResEdit uses the linked list of *ParentHandle*s to make sure that all the editors for that resource type are also closed.

- *name*—The second field contains a unique name for this instance of the *ParentRec*. For pickers, this field should contain the complete pathname of the picker's file. For editors, it contains the window name. More details about the naming conventions can be found in the Tips section at the end of this chapter. ResEdit normally sets the strings up for you so you won't have to worry about creating them yourself.

- *wind*—The *wind* field contains a pointer to the window that owns the *ParentRec*. This field allows ResEdit to traverse the linked list of *ParentHandle*s and still find the associated windows. Conversely,

ResEdit can traverse the linked list of windows and find the associated *ParentHandle*s since the window record's *refCon* field contains a handle to the *ParentRec* associated with the window.

- *rebuild*—*rebuild* indicates whether the window contents should be recalculated. This flag is usually set by a window opened by the window that owns the *ParentRec*. For example, when the 'ICON' editor changes an 'ICON', it sets the *rebuild* flag in the 'ICON' picker's *ParentRec* to let the 'ICON' picker know that it should rebuild its list of 'ICON's. As another example, the 'DLOG' editor sets the *rebuild* flag of the 'dctb' picker when a 'dctb' resource is added or removed ('dctb' resources add color to 'DLOG's). If it didn't set the flag, the 'dctb' picker's list wouldn't be accurate. Every picker (and any editor that can start another editor) should check the *rebuild* flag whenever an activate event is received.

- *resWasntLoaded*—The *resWasntLoaded* flag is only used by editors (it's replaced by a spare field in the *PickRec* definition). It's used to indicate whether the editor should release the resource that it's editing when its window is closed. It's important to avoid releasing a resource that's being used by someone else! Use of this field is described in more detail in Chapter 28.

Warning ▶

This isn't a fail-safe method of determining whether the resource is in use or not. For example, if some other part of ResEdit starts using the resource after the editor has been opened, the editor will release the resource when its window is closed, causing possible problems for the other user of the resource.

- *windowType*—The *windowType* field is used to tell ResEdit what type of window owns the *ParentRec*. The possible values are *typePickerWindow*, *resourcePickerWindow*, *folderInfoWindow*, *fileInfoWindow*, *resourceInfoWindow*, *editorWindow*, and *floatingWindow*.

- *theResType*—The *theResType* field contains the resource type of the resource being edited or picked.

- *theResFile*—The file number of the file that contains the resource being edited or picked is kept in *theResFile*.

- *codeResID*—The *codeResID* field holds the resource ID of the 'RSSC' resource containing the picker or editor. (The **ResEdID** procedure is used to fill in this field.)

- *theResToEdit*—A handle to the resource being edited is kept in *theResToEdit*. This field is used only by editors. It's replaced by a spare field in the *PickRec* structure.

▶ The *PickRec* Data Type

All pickers use the *PickRec* data type shown below, which is a superset of the *ParentRec* data structure.

```
typedef struct PickRec {
        ParentHandle        father;
        Str255              fName;
        WindowPtr           wind;
        Boolean             rebuild;
        Boolean             spare1;
        unsigned char       windowType;
        ResType             theResType;
        short               theResFile;
        short               codeResID;
        Handle              spare2;
        ResType             rType;
        long                rSize;
        short               minWindowWidth;
        short               minWindowHeight;
        ListHandle          instances;
        short               nInsts;
        short               viewBy;
        Boolean             showAttributes;
        ResType             ldefType;
        MenuHandle          theViewMenu;
        long                viewMenuMask;
        Cell                cellSize;
        STR255              optionCreateStr;
    } PickRec;
typedef PickRec     *PickPtr;
typedef PickPtr     *PickHandle;
```

As you can see, the first ten fields are the same as those in the *Parent-Rec* (except for a couple of fields that are called "spare" since they aren't used by pickers). The rest of the fields are used only by pickers. Here's a description of the additional fields.

- *rType—rType* is the resource type the picker is displaying. *rType* usually contains the same value as the *theResType* field. It might be different from *theResType* if an editor is also a picker. For example, the 'DLOG' editor pretends to be a picker when it opens the associated 'DITL' resource. It always keeps 'DLOG' in the *theResType* field, but when it's pretending to be a picker, it puts 'DITL' into the *rType* field so it can open the 'DITL' editor.

- *rSize—rSize* holds the size of a new empty resource. When the user creates a new resource, ResEdit automatically allocates a handle with *rSize* bytes.

- *minWindowWidth* and *minWindowHeight*—These two fields contain the minimum window size allowed when the user changes the size of the picker window.

- *instances—instances* is the handle to the List Manager list that contains the resources being displayed.

- *nInsts—nInsts* is the number of resources being displayed in the picker's list.

- *viewBy*—The current checked item on the picker's View menu is saved in the *viewBy* field. If you create a picker that shows resources in some new way (graphically, for example), you should initialize the *viewBy* field to *viewBySpecial* so the View by <type> item on the View menu will be enabled. Users will still be able to use the general picker to view by name, ID, size, or order, but if they pick View by <type>, your 'LDEF' is used.

- *showAttributes*—If *showAttributes* is true, the resource attributes are displayed when *viewBy* is set to any type except *viewBySpecial*. You should never set this field since its value is saved in the ResEdit Preferences file.

- *ldefType—ldefType* is the name of the 'LDEF' resource used to control the picker's list. Normally, *ldefType* is the same as *rType*, but sometimes one 'LDEF' can be used for several resource types (for example, the 'ICN#' picker uses the 'ICON' 'LDEF').

- *theViewMenu—theViewMenu* is a handle to the picker's View menu.

- *viewMenuMask—viewMenuMask* determines which items are enabled on the View menu. It can contain the values *viewNoSpecial*, *viewNoAttributes*, or *viewAll*.

- *cellSize—cellSize* determines the size of each cell in the list. This field is only used when View by Special is checked on the View menu.

- *optionCreateStr—optionCreateStr* replaces the normal CreateNew Resource text on the Resource menu when the Option key is pressed. The 'ppat' picker uses this string so the user will know that a relative pattern will be created if the Option key is pressed when a new pattern is created.

▶ Creating Your Own *ParentRec*

Your editor or picker will need to define its own equivalent of the *ParentRec* data structure. You'll call it something else, but remember to make the first few fields the same as the *ParentRec* or *PickRec*. For example, an editor that has its own menu might define the following *Parent-Rec* equivalent record.

```
typedef struct rABCDRec {
        ParentHandle      father;
        Str255            name;
        WindowPeek        wind;
        Boolean           rebuild;
        Boolean           resWasntLoaded;
        unsigned char     windowType;
        ResType           theResType;
        short             theResFile;
        short             codeResID;
        Handle            theResToEdit;
        MenuHandle        myMenu;
    } rABCDRec;
```

This editor has added only one new field: a handle to keep track of its menu. In a real editor, there would probably be many more fields including the undo state, preference values, selection information, and other data needed to edit the resource.

▶ How Editors and Pickers Communicate with ResEdit

Since editors and pickers are separate resources, you may be wondering how they communicate with the main part of ResEdit. You have to worry about communication both from your editor or picker to ResEdit and *vice versa*. We'll explain how ResEdit communicates with your editor or picker shortly. The only communication necessary in the other direction is when you want to use a procedure provided by the main part of ResEdit. You can do this by calling one of the 90 or so procedures that ResEdit provides (these are defined in the ResEd interface file). You'll link with a small assembly language dispatch module (ResDisp.a) that makes sure your call gets to the right procedure in ResEdit. The details of how to use each procedure can be found in Chapter 29.

▶ Entry Points for Editors and Pickers

Every picker (unless it's implemented using a 'PICK' resource) and editor must contain six procedures. These procedures provide the means for ResEdit to communicate with your editor or picker. The procedures are the same for both editors and pickers.

EditBirth

```
pascal void EditBirth(Handle theResource, ParentHandle dad)
```

EditBirth is the entry point for initializing editors. After locating and loading the appropriate 'RSSC' resource, ResEdit calls the **EditBirth** procedure with a handle to the resource to be edited. The *ParentHandle* of the window that's opening the editor (usually a picker) is passed in so it can be stored in the *father* field of the new editor's *ParentRec* to form a linked list of *ParentHandle*s. All the initialization the editor needs to perform should be done in this procedure. The editor should allocate its own *ParentRec* data structure and fill it in. A window should be allocated and made visible (don't draw the contents of the window—wait for an update event). Other data structures that will be needed later should be initialized and menus should be loaded.

PickBirth

```
pascal void PickBirth(ResType whichType, ParentHandle dad)
```

PickBirth is the entry point for initializing pickers. You usually won't need to do much in this procedure because ResEdit takes care of most of the housekeeping for you. You'll need to allocate a *PickRec* and initialize any other data structures you may need later. The *dad* parameter is the *ParentHandle* of the window that's opening the picker (usually the type picker) and should be stored in the *father* field of the picker's *PickRec* to form a linked list. The *whichType* parameter indicates the resource type the picker should display in its window. (Most pickers know how to display only one type, but the general picker displays whatever type is specified by the *whichType* parameter.)

DoMenu

```
pascal void DoMenu(short menu, short item, ParentHandle dad)
```

ResEdit calls **DoMenu** whenever the user chooses a menu command that affects a picker's or editor's window. The *ParentHandle* data structure that was allocated in **PickBirth** or **EditBirth** is passed in to allow access to global data. This routine needs to handle menu commands only as they apply to its window—other windows will handle the commands themselves, if necessary. Some commands (such as Save and Close) should be passed on by calling ResEdit's **PassMenu** procedure. This allows windows opened by this editor or picker to get a chance to act on the command. Other commands (like Cut and Open Editor) can be handled by this editor or picker and won't affect other windows.

DoEvent

```
pascal void DoEvent(EventRecord *evt, ParentHandle dad)
```

DoEvent is similar to **DoMenu** except that it handles all events other than menu commands. This routine is called only when there's an event waiting that affects its window. Don't try to detect the double-click shortcut since ResEdit automatically converts double clicks into Open commands, which are passed to the **DoMenu** procedure.

DoInfoUpdate

```
pascal void DoInfoUpdate(short oldID, short newID,
                         ParentHandle dad)
```

DoInfoUpdate is called whenever an info window has changed something (like the resource ID) that might affect an editor's or picker's window. All data structures should be updated to reflect the new resource attributes, name, and ID. Don't forget to update the window title and the name that's kept in the *ParentRec*.

IsThisYours

```
pascal Boolean IsThisYours(Handle thing, ParentHandle dad)
```

IsThisYours is called when ResEdit needs to know if a resource is in use. Pickers should always return false since they don't need exclusive access to any resources. Editors should check to see if the resource in question is the one they're editing and return true if so.

▶ Tips for Writing Pickers and Editors

Here is a collection of ideas to keep in mind when you write your picker or editor.

▶ No Globals!

Pickers and editors don't have access to normal global variables (except, of course, the low memory globals available to every Mac application) since they're not linked as part of the main program (which means register A5 isn't set up properly). All data you would normally save as global data (anything you need to save between calls to one of the entry points to your Picker or Editor) should be kept in your *ParentRec*. The ResEdit routine **GetQuickDrawVars** returns a pointer to the Quick-Draw globals (*thePort*, patterns, etc.) if you need to access them. For example, if you want to fill a rectangle with a 50% gray pattern, you could use the following code:

```
qdGlobals = GetQuickDrawVars();
FillRect (aRect, qdGlobals->gray);
```

▶ Double Clicks

You never have to worry about double clicks that are shortcuts for the Open command. When a double click is detected, ResEdit turns it into an Open command on the Resource menu (Open Picker, Open Resource Editor, and so on). Keep in mind that your code won't know about double clicks unless the Open item on the Resource menu is enabled. If ResEdit detects a double click and finds that the Open item on the Resource menu is disabled, it assumes that your editor or picker can't handle Open commands. ResEdit also won't convert double clicks to Open commands if the user double-clicks a control in the window. (That's so double-clicking a button or scroll bar won't open something).

If double clicks make sense in only part of your window, you can use the **NoDoubleClicksHere** procedure to disable them where they don't make sense. When your editor gets a mouse down event where double clicks aren't allowed, call **NoDoubleClicksHere**. For example, the 'DLOG' editor uses this technique to make sure that only double clicks inside the MiniScreen area of the window open the 'DITL' editor.

▶ The ResEdit Preferences File Is Always the Current Resource File

The ResEdit Preferences file is always the current resource file—not the file being edited. This is to avoid accidentally using resources from the file being edited. For example, if you were editing a different version of the System than the one you started your Mac with, you wouldn't want to accidentally use some of the possibly incompatible code resources from the file you're editing. You should always make sure you keep the current file set to the Preferences file. You can avoid bunches of bugs by always keeping this in mind. In fact, you rarely need to switch the current file to the file being edited. If you need information about the file being edited, use one of ResEdit's extended Resource Manager calls. For example, if you want to know how many resources of a particular type are in the file, use **RECount1Resources**. The only time you might want to set the current resource file to the file being edited is when you call a Toolbox procedure that uses **GetResource** to load a resource or that has the side effect of loading other resources. Toolbox procedures to watch out for include **GetFontName, GetPattern, Get Cursor, GetNewDialog** and **NewDialog**.

▶ Use **REGet1ResourceSpecial**

Whenever you need to get a resource from the file that's being edited, be sure to use **REGet1ResourceSpecial**. This procedure is similar to the toolbox procedure **Get1Resource** (and ResEdit's equivalent **REGet1-Resource**), except that it also indicates whether the resource was in use before you loaded it. This information allows you to properly dispose of the resource when your window is closed. Normally, when you're done with a resource, you should use **ReleaseResource** to free the memory it occupied. If the resource was already in use, however, you should leave it just as you found it.

▶ Never Use **GetResource**

This is really a corollary to the last two tips. The problem with the **GetResource** Toolbox procedure is that it looks through all open resource files starting at the current file until it finds a resource with the specified resource ID. When you use this procedure, you don't know what file the resource will be found in, and you could unknowingly edit resources from several different files! You should always use **REGet1ResourceSpecial** so you know exactly which file you'll get the resource from. The one time when it's OK (and even necessary) to use **GetResource** is when you're looking for a resource that's stored in ResEdit itself. To get a resource (such as a 'MENU' or 'DLOG') from ResEdit, you need to use **GetResource** so that the Resource Manager looks in the ResEdit Preferences file first before looking in ResEdit itself.

▶ Activate and Deactivate Events

Keep in mind that when pickers and editors are started, they don't always get an activate event before they get a deactivate event! If the user opens several windows at once, it's possible for a window to be initialized and receive update and deactivate events even though it was never activated. This means you should never clean up anything in your deactivate event processing code that you have done only in your activate event code. You must take care of all initialization in the **Edit-Birth** or **PickBirth** procedures.

▶ Window-Naming Conventions

It's important to make sure your windows follow the proper naming conventions. The window names in ResEdit aren't used just to give information about what the windows contain. When the user opens a picker or editor, ResEdit looks at the window title and the *name* field of the *ParentRec* of each window that's already open to make sure it doesn't open the same window twice. If you don't set up your windows with the proper names, ResEdit won't be able to detect that your window is already open. Needless to say, two editors editing the same resource can make quite a mess! Here's a recap of what the names should be for each window type.

The title of a type picker window should be the name of the file being edited. The *name* in the *ParentRec* should be the complete path of the file (such as Inspiration:Neat Applications:ResEdit). A resource picker's window title is of the form <resource type> from <file name> (ALRTs from Copy of System, for example). The *ParentRec* name is the same as for type pickers: the full pathname of the file.

Editors are a bit funnier. They have a window title like, <resource type> "<resource name>" ID = <resource ID> from <file name> (for example, MENU "File" ID = 2 from ResEdit). The *ParentRec* name should be the same as the window title.

▶ You're Nothing Without a Window

An editor or picker only exists because it has a window. The window contains two pieces of information that tell ResEdit everything it needs to know to communicate with the editor or picker. The first is the *windowKind* field (available in every window record), which contains the resource ID of the editor or picker. This ID is what ResEdit uses when it sends events to the editor or picker. The second is the *refCon* field, which contains a handle to the editor's or picker's *ParentRec* data structure. This structure contains the information that ResEdit needs to manage its windows properly. So, when it's time for your editor or picker to call it quits (or an error occurs during initialization), all you have to do is delete the window and the editor or picker disappears.

▶ Remember to Pass on Menu Commands

Usually, it's sufficient for your editor or picker to process its own events and not worry about other windows at all. Sometimes, however, it's necessary to pass a menu command on to other windows. The only windows you need to worry about are those the editor or picker has opened. For pickers, these could be other picker windows, editor windows, or info windows. For editors, these could be other editors, subeditors, or info windows. From the standard menus, only Close and Save need this special treatment. If you have your own menus, you may have other commands that need to be passed on. "So," you're asking, "when should I do it?" Any time the command itself, or the changes you make as a result of the command, will affect windows you've opened, you should pass on the command. The Save command needs to be processed by every window to make sure all open resources are ready to be saved to the file. When a window processes a Close command, it must make sure that any windows it opened (editors, pickers, subeditors, or info windows) are also closed. If the Close command isn't passed on, the linked list of *ParentHandle*s is broken, and ResEdit becomes very confused. You can pass a Close command on like this:

```
PassMenu(fileMenu, closeItem, myParentHandle);
```

Remember, **PassMenu** only passes the menu command to windows opened by the window doing the passing.

▶ Resource IDs for Editors, Pickers, and Their Resources

When you create your editor or picker, you'll have to pick a resource ID for your 'RSSC', 'PICK', and 'LDEF' resources, as well as any other resources (such as 'DLOG's and 'MENU's) used by your editor or picker. Apple has established some informal guidelines to help avoid resource conflicts. In ResEdit, Apple has reserved the resource IDs from 0 to 2,500 and from 3,000 to 10,000 for editors and pickers provided by Apple. This leaves the ranges from 2,500 to 3,000 and above 10,000 for use by people writing ResEdit extensions. To help minimize conflicts, pick a number between 2,500 and 3,000 for your editor's or picker's 'RSSC', 'PICK' and 'LDEF' resources, and use a range of up to ten resource IDs starting with a number ten times your editor's or picker's number for your other resources. For example, you might pick 2,550 for your editor, and 25,500 to 25,510 for your dialogs and menus.

▶ How to Set Up the Menus

When your editor or picker receives an activate event, you'll have to make sure all the menus are set up properly. For example, an editor should usually make sure the Open commands on the Resource menu and the Select Changed command on the Edit menu are dimmed. You may also want to change the text on the Edit and Resource menus to better reflect the actions the commands will invoke. To do this in the most efficient way you need to know what you have to change and what ResEdit takes care of for you. ResEdit guarantees the following when an editor or picker receives an activate event.

- *File menu*—All menu items are enabled.
- *Edit menu*—The text of all menu items except Select All and Select Changed is set to the default strings. (Select All and Select Changed usually aren't changed.) If a picker window is being activated, all menu items are enabled. If an editor or floating palette window is being activated, all items except Duplicate, Select All, and Select Changed are enabled.

- *Resource menu*—The text of all menu items except Get Resource Info is set to the default strings (Get Resource Info usually isn't changed). If a picker window is being activated, all items are enabled. If an editor or floating window is being activated, only Revert and Get Resource Info are enabled.

▶ When Is a *ParentHandle* Really a Parent?

Usually when a picker or editor calls a ResEdit procedure requiring a *ParentHandle* parameter, the window's own *ParentHandle* should be passed. Sometimes though, it's OK to pass the *ParentHandle* of the window's parent window (the same as the *dad* parameter of **EditBirth** and **PickBirth**). You can pass the parent window's *ParentHandle* to **Already-Open, EditorWindSetup, GetWindowTitle, PickerWindSetup, Call-InfoUpdate**, and **WindOrigin**.

▶ Summary

This chapter gives you an introduction to the process of extending Res-Edit by writing your own pickers and editors. We introduce the basic concepts, explain the example code and the build process, detail the main data structures, show you the procedures that are required, and show you several tips to make writing your editor or picker as easy as possible. In the next few chapters you can find more detailed information about writing pickers and editors, and a reference to the many procedures that ResEdit provides to simplify the process.

27 ▶ Writing a Picker

This chapter shows you how to write your own custom picker for Res-Edit. We'll talk about the general requirements for a picker, explain how to use a 'PICK' resource for a simple picker, and consider the changes you might want to make for a more sophisticated picker. Be sure you're familiar with the overview presented in the previous chapter before you dive into this chapter.

▶ What Is a Picker?

A picker is just code that displays in a window all the resources of a particular type from a single file. For very simple pickers, ResEdit takes care of all the event processing—all you have to provide is a 'PICK' resource to describe the picker and an 'LDEF' to draw the resources. If you look inside ResEdit, you'll see that most of the pickers are implemented using 'PICK' resources. A few ('snd ', 'FONT', and 'MENU') use 'RSSC' resources. Chances are good that you'll be able to simply create a 'PICK' resource and an 'LDEF' to implement your picker.

If a special picker doesn't exist for a resource type, ResEdit uses the built-in general picker. The general picker displays the resource ID, size, and name, and supports the View menu to allow the resources to be sorted by ID, size, name, and order in file. Even if you implement a special picker, the View menu will still allow the user to display your resources in various ways using the general picker. Your picker will only be invoked when View By <Type> is chosen from the View menu.

▶ Using 'PICK' Resources

A 'PICK' resource contains the data that tells ResEdit how to create a picker window and how that window should behave. Since ResEdit can't know how to draw your resource type, you also have to provide an 'LDEF' to draw the resources in the picker's window. We'll explain the example 'LDEF' in the next section. You can use a 'PICK' resource any time your goal is to provide a picker that draws the contents of its window in some appropriate way. In other words, if your picker doesn't need to provide any non-standard actions in response to events, 'PICK' resources will work for you. To give you an idea of what kinds of requirements keep you from using a 'PICK' resource, you can look at the few pickers in ResEdit that don't use them. For example, the 'snd ' picker adds a menu to the menu bar, and the 'MENU' picker makes sure the resource ID of a menu is the same as the ID stored inside the menu.

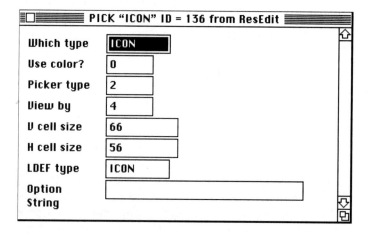

Figure 27-1. The template window for the 'PICK' resource used for the 'ICON' picker.

Figure 27-1 shows the template window for a 'PICK' resource. Notice that the resource contains fields similar to those stored in the *PickRec*. All ResEdit does is read the resource, initialize a *PickRec*, and allocate a window. As events are received that affect the picker's window, they're processed in the standard way. You can use the 'PICK' template to create and fill in new 'PICK' resources.

Here's what the fields of the 'PICK' resource mean.

- Which type—Which type is the resource type the picker will pick.
- Use color—Use color lets ResEdit know what kind of window to create. It should be *noColor* (0) for a standard black-and-white window, *canColor* (1) for a color window that will work properly if only black-and-white is available, and *requiresColor* (2) for a window that requires color.
- Picker type—ResEdit needs to know what kind of picker to create. Picker type can contain any of the values from the *PickerType* type defined in the ResEd file. Valid values are *textOnlyPicker*, *graphical-1DPicker*, or *graphical2DPicker* (0, 1, or 2). For example, ResEdit's standard picker that lists resources by name and ID is a *textOnlyPicker*. The 'SICN' and 'PAT#' pickers are *graphical1DPickers*. All of the pickers that list more than one resource in a row (such as the 'ICON' and 'PAT ' pickers) are *graphical2DPickers*.
- View by—When a picker window is opened, the initial view is specified by View by. Valid values are the same as defined in the *viewTypes* type from the ResEd file. The view is saved in the ResEdit Preferences file so this default is only used the first time a resource of this type is opened.
- V cell size and H cell size—The size of the cell allocated in the picker's list is determined by V cell size and H cell size. If 0 is specified in either of these fields, a default cell size is used.
- LDEF type—It's sometimes useful for several pickers to use the same 'LDEF'. To facilitate this, you can specify a different type here than was specified in the Which type field. For example, in ResEdit the 'ICON' and 'ICN#' pickers share the 'ICON' 'LDEF'.
- Option string—The string found in the Option string field is used to replace the text of the Create New Resource item on the Resource menu when the Option key is pressed. The 'ppat' picker uses this field to indicate that a relative pattern is created if the Option key is held down when a new pattern is created.

▶ What Is an 'LDEF'?

Pickers use lists managed by the List Manager to display all the resources of a particular type. (See *Inside Macintosh*, Volume IV for details about the List Manager.) The List Manager uses a list definition procedure to draw and highlight the items in the list. List definition procedures are stored in 'LDEF' resources and are loaded and called by the List Manager Package. List definition procedures are usually written in assembly language, but ResEdit includes a small assembly language module (LDEF.a) that allows you to write your 'LDEF' in C or Pascal. To write your 'LDEF' in C or Pascal, you must include a procedure named **DrawCell** in your C or Pascal module and link it with the LDEF.a file. *Inside Macintosh*, Volume IV, Chapter 30 describes how to use list definition procedures. Fortunately, ResEdit provides a procedure (**DrawLDEF**) that takes care of most of the work for you, as you'll see in the next section.

All of ResEdit's pickers set up their lists to provide the information needed by 'LDEF's in a consistent way. Each picker stores a handle to its PickRec data structure in the list's *refCon* field. This allows the 'LDEF' to access any of the values stored in the picker's *PickRec*. 'LDEF's also need to know the resource ID of the resource referenced by each cell. Pickers provide this information by setting the data for each cell to the resource ID of the resource referenced by that cell. When it comes time to draw the list, all the 'LDEF' has to do is look into the list to get the ID of the resource to draw. The next section shows you how easy it is to write an 'LDEF' for ResEdit.

▶ The LDEF Code

This section describes the details of the 'LDEF' used by the example 'ICON' picker. This 'LDEF' is also used by the 'ICN#' picker and illustrates how 'LDEF's can be shared by several pickers that display similar resources.

```
#define IconSize 128
```

IconSize specifies the size, in bytes, of the resource. This value is used to make sure the resource is valid before it's drawn.

```
pascal void DrawIcon (Rect *lRect, Handle theIcon) {
  if (SizeResource(tempH) >= IconSize)
    PlotIcon(lRect, theIcon);
}
```

The **DrawIcon** procedure draws the resource in the specified rectangle. In your 'LDEF', this procedure might need to perform more sophisticated drawing operations. For 'ICON's and 'ICN#'s, **PlotIcon** does all the work for you. If the resource is larger than it needs to be (it's an 'ICN#' or an invalid resource), the first 128 bytes are drawn. For your 'LDEF', it may be important to perform more thorough checking to make sure the resource is valid before it's drawn.

```
Handle IconFetch (Cell lCell, ListHandle lHandle,
                  short *id, Boolean *wasLoaded) {
  short      err;
  short      len = 2;
  Handle     tempH = nil;
  PickHandle tempPick;

  LGetCell((Ptr)id, &len, lCell, lHandle);
  if (len == 2) {          /* ID must be 2 bytes.        */
    tempPick = (PickHandle)((*lHandle)->refCon);
    tempH = REGet1ResourceSpecial((*tempPick)->theResFile,
                         (*tempPick)->rType, *id,
                         wasLoaded, &err);

  }
return tempH;
}
```

IconFetch is where this 'LDEF' does most of its work. It looks up the resource ID in the list data structure and gets a handle to the resource for the specified cell. **LGetCell** is called to get the contents of the cell. **REGet1ResourceSpecial** (described in Chapter 29) returns a handle to the resource that needs to be drawn. Remember, the list's *refCon* field contains a handle to the *PickRec* associated with the list. If your 'LDEF' draws only one resource type, you could use a constant instead of *rType*. The **was-Loaded** parameter is used to indicate whether the resource was already in memory and, therefore, should be left in memory when **DrawCell** is done.

```
pascal void DrawCell(short message, Boolean lSelect,
                   Rect *lRect, Point lCell,
                   short lDataOffset, short lDataLen,
                   ListHandle lHandle) {
  Handle theIcon;
  short id;
  Boolean wasLoaded;
```

DrawCell is the main entry point for the 'LDEF'. This is the procedure the List Manager calls to draw and highlight the resources in the list.

```
#pragma  unused (lDataOffset, lDataLen)
```

This *pragma* avoids warning messages from the compiler. The *lData-Offset* parameter is useful if you want to look directly into the list's data structure for the cell's data. The *lDataLen* parameter is useful if you're storing variable-length data in the list instead of the fixed-length resource IDs.

```
if ((message == lDrawMsg) || (message == lHiliteMsg)) {
  theIcon = IconFetch(lCell, lHandle, &id, &wasLoaded);
  DrawLDEF(message, lSelect, lRect, theIcon, id, "\p",
          32, 32, DrawIcon, lHandle);
  if ((theIcon ! = nil) && (! wasLoaded))
    HPurge (theIcon);
  }
```

The 'LDEF' only needs to respond to the draw and highlight messages—other messages can be ignored. ResEdit's **DrawLDEF** procedure handles the mechanics of drawing and highlighting the resource. It also draws the resource ID below the resource. **DrawLDEF** calls the **Draw-Icon** procedure just described to actually draw the resource. After the icon is drawn, the resource is made purgeable if it wasn't already in use when **DrawCell** was called.

That's all there is to writing an 'LDEF'. Of course, you don't have to use the **DrawLDEF** procedure. You could, instead, write your own code to draw anything you want in your picker's window. But, it's so easy to use **DrawLDEF**, why bother writing your own code?

▶ The 'ICON' Picker Code

If you need a more sophisticated picker than can be created with a 'PICK' resource, you'll have to write your own event processing code. The example picker code shows you a simple picker that displays 'ICON' resources and adds a menu to the menu bar. If you build this picker without changing its type, you'll need to delete the 'PICK' resource named 'ICON' from ResEdit before your code will be used. Next, we'll go through the picker code line by line, explaining how you can go about writing your own picker.

```
#define iconMenuID        10
```

```
#define listCellSizeH        0x38
#define listCellSizeV        0x42
```

iconMenuId defines the resource ID of the menu the picker will use. You'll need to supply your own menu since ID 10 is just a menu used by another part of ResEdit (and isn't even in the proper ID range for pickers). *listCellSizeH* and *listCellSizeV* define the cell size used in the list. The 'ICON' resource being displayed is only 32-by-32, but you need to leave room for a selection around the icon and the resource ID below it.

```
#define minIconsPerRow        2
#define ICONMinWindowWidth    (minIconsPerRow *
                               listCellSizeH) + theScrollBar
#define ICONMinWindowHeight   listCellSizeV
```

minIconsPerRow defines the minimum number of columns allowed in the list. When users resize the window, they won't be able to make it smaller than the width of two columns. If your picker is going to display a two-dimensional list (rows and columns of 'ICON's, for example), you must always show at least two columns. The number of columns is the only way ResEdit can tell the difference between a one-dimensional list (whose cells should get wider when the user expands the window) and a two-dimensional list (that should show more columns of fixed size cells). *ICONMinWindowWidth* and *ICONMinWindowHeight* define the minimum window size your picker will support. *theScrollBar* is the width of a scroll bar as defined in the ResEd file.

```
typedef struct IconPickRec {
    ParentHandle  father;
    ...
    Cell          cellSize;
    MenuHandle    iconMenu;
} IconPickRec;
typedef     IconPickRec  *IconPickPtr;
typedef     IconPickPtr  *IconPickHandle;
```

The *IconPickRec* structure defines the *PickRec* for this picker. It's identical to a *PickRec*, except for the name of the structure and the addition of the menu as the last field. When you define a new data structure, be sure to start with the definition of a *PickRec* and add to the bottom of it. In this way, other parts of ResEdit can still look at your data structure as if it were a *PickRec* and get the information they need.

```
pascal void EditBirth(Handle thing, ParentHandle dad) {
```

```
#pragma  unused (thing, dad)
}
```

EditBirth is used only for editors. You must include it here anyway since the RSSC.a file expects it.

```
pascal void PickBirth(ResType t, ParentHandle dad) {
  IconPickHandle   pick;
  IconPickPtr      p;                    /* temp ptr for *pick */
  MenuHandle       theIconMenu;
```

PickBirth is the initialization procedure for pickers. The *ResType* parameter *t* contains the resource type the picker should display. The *ParentHandle* points to the *ParentRec* of the window that's opening the picker (the type picker).

```
  pick = (IconPickHandle)NewHandle(sizeof(IconPickRec));
  p = *pick;
```

A handle (*pick*) is allocated to hold all of the picker's global data. Since this picker has added a menu to the standard *PickRec* structure, it has to allocate enough room for the slightly bigger *IconPickRec*. The variable *p* contains a pointer to the *IconPickRec* and is used to avoid dereferencing the handle each time it's used.

Warning ▶	Always be careful when you dereference handles. Since the handle isn't locked (which could have been done with the **HLock** Toolbox procedure), you must be careful not to do anything that may move memory. For each Toolbox procedure, *Inside Macintosh* indicates whether the procedure moves memory or not, so you can decide whether you need to lock the handle before making the call. If you're careful about locking handles, you'll avoid introducing bugs that are very hard to track down.

```
  p->father = dad;
  p->rType = t;
  p->viewBy = viewBySpecial;
  p->ldefType = t;
  p->cellSize.h = listCellSizeH;
  p->cellSize.v = listCellSizeV;
  p->minWindowWidth = ICONMinWindowWidth;
  p->minWindowHeight = ICONMinWindowHeight;
```

This code initializes the fields of the handle that was just allocated. These fields are explained in detail in Chapter 26.

```
1:    if (!DoPickBirth(noColor, true, graphical2DPicker,
2:                     ResEdID(), (PickHandle)pick)) {
3:      DisposHandle ((Handle)pick);
4:      }
5:    else {
6:      theIconMenu = GetMenu(iconMenuID);
7:      DetachResource((Handle)theIconMenu);
8:      (*pick)->iconMenu = theIconMenu;
9:      }
10:  }
```

By the Way ▶

Some code listings, like this one, have numbers at the left margin of each line of code. We've added these numbers so we can refer to specific lines of code. These numbers won't appear in the source code you compile.

In line 1, the **DoPickBirth** procedure sets up the window and creates the list for the picker—thus taking care of most of the hard work. It will return true if the window and list were successfully initialized, and false otherwise. If there was a problem, the *IconPickHandle* allocated earlier is disposed in line 3 and the picker exits—an appropriate error message has already been displayed by **DoPickBirth**. Line 6 loads the menu the picker will use, and line 7 detaches the menu handle. If you don't detach the handle, the picker will fight for control of the menu with pickers for other files. For example, if there are two 'ABCD' pickers open, both using the same 'MENU' resource, and the user closes one, releasing the 'MENU' resource, the other picker will have an invalid handle. Line 8 saves the menu handle in the *IconPickRec* structure.

```
pascal void DoEvent(EventRecord *evt, IconPickHandle pick) {
  PickEvent(evt, (PickHandle)pick);
  if (evt->what == activateEvt) {
    if (evt->modifiers & activeFlag)
      InsertMenu((*pick)->iconMenu, 0);
    else
      DeleteMenu(iconMenuID);
    DrawMBarLater (false);
    }
}
```

The **DoEvent** procedure handles all event processing for a picker. The picker can let the main part of ResEdit handle the standard events by calling the **PickEvent** procedure. When an activate event is received, **DoEvent** must also make sure the menu is inserted or deleted. Always use **DrawMBarLater** (described in Chapter 29) instead of the Toolbox procedure **DrawMenuBar** to avoid flickering of the menubar.

```
pascal void DoInfoUpdate(short oldID, short newID,
                         PickHandle pick) {
  PickInfoUp(oldID, newID, pick);
}
```

There's not much to say about this procedure—it's all handled by **PickInfoUp**. (Remember, this procedure is called when the user has changed a resource's attributes with the Get Resource Info command.) **PickInfoUp** scans through the list (using the handle in the *instances* field of the *PickRec*) in the picker's window and changes *oldID* to *newID*. If you have other data structures that depend on the ID, name, or attributes of the resources displayed in the picker window, you should update them in this procedure.

```
pascal Boolean IsThisYours (Handle thing, PickHandle pick) {
  #pragma  unused (thing, pick)
  return false;
}
```

A picker's **IsThisYours** procedure should always return false (true is returned when the resource is in use and shouldn't be used by other parts of ResEdit).

```
pascal void DoMenu(short menu, short item, IconPickHandle
                   pick) {
  if (menu == iconMenuID) {
    ;  /* Do something useful here. */
  }
  else {
    if ((menu == fileMenu) && (item == closeItem)) {
      DeleteMenu(iconMenuID);
      DrawMBarLater(false);
      DisposHandle((Handle)(*pick)->myMenu);
      }
    PickMenu(menu, item, (PickHandle)pick);
    }
}
```

DoMenu is the procedure that's called when the user picks a command from your menu, so here is where you'll do whatever is appropriate for their choice. This is also where you can intercept the Close command to make sure you remove and dispose of your menu before **PickMenu** does the final cleanup. Since the 'MENU' resource was detached, remember to use **DisposHandle** instead of **ReleaseResource**. (ResEdit had this bug for a long time!) **PickMenu** handles all the standard picker menu commands such as cutting, copying, duplicating, and reverting resources.

That's all there is to the standard picker example. All you need to add is the code to make it really do something!

▶ Fancy Pickers

As you've seen, ResEdit provides several procedures for you to call that will make your picker perform in the standard ways. Of course, you can override as much of the standard picker behavior as you want, but the more you override, the more work it is to get the picker working. An extreme example of this strategy is the 'FONT' picker, which overrides almost everything. If you want to expend the effort to provide a sophisticated picker, there are several procedures (such as **DoKeyScan**, **Scrap-Empty**, **DupPick**, and **ScrapCopy**) that can help simplify your job. These procedures are described in Chapter 29.

▶ Summary

In this chapter we show you how to create your own picker. First, we show you how to create a 'PICK' resource to describe your picker. Next, we describe what an 'LDEF' is and why you need one, and explain the example 'LDEF' code. We take you step by step through the example picker code. We also describe briefly how you can add your own extensions to the example picker. In the next chapter we show you how to create your own editor using the example editor code.

28 ▶ Writing an Editor

This chapter shows you how to write your own custom editor for ResEdit. We'll talk about the general requirements for an editor, explain the code for a simple editor, and give you some tips for making your editor work well with the other parts of ResEdit. If you're unsure whether you need to write your own editor, check out the information in Chapter 26.

▶ What Is an Editor?

An editor is just code to display a resource in a way that's useful for editing or browsing the resource. Editors can be very simple, like the 'PICT' editor, which only shows a 'PICT' in a window, or complex, like the 'KCHR' editor, which has an elaborate window, its own menus, and launches a related subeditor. The complexity of the editor depends entirely on the complexity of the resource to be edited and how fancy you want the editor to be. Before you tackle the job of writing an editor, you might want to see if you can get by with the much simpler job of creating a template for your resource. Chapters 24 and 26 give you all the information you'll need to decide whether you need to write an editor.

Since each editor has its own unique requirements, ResEdit can't give you as much help implementing an editor as it does for pickers. It provides many utility procedures to help make your editor a consistent member of the ResEdit family of editors, but you'll have to implement the bulk of the actual editing code yourself.

▶ The Example Editor Code

The best way to tell you how to write an editor is to show you how the example editor code works. The example editor edits 'XXXX' resources—a resource type made up just for the example and having no real use. It simply creates a small window and inverts it. (You can't really call that editing, but it gives you a framework on which to build a real editor.) We won't go through this code line by line, but we'll hit all the important parts. After we've explained the example code, we'll give you some hints about how you can make the example editor into an editor that really edits something. Be sure you're familiar with the description of how to use the example code presented in Chapter 26.

The example editor uses a structure called *rXXXXRec* for its data. We won't show the whole structure here since, other than the name of the structure and the name of the resource field (*hXXXX* instead of *the-ResToEdit*), this structure is identical to the *ParentRec* structure described in Chapter 26.

▶ GetNameAndTitle

The first procedure in the file is **GetNameAndTitle**. **GetNameAndTitle** creates the names that will be used by ResEdit to create the full name used for the window's title and the *name* field of the *rXXXXRec* structure.

```
void GetNameAndTitle(StringPtr windowTitle,
                     StringPtr windowName, Handle thing) {
  strcpy(windowTitle, "\pXXXX");
  SetETitle(thing, windowTitle);
  /* Add 1 for the length byte */
  strncpy(windowName, windowTitle, *windowTitle + 1);
}
```

The **SetETitle** procedure concatenates the resource ID and resource name of the *thing* parameter with the contents of the *windowTitle* parameter (for example, XXXX "My Resource" ID = 1234). The same value is returned in both the *windowName* and *windowTitle* parameters.

▶ EditBirth

The **EditBirth** procedure shown in Listing 28-1 creates a window for the editor and initializes its *rXXXXRec* data structure. The parameters to **EditBirth** are a handle to the resource to be edited and the *ParentHandle* of the window that opened the editor (the editor's parent window).

Listing 28-1 The **EditBirth** procedure

```
 1: pascal void EditBirth(Handle thing,ParentHandle dad) {
 2:   rXXXXHandle myXXXX;
 3:   WindowPtr   myWindow;
 4:   Str255      windowTitle, windowName;
 5:
 6:   GetNameAndTitle(windowTitle, windowName, thing);
 7:   myWindow = EditorWindSetup(noDialog, noColor,
 8:                              windowWidth, windowHeight,
 9:                              windowTitle, windowName,
10:                              true, ResEdID(), dad);
11:   if (myWindow != nil) {
12:     if (GetHandleSize(thing) == 0L)
13:       FixHand(sizeOfMyResource, thing);
14:
15:     myXXXX = (rXXXXHandle)NewHandle(sizeof(rXXXXRec));
16:     if (MemError() != noErr) {
17:       CloseWindow(myWindow);
18:       WindReturn(myWindow);
19:       return;
20:       }
21:     (*myXXXX)->father = dad;
22:     strncpy((*myXXXX)->name, windowName, windowName[0]+1);
23:     (*myXXXX)->wind = myWindow;
24:     (*myXXXX)->rebuild = false;
25:     (*myXXXX)->resWasntLoaded = !WasItLoaded();
26:     (*myXXXX)->windowType = editorWindow;
27:     (*myXXXX)->theResType = 'XXXX';
28:     (*myXXXX)->theResFile = HomeResFile(thing);
29:     (*myXXXX)->codeResID = ResEdID();
30:     (*myXXXX)->hXXXX = thing;
31:     ((WindowPeek)myWindow)->refCon = (long)myXXXX;
32:     }
33: }
```

The **EditorWindSetup** procedure called in line 7 allocates a window for use by the editor. It uses the *windowName* and *windowTitle* variables set by **GetNameAndTitle** to properly set up the window name and title. If your window will contain a dialog, you can specify its resource ID as the first parameter to **EditorWindSetup,** and specify 0 in place of the *windowWidth* and *windowHeight* constants.

Always be sure to verify that the window was created successfully. If it wasn't (indicated by **EditorWindSetup** returning nil), just exit the **EditBirth** procedure and your editor won't be opened (**EditorWind-Setup** will display an appropriate error message if it encounters a problem). If the window was successfully created, you'll need to make sure you have a valid resource. If ResEdit has just created the resource, it may have a length of 0, (depending on the contents of the picker's *rSize* field), and you should take whatever actions are necessary to make sure it's the right size and contains valid default data. The example editor doesn't care what the resource contains so, in line 13, it uses ResEdit's **FixHand** procedure to make sure it's the right size.

Now that the window is set up, it's time to allocate the *ParentRec* (or *rXXXXRec* in this case) and fill it in. If you write your editor in Pascal, you'll probably want to lock your handle down and dereference it in a WITH statement. It's important to call the **BubbleUp** procedure if you allocate any other memory before you unlock the handle. **BubbleUp** is similar to the Toolbox procedure **MoveHHi** in that it moves the handle as far out of the way as possible to avoid fragmentation. The code you might use would look like this.

```
BubbleUp(Handle(myXXXX));
HLock(Handle(myXXXX));
WITH myXXXX^^ DO
  BEGIN
  { Perform your memory allocations here. }
  END;
```

The code in Listing 28-1, lines 21 to 30, fills in every field of the structure that was just allocated. In line 25, the **WasItLoaded** procedure indicates whether the resource that's being edited was in use before the editor started. This information is used when the window is closed to determine if the resource should be released from memory (there's more about this when we talk about the **DoClose** procedure later in this chapter). In line 28, the **HomeResFile** Toolbox procedure returns the file reference number of the file that contains the resource being edited. ResEdit's **ResEdID** procedure used in line 29 returns the resource ID of the 'RSSC' resource that contains the editor. When ResEdit receives an event for the editor's window, it uses this number to make sure the editor's code (in the 'RSSC' resource) is loaded before it passes the event along. Line 31 places the *rXXXXHandle* into the window's *refCon* field, letting ResEdit know who owns the window.

▶ ## DoEvent

The **DoEvent** procedure shown in Listing 28-2 handles all events that affect the editor's window except menu events. Remember, the editor never receives events that don't affect its window (or its associated floating windows)—all that's taken care of for you by ResEdit. The parameters to **DoEvent** are the event record and the editor's *rXXXXHandle*.

Listing 28-2 The **DoEvent** procedure

```
 1: pascal void DoEvent(EventRecord *evt,
 2:                     rXXXXHandle myXXXX) {
 3: Point    mousePoint;
 4:
 5: BubbleUp((Handle)myXXXX);
 6: HLock((Handle)myXXXX);
 7: SetPort((*myXXXX)->windPtr);
 8: switch (evt->what) {
 9:   case mouseDown:
10:     mousePoint = evt->where;
11:     GlobalToLocal(&mousePoint);
12:     /* Add code to respond to the click here. */
13:     break;
14:
15:   case activateEvt:
16:     AbleMenu(editMenu, editNone);
17:     if (evt->modifiers & activeFlag) {
18:       /* Add activate code here. */
19:         }
20:     else {
21:       /* Add deactivate code here. */
22:         }
23:     break;
24:
25:   case updateEvt:
26:     PaintRect(&(*myXXXX)->windPtr->portRect);
27:     break;
28:
29:   case keyDown:
```

```
30:        if ((evt->message & charCodeMask) == deleteKey){
31:          DoMenu(editMenu, clearItem, myXXXX);
32:        }
33:      break;
34:
35:    case nullEvent:
36:      break;
37:    }
38:  HUnlock((Handle)myXXXX);
39:  }
```

Lines 5 and 6 aren't strictly needed here, but they probably would be needed in a real editor. If you save a pointer into *myXXXX* in a local variable or pass one of the fields of *myXXXX* to another procedure, you need to lock it down first. The **SetPort** Toolbox procedure called in line 7 makes sure any drawing you do ends up in the correct window. In Macintosh programming, one of the most common mistakes is to draw without first properly setting up the current port, so be careful.

The normal event processing switch statement starts on line 8. You can process any events that make sense for your editor here. Activate and update events are the only events you must process. The location of a mouse click is determined in lines 10 and 11, but you'll need to fill in the appropriate response to the click. Remember, don't try to detect double click events here—they're converted into Open commands on the Resource menu and sent to the **DoMenu** procedure.

Lines 16 to 23 handle activate and deactivate events. When an editor receives an activate event, it must make sure the menus are set up properly. The **AbleMenu** procedure sets the enable flags for an entire menu at once and redraws the menu bar if necessary. The ResEd file contains a set of constants you can use to set the menus to different states. For example, line 16 disables the entire Edit menu. In Chapter 26 we explained how ResEdit has configured the menus when you receive an activate event. It's also helpful to the user if you change the text of the items in the Edit and Resource menus to indicate exactly what they'll do in your editor. For example, the first item on the Resource menu is Create New Item in the 'MENU' editor, and Insert New Pattern in the 'PAT#' editor. If your editor has its own menu, you would insert it (with the **InsertMenu** Toolbox procedure) on activate and delete it (with the **DeleteMenu** Toolbox procedure) on deactivate.

Your editor should redraw the entire contents of its window when it receives an update event. Line 26 handles update events for the example editor by calling the **PaintRect** Toolbox procedure to simply fill the window with black. If your editor's window contains a dialog, you can use the **UpdtDialog** Toolbox procedure to redraw the contents of the window. All your editor has to do is redraw its window—ResEdit takes care of calling the **BeginUpdate** and **EndUpdate** Toolbox procedures for you.

Lines 30 and 31 handle key down events. You can do any processing that's appropriate when a key is pressed. In this case, the only processing converts the Delete key into a Clear command and sends it to the **DoMenu** procedure. **DeleteKey** and several other commonly used key constants are defined in the ResEd file.

The final event you might want to handle is the null event. There are a couple of situations that could be handled when a null event is received. If your window contains a dialog, you'll need to call the **DialogSelect** Toolbox procedure to make sure the insertion point blinks properly. You'll want to check the mouse location, and change the mouse pointer appropriately if you change the mouse pointer to different shapes depending on which part of the window the mouse is over. The last line of the **DoEvent** procedure unlocks the handle that was locked at the start of the procedure. Don't forget to unlock any handle you lock, or you might cause serious heap fragmentation problems.

▶ DoInfoUpdate

ResEdit calls the **DoInfoUpdate** procedure shown in Listing 28-3 when a Resource Info window makes a change in the information about the resource being edited and when a resource is being reverted. Any of the resource's information may be changed. It's important to update all of the editor's data structures as well as the window's title. It's also important to pass this call on to the window that opened the editor so that it, too, can update its data structures.

Listing 28-3 The **DoInfoUpdate** procedure

```
 1: pascal void DoInfoUpdate(short oldID, short newID,
 2:                          rXXXXHandle myXXXX) {
 3:  ParentHandle father = (*myXXXX)->father;
 4:  Str255      windowTitle,windowName;
 5:
 6:  HLock((Handle)myXXXX);
 7:  GetNameAndTitle(windowTitle, windowName,
 8:                  (Handle)(*myXXXX)->hXXXX);
 9:  GetWindowTitle(windowTitle, windowName, true,
10:                 (*myXXXX)->father);
11:
```

```
12:    strncpy((*myXXXX)->name, windowName,
13:            windowName[0]+1);
14:    SetWTitle((*myXXXX)->windPtr, windowTitle);
15:    (*father)->rebuild = true;
16:    CallInfoUpdate(oldID, newID, (long)father,
17:                   (*father)->wind->windowKind);
18:    HUnlock((Handle)myXXXX);
19:    }
```

It's very important to lock the handle at the beginning of **DoInfoUpdate** if any of its fields will be passed as parameters to procedures that may move memory. As described above, the **GetName-AndTitle** procedure called in line 7 returns a new *windowName* and *windowTitle*. The **GetWindowTitle** procedure then converts these strings into the standard ResEdit editor window title and name strings (title and name are the same for editors).

Lines 12 to 14 put the new *windowName* into the *ParentRec* data structure and set the window's title to *windowTitle*. Don't forget to add one to the string length any time you copy a Pascal-type string since the length byte isn't counted in the string length. And finally, lines 15 to 18 pass on the change and unlock the handle. If the window that opened the editor is a resource picker, setting its *rebuild* flag causes it to redisplay its list, so the name and ID of the resource are updated. The **CallInfoUpdate** procedure (called in line 16) calls the **DoInfoUpdate** procedure of the editor or picker with the specified *ParentHandle* and *windowKind*, letting that window also be updated.

▶ IsThisYours

The **IsThisYours** procedure shown in Listing 28-4 is called by ResEdit when it needs to find out whether a resource is already in use. Normally, your editor should only claim the resource that was passed to the **EditBirth** procedure. However, if your editor also works with auxiliary resources, you should also claim those. For example, the 'DLOG' editor claims both the 'DLOG' resource and the 'dctb' (dialog color table) resource with the same resource ID, if one exists.

Listing 28-4 The **IsThisYours** procedure

```
pascal Boolean IsThisYours(Handle thing,
                           rXXXXHandle myXXXX) {
  return (thing == (Handle)(*myXXXX)->hXXXX);
```

▶ DoMenu

The **DoMenu** procedure shown in Listing 28-5 processes all menu commands for the editor. If ResEdit receives a key down event and the Command key is down, it converts it into a menu ID and item number and sends it to the **DoMenu** procedure. The few exceptions to this rule include the Command key with the Enter, Return, and arrow keys.

Listing 28-5 The **DoMenu** procedure

```
 1: pascal void DoMenu(short menu, short item,
 2:                    rXXXXHandle myXXXX) {
 3:   BubbleUp((Handle)myXXXX);
 4:   HLock((Handle)myXXXX);
 5:   SetPort((*myXXXX)->windPtr);
 6:
 7:   switch (menu) {
 8:     case fileMenu:
 9:       switch (item) {
10:         case closeItem:
11:           if (DoClose(true, myXXXX)) {
12:             return;
13:             }
14:           break;
15:         case saveItem:
16:           PassMenu(fileMenu,saveItem,
17:                    (ParentHandle)myXXXX);
18:           break;
19:         case printItem:
20:           PrintWindow(nil);
21:           break;
22:       }
23:     case rsrcMenu:
24:       switch(item) {
25:         case rsrcRevertItem:
26:           if (NeedToRevert((*myXXXX)->windPtr,
27:                    (Handle)(*myXXXX)->hXXXX)){
28:             InvalRect(&(*myXXXX)->windPtr->portRect);
29:             if (!RevertThisResource(
30:                    (ParentHandle) myXXXX,
31:                    (Handle)(*myXXXX)->hXXXX)){
32:               (*((*myXXXX)->father))->rebuild = true;
33:               if (DoClose(false, myXXXX)) {
34:                 RERemoveAnyResource(
```

```
35:                                    (*myXXXX)->theResFile,
36:                                    (*myXXXX)->hXXXX);
37:                    DisposHandle((Handle)myXXXX);
38:                    return;
39:                    }
40:                  }
41:                }
42:             break;
43:          case rsrcGetInfoItem:
44:             ShowInfo((Handle)(*myXXXX)->hXXXX,
45:                       (ParentHandle)myXXXX);
46:             break;
47:          }

48:
49:    case editMenu: {
50:       switch (item) {
51:          case cutItem:
52:             break;
53:          case copyItem:
54:             break;
55:          case pasteItem:
56:             break;
57:          case clearItem:
58:             break;
59:          }
60:       }
61:    }
62: HUnlock (Handle) my XXXX);
63:   }
```

Just as in DoEvent, lines 3 through 5 move the *ParentHandle* up in memory, lock it down, and set the port to the editor's window so drawing can be done, if necessary. The rest of DoMenu is a switch statement that does whatever is necessary for each menu item. The Close item on the File menu is handled in line 11 by calling the DoClose procedure, shown in Listing 28-6. If DoClose returns true, DoEvent must return immediately since both its window and *ParentHandle* were freed by **DoClose.**

Editors generally don't need to do anything special for the Save command. If the editor doesn't edit the resource directly (it might edit a copy or convert the Resource Into a more convenient format for editing), the resource should be reconstructed when a Save command is received. It's also important to call **PassMenu** (as shown in line 16) to make sure any editor, subeditor or Resource Info windows opened by the editor are also saved. Printing in ResEdit doesn't produce beautiful output, but at least it's easy to implement in an editor! The **PrintWindow** procedure prints a copy of the contents of the window. You can, of course, implement a more sophisticated printing algorithm if it's important for the type of resource you're editing.

The next menu to check is the Resource menu (starting on line 23). The code from line 25 to line 42 takes care of the Revert This Resource command. The **NeedToRevert** procedure returns true if the resource has been changed. You may want to dim this menu item until the resource is changed. Since the resource is being reverted, the window will have to be redrawn. The **InvalRect** Toolbox procedure called in line 28 causes the entire window to be updated. In line 29, the **RevertThisResource** procedure takes care of actually reverting the resource. It returns false if the resource was new and therefore not found in the file.

If **RevertThisResource** returns false, the editor should remove the resource, close its window, and exit. Lines 32 through 38 take care of this situation. Since a resource is being removed, the resource picker's list should also be updated to remove the reference to the resource. This is accomplished by setting the *rebuild* flag of the window that opened the editor. Conveniently, the **DoClose** procedure takes care of all of the cleanup for the editor. The false parameter to **DoClose** indicates that **DoClose** shouldn't dispose of the *ParentRec* or release the resource as part of the Close process. After the window has been successfully closed, the **RERemoveAnyResource** procedure is called to remove the resource from the resource map. Since **DoClose** didn't dispose of the *ParentRec*, it's disposed of in line 37. After the resource has been removed and the window closed, it's a good idea to return immediately. If the resource wasn't newly added (**RevertThisResource** returns true) and the revert was successful, nothing else needs to be done.

A Resource Info window should be displayed in response to a Get Resource Info command. This is accomplished in line 44 by calling the **ShowInfo** procedure.

The rest of the menus can be checked next. The example editor contains code to check for the Edit menu but doesn't implement any Edit menu commands. If you add Edit menu commands, don't forget to enable the Edit menu itself when an activate event is received (in the **DoEvent** procedure). If you have a menu specific to your editor, you should check for it here, and do whatever is necessary for each command.

▶ DoClose

When the editor receives a Close command, it calls the **DoClose** procedure, shown in Listing 28-6.

Listing 28-6 The **DoClose** procedure

```
 1: static Boolean DoClose(Boolean notRevert,
 2:                             rXXXXHandle myXXXX) {
 3:   PassMenu(fileMenu, closeItem,
 4:           (ParentHandle)myXXXX);
 5:   if (WasAborted()) {
 6:     return false;
 7:     }
 8:   else {
 9:     CloseWindow((*myXXXX)->windPtr);
10:     WindReturn((*myXXXX)->windPtr);
11:     SetTheCursor(arrowCursor);
12:
13:     if (notRevert && ((*myXXXX)->resWasntLoaded) &&
14:         ((*((*myXXXX)->father)) >windowType!=
15:                 editorWindow))
16:       ReleaseResource((Handle)(*myXXXX)->hXXXX);
17:
18:     if (notRevert)
19:       DisposHandle((Handle)myXXXX);
20:     return true;
21:     }
22:   }
```

DoClose's *notRevert* parameter specifies that **DoClose** is not being called from the revert processing code. If a revert is in progress, it's important not to dispose of the *ParentRec* since it will be needed by Revert. The **PassMenu** procedure called in line 3 sends the Close command to any windows opened by the editor. Even if your editor doesn't open another editor or subeditor, you should still call **PassMenu** to make sure a Resource Info window is closed if one was opened with the Get Resource Info command. By the time control is returned to the **DoClose** procedure from the **PassMenu** procedure, all the windows opened by the editor will be closed. The **WasAborted** procedure is called in line 5 to see if any of the windows encountered an error and aborted the close. If your editor encounters an error during its close processing, it can set the abort flag by calling the **Abort** procedure.

The **CloseWindow** Toolbox procedure called in line 9 will free all the memory allocated to the window except the *windowPtr* itself. The *window-Ptr* can be returned to ResEdit to be reused by calling **WindReturn**. Since windows are non-relocatable blocks of memory, ResEdit tries to minimize heap fragmentation by preallocating the memory as high in the heap as possible and reusing the windows whenever possible. If you've changed the mouse pointer anywhere in your editor, it's a good idea to use the **Set-TheCursor** procedure to restore the normal arrow pointer. This is also the spot where you should delete any other data structures (including menus) that were allocated in the **EditBirth** procedure.

It's important to release the resource that the editor was editing if nothing was changed and no one else is using it. If you don't do this, the longer you use ResEdit, the more memory will be used up with unchanged resources that you're done with. You do have to be careful, though, because if another editor has a handle to the resource and you release it, fireworks soon follow! Fortunately, lines 13 to 15 show you a fairly easy way to tell if someone else might be using the resource. This code checks for three different situations in which the resource may be in use. The resource won't be released if *notRevert* is false since the revert processing code will be removing the resource after **DoClose** is finished. The *resWasntLoaded* flag was set in the **EditBirth** procedure and indicates whether the resource was in use before the editor started. It's safe to assume that if your editor was started by another editor, the other editor is probably using the resource. Line 14 checks this by looking into the *ParentRec* of the window that started the editor to see whether it's an editor. Another situation you might have to worry about is whether the editor itself has changed the resource. Obviously, you don't want to throw out your own changes. Fortunately, the **Release-Resource** Toolbox procedure won't release the resource if it has been changed (be sure to call the **SetResChanged** procedure whenever you make a change).

As you can see in lines 8, 9, and 20, all that's left to do is dispose of the *ParentHandle* that was allocated in **EditBirth** and return true to indicate the window was successfully closed. As was already mentioned, the hadle isn't disposed if **DoClose** is called from the revert processing code.

▶ Tips for Writing an Editor

The following sections provide a collection of tips that should speed the development time for your editor, reduce the bugs you encounter, and make your editor more compatible with the rest of ResEdit.

▶ How to Add a Menu to Your Editor

Probably one of the first changes you'll want to make to the example editor is to add a menu. Adding a menu to an editor is very simple, so we'll give you a brief run-through of the changes you'll need to make.

First, you'll need to define a constant to indicate what the resource ID of your menu will be. Don't forget to follow the rules outlined in Chapter 26 when you pick the resource ID for your menu. Next, you'll need to add a field to the end of the *rXXXXRec* data structure to hold the menu. Both of these changes are shown in the following code.

```
#define  XXXXMenuID  1600
typedef struct rXXXXRec {
    ParentHandle      father;
    ...
    Handle            hXXXX;
    MenuHandle        XXXXMenu;
    } rXXXXRec;
```

To initialize the menu, you'll need to add a couple of lines of code to the **EditBirth** procedure.

```
(*myXXXX)->XXXXMenu = GetMenu(XXXXMenuID);
DetachResource((Handle)(*myXXXX)->XXXXMenu);
```

The **DetachResource** Toolbox procedure removes the menu's handle from the resource map, so you have your own copy that no one else can interfere with. Be sure your menu is not purgeable or it may be removed from memory when memory starts getting full. Now that the menu has been loaded, you'll need to add it to the menu bar.

```
if (evt->modifiers & activeFlag) {
  InsertMenu((*myXXXX)->XXXXMenu, 0);
  }
else {
  DeleteMenu(XXXXMenuID);
  }
DrawMBarLater(false);
```

You add this code to the **DoEvent** procedure's *activateEvt* processing code. The **DrawMBarLater** procedure helps avoid flashing the menu bar each time a menu is inserted, deleted, enabled, or disabled by waiting until nothing else is going on to actually draw the menu bar. The code that follows takes care of removing and disposing of your handle and should be added to the **DoClose** procedure.

```
DeleteMenu(XXXXMenuID);
DrawMBarLater(false);
DisposHandle((Handle)(*myXXXX)->XXXXMenu);
```

Don't forget to dispose of the handle since it was detached in **Edit-Birth**. Finally, you've got the setup code out of the way and you can add the code that really does something with your menu. You'll need to add a new case to the end of your **DoMenu** procedure.

```
case XXXXMenuID:
    switch (item) {
        /* Implement the XXXX menu here. */
        }
```

Of course, you'll have to add the appropriate code to implement your menu, but that's the fun part.

▶ How to Use a Dialog for Your Window

In many cases, using a dialog simplifies the job of implementing an editor. Why do the work yourself if you can let the Dialog Manager do it for you? Many of ResEdit's editors use dialogs, including the 'DLOG', 'ALRT', 'WIND', 'itl0', 'itl1', 'BNDL', and 'pltt' editors. Unfortunately, you can't just drop in a dialog and have it work for you. You'll have to make changes in quite a few places in the example code, but when you're done, you'll have a much more complete editor. Remember, we're going to show you here how to make a few changes to the example code to make it display a dialog, but you'll need to add a lot more code to actually get it to do anything with that dialog.

The first order of business is to design the dialog. This is the most important step. Take some time and think about the best layout. You can use ResEdit's 'DITL' editor to help with the design. Of course, you'll find yourself changing it as your design progresses, but you'll be much better off if you start from a solid base. The first addition you'll need to make to the code will be a constant to specify the resource ID of the dialog you're going to use. You could use this constant for an editor with ID 2500.

```
#define            myDLOGID            25000
```

You'll use this ID in the call to the **EditorWindSetup** procedure in the following way.

```
myWindow = EditorWindSetup(myDLOGID, noColor, 0, 0,
                          windowTitle, windowName,
                          true, ResEdID(), dad);
```

There are two differences between this use of **EditorWindSetup** and the original example code. The first difference is the use of the *myDLOGID* constant, and the second is the use of 0 in place of the *windowWidth* and *windowHeight* constants. Specifying 0 for *windowWidth* and *windowHeight* indicates that the size of the dialog found in the 'DLOG' resource should be used. The bulk of the changes are in the **DoEvent** procedure. Listing 28-7 shows a whole new switch statement that takes care of each type of event.

Listing 28-7 Decoding events in the **DoEvent** procedure

```
switch (evt->what) {
    case mouseDown:
        mousePoint = evt->where;
        GlobalToLocal(&mousePoint);
        if (DialogSelect(evt,
                    &((DialogPtr)(*myXXXX)->windPtr),
                    &theItem)) {
            switch(theItem) {
                /* Handle your buttons, user items, etc.
                    here. */
                }
            }
        break;
    case activateEvt:
        AbleMenu(editMenu, editNone);
        if (evt->modifiers & activeFlag) {
            /* Do activate processing here.   */
            }
        else {
            /* Do deactivate processing here. */
            }
        /* Don't care about the result. */
        DialogSelect(evt, &tempDialogPtr, &itemHit);
        break;
    case updateEvt:
        UpdtDialog((DialogPtr)(*myXXXX)->windPtr,
```

```
                ((DialogPtr)(*myXXXX)->windPtr)->visRgn);
        break;
    case keyDown:
        if (DialogSelect(evt, &tempDialogPtr,&itemHit)) {
            /* Do any special key processing here. */
        }
        break;
    case nullEvent:
        /* Don't care about the result. */
        DialogSelect(evt, &tempDialogPtr, &itemHit);
        break;
    }
```

In Listing 28-7 you can see that each type of event now makes a call to the Dialog Manager to do some processing. It's probably not a good idea to call the **DialogSelect** Toolbox procedure once instead of calling it for each type of event, since you'll undoubtedly want to take different actions for different types of events. For example, you probably don't want to do anything at all after calling **DialogSelect** for null and activate events. For *mouseDown* events, however, you'll want to do some extra processing, depending on which dialog item was clicked. For example, if you have buttons in your window, you'll perform whatever action corresponds to the button that was clicked. It's important to note that you can't call **DialogSelect** for update events. This is because Res-Edit has already called the **BeginUpdate** Toolbox procedure and **Dialog-Select** would call it again, leading to weird and unexpected results.

The only other change you'll need to make is in the **DoClose** procedure. You should change the call to **CloseWindow** to a call to **CloseDialog** instead. And that's it! If you put in these changes, you'll see a dialog appear when you select one of your resources. Of course, the dialog won't do much more than draw itself until you add more code, but that's when the fun begins, right?

▶ How to Use User Items in a Window

If you use a dialog to implement your editor, you'll probably use at least one *userItem* field. User items can be convenient, but you have to be very careful when using them with ResEdit. To minimize heap fragmentation, the 'RSSC' resource containing your editor is unlocked at the end of every event the editor processes. It's relocked before the editor is called with the next event. Since it's possible that the resource might move to a different memory location between events, the pointer to the procedure that handles your user items may no longer be valid. Fortunately, it's easy to get around this problem—just reinstall your user item handlers (using the **GetDItem** and **SetDItem** Toolbox procedures) at the beginning of your **DoEvent** and **DoMenu** procedures, and everything should work fine.

▶ Events: Who's in Charge

ResEdit helps out by taking care of many of the events an application normally has to process. It can be pretty confusing, though, if you don't know which ones ResEdit handles and which ones you're responsible for. Tables 28-1, 28-2, and 28-3 list each event type and who should handle it.

Table 28-1. Events Handled by ResEdit

Event Type	Notes
mouseDown	
inDesk	
inMenuBar	
inSysWindow	
inDrag	
inGoAway	Converted to a Close command
autoKey	Turned into keyDown events
diskEvt	

Table 28-2. Events Partially Handled by ResEdit

Event Type	Notes
keyDown	ResEdit translates keys from the extended keyboard to their equivalent on the smaller keyboard. Command keys are sent to DoMenu, others are sent to DoEvent.
updateEvt	ResEdit calls BeginUpdate and EndUpdate for you.
app4Evt	MultiFinder suspend and resume events are converted to normal activate and deactivate events and sent to the DoEvent procedure.

Table 28-3. Events Your Editor Must Handle

Event Type	Notes
nullEvent	
mouseDown	
inContent	Double clicks are converted to Open Resource commands.
inGrow	
inZoomIn	TrackBox already called
inZoomOut	TrackBox already called
keyDown	Except as noted in Table 28-2
updateEvt	Draw only the contents of your window
activateEvt	
All other events	

▶ Menus: Who's in Charge

As with events, menus are partially handled by ResEdit and partially handled by your editor. ResEdit handles the Apple and Window menus and any menu commands received while a desk accessory is the front window. You have to handle the Resource and Edit menus completely on your own. Table 28-4 shows the File menu commands you'll have to handle.

Table 28-4. File Menu Commands Your Editor Must Handle

Command	Notes
Close	Handled completely by the Editor.
Save	ResEdit saves the file, but each editor has to make sure its resource is ready to save.
Print	Handled completely by the Editor.
Quit	ResEdit sends a close to each editor.

▶ Don't Forget to Call **SetResChanged**

The only way ResEdit can know to save your resource is if you call the **SetResChanged** procedure each time you make a change to the resource being edited. Be sure to use **SetResChanged** and not the **Changed-Resource** Toolbox procedure.

▶ Saving Preference Information in the ResEdit Preferences File

ResEdit introduced a Preferences file in version 2.0. This file is kept in the System Folder (or in the Preferences Folder under System 7). Res-Edit stores all kinds of preference information in this file, and you can store preference information for your editor there, also. All you have to do is package your preferences in a structure and add the handle to the structure to the ResEdit Preferences file as a new resource. Your editor can follow the strategy used by most of ResEdit's editors by keeping its preference information in a resource of type 'PREF'. You should use the same rules for picking your resource ID as you do for any other re-source you create (ten times the ID of your editor). In this way, you won't have to worry about someone else overwriting your preferences, or *vice versa*.

We'll show you some code fragments for two procedures: one to write your preferences, and one to read them. First you'll need to add a struc-ture to define your preferences and a few types to define the resource you'll save your preferences in.

```
#define         myPrefsType     'PREF'
#define         myPrefsID       1600
#define         myPrefsName     "\pXXXX editor"
typedef struct PrefsRec
          {
          short prefVersion;
          /* other prefs here */
          } PrefsRec;
typedef PrefsRec      *PrefsPtr;
typedef PrefsPtr      *PrefsHandle;
```

Of course, you'll want to add your own preferences to the *PrefsRec* structure. It's a good idea to keep a preferences version so you'll be able to make changes in future versions and still be compatible with older versions of your preferences resource. You'll also need to add a prefer-ences handle to the end of your *rXXXXRec* data structure.

You'll need to initialize *myPrefs* in your **EditBirth** procedure by calling the **ReadMyPrefs** procedure, shown in Listing 28-8.

Listing 28-8 The **ReadMyPrefs** procedure

```
 1: void ReadMyPrefs (rXXXXHandle myXXXX) {
 2:   PrefsHandle myPrefs;
 3:
 4:   myPrefs = (PrefsHandle)Get1NamedResource(myPrefsType,
 5:                                            myPrefsName);
 6:   (*myXXXX)->myPrefs = myPrefs;
 7:   if ((myPrefs == nil) || (ResError() != noErr))
 8:     {         /* set up the default preferences */
 9:     myPrefs = (PrefsHandle)NewHandle(sizeof(PrefsRec));
10:     (*myPrefs)->prefVersion = 1;
11:     /* Fill in the other preferences here. */
12:     (*myXXXX)->myPrefs = myPrefs;
13:     WriteMyPrefs (myXXXX);
14:     }
15:     else
16:       DetachResource((Handle)prefs);
17:   }
```

The **ReadMyPrefs** procedure, shown in Listing 28-8, reads a preference resource from the ResEdit Preferences file. The **Get1Named-Resource** procedure called in line 4 is used to make sure the correct resource is loaded—chances are small that someone else will pick the same resource name for their preferences resource. It's OK to use **Get1-NamedResource** here instead of **REGet1NamedResource** since you know the current resource file is set to the ResEdit Preferences file. If the resource isn't found, a *prefsHandle* is allocated and a default set of preferences are set up and written to the Preferences file (**WriteMyPrefs** is shown in Listing 28-9). If the resource is found, it's detached in line 16. Be sure to dispose of the preferences handle in your DoClose procedure.

This code assumes you're still on version 1 of your preferences resource. If you've incremented your version number, you'll need to convert old version resources to the new format in this procedure. You should try to make sure your preferences are both forward- and backward-compatible. Whenever the user changes the preferences, you can write them out by calling the **WriteMyPrefs** procedure, shown in Listing 28-9. As you can see from the listing, ResEdit makes writing the preferences pretty easy by providing the **WritePreferences** procedure.

Listing 28-9 The **WriteMyPrefs** procedure

```
void WriteMyPrefs (rXXXXHandle myXXXX) {
```

```
WritePreferences (myPrefsType, myPrefsID, myPrefsName,
                  (Handle)(*myXXXX)->myPrefs);
}
```

▶ ## How to Implement the Edit Menu

If you're using a dialog for your window, you can use the code in Listing 28-10 to implement the Edit menu.

Listing 28-10 A simple edit menu

```
case editMenu: {
  switch(item) {
    case undoItem:
      DoMyUndo(myXXXX);
      break;
    case cutItem:
      SaveUndoState(item, myXXXX);
      DlgCut((DialogPtr)(*myXXXX)->windPtr);
      err = (OSErr)ZeroScrap();
      err = TEToScrap();        // put it in the scrap
      break;
    case copyItem:
      DlgCopy((DialogPtr)(*myXXXX)->windPtr);
      err = (OSErr)ZeroScrap();
      err = TEToScrap();        // put it in the scrap
      break;
    case pasteItem:
      SaveUndoState(item, myXXXX);
      err = TEFromScrap();       // Get it from the scrap
      DlgPaste((DialogPtr)(*myXXXX)->windPtr);
      break;
    case clearItem:
      SaveUndoState(item, myXXXX);
      DlgDelete((DialogPtr)(*myXXXX)->windPtr);
      break;
  }
}
```

Most of the procedures used in Listing 28-10 are Toolbox procedures, but a couple are procedures you'll need to provide. If you want to implement the Undo command, you'll have to provide the **DoMyUndo** and **SaveUndoState** procedures. The next tip gives you some hints about implementing undo.

▶ Implementing Undo

Undo has a reputation for being very difficult to implement, but this doesn't have to be the case. Depending on the complexity of your editor, Undo might be fairly easy to implement. The easiest way to implement Undo is to save a copy of your resource before every change. Then all you have to do for Undo is reinitialize your editor from the saved copy of your resource! Be sure to save the current resource before you restore the saved resource so you can Redo the change if necessary. The user will also appreciate it if you make sure the Edit menu accurately reflects the action that will be performed when the Undo command is selected. For example, you should dim the menu item if there's nothing to undo, change the text to indicate what will be undone (Undo Paste, for example), and change the text to Redo after they have undone a change (Redo Paste, for example). If you really want to do it right, you should also save and restore the contents of the scrap (you won't find many parts of ResEdit that do this).

▶ When Is Your Window Activated?

Don't assume your window is active just because its **EditBirth** procedure is called. In fact, if the user opens two editors at the same time, one will be active and the other will be inactive. If you don't watch out for situations like this, you'll end up with an inactive window that contains an active selection—a definite human interface no-no. Until you receive an activate event, make sure Text Edit fields and List Manager lists are inactive and don't insert your menus.

▶ How to Implement Fancier Printing

The default printing that most editors provide is sufficient if the editor window doesn't scroll or contain important information that's hidden. If fancier printing is important to you, you have a couple of options. The **PrintWindow** procedure takes a *PicHandle* as a parameter. Usually, editors call **PrintWindow** with a nil parameter to indicate that a picture of the contents of the editor's window should be printed. However, an editor can pass in any *PicHandle* and it will be printed instead of the normal picture. Unfortunately, most editors don't have a spare picture laying around that they can print.

The other alternative for printing is to handle the whole job yourself, just as you would in a normal application. Apple's *Macintosh Technical Note* number 161 thoroughly describes how to write a printing loop and includes both C and Pascal code samples. You can call ResEdit's **PrintSetup** procedure at the beginning of your print code to make sure the Page Setup dialog has been filled in and to return a *THPrint* handle for you. Other than that, you're on your own.

▶ Using Floating Windows

If you want to implement a really fancy editor, you might want to include floating palette windows. Floating windows can be convenient for several reasons. The biggest advantage is that users can put them wherever they want. If your window is a bit too big for an SE screen, you might want to remove a fixed palette and let the user move it out of the way. ResEdit makes this easy by providing the **FloatingWindowSetup** procedure. All your editor needs to do is set up the floating window in **EditBirth** and check in **DoEvent** to see if the event occurred in the floating window. Once the floating window is set up, all the events that occur in the floating window are passed to your main window. Here's how you can initialize the floating window in **EditBirth**.

```
myFW = (FloatingWindowHandle)
            NewHandleClear(sizeof(FloatingWindowRec));
where.h = 0;
where.v = 0;
floatingWindow = FloatingWindowSetup(windID, myFW,
                        (ParentHandle)myDITL, where);
if (floatingWindow == nil)
  /* Take care of errors here. */
else
  (*myXXXX)->floatingWindow = floatingWindow;
```

The *FloatingWindowRec* structure is defined in the ResEd file. It's just another variation of the *ParentRec* structure that includes a *windowPtr* to identify the editor window that owns the floating window. The first parameter to **FloatingWindowSetup** is the resource ID of a 'WIND' resource that defines the shape of your floating window. You'll need to add a field to the *XXXXRec* structure to save the floating window's *windowPtr*. Be sure to check for a return value of nil from **FloatingWindowSetup** in case there wasn't enough memory to allocate the window. More details about **FloatingWindowSetup** can be found in Chapter 29. You can either do normal update event processing to draw your floating window, or you can install a window picture that the Window Manager will update for you. Here's how you can use a window picture.

```
palettePict = GetPicture(paletteID);
if(palettePict == nil)
  /* Take care of errors here. */
else {
  DetachResource((Handle)palettePict);
  SetWindowPic((*myXXXX)->floatingWindow, palettePict);
  }
```

Be sure you detach the handle to the picture. If you don't, you might end up with two instances of your editor editing two different resources, and both using the same picture handle. This is OK until one of the editors is closed and releases the shared resource. You'll need to clean up the palette when your editor receives a Close command. Here's what you need to do.

```
CloseWindow((*myXXXX)->floatingWindow);
WindReturn((*myXXXX)->floatingWindow);
```

That's it for maintaining the floating window. Now all you have to do is make it work. You'll probably want to detect mouseDown events in the floating window and take some appropriate action. Here's how you can tell whether the mouse is in the main editor window or the floating window.

```
mouseCode = FindWindow(event->where, &whichWindow);
if (whichWindow == (*myXXXX)->floatingWindow)
    /* Mouse is down in the floating window. */
```

▶ Using Pop-up Menus

ResEdit provides a couple of procedures that make implementing pop-up menus a snap. In your **EditBirth** procedure, you have to load and detach the menu just as if you were going to add it to the menu bar. When you receive an update event for your window, just call **Draw-Popup** to take care of drawing the current value of your menu. When you receive a mouseDown event in your pop-up menu, call **DoPopup** to take care of displaying the menu and tracking the mouse as the user selects a new menu item. When your window is closed, you need to dispose of the handle to the menu. That's all there is to it. The interfaces to the **DrawPopup** and **DoPopup** procedures are discussed in Chapter 29.

▶ Using Color Palette Pop-up Menus

ResEdit provides a set of four procedures to manage color palette pop-up menus. These pop-up menus are used by several editors, including the 'MENU' editor and the 'DLOG' editor. The easiest way to use color pop-up menus is to define user items in a dialog that will contain the color swatches. Using user items lets you rely on the Dialog Manager for much of the maintenance of your window—the use of user items and dialogs was described in an earlier tip. You'll need to call **InstallColorPalettePopup** to initialize the pop-up in your **EditBirth** procedure and when you receive a Revert This Resource command or an update event. When you receive a mouseDown event in one of your color swatches, you can show the pop-up menu and track the mouse like this.

```
if ColorPalettePopupSelect(windPtr, &itemBox,
                           &newColor, hasColorQd) {
    /* Save the new color selected by the user. */
    }
```

ColorPalettePopupSelect takes care of everything for you, including displaying the pop-up menu and tracking the selected color in the color swatch. You should call **DrawColorPopup** from the draw procedure for your color swatch user items. Call **DeinstallColorPalettePopup** from your **DoClose** procedure when you're done with the color palette.

▶ **Summary**

This chapter gives lots of details about how to write your own editor. We take you step by step through the example code, and give you several tips and suggestions to help you write your editor. Now it's up to you. Take the example code and get busy! In the next chapter we give you details about all the procedures available in ResEdit for you to use.

29 ▶ The ResEd Interface

In this chapter we describe all the procedures ResEdit provides for use by your editor or picker. Because lots of procedures are available, we group them by function so you can find the procedure you're looking for. Since there are so many procedures, it may be difficult to know whether ResEdit provides the service you want. If what you're doing is done in other editors provided with ResEdit, chances are pretty good that ResEdit has a procedure or two to help implement the feature. If you follow the instructions and examples provided in Chapters 26, 27, and 28, you should be pretty familiar with the procedures described in this chapter by the time you need to strike out on your own.

▶ Constants and Structures

The first half of the ResEd file provides constant and structure definitions used by all editors and pickers. The first set of constants are used with ResEdit's menus. Each menu (File, Edit, Resource, and View) has three sets of constants: a set that represents the menu items themselves, a set of masks to enable or disable each menu item, and a set of commonly used mask combinations. In the DoMenu procedure, you'll use the constants that define the menu items (such as newFileItem or undoItem) in the switch statement that decodes the menu command. You'll use the mask combinations when you call the AbleMenu procedure in response to an activate or deactivate event. You'll use the masks themselves if you need to create a mask combination that isn't provided for you.

After the menu constants, you'll find a lot of constant definitions for strings you might want to use. There are strings containing the text from the Resource menu, several error strings, and various other strings. You can access any of these strings with either the **GetNamedStr** or **GetStr** procedure. Following the definition of these constants are the structures used by all editors and pickers. This is where you'll find the *PickRec* and *ParentRec* structure that each picker and editor must use. You'll also find a few other structures that are described with the procedures that use them.

▶ ResEd Procedures

▶ Window Utilities

```
pascal Boolean AlreadyOpen(StringPtr windowTitle,
              StringPtr windowName, ParentHandle parent);
```

The **AlreadyOpen** procedure should be used to make sure an editor or picker window is not opened twice for the same resource or resource type. You normally won't need to call this procedure because it's called for you by **EditorWindSetup** and **PickerWindSetup**. If a window is already open, **AlreadyOpen** activates it and returns true. **AlreadyOpen** uses the *windowTitle* and *windowName* parameters (described with the **EditorWindSetup** procedure) to identify the window.

```
pascal WindowPtr EditorWindSetup(short dlogID,
              ColorType colorKind, short width,
              short height,StringPtr windowTitle,
              StringPtr windowName, Boolean addFrom,
              short windowKind, ParentHandle parent);
```

EditorWindSetup is used by almost every editor to set up its window. It takes care of most of the details necessary to get an editor started. The use of this procedure is described in Chapter 28. The *dlogID* parameter allows you to specify the resource ID of a 'DLOG' resource to use for your window. The "Tips" section of Chapter 28 shows you how to use a 'DLOG' with your editor. The *colorKind* parameter determines whether a color or black-and-white window is created. It can contain the values *noColor*, *canColor*, or *requiresColor*. If you specify *requiresColor* and color

QuickDraw isn't available, **EditorWindSetup** displays an error message and returns a *nil* pointer. If your editor can make use of color but doesn't require color, you should specify *canColor*. The *width* and *height* parameters determine the size of the window that's created. If you want to use the size specified in the 'DLOG' resource, set *width* and *height* to zero. The *windowTitle* and *windowName* parameters should contain the same string set to something like "XXXX id = 300". The *addFrom* boolean determines whether the "from FileName" string is added to *windowTitle* and *windowName*. Editors should always set *addFrom* to true. The *windowKind* parameter should be set to the resource ID of the editor (you can get this ID by calling **ResEdID**). And, finally, the *parent* parameter is the *ParentHandle* of the window that opened the editor (the same as the *dad* parameter to **EditBirth**). If a window can't be allocated, **EditorWindSetup** returns nil and the **EditBirth** procedure should be aborted.

```
pascal WindowPtr FloatingWindowSetup(short WINDID,
                FloatingWindowHandle fw, ParentHandle owner,
                Point where);
```

FloatingWindowSetup is used to allocate a floating palette window, which can be attached to any editor's window. ResEdit takes care of hiding and showing the window when it's activated or deactivated. *WINDID* is the resource ID of a 'WIND' resource that defines the floating window. The *fw* parameter is a handle to a *FloatingWindowRec* that will be filled in by **FloatingWindowSetup**. Before **FloatingWindowSetup** is called, *fw* should be allocated by calling the **NewHandleClear** Toolbox procedure. The *owner* parameter specifies the *ParentHandle* of the window that owns the floating window and will process its events. The *where* parameter specifies the location, in global coordinates, of the top left corner of the floating window. If *where.h* and *where.v* are both 0, the floating window is placed near the owning window. When your editor receives an event, it should check to see which window received the event and process it accordingly. Chapter 28 shows you how to use floating palette windows.

```
pascal void GetWindowTitle(StringPtr windowTitle,
                StringPtr windowName, Boolean addFrom,
                ParentHandle parent);
```

The **GetWindowTitle** procedure sets up the strings that are used for a window's name (in the *ParentRec* data structure) and title (in the *Win-*

dowRecord data structure). Normally, pickers won't need to call **GetWindowTitle** since the **DoPickBirth** and **PickInfoUp** procedures take care of setting up the window's name and title. For editors, this procedure is called for you by the **EditorWindSetup** procedure, so you'll only need to use it in your editor's **DoInfoUpdate** procedure. When you call **GetWindowTitle**, the strings should be set up just as they are when you call **EditorWindSetup**. The *addFrom* parameter determines whether "from FileName" is appended to each string. Editors should always set *addFrom* to true. The *parent* parameter should be the *ParentHandle* of the window that opened the editor.

```
pascal WindowPtr PickerWindSetup(ColorType colorKind,
           Boolean showTheWindow, short width,
           short height, StringPtr windowTitle,
           short windowKind, ParentHandle parent);
```

PickerWindSetup takes care of almost everything necessary to set up a window for a picker. You usually won't need to call this procedure since it's called for you by the **DoPickBirth** procedure. The *colorKind* parameter determines whether a color window is allocated. You can find more information about *colorKind* with the description of **DoPickBirth**. The *showTheWindow* parameter indicates whether the window should be displayed after it's initialized. The *width* and *height* parameters define the size of the window that will be allocated. The *windowTitle* parameter should contain the resource type with an *s* appended (MENUs, for example). The "from a File" string will be added for you, so the window title will be something like "MENUs from a File." The *windowKind* parameter should contain the resource ID of the picker. This resource ID is used to access the 'LDEF' (list definition procedure that's used to draw the items in the list). The last parameter, *parent,* should contain the *ParentHandle* of the window that opened the picker. **PickerWindSetup** returns nil if the window couldn't be allocated or a picker for the resource type is already open.

```
pascal void SetETitle(Handle h, StringPtr str);
```

SetETitle (Set Editor Title) appends the resource ID and name of the *h* parameter to the string specified in the *str* parameter. For example, calling **SetETitle** with a handle to a resource with ID 128 and name "Spaghetti" would append '"Spaghetti" ID = 128' to the contents of the *str* parameter. You should use the **SetETitle** procedure to create your window's name and title before you call **EditorWindSetup** or **GetWindowTitle**.

```
pascal WindowPtr WindAlloc(void);
```

WindAlloc allocates memory for a color or black-and-white window. Normally, you won't need to use **WindAlloc** since window allocation is taken care of by **EditorWindSetup** and **PickerWindSetup**. ResEdit attempts to avoid heap fragmentation by keeping the window records as low in memory as possible. Pointers allocated with **WindAlloc** should be returned by calling **WindReturn** instead of **DisposPtr**.

```
pascal void WindReturn(WindowPtr w);
```

WindReturn should be used to free window pointers allocated by **WindAlloc**, **EditorWindSetup**, **PickerWindSetup**, or **FloatingWindowSetup**. Using **WindReturn** instead of **DisposPtr** helps ResEdit better manage its use of memory and avoid heap fragmentation.

▶ Extended Resource Manager

The extended Resource Manager calls should always be used instead of the corresponding Toolbox procedures. Unless otherwise noted, the only difference between ResEdit's resource calls and the Toolbox equivalents is that ResEdit's versions take a resource file as a parameter. Since the current resource file is always set to the ResEdit Preferences file, you need to be able to access resources from the file being edited by specifying the resource file.

```
pascal Boolean REAddNewRes(short resFile, Handle hNew,
                 ResType t, short idNew, const Str255 s);
```

REAddNewRes adds the handle *hNew* to the current resource file. The resource is given type *t*, ID *idNew*, and name *s*. The only differences between **REAddNewRes** and the **AddResource** Toolbox procedure are that **REAddNewRes** takes the resource file as a parameter, displays an alert if an error occurs, and returns a boolean to indicate whether the addition was successful. If the new resource was added successfully, true is returned.

```
pascal void REAddResource(short resFile, Handle theResource,
              ResType theType, short theID, const Str255
              name);
```

REAddResource is the same as the AddResource Toolbox procedure, except that it takes the resource file as a parameter.

```
pascal short REBeautifulUnique1ID(short resFile,
              ResType WhichType);
```

REBeautifulUnique1ID returns a new resource ID that is guaranteed to be unique within the specified resource file. **REBeautifulUnique1ID** differs from the **Unique1ID** Toolbox procedure in the way it calculates the new ID. **REBeautifulUnique1ID** returns the first available ID greater than 128, whereas **Unique1ID** returns a random ID greater than 0.

```
pascal short RECount1Resources(short resFile,
              ResType theType);
```

RECount1Resources is the same as the **Count1Resource** Toolbox pro-cedure, except that it takes the resource file as a parameter.

```
pascal short RECount1Types(short resFile);
```

RECount1Types is the same as the **Count1Types** Toolbox procedure, except that it takes the resource file as a parameter.

```
pascal Handle REGet1IndResource(short resFile,
              ResType theType, short index);
```

REGet1IndResource is nearly identical to the **Get1IndResource** Toolbox procedure. The differences are that **REGet1IndResource** takes a resource file as a parameter and, if the resource isn't found, sets the *resErr* low memory global to *resNotFound* as well as returning a nil handle.

```
pascal void REGet1IndType(short resFile,
              ResType *theType, short index);
```

REGet1IndType is the same as the **Get1IndType** Toolbox procedure, except that it takes the resource file as a parameter.

```
pascal Handle REGet1NamedResource(short resFile,
             ResType theType, const Str255 name);
```

REGet1NamedResource is the same as the **Get1NamedResource** Toolbox procedure, except that it takes the resource file as a parameter.

```
pascal Handle REGet1Resource(short resFile, ResType theType,
             short theID);
```

REGet1Resource is nearly identical to the **Get1Resource** Toolbox pro-cedure. As with **REGet1IndResource**, the only difference is that **REGet1Resource** sets the *resErr* low memory global if the resource isn't found and takes the resource file as a parameter.

```
pascal Handle REGet1ResourceSpecial(short resFile,
             ResType theType, short ID,
             Boolean *wasLoaded, short *error);
```

REGet1ResourceSpecial is similar to the **REGet1Resource** procedure, except it returns a boolean to indicate whether the resource was in use or not. Whenever you're loading a resource from a file opened by the user, you should use **REGet1ResourceSpecial** instead of **REGet1-Resource** or **Get1Resource**. The *wasLoaded* parameter returns true if the resource was already in memory, belongs to ResEdit or the System file, and wasn't purgeable, or if the resource is in use by another ResEdit editor. If *wasLoaded* is returned true, the caller should never use the **Re-leaseResource** Toolbox procedure to release the resource.

```
pascal Handle RENewUniqueRes(short resFile, long s,
             ResType t);
```

RENewUniqueRes adds a resource with *s* bytes and resource type *t* to the specified resource file. The new resource is assigned a unique resource ID by calling **REBeautifulUnique1ID**. A handle to the new resource is returned. A nil handle is returned if the resource couldn't be added.

```
pascal void RERemoveAnyResource(short resFile,
             Handle theRes);
```

RERemoveAnyResource is similar to the **RmveResource** Toolbox procedure. The only difference is that **RERemoveAnyResource** will allow a resource to be removed even if the *resProtected* resource attribute is set. **RERemoveAnyResource** should always be used in place of **RmveResource**. You should use this procedure in your editor if **Revert-ThisResource** indicates the resource should be removed because it was newly added since the file was opened or saved.

```
pascal Boolean RevertThisResource(ParentHandle parent,
                 Handle theRes);
```

RevertThisResource restores the resource *theRes* to its state when the file was opened or last saved. The *parent* parameter should be the *ParentHandle* of the window that owns the resource being reverted (for example, an editor would pass its *ParentHand*). If the revert is successful, **RevertThisResource** returns true. If the resource didn't exist in the file at the time of the last save (it was recently created), **RevertThis Resource** returns false and the caller should remove the resource (using **RERemoveAnyResource**). If the caller is an editor and false is returned, the editor should remove the resource and close its window just as if it had received a Close command. **RevertThisResource** automatically calls **PassMenu** with a Close command to make sure any windows opened by the caller are closed since they probably have an out-of-date copy of the resource. If the resource hasn't been changed, **RevertThisResource** does nothing and returns true.

▶ Routines Used by Pickers

```
pascal short DefaultListCellSize(void);
```

DefaultListCellSize returns the height (in pixels) of a standard row in a picker window (ascent plus descent plus leading of the application font). You normally won't use this procedure since **DoPickBirth** takes care of calculating your window size for you. This value is useful if you're implementing a picker that displays the resource information as rows of text.

```
pascal Boolean DoPickBirth(ColorType colorKind,
                 Boolean buildList,
                 PickerType which,
                 short pickerResId, PickHandle pick);
```

DoPickBirth takes care of most initialization for a picker. The *color-Kind* parameter determines whether a color or black-and-white window is created. It can contain the values *noColor, canColor*, or *requiresColor*. If you specify *requiresColor* and color QuickDraw isn't available, the default picker is started and false is returned. If your picker can make use of color, but doesn't require color, you should specify *canColor*. If *buildList* is true, a List Manager list of resources will be created. The *which* parameter determines the size of the window created and the type of list it contains. The possible values are *textOnlyPicker* (for the default type of resource list that shows the resource IDs and names of the resources), *graphical1DPicker* (for graphical resources such as 'PAT#' that use one-column lists), and *graphical2DPicker* (for graphical re-sources such as 'ICON' that use two-dimensional lists). The resource ID of the picker itself is specified in the *pickerResId* parameter. *Pick* is the handle to the pickers *PickRec* structure. You must initialize the *father, rType, viewBy, cellSize, ldefType, minWindowWidth,* and *minWindowHeight* fields before calling **DoPickBirth**. Chapter 27 shows more details about the use of **DoPickBirth**.

```
pascal void DrawLDEF(short message, Boolean lSelect,
                const Rect *lRect, Handle theRes, short id,
                StringPtr title, short maxH, short maxV,
                DrawResProcPtr DrawResource, ListHandle lh);
```

DrawLDEF is a procedure shared by every picker that displays a list of graphical elements (icons, patterns, etc.). **DrawLDEF** should be called from your picker's 'LDEF' (list definition procedure). The "List Manager" chapter of *Inside Macintosh*, Volume IV explains in detail how to use list definition procedures, and **DrawLDEF**'s use is described in some detail in Chapter 27. The *message, lSelect,* and *lRect* parameters are the same as the first three parameters of your list definition procedure. If the *title* parameter is an empty string, the *id* is converted to a string and used as the title (the title is drawn under the graphic element). The *maxH* and *maxV* parameters specify the size of the graphical part of the cell. This size is used when placing the title text. The *DrawResource* parameter is a pointer to a procedure that draws the graphical part of the cell. It should have an interface like this.

```
pascal void DrawResource(Rect lRect, Handle theRes)
```

```
pascal void GrowMyWindow(short minWidth, short minHeight,
                WindowPtr windPtr, ListHandle lh);
```

GrowMyWindow should be called when the user clicks in the size box of a picker's window. You normally won't need to call **GrowMy-Window** because it's called for you by **PickEvent**. **GrowMyWindow** resizes and redraws the window and list. The list is modified to make sure the maximum number of rows and columns are displayed without requiring horizontal scrolling.

```
pascal void PickEvent(EventRecord *evt, PickHandle pick);
```

PickEvent handles events for pickers. It's usually unnecessary to do anything in your picker's **DoEvent** procedure except call **PickEvent**.

```
pascal void PickInfoUp(short oldID, short newID,
               PickHandle pick);
```

PickInfoUp should be called from your picker's **DoInfoUpdate** procedure. Normally calling **PickInfoUp** satisfies all the requirements of the **DoInfoUpdate** procedure.

```
pascal void PickMenu(short menu, short item,
               PickHandle pick);
```

PickMenu handles menu commands for pickers. Unless your picker has its own menu, **PickMenu** takes care of all menu commands for you.

```
pascal short PickStdHeight(void);
```

PickStdHeight returns the picker height (in pixels) set in the ResEdit Preferences dialog. You should never need to use this procedure since the window size is set up for you by **DoPickBirth**.

```
pascal short PickStdWidth(void);
```

PickStdWidth returns the picker width (in pixels) set in the ResEdit Preferences dialog. You should never need to call this procedure since the window size is set up for you by **DoPickBirth**.

▶ Routines Used by Editors

```
pascal Boolean CloseNoSave(void);
```

CloseNoSave returns true if it's OK for an editor to throw away its changes when it receives a Close command. It's especially important to call **CloseNoSave** if it's possible for your editor to detect an error during the normal Close processing. You wouldn't want an error alert to pop up right after the user has clicked the No button in the Save dialog! **CloseNoSave** returns true when a file is being closed but not saved and when a resource is being reverted or deleted from a picker.

```
pascal Boolean NeedToRevert(WindowPtr myWindow,
                Handle theRes);
```

The **NeedToRevert** procedure should be called in response to a Revert This Resource command. If *myWindow* is the front window and the resource specified by *theRes* has changed, **NeedToRevert** displays an alert to verify that the user really wants to discard changes to the resource. A result of true is returned only if the user OKs the revert.

```
pascal void NoDoubleClicksHere(void);
```

NoDoubleClicksHere is useful in editors that have only part of their window in which it makes sense to convert double clicks into Open commands. For example, in the 'DLOG' editor, a double click in the mini-screen should open the associated 'DITL' resource, but a double click in the Top field should select the number. Normally, ResEdit converts a double click into an Open command from the Resource menu. In the 'DLOG' editor's case, this would only make sense if the double click were inside the mini-screen—otherwise the double click should be passed on to the **DialogSelect** Toolbox procedure. An editor can get around this by checking the location of the click on each mouseDown event. If the click is outside the area where an Open command makes sense, calling **NoDoubleClicksHere** will make sure the double click is handled correctly.

```
pascal void SetResChanged(Handle h);
```

SetResChanged should be called whenever you've changed the resource *h*. **SetResChanged** should always be called instead of the **ChangedResource** Toolbox procedure.

```
pascal Boolean WasItLoaded(void);
```

WasItLoaded should be called in the **EditBirth** procedure of every editor. The return value should be saved in the *ParentRec* structure so it can be checked later, when the editor receives a close command. **WasIt-Loaded** returns true if the resource was in use by ResEdit or the System before it was opened for editing. If **WasItLoaded** returns true, you must be careful to never release the resource.

▶ Starting Editors and Pickers

```pascal
pascal void GiveEBirth(Handle resHandle, PickHandle pick);
```

GiveEBirth is used to start an editor for a particular resource. Calling this procedure is effectively the same as calling the appropriate editor's **EditBirth** procedure. Control won't return to the calling editor or picker until the new editor's **EditBirth** procedure has been completed. The *resHandle* parameter should be a handle to a resource—be sure not to use a handle that's not really a resource. The *pick* parameter is a handle to a *ParentRec* structure. It's OK to call this procedure from an editor instead of a picker as long as the editor's *ParentRec* includes the *rType* and *rSize* fields normally found in a *PickRec*. These fields must be in the appropriate place in the *ParentRec* structure (the same place they're found in the *PickRec*) and must be initialized with the resource type of the resource being edited (for *rType*) and the default size of a new resource of that type (for *rSize*).

Normally, **GiveEBirth** looks for a custom editor to edit the resource. If one isn't found, it looks for a template to use with the resource. As a last resort, the hexadecimal editor is used. This scenario changes depending on the modifier keys held down when the last event was received. If the Option and Command keys were both held down, a dialog is displayed to ask the user which template they would like to use to edit the resource (the same as selecting Open Using Template from the Resource menu). If a template exists for the resource, it's used as the default in the dialog. If the Option key is held down, the hexadecimal editor is opened (the same as selecting Open Using Hex Editor from the Resource menu). The editor that's started can also be changed using an 'RMAP' resource as described in Chapter 25.

```pascal
pascal void GiveSubEBirth(Handle resHandle,
                PickHandle pick);
```

GiveSubEBirth starts a subeditor with the specified handle. This procedure is similar to **GiveEBirth**, except that it starts only the subeditor for the specified resource—it never starts the template or hexadecimal editor. Since subeditors are really part of the main editor, it's OK to pass a normal handle rather than a resource in the *resHandle* parameter. You're guaranteed that only the main editor and the subeditor will use the contents of this handle, so you can define it to contain anything you want. Remember, the real difference between a normal editor and a subeditor is that a normal editor's resource name begins with an @ character, and a subeditor's resource name begins with a $ character.

```
pascal void GiveThisEBirth(Handle resHandle,
                PickHandle pick, ResType openThisType);
```

GiveThisEBirth is similar to **GiveEBirth,** except the caller can specify the resource type to use. This way you can have more control over how an editor is chosen for the resource. The modifier keys are also ignored by this procedure (holding down the Option or Command key will not affect which type of editor is opened). No matter what type of resource is passed in the *resHandle* parameter, it's treated as if it were a resource of type *openThisType*. As with **GiveEBirth**, ResEdit tries to use a custom editor first, a template second, and the hexadecimal editor as a last resort.

▶ Sending Events and Menu Commands

```
pascal void CallDoEvent(EventRecord *evt,
                WindowPtr theWindow);
```

With the **CallDoEvent** procedure you can send an event to any window. You'll probably never need to use this procedure. One possible use is described with the discussion of the **PassEvent** procedure.

```
pascal void CallInfoUpdate(short oldID, short newID,
                long object, short id);
```

The **CallInfoUpdate** procedure calls the specified window's Do-InfoUpdate procedure. The window is specified by its *ParentHandle* (*object*) and the resource ID of the editor or picker that owns the window (*id*). When the user makes a change in an info window (displayed with the Get Resource Info command on the Resource menu), it's important to make sure all windows displaying the information that was changed get a chance to update themselves. The info window facilitates this by calling the **DoInfoUpdate** procedure of the window that opened it. An editor should make sure it keeps the information flowing by calling **CallInfoUpdate** to pass the information on to the window that opened it. An editor can pass on the info update command by using the following code.

```
CallInfoUpdate(oldID, newID,
               (long)(*myObj)->father,
               (*(*myObj)->father)->wind->windowkind);
```

```
pascal void PassEvent(EventRecord *evt,
               ParentHandle parent);
```

The **PassEvent** procedure is used to send events to any windows opened by the window that owns the *parent* parameter. You'll rarely need to use this procedure. One use of this procedure would be to implement a cheap version of inter-editor communication using *app1* events. If you have an editor that opens subeditors, you might want to send them information. You could do this by using **PassEvent** to send them an *app1* event. The *message* field of the *evt* record could be used to hold whatever information you want to send to the subeditor. If you need to send information from the subeditor to the editor, you can use the **CallDoEvent** procedure.

```
pascal void PassMenu(short menu, short item,
               ParentHandle parent);
```

PassMenu is similar to **PassEvent**, except it passes on menu com-mands. For example, if your editor opens two subeditor windows and a resource info window, **PassMenu** sends a menu command to all three windows. **PassMenu** should be used to pass along any menu com-mand that can affect more than one window. For the standard ResEdit menus, this includes the Save and Close commands. If your editor has opened other windows, it's important that they be closed before your editor is closed. If they aren't closed, the linked list of *ParentHandle*s will be broken.

▶ Miscellaneous Utilities

```
pascal void Abort(void);
```

The **Abort** procedure can be used to abort Close, Quit, or Save commands. You can find out if an operation was aborted by calling **WasAborted**.

```
pascal void AbleMenu(short menu, long enable);
```

AbleMenu is a shortcut way to set the enable flags for an entire menu at once. For example, to enable every item on the File menu, you could call **AbleMenu** with the *enable* parameter set to *fileAll*. The ResEd file contains constants for many common combinations of enabled and disabled items for the File, Edit, Resource, and View menus. The *menu* parameter specifies the ID of the menu to be enabled, and *enable* specifies the enable flags for each menu item and the menu itself.

```
pascal void BubbleUp(Handle);
```

BubbleUp is ResEdit's version of the **MoveHHi** Toolbox procedure. **BubbleUp** should always be used in place of **MoveHHi** to make sure the heap zone is set up correctly. It's a good idea to call **BubbleUp** before you lock a handle if it will be locked for a long time. **BubbleUp** may have to move large chunks of memory around and could, therefore, be very slow.

```
pascal void CenterDialog(ResType theType, short dialog);
```

CenterDialog loads a dialog or alert into memory and centers its boundsRect. The caller can then call **GetNewDialog**, **Alert**, **Caution-Alert**, **NoteAlert**, or **StopAlert** to use the centered dialog or alert. You should always call **CenterDialog** before you display a dialog or alert so it appears where the user expects it. The *theType* parameter specifies whether a 'DLOG' or 'ALRT' resource should be loaded, and the *dialog* parameter specifies the ID of the dialog or alert resource. The dialog or alert is centered on the same screen that contains the current port. If the dialog or alert has an associated color table ('dctb' or 'actb'), it's centered on the screen that can show the most colors and contains any portion of the current port. If the dialog or alert doesn't contain color and the last command was selected from a menu, the dialog is centered on the screen with the menu bar.

```
pascal Boolean CheckError(short err, short msgID);
```

CheckError displays an error alert and returns false if the *err* para-meter is not 0. If *err* is 0, true is returned. **CheckError** has built-in error messages for many different errors. If the *err* isn't one of these built-in errors, the message specified by *msgID* is displayed. *msgID* should be an index into the 'STR#' resource in ResEdit named "Misc.". If *msgID* is 0, the default message "I/O Error. [#]" is displayed. The actual error number (*err*) is always displayed in square brackets at the end of the error message. If *msgID* is negative, it's assumed to be an index into the 'STR#' resource with ID 128. This resource is guaranteed to be available in memory (it's preloaded when ResEdit starts) and should be used only for serious, unrecoverable errors.

```
pascal Boolean ChooseIcon(ParentHandle parent,
              short *IconResID, IconType *IconKind,
              short dialogID );
```

ChooseIcon can be used by an editor to display a dialog allowing the user to select an icon. *parent* is the editor's *ParentHandle*. *IconResID* is the resource ID of the initially selected icon. If there's no initial selection, pass an unused resource ID (call **ReBeautifulUnique1ID** to get an un-used ID). The *IconKind* parameter can be either *onlyIcon* or *only-ICNPound*—other values are used by the 'MENU' editor and aren't useful for other editors. The *dialogID* parameter is the resource ID of the dialog that should be used. You should either use one of the existing dialogs from ResEdit or make a copy of an existing dialog and make small changes. Don't delete or renumber any of the first nine dialog items—if you don't want to use all the items, you can make them invisible by moving them outside of the window bounds.

```
pascal Boolean ColorAvailable(Boolean needColorQD);
```

ColorAvailable returns true if Color QuickDraw is available and false otherwise. If *needColorQD* is true and Color QuickDraw isn't available, an error alert is displayed. Remember, just because color QuickDraw is available doesn't mean a color or gray-scale monitor is attached.

```
pascal void ConcatStr(StringPtr str1, StringPtr str2);
```

ConcatStr concatenates two strings by adding *str2* to the end of *str1*. No length checking is done, so make sure the total length of the two strings is less than 255 characters before you call **ConcatStr**.

```
pascal short DisplayAlert(AlertType which, short id);
```

DisplayAlert displays an alert with resource ID *id*. The *which* parameter indicates the kind of alert that should be displayed. Possible values are shown in Table 29-1.

Table 29-1. Types of Alerts

Alert Type	Action
displayTheAlert	Normal alert using **Alert** procedure
displayStopAlert	Stop alert using **StopAlert** procedure
displayNoteAlert	Note alert using **NoteAlert** procedure
displayCautionAlert	Caution alert using **CautionAlert** procedure
displayYNAlert	Yes, No alert using **CautionAlert** procedure
displayYNCAlert	Yes, No, Cancel alert using **CautionAlert** procedure
displayYNCStopAlert	Yes, No, Cancel alert using **StopAlert** procedure

The last three alerts in Table 29-1 assume the alert contains either Yes and No or Yes, No, and Cancel buttons. Filtering is provided to make the standard keys work with the alert. Typing the *Y, N,* or *C* key is the same as clicking the button starting with the same letter. The Return and Enter keys are equivalent to clicking the Yes button, and pressing the Escape key or Command-period is the same as clicking the Cancel button.

```
pascal Boolean DisplaySTRAlert(AlertType which,
             StringPtr STRName, short STRIndex);
```

This procedure is similar to **DisplayAlert,** except you specify a string rather than an 'ALRT' resource ID. ResEdit has a built-in 'ALRT' resource which is used to display almost all of its alerts—the appropriate text is simply substituted into the alert before it's displayed. The *which* parameter specifies the type of alert to display, as shown in Table 29-1. **DisplayStrAlert** doesn't support either of the Yes, No, Cancel alerts. The *strName* parameter specifies the name of an 'STR#' resource in ResEdit (or the ResEdit Preferences file) that contains the string. *STRIndex* is the index into the 'STR#' resource. True is returned if the OK or Yes button is clicked.

```
pascal void DrawMBarLater(Boolean forceItNow);
```

DrawMBarLater sets a flag to indicate that the menu bar should be drawn at the next opportunity. You should always call **DrawMBarLater** instead of the **DrawMenuBar** Toolbox procedure so the menu bar doesn't flash. When an editor or picker is activated, it often needs to change the state of several menus as well as add its own menus to the menu bar. If each of these changes drew the menu bar, it would flash annoyingly. **DrawMBarLater** remembers that the menu bar needs to be drawn but doesn't actually draw it until there are no other events waiting to be processed. In some special circumstances (such as when the 'MENU' editor puts its fake menu on the menu bar), you might need to force the menu bar to be drawn immediately instead of waiting until later. You can do this by setting *forceItNow* to true. Calling **DrawMBar-Later** with *forceItNow* set to true is not the same as calling **Draw-MenuBar**, because **DrawMBarLater** also clears any other pending menu bar updates.

```
pascal WindowPtr FindOwnerWindow(Handle theRes);
```

FindOwnerWindow returns a pointer to the window that's editing the resource specified by *theRes*. If no editor is using the resource, nil is returned. **FindOwnerWindow** should be used by editors that can edit more than one resource. Editors must be very careful not to make changes to a resource that might be in use by another editor, so before releasing or editing a resource, other than the one passed to **EditBirth**, call **FindOwnerWindow**.

```
pascal void FixHand(long s, Handle h);
```

FixHand makes sure the resource *h* contains *s* bytes, shrinking or growing it as necessary. If the resource is grown, the extra bytes are filled with zeros.

```
pascal void FlashDialogItem(DialogPtr dp, short item);
```

FlashDialogItem briefly highlights the control with item number *item* in dialog *dp*. When a key (such as Return or Enter) is used as a shortcut for clicking a button, **FlashDialogItem** should be used to "flash" the button when the shortcut key is pressed so the user knows which button was selected.

```
pascal void FrameDialogItem(DialogPtr dp, short item);
```

FrameDialogItem draws a three-pixel border around a button in a dialog to show that it's the default button. If the item is dim (not enabled), a dim frame (gray) is drawn. **FrameDialogItem** should be called from a dialog's filter procedure when an update event is received.

```
pascal void GetNamedStr(short index, const StringPtr name,
              StringPtr str);
```

GetNamedStr returns a string from an 'STR#' resource. *name* is the resource name of the 'STR#' resource, and *index* indicates which string should be returned. (The first string in an 'STR#' resource has an *index* of 1.)

```
pascal pQuickDrawVars GetQuickDrawVars(void);
```

GetQuickDrawVars returns a pointer to a structure containing the normal QuickDraw variables (such as *thePort*, *screenBits*, and *dkGray*). Editors and pickers don't normally have access to the QuickDraw variables because they reside in stand-alone resources and register A5 isn't set up correctly (the same reason they can't have global variables).

```
pascal Rect GetScreenRect(Boolean roomForIcons,
              WindowPtr wind);
```

GetScreenRect returns the size of the screen that contains the majority of the specified window. If the window is on the main screen (the one with the menubar), the size returned doesn't include the menu bar. If the screen containing the window is large (larger than 400 by 600), is the main screen, and *roomForIcons* is true, approximately 50 is subtracted from the right side of the rectangle to leave room to see icons on the desktop.

```
pascal void GetStr(short index, short resID, StringPtr str);
```

GetStr is similar to **GetNamedStr**, except it looks up the 'STR#' resource by resource ID rather than by resource name.

```
pascal Boolean HandleCheck(Handle h, short msgID);
```

HandleCheck can be called after loading a resource. It displays an error alert and returns false if the **ResError** Toolbox procedure returns a non-zero error number or if the resource handle *h* is nil or purged (**h* is nil). If the resource is OK, true is returned. If an error is detected, **Check-Error** is called with the error number and the *msgID* parameter. If the handle is nil or purged, an error is displayed using the string found at index *msgID* in the 'STR#' resource named "Misc."

```
pascal void MetaKeys(Boolean *cmd, Boolean *shift,
                Boolean *opt);
```

MetaKeys returns the state of the Command, Shift, and Option keys when the last event was processed by ResEdit. If you want to use one of the modifier keys to implement a shortcut, use **MetaKeys** to find out which keys are pressed. It's important to use this procedure rather than looking in the event record because ResEdit occasionally "pretends" some of the keys were pressed when they really weren't. For example, when the user chooses the Open Using Hex Editor command from the Resource menu, ResEdit pretends the Option key was pressed (this is why Option-double-click opens the hexadecimal editor).

```
pascal Handle PrintSetup(void);
```

PrintSetup can be used to set up a print record if you're doing your own printing instead of using **PrintWindow**. The return parameter is really of type *THPrint*. Printing is discussed in the "Tips" section of Chapter 28.

```
pascal void PrintWindow(PicHandle toPrint);
```

PrintWindow can be used to print the contents of your window. If *toPrint* isn't nil, the *toPrint* picture will be printed instead of the window's contents. Most editors should call **PrintWindow** with *toPrint* set to nil. **PrintWindow** prints an editor's window by opening a Quick-

Draw picture and then forcing the editor to redraw the contents of its window. The resulting picture is then printed.

```pascal
pascal short ResEdID(void);
```

ResEdID returns the resource ID of the calling editor or picker. This resource ID should be stored in the *codeResID* field of the *ParentRec* structure. Editors that don't use **EditorWindSetup** should also save their resource ID in the *windowKind* field of their window.

```pascal
pascal void SetTheCursor(short whichCursor);
```

SetTheCursor sets the mouse pointer to the 'CURS' resource with resource ID *whichCursor*. The special constant *arrowCursor* defined in the ResEd file can be used to set the arrow cursor. Any cursor located in the ResEdit Preferences file, ResEdit, or the System can be set with **SetThe-Cursor**.

```pascal
pascal void ShowInfo(Handle h, ParentHandle parent);
```

ShowInfo displays a resource information window for the resource specified by *h*. The *parent* parameter is the caller's *ParentHandle*. **Show-Info** should be called in response to a Get Resource Info command.

```pascal
pascal Boolean StandardFilter(DialogPtr theDialog,
                 EventRecord *theEvent, short *itemHit);
```

StandardFilter is a standard filter procedure for use with modal dialogs. It assumes that the OK button is item number 1, and the cancel button is item number 2. A dark border is drawn around the OK button, and the button is flashed when the Return or Enter key is pressed. If the OK button is disabled, the border is drawn in gray rather than black. If there are editable fields in the dialog, Cut, Copy and Paste are supported.

```pascal
pascal void TypeToString(ResType t, StringPtr s);
```

TypeToString converts the resource type *t* to a string *s*. Storage for the string must be preallocated.

```pascal
pascal void UseAppRes(void);
```

UseAppRes sets the current resource file to the ResEdit Preferences file. You should call **UseAppRes** after you've changed the resource file by calling the **UseResFile** Toolbox procedure.

```
pascal Boolean WasAborted(void);
```

WasAborted returns true if the current event was aborted. For example, if a Close command was passed on to other windows that were opened by an editor (using the **PassMenu** procedure), you can check to see if the other windows closed successfully by calling **WasAborted**. You can set the aborted flag to true by calling the **Abort** procedure. The aborted flag is set to false before each event is processed.

▶ Pop-up Menus

ResEdit provides support for two different kinds of pop-up menus. Normal pop-up menus use the **DoPopup** and **DrawPop** procedures. Color palette pop-up menus are supported by **InstallColorPalettePopup, DeinstallColorPalettePopup, DrawColorPopup** and **ColorPalettePopupSelect.**

```
pascal Boolean ColorPalettePopupSelect(WindowPtr whichWindow,
            Rect *itemBox, RGBColor *whichColor,
            Boolean CQDishere, Boolean useColorPicker);
```

ColorPalettePopupSelect handles mouseDown events in color palette pop-up menus. Call this procedure whenever you receive a mouse-Down event in one of your color patches. *whichWindow* is the window containing the pop-up, *itemBox* is the *Rect* to be used to draw the color swatch, *whichColor* is the *RGBColor* to be used as the default color, and *CQDishere* is true when Color QuickDraw is available. If *useColorPicker* is true, the color picker dialog is displayed rather than the color palette pop-up. On exit, *whichColor* contains the *RGBColor* selected by the user.

```
pascal void DeinstallColorPalettePopup(WindowPtr whichWindow,
            Boolean CQDishere);
```

DeinstallColorPalettePopup removes the palette from the window. Call this procedure before closing your window.

```
pascal void DoPopup(DialogPtr whichDialog,
            short promptDialogItem,
            short popupDialogItem,
            short *menuItem, MenuHandle whichMenu);
```

Call **DoPopup** when you receive a mouseDown event in the dialog item that contains a pop-up menu. You can use this procedure along with the **DrawPopup** procedure to implement pop-up menus in your editor or dialog. *whichDialog* is the window that contains the pop-up menu. *promptDialogItem* is the item in the dialog that shows the pop-up menu's prompt, and *popupDialogItem* is the dialog item that actually contains the pop-up menu. *menuItem* contains the current setting when you call **DoPopup** and returns the new menu choice. *whichMenu* is the handle to the menu itself.

```
pascal void DrawColorPopup(WindowPtr whichWindow,
            Rect *itemBox, RGBColor *whichColor,
            Boolean CQDishere);
```

DrawColorPopup draws the color swatch and a drop shadow indicating that the color swatch is actually a pop-up menu. Call this procedure for every pop-up palette whenever you need to update the window contents. *whichWindow* is the window containing the pop-up menu, *itemBox* is the *Rect* to be used to draw the color swatch, *whichColor* is the *RGBColor* to be drawn, and *CQDishere* is true when Color QuickDraw is available.

```
pascal void DrawPopup(DialogPtr whichDialog,
            short whichDialogItem, short whichMenuItem,
            MenuHandle whichMenu);
```

When you receive an update event, call **DrawPopup** to draw the current contents of a pop-up menu. The *whichDialog* parameter is the *DialogPtr* of the window containing the pop-up menu. *whichDialogItem* is the item in the dialog that represents the pop-up menu and *which-MenuItem* is the current menu choice. *whichMenu* is the handle to the actual pop-up menu. You can use this procedure along with the **DoPopup** procedure to implement pop-up menus in your editor or dialog.

```
pascal void InstallColorPalettePopup(WindowPtr whichWindow,
            Boolean CQDishere, Boolean isActive);
```

InstallColorPalettePopup sets up a palette for the window containing the system colors for the deepest available device. The use of the color pop-up menu is described in Chapter 28. Call this procedure immediately after opening your window and whenever you receive an update event. It's OK to call **InstallColorPalettePopup** multiple times without calling **DeinstallColorPalettePopup**. *whichWindow* is the window containing the pop-up menu, *CQDishere* is true when Color QuickDraw is available, and *isActive* is true when *whichWindow* is the frontmost window.

▶ Other Procedures

```pascal
pascal short BuildType(ResType t, ListHandle lh);
```

BuildType adds resources to an initialized List Manager list. You can use **BuildType** in your picker if it doesn't use **DoPickBirth**, **PickEvent**, and **PickMenu**. **BuildType** assumes that the lists *refCon* field contains the *PickHandle* of the picker that owns the list. When **BuildType** is through, the list will contain the resource IDs of all resources of type *t* in the pickers resource file in the order they appear in the file. The number of resource IDs in the list is returned.

```pascal
pascal void DoKeyScan(EventRecord *evt, short offset,
                ListHandle lh);
```

DoKeyScan handles key events for pickers. Since it's called for you by **PickEvent**, you shouldn't need to call this procedure. **DoKeyScan** takes care of moving to the appropriate cell as the user types characters (for example, in a resource picker, typing a resource ID or name moves the selection to the resource with the closest match). The *offset* parameter is the byte offset into a cell's data where the string to match starts.

```pascal
pascal Handle DupPick(Handle h, Cell c, PickHandle pick);
```

DupPick duplicates the resource *h* and adds it to the list owned by the picker ((*pick*)->instances). A handle to the new resource is returned. **DupPick** is normally called for you by **PickMenu**.

```pascal
pascal void GetErrorText(short error, StringPtr errorText);
```

GetErrorText returns text explaining the error specified in *error*. If the error is not one with a built-in error message, "I/O Error. [#]" is returned. *errorText* should be a pointer to a preallocated string containing room for 25 characters.

```
pascal short GetResEditScrapFile(void);
```

GetResEditScrapFile returns the resource file number of the ResEdit scrap file. If you need to do your own scrap manipulation, you can read and write the ResEdit scrap file directly. **GetResEditScrapFile** transfers any resources on the desk scrap into the ResEdit scrap before returning. The constant *noScrap* is returned if an error occurred while creating the scrap file. You can use the **ScrapEmpty** procedure to clear the ResEdit scrap file before writing to it.

```
pascal Boolean GetType(Boolean templatesOnly, StringPtr s);
```

GetType returns in the string *s* a resource type selected by the user. **GetType** displays a dialog with a list of types for the user to choose from along with an editable field for entering a type not included in the list. If *templatesOnly* is true, the list is made up of resource types that have templates available; otherwise, editors are also included in the list. On input, *theType* is the default type used to initialize the editable field. True is returned if a resource type was selected, false is returned if the user canceled the dialog. *s* should point to a string of at least 4 bytes.

```
pascal ResType MapResourceType(Boolean editor,
               Handle theRes, ResType origResType);
```

MapResourceType uses the 'RMAP' resource to see what editor or template should be used with a resource type of *origResType*. If an 'RMAP' resource is found, the resource ID of *theRes* is used to see if additional resource ID mapping should be done. Chapter 25 explains 'RMAP' resources.

```
pascal Boolean PlaySyncSound(short which, Handle sndHandle);
```

PlaySyncSound plays the sound contained in *sndHandle*. *which* can be set to 1 to simply play the sound, 2 to play the sound as a HyperCard sound, and 3 to play a scale using the sound. **PlaySyncSound** is used by the 'snd ' picker.

```
pascal short ResEditRes(void);
```

ResEditRes is a simple inline procedure that returns the resource file number of ResEdit.

```
pascal void ResourceIDHasChanged(ParentHandle parent,
              ResType theType, short theOldId,
              short theNewId);
```

ResourceIDHasChanged should be called whenever you change a resource's ID so the revert commands will work properly.

```
pascal Boolean RestoreRemovedResources(PickHandle pick);
```

You should call **RestoreRemovedResources** during a revert if you have deleted any resources. For example, the 'BNDL' editor calls this to restore 'FREF' resources that it has deleted. All resources of type (*pick)->rType that have been deleted are restored. True is returned if the calling picker's list needs to be rebuilt.

```
pascal void ScrapCopy(ResType theType, Handle *h);
```

ScrapCopy puts the handle *h* into the ResEdit scrap file. If the handle *h* isn't a resource it's added to the scrap file with the resource type specified by *theType*.

```
pascal void ScrapEmpty(void);
```

ScrapEmpty clears out the ResEdit scrap file.

```
pascal void SendRebuildToPicker(ResType theType,
              ParentHandle parent);
```

SendRebuildToPicker sets the rebuild flag in the *PickRec* of the picker for resources of type *theType* for the file that *parent* belongs to. If an editor changes information (such as the resource ID or name) of a resource of another type, it's a good idea to call this procedure to make sure the picker window is up-to-date.

```
pascal void SendRebuildToPickerAndFile(ResType theType,
              ParentHandle parent);
```

SendRebuildToPickerAndFile is similar to **SendRebuildToPicker**, except it also sets the rebuild flag for the type picker. (What a surprise!) An editor should call this procedure if it creates a resource of another type.

```
pascal short SysResFile(void);
```

SysResFile returns the resource file number of the System file.

```
pascal ListHandle WindList(WindowPtr w, short nAcross,
                Point cSize, short drawProc);
```

Pickers can use **WindList** to set up the List Manager list in their window. You only need to use this procedure if you can't call **DoPickBirth**. The *nAcross* parameter specifies how many columns the list should contain, *cSize* specifies the size (in pixels) of each cell in the list, and *drawProc* specifies the resource ID of the 'LDEF' that draws the list.

```
pascal void WindOrigin(WindowPtr w, ParentHandle parent);
```

WindOrigin moves the specified window so that it's in the correct position on the screen relative to other ResEdit windows. You only need to call this procedure if you don't use **EditorWindSetup** or **PickerWindSetup**.

```
pascal void WritePreferences (ResType prefType, short prefId,
                const Str255 prefName, Handle prefHandle);
```

WritePreferences writes *prefHandle* to the ResEdit Preferences file with a resource type of *prefType*, ID of *prefId*, and name of *prefName*. Chapter 28 explains how to read and write preferences.

▶ Summary

This chapter gives you a brief overview of the ResEd file and then launches into descriptions of each procedure that ResEdit provides for your editor or picker to call. Over 90 procedures are described, and many include brief examples. Many of the procedures are also discussed in Chapters 26, 27, and 28, where you'll find examples that help clarify how they should be used. With this chapter as a reference and the examples presented in previous chapters, you should now be ready to dive in and write your own editor or picker.

Appendix A
Shortcuts and Hints

▶ **General Macintosh**

- If you normally use MultiFinder, you can restart using just the Finder by holding down the Command key when you restart your Mac. You can't restart without MultiFinder if you're using System 7.
- You can rebuild your Desktop file (or your Desktop database in System 7) by holding down the Command and Option keys when you restart your Mac.
- Within an application you can move a window without making it the active window by holding down the Command key while you drag the window by its title bar.

▶ **General ResEdit**

- When the splash screen is displayed, any event causes the splash screen to go away, and ResEdit also acts upon the event. For example, clicking the menu bar removes the splash screen and pulls down the selected menu. Similarly, typing a Command key removes the splash screen, and ResEdit acts on the command.

- If you press the Option key while you click the close box of a window, all that file's windows will close except the type picker.
- Pressing the Option key while opening a resource picker causes the resource picker to appear in view by ID.
- If you're having trouble editing a file (if you get bombs when you try to edit it, for example), try using the Verify command on the File menu to make sure the file is OK.
- To be on the safe side, check the "Verify files when they are opened" check box in the Preferences dialog. This makes opening a file take longer, but you'll know the file is OK.
- If you press the Option key when you open a file (if "Verify files when they are opened" is checked in the Preferences dialog) or when you verify a file, you see a diagnostic window that lists details of any damage.
- If you have a few files that you use frequently with ResEdit, try adding them to the Open Special menu so you can give them Command key shortcuts. That way you can open them from the splash screen, or any time you want to get to them quickly.
- You can customize or override any resource in ResEdit by placing your own version of the resource in ResEdit's Preferences file. This way you only have to remove the Preferences file from your System Folder to put ResEdit back in its original, default state. Plus, you won't lose your changes when you update to a new version of ResEdit.

▶ Resource Pickers

- Pressing the Option key when you copy or cut one or more resources adds them to any resources already on ResEdit's clipboard. Normally, when you cut or copy, you replace the contents of the clipboard.
- Pressing the Option key while double-clicking a resource opens the resource in the hexadecimal editor. This is the same as selecting Open Using Hex-Editor from the Resource menu.
- Pressing the Option and Command keys while double-clicking a resource opens the template editor instead of the normal custom editor. You see a dialog asking you to select the template you want

to use. This is the same as selecting Open Using Template from the Resource menu.

▶ Fatbits Editors (except the 'FONT' editor)

- Double-clicking the eraser clears the fatbits editing area.
- Double-clicking the rectangular selection tool selects the whole fatbits editing area. Select All on the Edit menu gives the same result.
- If you hold down the Option key while you drag a selection, you'll duplicate the selection.
- You can use the arrow keys to move a selection one bit in the desired direction as a shortcut for selecting the nudge commands from the Transform menu.
- Pressing the Shift key constrains several of the drawing tools:

    The line tool draws lines only at 45- and 90-degree angles,

    The empty and filled rectangle tools draw only squares,

    The empty and filled rounded rectangle tools draw only rounded squares,

    The empty and filled oval tools draw only circles,

    The pencil and eraser are constrained to horizontal or vertical lines.

- You can tear off the pattern and color pop-up palettes.
- In editors with multiple views (icon and mask in the 'ICN#' editor, for example), you can fill in any of the views by dragging the image from one view to another.
- In the list editors ('SICN', 'PAT#', and 'ppt#') you can reorder elements in the list by dragging. (This is most useful during software development. Be careful about reordering existing list resources.)
- You can add your own patterns to ResEdit's pop-up pattern palettes. Open ResEdit and find the 'ppt#' (for color patterns) or 'PAT#' resource named Fill Pattern. Copy the resource and paste it into the ResEdit Preferences file. Add, remove, or update the patterns until you have the set you want to use. For consistency, it's a good idea to keep the black-and-white patterns (both in the

'PAT#' resource and in each pattern of the 'ppt#' resource) the same as the color patterns.

- In the color fatpixels editors, pressing the Command key when picking a color from the foreground color palette changes all pixels of the current foreground color to the selected color.

- In the color fatpixels editors, pressing the Option key temporarily changes any of the drawing tools (except the selection tools, eraser, or hot spot tool) into the eyedropper tool.

- In the color editors, you can add your own sets of colors to the Color menu by putting a 'clut' resource in the ResEdit Preferences file. (You won't see them in the icon family editor, however, because these resources use fixed color tables.)

- Pressing the Option key when you create a color pattern (from the 'ppat' picker or the 'ppt#' editor) creates a relative pattern.

▶ 'DLOG', 'ALRT', and 'WIND' Editors

- You can use the arrow keys to move the window on the Mini-Screen one bit in the specified direction.

- When you create a new 'WIND', 'ALRT', or 'DLOG', the default values are taken from a resource in ResEdit named "Default." You can override these with your own defaults by placing a resource of the appropriate type in your ResEdit Preferences file in the System Folder. Make sure your resource has the name "Default."

- You can double-click the mini-dialog or mini-alert, or press the Return or Enter key to open the associated 'DITL' resource.

▶ 'MENU' Editor

- Pressing the Return key moves the selection to the next menu item in the list. If the selection is already at the end of the list, a new item is added.

- When you're designing a menu, you can reorder items by simply dragging an item to its new location. (Don't do this when customizing an existing menu!)

▶ 'DITL' Editor

- Holding down the Option key temporarily toggles the Show Item Numbers command. If Show Item Numbers is off, pressing the Option key will show the item numbers. If Show Item Numbers is on, pressing the Option key will hide the item numbers.

- Pressing the Return or Enter key opens item editor windows for all selected items.

Appendix B
Resource Types

This appendix lists some standard resource types and a brief description of each. The "Editor" column tells you whether ResEdit has a special editor (E) or a template (T) for that resource type.

Type	Editor	Description
'actb'	E,T	Alert color look-up table. Edited by 'ALRT' editor
'acur'	T	Animated cursor resource
'ADBS'		ADB (Apple Desktop Bus) driver code
'alis'		System 7 file alias information
'ALRT'	E,T	Location and size of an alert window
'APPL'	T	Application list from the Desktop file
'bmap'		BitMap used by old versions of the Control Panel
'boot'		Boot blocks in System file
'BNDL'	E,T	Bundle resource used to attach icons to applications and their documents
'CACH'		RAM cache control code
'card'		Contains the name of a video card
'cctb'	T	Control color look-up table
'CDEF'		Code for drawing controls (Control DEFinition)
'cdev'		Code for a Control Panel device
'cicn'	E	Color icon

Type	Editor	Description
'clst'		Cached icon lists used by the Chooser and Control Panel
'clut'	E,T	Color look-up table
'CMDK'	T	List of Command keys used in ResEdit
'CMDO'		Used for MPW Commando interface
'cmnu'	E,T	MacApp temporary menu resource
'CMNU'	E,T	Command menu. MacApp menu resource
'CNTL'	T	Definition data for controls such as scroll bars
'CODE'		Application code
'crsr'	E	Color mouse pointer
'CTY#'	T	City list from MAP Control Panel device
'CURS'	E	Mouse pointer
'dctb'	E,T	Dialog color look-up table. Edited by 'DLOG' editor
'DITL'	E,T	Dialog Item List. Defines the contents of dialogs and alerts
'DLOG'	E,T	Defines the location and size of a dialog window
'dpsr'		System 7 Edition Manager section information
'DRVR'	T	Driver (printer, network, etc.) or desk accessory
'DSAT'		Startup and bomb alerts and code to display them
'FBTN'	T	MiniFinder button
'fctb'	T	Font color look-up table
'FCMT'	T	Finder's GetInfo comments stored in the Desktop file
'FDIR'	T	MiniFinder button directory ID
'FILE'		Contents of ResEdit's Open Special menu (found in the ResEdit Preferences file)
'finf'	T	Font information
'FKEY'		Function key code usually found in the System file
'fld#'	T	List of folder names
'FMTR'		Format record for 3½ inch disks
'fmts'		System 7 Edition Manager available formats
'FOBJ'		Information about folders
'FOND'	T	Font family description
'FONT'	E,T	Font description
'FREF'	E,T	File reference
'fval'	T	System 7 Finder's data (similar to the 'LAYO' resource used by earlier Finders)

Type	Editor	Description
'FRSV'	T	Resource IDs of ROM font resources
'FWID'	T	Font width table
'gama'		Gamma table—color correction for monitors
'GNRL'	T	ResEdit's preference information (stored in the ResEdit Preferences file)
'hmnu'		System 7 help for menus
'hdlg'		System 7 help for dialogs
'hwin'	T	System 7 help for windows
'hrct'		System 7 help rectangles
'icl4'	E	System 7, 4-bit large (32 x 32) Finder icon
'icl8'	E	System 7, 8-bit large (32 x 32) Finder icon
'icmt'	T	Comment for Installer 3.0 and later
'ICN#'	E	Black-and-white Finder icon with mask
'ICON'	E	Icon used in dialogs, menus, etc.
'ics#'	E	System 7, black-and-white small (16 x 16) Finder icon with mask
'ics4'	E	System 7, 4-bit small (16 x 16) Finder icon
'ics8'	E	System 7, 8-bit small (16 x 16) Finder icon
'ictb'		Color dialog item list
'inbb'	T	Installer scripts for Installer 3.0 and later
'indm'	T	Installer scripts for Installer 3.0 and later
'infa'	T	Installer scripts for Installer 3.0 and later
'infs'	T	Installer scripts for Installer 3.0 and later
'INIT'		Code run at System startup time
'inpk'	T	Installer scripts for Installer 3.0 and later
'inra'	T	Installer scripts for Installer 3.0 and later
'insc'	T	Installer script
'INT#'		Integer list used by Find File DA
'INTL'	E	Old style 'itl0' and 'itl1'
'itl0'	E	Date, time, and number formats
'itl1'	E	International date/time information
'itl2'		International string comparision code
'itl4'		Tables needed for international number formatting and conversion
'itlb'	T	International script bundle that determines which keyboard and which international formats to use

Type	*Editor*	*Description*
'itlc'	T	International script configuration
'itlk'	T	International exception dictionary for 'KCHR' resource
'KCAP'		Physical layout of the keyboard
'KCHR'	E	Mapping of virtual key codes to character codes
'KEYC'		Old keyboard layout
'KMAP'		Keyboard mapping from raw keycode (generated by the keyboard) to virtual keycode
'kscn'		Small icons that correspond to 'KCHR' resources
'KSWP'		Key-plus-modifier combinations that can be used to toggle international keyboard scripts
'LAYO'	T	Finder layout resource
'LDEF'		Code used by the List Manager to draw lists
'lmem'		Globals to be switched by MultiFinder
'mach'		'cdev' filtering
'MACS'	T	Version number in System file
'MBAR'	T	Set of 'MENU's to be displayed together on the menu bar
'MBDF'		Menu bar definition code
'mcky'	T	Speed associated with the different choices in the mouse Control Panel
'mctb'	E,T	Menu color look-up table. Edited by 'MENU' editor
'mcod'		MacroMaker information
'mdct'		MacroMaker information
'MDEF'		Code for drawing menus
'mem!'		MacApp memory utilization
'MENU'	E,T	Definition for a standard menu
'minf'	T	MacroMaker macro information
'mitq'		Default queue sizes for the MakeITable procedure
'MMAP'		Mouse tracking code
'mntb'		Relates a command number to a menu in MacApp
'mntr'		Monitor extension code—adds items to the Options dialog displayed by the Monitors Control Panel device
'mppc'		MPP configuration resource
'mst#'		MultiFinder string list used to identify menu and item used for Quit and Open commands
'mstr'		MultiFinder string used to identify menu and item used for Quit and Open commands

Type	Editor	Description
'NFNT'		New font description; similar to 'FONT' resource
'nrct'	T	Rectangle position list
'PACK'		Packages of code used as ROM extensions
'PAPA'	T	Printer access protocol address used for AppleTalk
'PAT '	E	8-by-8-bit black-and-white pattern
'PAT#'	E	A list of 'PAT ' resources
'PDEF'		Printer driver code
'PICK'	T	ResEdit's picker definitions
'PICT'	E,T	Picture used by many drawing programs
'pltt'	E,T	Palette of colors
'POST'	T	PostScript code
'ppat'	E,T	Pixel pattern, color patterns of variable size
'ppt#'	E	List of 'ppat' resources
'PREC'	T	Printer driver's private data storage. ID 0 contains the default page setup info
'PREF'		ResEdit editors' preference information
'PRER'		Non-serial printer Chooser code
'PRES'		Serial printer Chooser code
'prvw'		System 7 Edition manager—similar to a 'PICT'
'PTCH'		Code to patch the ROM
'ptch'		Code to patch the ROM
'qrsc'	T	System 7 Database Access Manager query record
'RDEV'		Network Chooser code
'RECT'		Coordinates of a single rectangle
'resf'	T	System 7 reserved fonts
'RMAP'	T	ResEdit resource map
'ROv#'	T	List of ROM resources to override
'ROvr'		ROM override code
'RSSC'		ResEdit editors and pickers
'RVEW'	T	ResEdit picker view information
'scrn'	T	Screen configuration
'seg!'		MacApp segmentation control
'SERD'		RAM serial driver code
'sfnt'		True Type outline font description
'SICN'	E	List of small (16-by-16) icons

Type	Editor	Description
'SIZE'	T	MultiFinder size information
'snd '		Sound used for the System beep, HyperCard ,and other applications
'snth'		Sound synthesizer code
'STR '	T	String of characters
'STR#'	T	List of strings
'styl'	E	Style information for characters in 'TEXT' resource
'TEXT'	E,T	Unformatted text—formatting can be provided in a 'styl' resource
'tlst'		Title list
'TMPL'	T	ResEdit template
'TOOL'	T	ResEdit fatbits editors tool layout
'vers'	E,T	Version information used in the Finder's GetInfo window
'wctb'	E,T	Window color look-up table. Edited by 'WIND' editor
'WDEF'		Window definition code for drawing the structure part (title bar, frame, etc.) of windows
'WIND'	E,T	Size, location , and type of a window
'wstr'	T	Query string used by 'qrsc' resource

Appendix C
Editing Resources in Hexadecimal

Sometimes you'll have to dip down into the hexadecimal editor to change a resource that doesn't have an editor or a template. There's really nothing scary about the hex editor if you understand a little about the editor and how the hexadecimal number system works.

▶ The Hexadecimal Number System

Hexadecimal is a base-16 number system, which is a convenient system for computers because two hex digits can represent one byte. The numbers 1 through 9 are the same in decimal as they are in hexadecimal. The numbers 10 through 15 are represented as shown in Table C-1.

Table C-1. Hexadecimal Equivalents of Decimal Numbers

Decimal	Hexadecimal
10	A
11	B
12	C
13	D
14	E
15	F

Table C-2 shows some examples that should help you get the hang of converting from decimal to hexadecimal and back.

Table C-2. Hexadecimal to Decimal Conversions

Hexadecimal	Conversion	Decimal
10	1 x 16	16
23	2 x 16 + 3	35
2A	2 x 16 + 10	42
56	5 x 16 + 6	86
C5	12 x 16 + 5	197
FF	15 x 16 + 15	255

▶ The Hexadecimal Editor

When you open a resource with the hexadecimal editor, you see a window like the one shown in Figure C-1. The left side of the window shows the offset (the number of bytes from the beginning of the resource) in hexadecimal, of course; the middle of the window shows hexadecimal numbers; and the right side shows their text equivalents. Each row displays eight bytes of the resource. Since many numbers don't have understandable text equivalents, the right side of the window is often unintelligible, as you can see in the figure.

You can edit either the numbers or the text—just click the part of the window you want to edit. Entering text in the text side of the window works just like you'd expect—simply type the characters you want to add. Adding or changing numbers in the middle of the window is not quite as straightforward. Digits in the hex editor always come in pairs, so if you want to change a number, you have to change two digits. Res-Edit tries to help you keep the digits in pairs by adding a 0 whenever you enter just one digit. For example, if you type a 3, 03 appears in the window. If you then type a 4, you'll have 34 (the added 0 will be removed). Likewise, since digits always come in pairs, you can't select just one digit—you always have to select pairs of digits.

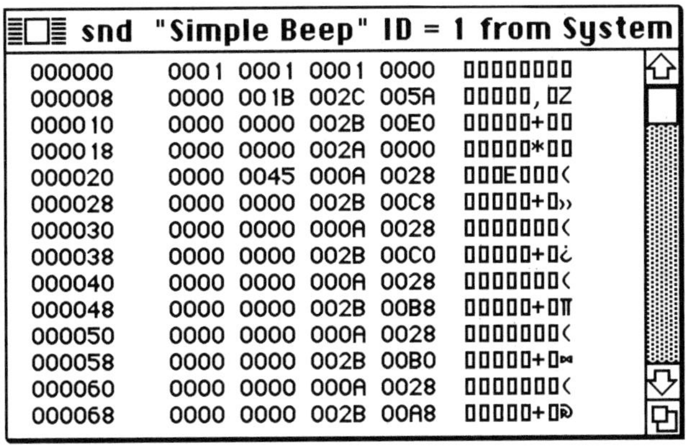

≣□≣ snd "Simple Beep" ID = 1 from System					
000000	0001	0001	0001	0000	00000000
000008	0000	001B	002C	005A	00000,0Z
000010	0000	0000	002B	00E0	00000+00
000018	0000	0000	002A	0000	00000*00
000020	0000	0045	000A	0028	000E000<
000028	0000	0000	002B	00C8	00000+0»
000030	0000	0000	000A	0028	0000000<
000038	0000	0000	002B	00C0	00000+0¿
000040	0000	0000	000A	0028	0000000<
000048	0000	0000	002B	00B8	00000+0π
000050	0000	0000	000A	0028	0000000<
000058	0000	0000	002B	00B0	00000+0∞
000060	0000	0000	000A	0028	0000000<
000068	0000	0000	002B	00A8	00000+0℗

Figure C-1. The hexadecimal editor shows offsets on the left, numbers in the middle, and text on the right.

You can use all the standard editing commands on either the numbers or the text. If you want to copy between two resources, just select the numbers you want, copy them, and paste them into the other resource. If you paste when numbers or text are selected, the selection is replaced. If you paste when there's no selection, the Clipboard contents are inserted at the insertion point.

The hexadecimal editor has a Find menu to help you find your way around the resource. The Find Hex command lets you find and change hexadecimal numbers. The Find Hex window doesn't help you make sure you enter only pairs of digits, so you have to check that for yourself. The Find ASCII command lets you search for and change a string in the text part of the window. The Find Offset command just moves the insertion point to the specified offset within the resource. All these dialogs are non-modal windows, so you can leave them open while you're working on the resource.

Appendix D
Resources in ROM

Table D-1. 128K ROM

Type	ID	Description
'CURS'	1	I-beam cursor
'CURS'	2	Cross cursor
'CURS'	3	Plus cursor
'CURS'	4	Watch cursor
'DRVR'	3	Sound driver
'DRVR'	4	Disk driver
'DRVR'	9	AppleTalk driver
'DRVR'	10	AppleTalk driver
'FONT'	0	Name of System font
'FONT'	12	System font
'PACK'	4	Floating-Point Arithmetic Package
'PACK'	5	Transcendental Functions Package

Table D-1. 128K ROM (continued)

Type	ID	Description
'PACK'	7	Binary-Decimal Conversion Package
'SERD'	0	Serial driver
'WDEF'	0	Default window definition function

Table D-2. SE

Type	ID	Description
'CDEF'	0	Default button definition procedure
'CDEF'	1	Default scroll bar definition procedure
'CURS'	1	I-beam cursor
'CURS'	2	Cross cursor
'CURS'	3	Plus cursor
'CURS'	4	Watch cursor
'DRVR'	3	Sound driver
'DRVR'	4	Disk driver
'DRVR'	9	AppleTalk driver
'DRVR'	10	AppleTalk driver
'DRVR'	40	AppleTalk driver
'FONT'	0	Name of System font
'FONT'	12	System font (Chicago 12)
'FONT'	393	Geneva 9 font
'FONT'	396	Geneva 12 font
'FONT'	521	Monaco 9 font
'KMAP'	0	Keyboard map for keyboard driver
'MBDF'	0	Default menu bar procedure
'PACK'	4	Floating-Point Arithmetic Package
'PACK'	5	Transcendental Functions Package
'PACK'	7	Binary-Decimal Conversion Package
'SERD'	0	Serial driver
'WDEF'	0	Default window definition function (document window)
'WDEF'	1	Default window definition function (rounded window)

Table D-3. Mac II

Type	ID	Description
'CDEF'	1	Default scroll bar definition procedure
'CURS'	1	I-beam cursor
'CURS'	2	Cross cursor
'CURS'	3	Plus cursor
'CURS'	4	Watch cursor
'DRVR'	3	Sound driver
'DRVR'	4	Disk driver
'DRVR'	9	AppleTalk driver
'DRVR'	10	AppleTalk driver
'DRVR'	40	AppleTalk driver
'FONT'	0	Name of System font
'FONT'	12	System font (Chicago 12)
'FONT'	384	Name of Geneva font
'FONT'	393	Geneva 9 font
'FONT'	396	Geneva 12 font
'FONT'	512	Name of Monaco font
'FONT'	521	Monaco 9 font
'KMAP'	0	Keyboard mapping (hardware)
'NFNT'	2	Chicago 12 font (4-bit)
'NFNT'	3	Chicago 12 font (8-bit)
'NFNT'	34	Geneva 9 font (4-bit)
'PACK'	4	Floating-Point Arithmetic Package
'PACK'	5	Transcendental Functions Package
'PACK'	7	Binary-Decimal Conversion Package
'SERD'	0	Serial driver
'WDEF'	0	Default window definition function (document window)
'WDEF'	1	Default window definition function (rounded window)
'cctb'	0	Control color table

Table D-3. Mac II (continued)

Type	ID	Description
'clut'	2	Color look-up table (black, white, light gray, dark gray)
'clut'	4	Color look-up table (System 16 colors)
'clut'	8	Color look-up table (System 256 colors)
'clut'	127	Color look-up table (original eight QuickDraw colors)
'gama'	0	Color correction table
'mitq'	0	Internal memory requirements for MakeITable
'snd '	1	Brass horn
'wctb'	0	Window color table

Appendix E
Translating Applications for Other Languages

People all over the world use the Macintosh, so software applications can follow this international machine anywhere. Adapting software to a particular region, language, or country is called *localization*. The best time to consider localization is when designing a program, because it isn't necessarily as simple as translating all the text a user sees. Many of your assumptions become meaningless (or worse) when you consider other languages and countries. You can't assume text always flows from left to right, and not all languages use the same alphabet, so alphabetizing and sorting rules can also vary. You have to allow for different punctuation, word order, and message length. (For example, translating from English often increases the amount of text.) Phone numbers and addresses most likely have a different format. In addition, keyboards vary from country to country, as does the standard paper size. These are just some of the things you have to consider.

Fortunately, Apple's localization engineers solved many country-compatibility problems at the outset. You can assume that most Mac owners have purchased systems compatible with their country and language. This means the System file, Finder, DAs, fonts, time and date format, other pertinent files and resources, and even the keyboard are appropriately localized for the country in which they are sold. Obviously, you can't work in a vacuum, so you need to be up-to-date on which parts of the Macintosh environment differ, and how. Several books available through the Apple Programmer's and Developer's Association (APDA) offer more technical details concerning how to make your software compatible throughout the world.

This appendix briefly summarizes the resources that may contain text and would, therefore, need to be modified during localization. These resources and their editors have been covered in the body of this book, so here we merely discuss considerations for localization. The bulk of your translation efforts will occur in menus ('MENU'), strings ('STR ' and 'STR#'), and dialog item lists ('DITL').

▶ 'ALRT', 'DLOG', and 'DITL' Resources

'ALRT' and 'DLOG' resources get their contents from 'DITL' resources, which can include various buttons and other controls ('CNTL's), as well as static and edit text. Some of these items might need to become larger to incorporate translated text. If so, you may need to enlarge the appropriate 'DITL' components. Depending on how much room you have, and how much the translated 'DITL' items change in size, the associated 'ALRT' or 'DLOG' resources may have to change size, too. Ideally, these resources should initially be built with a little room to grow.

Don't forget that dialogs may have titles. Choose Set Characteristics from the 'DLOG' menu to change a title.

▶ 'MENU' or 'CMNU'

Clearly, menus—including submenus and pop-up menus—require a great deal of careful translation. Try to keep the translations as short as possible so the menu bar doesn't get crowded, and don't reorder menu items. You should never change the standard Command-key shortcuts (Undo, Cut, Copy, Paste, and Quit, for instance), but if your foreign users aren't already familiar with the English version, you might want to consider reassigning a few application-specific Command keys so the mnemonics make sense.

▶ 'STR ' and 'STR#' Resources

String resources constitute a major chunk of your translation project. Try to keep the translations short without losing clarity. Remember not to delete variables such as ^0. You may have to change the order of multiple variables within a message to make it grammatically correct.

▶ 'WIND'

Generally, all you have to worry about here are possible window titles. Choose Set Characteristics from the 'WIND' menu to change a title.

▶ Other Resource Types

A few other resource types occasionally require translation, so they're worth checking: 'PICT', 'TEXT', 'CNTL', 'vers', and 'itl0' and 'itl1' (if you have your own special versions).

Afterword by Scott Knaster

According to Silicon Valley legend, the Macintosh was already far along in its development when an engineer named Bruce Horn got a Great Idea. He invented a way to separate the human-language-specific parts of a program, the stuff that has to be translated from English to French to Swahili to who-knows-what, from the code of the program, which can stay the same all around the world. This idea was called *resources*, and was embodied in a part of the Macintosh system software called the Resource Manager.

Every Macintosh programmer knows that resources have become one of the most interesting and unique (and sometimes agonizing) features of the Macintosh. In addition to letting folks translate programs into different human languages, resources let users fiddle with their applications in unprecedented ways, as Peter and Carolyn have told you in this book. The Macintosh is a great computer for regular people who like to mess around with their computer environment, and this book shows you how to do that in dozens of different ways.

Inventing the Resource Manager was only part of the story, though. A key part of the promising vision of resources was an application that would allow non-technical users to examine and modify a program's resources. This was the tool that would be used to translate a program's text into other languages. And that's how ResEdit was born. Except it wasn't quite that easy.

Creating ResEdit turned out to be a daunting task, something like a tiger trying to catch its own tail. The effort was started by Rony Sebok and Steve Capps, whose names (or at least initials) are immortalized by the 'RSSC' resource type that ResEdit still uses, furthered by Gene Pope, and now carried on by Peter Alley. Through their incredible efforts, ResEdit has evolved to its current advanced state.

ResEdit and this book provide a great example of why the Macintosh is still uniquely powerful, even in today's world of hey-look-at-my-graphical-user-interface. The tricks and customizations that you've learned in this book just aren't possible on any other computer that has the Macintosh's rich world of applications.

The creation of the Resource Manager in the original Macintosh was the first part of the dream of translating text and customizing software through resources. The second part of the idea was realized when ResEdit was written, making an easy way to see and change resources. Now, with *ResEdit Complete*, a third milestone has been achieved: There's a guidebook that makes it possible for every Macintosh user to take advantage of the power of resources. I think that was kind of the idea in the first place.

Scott Knaster
Macintosh Inside Out Series Editor

Index

Titles in the Macintosh Inside Out Series

▶ **Extending the Macintosh® Toolbox**
Programming Menus, Windows, Dialogs, and More
John C. May and Judy B. Whittle
A complete guide to programming the Macintosh interface.
352 pages, $24.95, paperback, order #57722

▶ **Programming QuickDraw™**
Includes Color QuickDraw and 32-Bit QuickDraw
David A. Surovell, Fred M. Hall, and Konstantin Othmer
The first in-depth reference to the Macintosh graphics system.
448 pages, $24.95, paperback, order #57019

▶ **Programming for System 7**
Gary Little and Tim Swihart
A complete programmer's handbook to the newest version of the Macintosh system software.
384 pages, $26.95, paperback, order #56770

▶ **Programming with AppleTalk®**
Michael Peirce
An accessible guide to creating applications that run with AppleTalk.
288 pages, $24.95, paperback, order #57780

▶ **The A/UX® 2.0 Handbook**
Jan L. Harrington
A complete and up-to-date introduction to UNIX on the Macintosh.
448 pages, $26.95, paperback, order #56784

▶ **System 7 Revealed**
Anthony Meadow
A first look inside the important new Macintosh system software from Apple.
400 pages, $22.95, paperback, order #55040

▶ **ResEdit™ Complete**
Peter Alley and Carolyn Strange
Contains the popular ResEdit software and complete information on how to use it.
576 pages, $32.95, book/disk, order #55075

▶ **The Complete Book of HyperTalk® 2**
Dan Shafer
Practical guide to HyperTalk 2.0 commands, operators, and functions.
480 pages, $26.95, paperback, order #57082

▶ **Programming the LaserWriter®**
David A. Holzgang
Now Macintosh programmers can unlock the full power of the LaserWriter.
480 pages, $24.95, paperback, order #57068

▶ **Debugging Macintosh® Software with MacsBug**
Includes MacsBug 6.2
Konstantin Othmer and Jim Straus
Everything a programmer needs to start debugging Macintosh software.
576 pages, $34.95, book/disk, order #57049

► **Developing Object-Oriented Software for the Macintosh®**
Analysis, Design, and Programming
Neal Goldstein and Jeff Alger
An in-depth look at object-oriented programming on the Macintosh.
368 pages, $26.95, paperback, order #57065

► **Writing Localizable Software for the Macintosh®**
Daniel R. Carter
A step-by-step guide which opens up international markets to Macintosh software developers.
496 pages, $26.95, paperback, order #57013

► **Programmer's Guide to MPW®, Volume I**
Exploring the Macintosh® Programmer's Workshop
Mark Andrews
Volume I covers the MPW shell and shows how to develop an application.
608 pages, $26.95, paperback, order #57011

► **Programmer's Guide to MPW®, Volume II**
Mastering the Macintosh® Programmer's Workshop
Mark Andrews and Neil Rhodes
Volume II examines the tools and programming language designed to be used with MPW.
608 pages, $32.95, paperback, order #57012

► **Elements of C++ Macintosh® Programming**
Dan Weston
Teaches the basic elements of C++ programming, concentrating on object-oriented style and syntax.
512 pages, $22.95, paperback, order #55025

► **Programming with MacApp®**
David A. Wilson, Larry S. Rosenstein, and Dan Shafer
Hands-on tutorial on everything you need to know about MacApp.
576 pages, $24.95, paperback, order #09784
576 pages, $34.95, book/disk, order #55062

► **C++ Programming with MacApp®**
David A. Wilson, Larry S. Rosenstein, and Dan Shafer
Learn the secrets to unlocking the power of MacApp and C++.
624 pages, $24.95, paperback, order #57020
624 pages, $34.95, book/disk, order #57021

Order Number	Quantity	Price	Total	
————	———	——	———	Name _____
————	———	——	———	Address _____
————	———	——	———	_____
————	———	——	———	City/State/Zip _____
————	———	——	———	Signature (required)_____

TOTAL ORDER _____   ___Visa   ___MasterCard   ___AmEx

Shipping and state sales tax will be added automatically.

Credit card orders only please.

Offer good in USA only. Prices and availability subject to change without notice.

Account # _____ Exp. Date _____

Addison-Wesley Publishing Company
Order Department
Route 128
Reading, MA 01867
To order by phone, call (617) 944-3700